MINDING MR. MARKET

MINDING
MR. MARKET

TEN YEARS ON WALL STREET
WITH GRANT'S INTEREST RATE
OBSERVER

James Grant

FARRAR STRAUS GIROUX

NEW YORK

To
JOHN W. HOLMAN, JR.

CONTENTS

Introduction

I. MR. MARKET CHANGES HIS MIND

II. GOOD BANKS AND BAD

III. IT'S A NEW ERA

VII. THE RISE AND FALL OF DEBT

VIII. THE FINE ART OF CORPORATE FINANCE

IX. PUBLIC FINANCE

The sheer number of words in this book may properly arouse suspicion. The past decade was the Age of Bull Markets, and the best financial advice was that which was the most concise. With perfect foresight, an interest rate analyst could have confined himself to saying "down," and a stock market forecaster to saying "up." He or she could have repeated those single words for emphasis at intervals beginning about 1982.

All of these essays first appeared in *Grant's Interest Rate Observer*, which began publication ten years ago. INTEREST RATES RISE was the headline on the front page of volume one, number one, dated November 8, 1983. Even then we did not give in to sensationalism.

I had left the staff of *Barron's* in the summer of 1983, believing that the world needed something else to read. In particular, I thought, it could use a twelve-page, twice-monthly publication devoted to interest rates and related financial topics ("a journal for this age of monetary upset and volatility," the first issue said). I wouldn't try to forecast interest rates because I couldn't. I would merely provide the necessary clarification.

Clarity was not an immediate bestseller, however, and the takeoff of *Grant's* was soon followed by a series of near crash landings. James B. Rogers, Jr., the New York investor, immediately subscribed, but the thousands of others who eventually followed him did not rush in all at once. Clearly, what they wanted to know about interest rates was something I couldn't tell them. Actually, in June and July 1984, I did tell them: Rates were headed down, I correctly forecasted, but they took no particular notice, perhaps suspecting that this one dazzlingly accurate prediction would be inevitably offset by others just as dazzlingly inaccurate (as indeed it was).

In truth, I had gotten off on the wrong analytical foot. Inflation was then at the top of the *Grant's* agenda. As we all know today, however, and as I should have appreciated at the time, inflation was already in full retreat. The Federal Reserve and its policies were another evergreen topic of ours, but so they were for nearly every other economic analyst on Wall Street, and I could bring no unique insight to bear on them. Then in the summer of 1984, in the midst of *Grant's* own formative financial crisis, I was introduced to Drexel Burnham Lambert and the financial crisis of the future.

The occasion was dinner for three in New York. One of the diners was James S. Chanos, a young analyst who in 1982, only two years out of Yale, had diagnosed the terminal financial disease of Baldwin United, the big life- and mortgage-insurance company. He talked about Drexel, its star junk-bond financier, Michael Milken, and the strange circle of Drexel's junk-bond-buying clients. A second diner, William M. McGarr, a professional short seller, discussed Caterpillar Tractor, which he happened to be short, having sold borrowed shares in expectation of a fall in the price of stock. I discussed Treasury bonds. By the end of the evening, we sat in wreaths of mutual esteem, perfectly understanding the unsound tendencies in banking and corporate finance that would shorten the economic expansion and damage the stock market (then hovering just over 1,000 on the Dow Jones Industrial Average, as opposed to 3,300 at this writing). The bear market could begin at any moment.

It did not, although it is a testament to the investment acumen of McGarr and Chanos that they were able to prosper, not merely survive, by selling stocks short in the boom years. It is a feat that might be compared to running a successful surfboard rental business in Omaha. Integrated Resources, a tax shelter purveyor and real estate syndicator that Chanos correctly identified that evening as a future bankrupt, survived until 1989. Drexel itself didn't go broke until 1990. Caterpillar, which in fact failed to deliver what Wall Street had expected of it, suffered a bad patch in the market but then went back up. The years 1984, 1985, 1986, 1987, and 1988 were conspicuous for the fact that the credit expansion we had talked about didn't stop. As for the stock market crash, nothing would have surprised us less if it had occurred in the fall of 1984. As it was, it happened on October 19, 1987, more than three years after we walked out of the restaurant (and from heights we did not imagine). Then the market proceeded to go right back up: a crash in reverse.

The rise of debt and the levitation in the prices of things that debt could finance occurred over the strenuous, sometimes exasperated objections, of *Grant's*. Starting in mid-1984, the focus of the magazine turned away from the great, imponderable macroeconomic questions toward the little, discrete microeconomic questions, for instance the vogue in junk bonds and soon-to-be empty office buildings. Our editorial approach was to ask the deceptively simple question, "What's next in financial markets?" In September 1984, our "gala junk issue" was devoted to Drexel and its pocket junk-bond-buying accounts. It was a lucky change of direction because Wall Street is constitutionally incapable of criticizing itself or its securities.

Grant's developed a niche in truth-telling, which sometimes amounted to nothing more than quoting the hair-raising legal language of the bond prospectuses that described (in accordance with the law) a specific emission of speculative-grade debt. As for inflation, the scourge of the late 1970s, we increasingly became absorbed in its opposite number, deflation. In a deflation, prices fall and the value of money appreciates. As loan collateral becomes impaired, banks fail and bonds default. In the United States in the 1980s, there was no deflation. There was, however, a confluence of deflationary symptoms here and abroad. Real estate entered a bear market, airlines became overleveraged, and banks absorbed huge, disabling losses.

A critic complained that *Money of the Mind*, my recent history of American finance, was like an account of the interstate highway system written from the point of view of the accidents. The same might be said, both fairly and unfairly, of *Grant's*. Where most observers of the 1980s emphasized the rewards, we dwelled mainly on the risks. In the junk bond market, in the reckless patterns of bank lending, in the dementia of Japanese finance, in the riot of the Treasury's borrowing, we saw not the bull market of today but the comeuppance of tomorrow. Undoubtedly, *Grant's* drank less champagne and took fewer wooden nickels than almost any other financial publication in the West, and we anticipated many of the biggest disasters of the day. The cost of this upright and godly living was that not a few of the nickels we spurned turned out to be speculative gold pieces. Day by day and month by month we bore the stigma of being wrong. I felt it keenly and from time to time doubted not only my sanity but also my ability to do arithmetic and read simple declarative sentences for comprehension. The people I chose for the occasional *Grant's* profile were not only intelligent and accomplished but also, usually, like-minded. They were fellow sufferers, and I was drawn to them partly to ratify my own judgment, even my coherence. If I may say so, however, the years have been more generous in their appraisal than the days and months. *Grant's* has been vindicated on many things, not least the homely truth that trees don't grow to the sky. It only seemed as if they could. Indeed, it seemed so for years. It is a lesson that future generations of skeptics may take to heart. (No doubt the stock and bond markets will one day become just as unreasonably loathed as they are now uncritically loved. It will behoove all of us to remember then that the sky doesn't fall.)

In financial markets, progress is cyclical, not cumulative. As the material lot of the industrialized countries is generally improving, equity markets are usually rising. Investment technology is better than ever, and information is becoming more widely disseminated all the time. Yet there is no observed improvement in the emotional stability of the average investor, notwithstanding dramatic advances in financial literacy or in the sophistication of computer software. The investor of the 1990s is probably no less prone to excitability and self-delusion than the investor of the 1920s. Paul Macrae Montgomery, about whom *Grant's* wrote in 1984, has made a lifelong study of the role of perception in the financial markets. There is the logical and calculating part of the human mind, Montgomery has observed, but there is also the emotional and impulsive region. Each plays its role in the supposedly cold-blooded calculations of buying and selling stocks and bonds. To suppose that the value of a common stock is determined purely by a corporation's earnings discounted by the relevant interest rate and adjusted for the marginal tax rate is to forget that people have burned witches, gone to war on a whim, risen to the defense of Joseph Stalin, and believed Orson Welles when he told them over the radio that the Martians had landed. Investors are prone to be bullish at the top of the market when prices are high, and bearish at the bottom when prices are low. Like war, speculation is a social activity. It is carried on by groups.

In the early years, *Grant's* was an individual, me. When Elizabeth H. McCormack, my secretary, was out, my thoughts and moods had the full run of the office. Isolation is conducive to eccentricity (or perhaps eccentricity seeks out isolation). Sitting alone in a room, I proceeded to champion orthodoxy. As Wall Street pushed the New Era, I defended conservatism. I became the champion of such lost causes as investment-grade bond ratings, cash, equity, conventional underwriting standards, and (most unprofitably) gold bullion. Our second issue contained a profile of a fascinating, deflation-minded gold mine developer, Evans Dick.

There was a healthy measure of conceit in this attitude, I know. Brilliant people come to Wall Street, and they are paid to think. Innovation is the life force of the financial markets, and orthodoxy for its own sake avails nothing except nostalgia. As everybody knows, however, Wall Street exists for a purpose: not to produce disinterested research, not to provide "service," not to raise capital for a growing America, but to sell stocks and bonds.

The higher the market, the easier it is to sell but the more disingenuous the sales pitch becomes. (In almost every other walk of commercial life, people buy more at lower prices; in the stock and bond markets, they seem to buy more at higher prices.) By the late 1980s, I believed, Wall Street was rationalizing the indefensible. "In terms of fundamentals [that is, facts]," wrote one brokerage firm about the stock of Japan Air Lines in 1987, "JAL remains unattractive. However, fundamentals have historically proved irrelevant to JAL's price movement." Even more stupefying than that statement, which by the way was not unusual, was that it wasn't disproven until 1991–92. The facts didn't matter until they did.

As for my own motives, I had to draw attention to *Grant's*, first and foremost, and I could hardly do that by falling in with the crowd. KUDOS TO MERRILL LYNCH! is a headline that would not have sold many subscriptions, even to Merrill Lynch and even at the low 1984 rate of $250 a year. Then, too, I am almost physically incapable of lining up with a consensus; agreement inflames my native obstinacy.

In speculation, interestingly enough, contrary-mindedness is often a virtue. A layman might suppose that profits lie with the majority. Because the mass of people have the weight of the money, he might imagine that the crowd would tend to be on the winning side of things. Not for long, in my experience. If the majority confidently knows something, that one thing is probably already reflected in the structure of prices, and the market is vulnerable to a surprise. Markets are moved by the unexpected, and the unexpected is what the crowd isn't anticipating. The financial future may be imagined, but it can never be positively known. What people know is the past and present, and they often project the familiar out into the unknown, with unsatisfying results.

Still, it is an ever-present risk for the self-styled contrarian that the past literally does repeat itself and that the crowd outsmarts the remnant. Indeed, the past repeats itself almost constantly, as witness the multitude of Tuesdays that are virtually indistinguishable from the multitude of preceding Mondays. Disruptive, let alone epochal, change is necessarily rare, and the avant-garde thinker is prone to see shadows or to shoot at ghosts. Extensive experience has taught me that there are many ways to be wrong about markets: through shortsightedness, of course, but also through excessive farsightedness; through pride, ignorance, bad luck, impatience, imagination, or sophistry. My signature variation on this latter pitfall is to misapply "the lessons of financial history." History undoubtedly teaches lessons about investment, but it does not say which lesson to apply when. "Find value, always" is as good a precept as any, but value is subjective and its definition is liable to change. In highly speculative markets, value means "it is going up." One must stay abreast.

Two underappreciated forces in financial markets are irony and paradox. Time and again in investing, things are not what they seem. One's best, most profitable ideas frequently begin unprofitably. Pride goeth before a fall—also publicity, handshakes, and celebrity. The biblical injunction about the first and the last trading places often has literal truth. Thus, stocks and bonds, which fared poorly in the inflationary 1970s, excelled in the disinflationary 1980s (and up to this writing in the 1990s). Gold, oil, and stamp collections appreciated in the 1970s but depreciated in the 1980s. The country's "most admired" companies (as listed annually in the glossy business magazines) are frequently on their way to becoming among the country's least admired investments. When a cynical investor hears that there are too many optimists in the market, he will begin to worry. By the same token, an overabundance of pessimists will give him courage. After all, he may ask, if everyone is already bearish, who is left to sell?

Everyone was not bearish in the 1980s (except perhaps on the morning of October 20, 1987). On the contrary, credulity enjoyed one of its greatest bull markets. The bankers believed the real estate developers, and the bank-stock investors (for a time) believed the bankers. The buyers of junk bonds believed the promoters, and the promoters believed themselves. The government bond market believed the politicians (who in 1985 promised that the Gramm-Rudman-Hollings Act would stop the growth of the public debt).

In bull markets there is no clear demarcation between progress and fantasy. In the 1980s, tax rates, inflation rates, and interest rates fell. Entrepreneurial activity increased, and if economic growth was slower than it had been during the 1960s and even during the mid-1970s, the Reagan expansion was long-lived. In 1980, the last year of the Carter administration, the top marginal income tax rate was 70 percent. Under the then-ruinous inflation rate of 13 percent, more and more middle-class people were being cast unfairly into the higher tax brackets with every passing year. The bad old inflationary days ended with an $850 gold price in 1980 and a 15 percent Treasury bond yield in 1981. In the mind's eye of 1980–81, people could see the wheelbarrows of Weimar brimful with worthless currency. What they failed to reckon with was the power of tight money and the inevitability of supply and demand. Oil never got to $100 a barrel because consumers used less of it and producers lifted more of it. Presently, people changed their minds about inflation. In August 1982, they proceeded to buy bonds and stocks, and they are still buying them more than a decade later at prices and valuations not seen in the memory of even middle-aged onlookers.

Grant's, busily blighting junk-debt prospectuses, failed to reckon with the bullish side of the debt phenomenon. Bullish it was, however, until it stopped (and indeed, for the stock market as a whole, it was bullish even then). The stewards of American finance would apparently do anything. Bankers lent to Donald Trump and those who would be like Trump. Investment bankers designed debt-laden transactions that would fail unless serendipity struck the borrowing company. Republicans acceded to the quadrupling of the public debt and presided over an expansion of government guarantees for lenders and borrowers that socialists might have envied.

I wrote hundreds of thousands of foreboding words, and not every one of them found its target. I could make a list of examples. To pick only one, the Federal National Mortgage Corp. did not suffer debilitating losses in the mid-1980s because of its lending in Texas. Texas house prices dropped and credit-related losses increased, but Fannie Mae (as the vast, federally sponsored mortgage lender is known) brushed aside these troubles. Falling interest rates helped it far more than falling house prices harmed it. The 1980s were an innovative decade, capitalism is a dynamic system, and any disciple of the late, great Grover Cleveland (as I happen to be) is liable to be brought up short by the rate of change. New markets and investments proliferated—in futures, options, swaps, and securities fashioned from anything and everything, not excluding credit card receivables and boat loans. Financial activity soared, whereas a good many fields of nonfinancial activity—industrial production, for instance—conspicuously did not. Banks lost customers to the securities markets, and the investment-grade bond market relinquished its place in the sun to the junk bond market.

But—and I did not imagine this—progress cut with a manic edge. People *would* look on the bright side, and by early 1993 doubt had almost been driven from Wall Street. The overriding lesson of the preceding decade was reducible to the single idea that stocks and bonds went up ("cash is trash," the more poetically inclined brokers said). As for the 1987 stock market crash and the 1989–90 junk-bond market crash, they were flukes, the majority believed. More than that, they were opportunities. If because of some government policy blunder or a miscalculation by some financial engineer, stock prices actually went down, so much the better. One could invest on the cheap for the next inevitable rise.

Thus, a new utopianism entered financial thinking, and nowhere was it more evident than on the editorial page of *The Wall Street Journal*. "The Victorians were people who, discovering sex, thought the human race was about to vanish," wrote Robert L. Bartley, the *Journal*'s editor, in his book, *The Seven Fat Years*. "In 1990 the Americans discovered credit." In fact, by 1990 Americans were fully conversant with the subject, having pushed up the ratio of debt to national output to about 190 percent from 140 percent only six years earlier. Did they—individuals, corporations, and governments—borrow excessively during the boom? On this, little *Grant's* and the big *Journal* disagreed, with *Grant's* taking the affirmative position. The *Grant's* view proceeded from a belief that people could and did make collective errors of judgment. The *Journal's* position stemmed from the view that if something went wrong in the economy—a recession, for instance, or a credit contraction—it was the government's fault. *Grant's* was perhaps even more antistate than the *Journal*, and we criticized freely and without partisanship. Our line, then and now, is that under Reagan and Bush the risk of loss was increasingly socialized through the doctrine that some banks were too big to fail and by the expansion of federal guarantees of mortgages. (The Austrian economists Ludwig von Mises and Friedrich von Hayek taught that excessive lending and borrowing distorts investment decisions and therefore the structure of production. These distortions cause or aggravate downturns in the business cycle. However, they reckoned before the U.S. government, in the form of federal deposit insurance and allied credit guarantees, could perpetuate the expansion phase and postpone or mitigate the contraction phase. Altogether, the 1980s plowed new ground in overdoing it.) "Victorian finance" was the *Journal's* disparaging rubric for the revival of conservative financial tendencies in America. The country's most economically influential opinion page viewed the new conservatism not as a return to the underwriting standards of only a decade before but as a retrograde movement imposed by regulators on a blameless banking profession. As Michael Milken had been physically jailed, so the nation's credit had been financially locked up. Washington did it by fiat.

Whatever the government did, however, it did not make Wall Street underwrite the bond issues of Robert Campeau or force bankers to line up to finance the hoped-for (but luckily unconsummated) leveraged buyout of UAL Corp., parent of United Air Lines. The government may fairly be blamed for the forced sale of junk bonds by savings and loans in 1989–90, but it did not cause the issuers of those bonds to default in record numbers. Nor did it create the circumstances that caused the bond-rating agencies to downgrade twice as many corporate issuers as they upgraded in the mid- and late 1980s, or the circumstances that brought about the steady deterioration in the quality of the junk bonds that came to market until about 1989. The rate of bankruptcy filings among individuals skyrocketed, but the government had not coerced Americans to borrow the money that they subsequently were unable to repay. If the rebuttal to these claims is that, in corporate finance, the tax code favored debt over equity, the rejoinder is that it has always done so, ever since the 1916 Revenue Act. Nothing in the tax treatment of corporate debt changed fundamentally in the 1980s. Indeed, the zaniest offenses against the canons of sound banking occurred outside the reach of the Internal Revenue Service, in Japan. Not even Switzerland was spared from a bank-financed bear market in real estate. In one country after another, lenders replicated the blockheaded practices of the Texas bankers during the early and mid-1980s. On the evidence, nobody was reading the newspapers.

There is little or no permanent truth in financial markets. It is a business for philosophical relativists, and *Grant's* has made its greatest errors in mistaking one fact or, worse, one hope for the shining light of the truth. In February 1991, convinced that neither the recession nor the credit contraction was ending, I wrote several essays proving beyond the shadow of a doubt that the stock market could not go up. They were first-rate pieces, marred only by the fact that the market did go up.

Financial ideas have their seasons. In 1983, the year we started publishing, everybody wanted growth stocks. By the mid-1980s, the watchword was business "franchises," or brand names like Marlboro. Then came leveraged buyouts and takeover candidates and—for what seemed to be an eternity—Japanese stocks at pre-posterous valuations. Sometimes fashions evolve over decades. The analyst David C. Cates recalled that in the 1950s bank stocks were valued by one criterion only: book value, or what the stockholders own. The tenet of the generation that had weathered the Great Depression was: "We know what banks owe, not what they own." By the 1960s the market dared to think of banks as it did other growing businesses, and it valued their stocks according to their profits. However, more than a few banks achieved growth through inordinate risk-taking. It came to light in the mid- and late 1980s that, in many cases, reported profits were in fact nonexistent. Lending to a real estate developer, a bank took a fee. The

"Oh dear. Was Mr. Market out of sorts today?"

trouble only began when the developer defaulted. So in 1990 it was back to book value again. Now that the economic sun has once more come out from behind the clouds, profits are back in fashion. The cycles of fashion have become compressed.

The inspiration for the title of this book (and for the illuminating Hank Blaustein cartoon) was a parable told by Benjamin Graham and by his celebrated student, Warren E. Buffett. There was a small, private business, wrote Graham, and one of the owners was a man named Market. Every day Mr. Market had a new opinion of what the business was worth, and at that price stood ready to buy your interest or sell you his. As excitable as he was opinionated, Mr. Market presented a constant distraction to his fellow owners. "What does he know?" they would wonder, as he bid them an extraordinarily high price or a depressingly low one. It was Graham's opinion, and Buffett's, too, that the gentleman knew little or nothing. "You may be happy to sell out to him when he quotes you a ridiculously high price, and equally happy to buy from him when his price is low," wrote Graham. "But the rest of the time you will be wiser to form your own ideas of the value of your holdings, based on full reports from the company about its operations and financial position."

It has always been easier to praise these words than to live by them, and *Grant's* and Mr. Market have had their differences. I think that Graham would approve of this friction, although he may not have foreseen the time when so many people would be prepared to treat this manic-depressive as a seer.

If *Grant's* once was an individual, it is so no more, and the growing depth of the personnel is apparent in the improvement of the journalism. Let me therefore thank the staff who have so signally contributed to this book. Our indispensable publisher, Jay Diamond, was formerly an investment banker, and he brings the analytical skills of that dark profession to all our corporate finance investigations. Sue Egan, who administers the office and the magazine, helped to administer the book. John P. Britton, Kathleen F. Turner, and Carolina Guevara-Lightcap—staff members past and present—all rendered assistance, as did numerous friends who are not on the payroll, including Charles Peabody of East Shore Partners; Mariel Clemenson, formerly director of high-yield research at Lehman Brothers; and Fred D. Kalkstein of Janney Montgomery Scott.

Hank Blaustein, our nonpareil artist, drew the sketches, Ruth Hlavacek, our all-seeing copy editor, read proof. Farrar, Straus and Giroux has paid *Grant's* the highest compliment in publishing a collection of financial essays, an especially perishable form of journalism. Thanks, then, to Jonathan Galassi, editor in chief; Elisheva Urbas, managing editor; and Rose Ann Ferrick, copy editor.

I have one co-author in Frederick E. ("Shad") Rowe, who contributed the piece on "Bulldog," the Texas repo man, and another in Patricia Kavanagh, my wife and the former publisher of *Grant's* (and now the president of our holding company). She helped to support me in the formative years when skepticism not only paid no dividends but also earned no salary.

MINDING MR. MARKET

PART ONE

MR. MARKET CHANGES HIS MIND

TIMING ARTIST

June 18, 1984

A fraternal article of faith among the people who try to forecast interest rates for a living is that nobody can hope to succeed at his job consistently. Saying this, the forecasters don't mean to disparage laymen. They mean that the experts can't do it either. So long has this doctrine of low expectations been repeated and so deeply has it taken root on Wall Street that any professional investor who complains about an inaccurate forecast or who blames an erroneous forecast for a market loss runs the risk of making himself a laughingstock. The rationale for this code of behavior is not so much the irreproachable idea that every adult should bear the blame for his or her own errors of judgment. It is, rather, that to demand a high predictive batting average from a bond market analyst amounts to a confession of gullibility on the part of the person who believed that such a thing was possible in the first place.

Another credo of the forecasting profession, and one that betrays a measure of self-esteem equally as low as the first, is that someone who *could* predict interest rates soon would be able to retire from having to predict anything. Thus, through a kind of reverse natural selection, the people who continue to forecast are, almost by definition, the ones who can't succeed at it. At all events, when Paul Macrae Montgomery, a laconic, sharp-featured Virginian, stepped to the rostrum of the fourth annual bond seminar of the Financial Analysts Federation in New York this past March to deliver a talk titled "Logical Limits and Practical Possibilities of Interest Rate Forecasting: A Case for Technical Analysis," the professional fore-

casters and investors in attendance were unreceptive. Montgomery, who is given to self-deprecating humor, recalls the reaction he received: "The speech fell stillborn from the dais. No comments, pro or con. No murmurs."

On most financial daises, Montgomery would cut an unconventional figure. For one thing, he wears thick, horn-rimmed glasses, the bows of which are discolored. He shuns typical Wall Street suits and wears his hair longer than the usual business length. He is forty-two years old but could almost pass for thirty, and says that he does pass for twenty-eight, "in the dating bars." For another thing, his intellectual tastes run to Shakespeare and the history of science, and he likes to drop technical terms and literary phrases unexpectedly into his financial presentations. Also, his forecasting record is so extraordinary that it often excites either envy or incredulity, which can set an audience against him before he even starts to speak. (To the inevitable question of why he bothers to forecast, if he really *can* forecast, Montgomery answers that he happens to like it. On the other hand, he says, he doesn't like to speculate, and he has a positive dread of speculating on margin. It's not that he isn't right; it's that he has trouble with the practical problems of speculation, such as deciding when to hold fast to a position or when to take a loss. "Your strong points determine your potential in the market," he likes to say, "but your weak points determine your actual results. And my weak point is management.")

In New York that morning, Montgomery led his audience on a tour of what, for them, might have seemed unfamiliar and inhospitable terrain. Not only did he assert that such conventional interest rate forecasting techniques as money-supply analysis and budget-deficit watching were ineffective, but he also explained why they had failed and why they were bound to fail again in the future.

Blaming "false principles of science," he elaborated in considerable detail, in his Southern accent, as follows:

> Whereas physical systems concern material objects, the central nexus of economics is *value*, which is not inherent in any physical object but rather derives exclusively from human *desire* for particular objects at certain particular times. Therefore, the ultimate subject of economics is not gold or savings accounts or money supply or houses or any physical goods whatsoever—but immaterial mental and emotional states. The fundamental difference between the values, or mental states, which are the subject of economic science, and the material objects, which are the subject of physical science, is that mental states do not obey the Law of Conservation of Momentum. This law states that an isolated object in motion will continue in motion with the same momentum throughout time, and it is this conservation principle that provides order and permits precise prediction in physics. . . . Unfortunately, mental states, and hence economic values, unlike physical phenomena, do not remain constant with time. Mental states rather are in constant flux, and these fluctuations through time are due to myriad causes, many of which are unknown, and many if not most of which lie far beyond the

purview of economic theory. *Therefore, a scientific economic dynamic, and hence consistently accurate interest rate prediction, is logically impossible within the framework of classical economic theory and methodology.*

The next thing Montgomery said was perhaps more worrisome to his listeners than this indictment of the ideas by which most of them were making a comfortable living in the financial markets. It was that since new information is so quickly digested by investors and speculators, nobody should expect to turn a bond market trading profit merely by recycling the same old data. Thus, said Montgomery, if he was right—if human emotion does play a vital, unacknowledged role in interest-rate movements, and if so-called fundamental data are reflected in market prices almost instantly upon their public dissemination—it followed that new forecasting techniques were needed. "It is the suggestion of this paper," he said, "that some of the radically different primitive concepts of 'technical' analysis may suggest some methodologies very helpful in forecasting interest rates."

In fact, Montgomery went on, technical analysis had been most helpful to him. He related that, of the forty-one short-term buy and sell signals he had issued to his bond clients since March 14, 1981, all but four had been profitable, and he added, for good measure, "The binomial probability of this record occurring by chance is approximately .0000000929." He attributed his forecasting success to chart patterns, time cycles, Elliott Waves, Fibonacci numbers, and other such technical apparatus, devices which, as far as mainstream opinion is concerned, bear the same relation to economics as divining rods do to geology.

To his knowledge, Montgomery says, he has never been nominated for the *Institutional Investor*'s research "All-Star Team," Wall Street's equivalent of the Tony awards, although his forecasting record stands head and shoulders above that of the economists who consistently are on it. He has fewer than thirty clients, and when once, a couple of years ago, he circulated a marketing letter to a list of approximately five hundred institutional bond prospects, he received just two replies. However, he has earned the gratitude of a few investors and gained a measure of recognition in the financial press, both for the accuracy of his forecasts ("eerily accurate"—

Barron's) and for the inventiveness of some of his market research. One paper he wrote, heavily footnoted and mock-heroically titled "The Hemline Indicator of the Stock Market: Some Theoretic and Empiric Support," made the rounds in 1975 and is still being read. He concluded that stock prices do, after all, move up and down with hemlines and that, in the days before movable hemlines, prices rose and fell with necklines. More recently, his discovery of the contrary investment implications of *Time* magazine covers brought him a splash of ink.

The *Time* system, which Montgomery tossed off for fun, is a textbook application of the theory of contrary opinion, which holds that the crowd tends to wind up on the wrong side of the market. (Specifically, he found for a few months following the cover date, the financial trend that *Time* has reported takes the course implied by the cover story. Within a year of publication, however, it has gone 180 degrees the other way, refuting the cover.) Montgomery, who likes to give the consensus the widest possible berth, is nonetheless generous in his estimation of the people who usually populate the crowd and about the financial and economic establishment that, for the most part, has given *him* wide berth. "These guys are not dummies," he said the other day in his office. "Somebody like [Paul] Samuelson, I don't even understand the titles of some of his papers. . . . They're brilliant men, and I have a lot of respect for them. But the methodology they use is not appropriate to the problem, and that's why they haven't been able to forecast better than chance."

In the nonestablishment world of fixed-income timing, Montgomery is most often compared to Ned Davis of Ned Davis Associates; John Mendelson, the Dean Witter market technician who *has* kept a foot in the investment mainstream; and to Robert Prechter, editor of *The Elliott Wave Theorist*. Prechter, for his part, calls Montgomery "probably the best interest-rate forecaster in the world." A Canadian bond investor who keeps tabs on what all four timers have been saying still stands in awe of Montgomery for his bullish call of October 1, 1981, which happened to coincide exactly with the bottom of the market in Treasury bonds. Montgomery himself calls his precision that day a fluke, and to anyone who asks whether he ever made a mistake, he mentions his ill-fated sell signal of October 1, 1982. ("Although the market has gone against us for only several days," he wrote his subscribers in mid-October, "these must have been about the worst several days in history to have been underinvested in bonds. Since any clients who might have reduced positions have suffered significant opportunity loss, we feel obliged to return this quarter's advisory fees.") He says that the forecasting business subtly tends to inflate one's sense of self-importance because a forecaster, just by making a prediction, presumes to know what people will do with their money before they do. Ever since 1974, he continues, when his clients and he lost heavily in the gold market because of his own pride of opinion, he has tried to keep his ego out of his forecasts. If you ask him what he thinks, he will describe what his indicators are saying. He has about 220 of them, and he and his research associate, Michelle James, collect and post them laboriously. Montgomery doesn't use a computer; until a few years ago, he didn't use a pocket calculator.

Montgomery was born in Newport News on June 6, 1942. He was graduated from the College of William and Mary and from the Colgate Darden Graduate School of Business of the University of Virginia. After some work in his family's real estate business, he began his career in the market as a stock broker in 1971. He started with Legg Mason & Co. and has never changed firms; he began to specialize in bonds in 1979. (Legg, however, did change names: in 1973 it became Legg Mason Wood Walker, Inc. Its office in Newport News is situated on the ground floor of what used to be the First & Merchants Bank Building on Washington Avenue. But when the bank changed its name to the Sovran Bank, the old name was pulled off the facing.)

He relates that he was a champion pole vaulter in high school and that he did his best athletic and scholastic work in the warm weather. In the winter he was prone to bouts of depression. Once, he said, as a college freshman, he underwent shock treatment for depression at the Norfolk General Hospital, and he likes to say that he learned more about markets during that hospitalization than he subsequently absorbed at business school. In general, he insists, "two weeks at Bellevue is worth two years at Wharton. . . . It was by trying to understand these mood swings that were periodic and not related to anything mechanical that I turned to the study of cycles." By cycles Montgomery means recurring patterns of behavior and market action. Citing the work of the Foundation for the Study of Cycles in Pittsburgh, he says that a dozen interest rate cycles, ranging from six months to fifty-four years in length, have been identified by other investigators (notably, in the case of the long cycle, by Nikolai D. Kondratieff) and that he has discovered some new ones himself. Without tipping his hand, he says that some of his cycles are designed to predict the emotional ups and downs of investors. Like the late R. N. Elliott, who propounded the notion that market patterns tend to move in a series of five waves, Montgomery believes that human emotions are rhythmical and, to that extent, predictable.

The crux of his forecasting approach is time. He doesn't predict the level of interest rates but rather the direction of rates from one of his signals to the next. He monitors the bond market from three different vantage points, short term (one week to five weeks), intermediate term (one month to five months), and long term (six months to a year). At the moment, he reports, his long-term model, which turned bearish in June 1983, remains bearish, although it's become less so recently. His intermediate-term work is also bearish, but on June 4 he decided that it was almost bullish, and he called his clients to tell them that. His short-term model propitiously flashed "buy" on May 30. All in all, Montgomery says, "it looks as good as it's looked since last December."*

A good part of his day is spent saying that, or something like it, to his clients over the phone. Sometimes the talk turns to Elliott Wave counts and chart formations or to Fibonacci numbers, a numerical series with alleged predictive and quasi-mystical properties. What it never dwells on, if Montgomery can help it, is M-1, the geopolitical situation, the budget deficit, or the burden of private credit demand, most of which factors, he believes, are usually discounted by prices even as economists are talking about them. Interestingly, Montgomery draws a distinction between monetary forces, like market interest rates and the turnover rate of money,

---

* Nine years later bonds were yielding less than 7 percent, and they were as much beloved as they had been hated in the spring of 1984 when they yielded 14 percent. I asked Montgomery to venture a long-term, hardcover-book horizon forecast on the future of the bond market, and he wrote on February 26, 1993: "While the pieces are not *all* in place today, before too long bond prices should embark on an extended move to the downside. *If* the U.S. dollar maintains its fundamental integrity, then any such down move may well be just a very uncomfortable interruption within a bull market which will continue in halting fashion until the turn of the century. If it does not, the great bull market in bonds will likely have ended for good."

on the one hand, and the Federal Reserve, on the other. He maintains that, for the most part, the market leads the Fed rather than vice versa. Another eccentricity of his is that he never instructs the Fed or the national government in public policy. He says he would consider it irrelevant to his clients' needs to testify before a committee of Congress, even if somebody asked him to.

As much as the accuracy of his calls ("uncannily accurate"—*Grant's*), what sets Montgomery apart from the bond market crowd is his eclectic taste in ideas. After the appearance of a critical article about Elliott Wave analysis a couple of years back, Montgomery sent its author a gently chiding letter. "Elliott is speculative at best," he wrote, "and unlike Prechter, I don't have the eye to use it effectively. Yet to deny that it has any basis would be tantamount to a tone deaf person's denying there is such a thing as music."

In the same letter Montgomery also enclosed an excerpt from a paper he had written on John Milton, in which he discussed, among other nonliterary subjects, the atomic properties of gold. "Thought you might add this to your collection of outré analysis," he suggested. "*Everyone* says that footnote 85 of my Milton paper is the *worst* thing I ever did (in a market letter), so it may be correspondingly important. Pull it out when I die broke and/or in the funny farm."

HAPPY DOWNSIDE

July 2, 1984

L ast fall William M. McGarr, founder and general partner of the McGarr Fund, decided that things would be different in the stock market this time around. He decided (as he explained to his investors in two concise paragraphs) that the oft-predicted inflationary liftoff would fail to ignite and that the earnings of leveraged, inflation-dependent corporations would suffer accordingly. Having made up his mind, he acted. He sold short the shares of capital-goods companies, farm equipment makers, and commodity producers.

The other day, just before the books were closed on the second quarter, he added up the 1984 results to date. They were: McGarr Fund, up 26 percent; Dow Jones Industrial Average, down 10 percent.

In order to get from here to there, McGarr, who managed money at Morgan Stanley before starting his limited partnership last year, applied some out-of-the-way financial ideas. Once he told a prospective client: "Nowadays, the best inflation hedge is cash." He meant that the bond and money markets would no longer sit still for negative "real" interest rates and that yields would more than keep pace with rising prices (which, of course, so far they have). McGarr contends that deflation has gained the upper hand over inflation and that commodity prices will stagnate. Furthermore, he insists on actually reading the annual reports of the companies in which he's preparing to take a position, and he studies the commodities tables in *The Wall Street Journal*. (It should be stated, in the interests of full disclosure, that McGarr is a paid-up subscriber to this publication. He reads it selectively, skipping over the inflation-scare material.) Late last summer he began to notice a common thread in the investment news. The capital, farm equipment, and raw-materials companies that had done so well in the seventies were making heavy weather of it. Their margins were under pressure, and they couldn't raise prices fast enough. Furthermore—here was the opportunity, McGarr thought—there was a widening disparity between the facts and what Wall Street believed.

The Street, as McGarr sized it up, believed that inflation was around the corner. It was an uninformed view, he says, because the investment strategists who propounded it were often in the dark about the operating facts of the companies they recommended. From his own digging, McGarr had decided that if anything was around the cyclical bend, it was the oncoming train of deflation. One of the stocks he sold was Caterpillar Tractor. ("Look at that chart," says McGarr. "You've got ten years' supply at fifty.")

Cat wasn't then, and isn't now, his biggest or most profitable short position, but it was the one that brought him the most solicitous attention from his bullish friends. As he sold, in late 1983 and early 1984, a half-dozen brokerage houses were urging their clients to buy. The sheer weight of his selling couldn't have frightened anybody, McGarr noted—his fund has yet to pass the $10 million mark in assets—but something about his investment approach got under the skins of the bulls. "I'd get unsolicited calls," he says. "They'd say, 'You ought to cover that stock.' " He had sold at prices as low as 43⅛ and as high as 49⅝. Last week when the price hit 37, a fifty-two-week low, he was thinking about selling some more.

Without going into details, McGarr will say that he's short of twenty or so stocks and long in just a few. "I don't have an underlying strategy for the long side," he says. "I haven't done much in it, and I haven't made much money at it." He says that he doesn't believe in puts and calls, nor does he follow a mechanical trading system that would cause him to liquidate a stock after a particular percentage loss. He says that he likes to do his homework, to stake out a position, and then to wait.

MAX

October 22, 1984

The *New York Post*, the fourth largest daily newspaper in the United States and the American flagship of Rupert Murdoch, the Australian publishing magnate, is a tabloid's tabloid. Its strongest editorial suit is sports, and its front page blares the kind of headline that makes a quick impression on bustling Manhattan commuters (SUBWAY RIDER'S THROAT SLASHED). Its outlook is conservative, but not so conservative as to inhibit the editors in their selection of feature material (WIDOW SUES FOR HUSBAND'S SPERM).

From the turn of the century to the 1930s, the *Post* (or the *Evening Post*, as it used to be known) was the most highbrow daily in town. It became a tabloid in 1942, and it was acquired by Murdoch in 1976. To make his own conservative sensational imprint on what had been a politically liberal and, to his taste, insufficiently sensational sheet, Murdoch imported a cadre of Australian editors. Later on, in the summer of 1980, he brought in an ambassadorial-looking, Australian financial editor, Maxwell Newton.

Both by dint of his boss's acquisitiveness and his own enterprise, Maxwell Newton today is one of the most widely read writers on money and interest rates in the world. His column appears six times a week in the *Post* and also, from time to time, in two of Murdoch's out-of-town American dailies, the *Boston-Herald* and *Chicago Sun-Times*. It appears overseas in the *London Times* (Murdoch's consummate nontabloid) and in a quintet of Murdoch's Australian papers, *The Australian*, *Adelaide News*, *Sydney Daily Mirror*, *Sydney Daily Telegraph*, and *Brisbane Sun*. Furthermore, Max consults with professional investors in the United States, the United Kingdom, Japan, and Australia. He publishes a daily *New York Money Market Report*, which deals with the credit markets, foreign exchange, and commodities. On Saturday nights, he writes about 2,500 words for his

Weekend New York Money Market Report, and on Sunday he edits his *Chicago Weekly Report*. (He says that the only night he *doesn't* write is Friday.) He bats out a couple of columns a month for his clients' newsletters, and he makes an occasional speech. He's written one book, *The Fed*, a sharp critique of the Federal Reserve System, and he's at work on a second book, provisionally titled *Two Americas: One Hundred Million Workers and One Hundred Million Dependents*. Max gives two reasons for his staggering output: first, that he loves his work, and second, that once he starts to write, he never looks back and never revises.

Unlike most of his colleagues in the financial press, who lack the nerve, the inclination or the opportunity to blast Henry Kaufman by name, or to charge (as Max did) that the new president of the Federal Reserve Bank of New York, E. Gerald Corrigan, is a bureaucratic nullity, Max writes from the heart. He calls the markets as he sees them. He was bullish on bonds in the fall of 1983, a bad call, but he was also bullish at the bottom last spring, a good call. He likes the bond market now. He was bullish on bonds in the summer of 1982, just before the rally, but he was bearish on stocks even as that market was roaring (DON'T BE FOOLED BY STOCK SURGE). He flatters his friends ("James Grant, owner of the prestigious fortnightly *Grant's Interest Rate Observer* . . .") and ridicules his enemies, including Kaufman, Albert Wojnilower, various Keynesian economists, and the Federal Reserve Board. More than most financial writers, Max takes Wall Street personally. He holds its forecasters individually accountable for bad predictions, and he doesn't scruple at name-calling. If he didn't invent the sobriquet "Dr. Death and Dr. Doom" for Kaufman and Wojnilower (Max himself isn't sure), he popularized it and expanded on it. Now Kaufman (who, through a spokesman, declines to comment on Max) is "Mr. Confusion." Sometimes the hero of one column resurfaces as the goat of a subsequent column. When Max was a monetarist, the disciples of Milton Friedman led a charmed life in the Newton corner of the Murdoch press. Since his own recantation of "rigid monetarism," however, which followed the major revisions of last years' money-supply data, the same economists have suffered Max's brickbats.

So big is Max's circulation and so closely is he read by investors, professionals, and amateurs alike that his columns can move markets (and generate leads: "When he was writing good things about me," said a Wall Street economist who has since incurred Max's displeasure, "my phone was ringing off the hook, and my mail was twelve inches high"). For instance, on Monday, June 4, he reported that "the U.S. Treasury and the Federal Reserve are currently planning a massive bailout for the American banks," and he went on to claim that the "U.S. Treasury will issue a special fifty-year security which the banks will be allowed to count as part of their capital."

On the face of it, the story might have seemed preposterous, but Max is known to have a well-placed source at the Treasury in the person of the Undersecretary for Monetary Affairs, Beryl Sprinkel, and the Continental Illinois affair was fresh in mind. At all events, as Max himself modestly noted next day, the bailout column "was accompanied by (I am not saying that it caused) large rises in the stock markets of Australia, England, and the United States." (Interestingly, in New York, Telerate attributed Max's scoop to the *London Times*, although the same column had appeared the same morning in the more accessible if less august pages of the *New York Post*.) As for the bailout, it hasn't happened yet, Sprinkel has denied that it was ever planned, and Max, for one, has stopped predicting it.

Max talks in a full-throttle Australian accent, stands six feet one inch tall, wears Texas-style string ties and silver collar points, and is married to the former Olivia Waldron of Black Rock, Melbourne, Victoria, Australia. The son of a plumber, Max was born in Perth, Western Australia, in 1929. After graduating with First Class Honors in Economics from the University of Western Australia in 1951, he studied at Cambridge University, England, where, in 1953, he was awarded First Class Honors and the prestigious Wrenbury Scholarship for Economics. Norman Podhoretz, now the editor of *Commentary*, a publication very different from the *Post*, shared rooms with Max at Cambridge. He recalls that Max "was kind of a wild young man. At least that was his pose—from the bush in Australia. He was very brilliant and did very well. . . . Although he pretended to be a barbarian, he was a man of quite exquisite taste and intellectual quality." So idiomatic and fluent was Max's French, Podhoretz relates, that the French, listening to him, would mistake him for a Belgian. According to Podhoretz, Max admired the United States, rejected the prevailing anti-Americanism in Europe, and was contemptuous of the British. Max himself amends this last point slightly: "I loved the English. I still do. I only like to go back there now when I have money. I like to watch the English grovel. They grovel beautifully for money."

Returning to Australia in 1954, Max took a job with the Treasury in Canberra but quickly resigned, moved to Sydney, and sold car batteries by mail. Next he joined the economics department of the Bank of New South Wales. Time was heavy on his hands, and he wrote a series of letters to the editor of the *Sydney Morning Herald* in the spring of 1956. The letters attracted the attention of R. A. G. Henderson, managing director of the *Herald*, who promptly gave him a job. In short order, Max became the *Herald*'s political correspondent. He moved on to become managing editor of the *Australian Financial Review* and the founding editor of Rupert Murdoch's *The Australian*. When Murdoch and he parted company in 1965, Max went into the publishing business for himself. He accumulated a lucrative stable of trade publications and joined battle with the government over protectionism, espousing then, as he faithfully does now, free trade and free markets. In 1971 he founded the sensational *Melbourne Observer*, "a mixture," he recalls with mock wistfulness, "of the *New York Post* and the *Star*, a charming mixture. People used to ask me, 'Mr. Newton, what is your editorial formula?' And I'd say, 'the Four Ts—tits, trots, track, and TV.' "

In retrospect, Max identifies his publishing apex as the Football Grand Final edition of the *Sunday Observer* in October 1974, which, he says, sold 212,000 copies at the "unprecedented, unheard of, and never-to-be-repeated price of 40 cents. That was the peak. After that it was downhill all the way. Within three years, I was bankrupt." By 1977 his net worth, which was $3 million or so at the top, hit zero, and he was rebuilding his fortunes in pornographic books and sexual paraphernalia. Smut was the logical next step, Max relates, because he'd been printing dirty magazines in order to spread the costs of his printing operations over a wider base. It was Murdoch who helped him back into journalism, Max says, first, by refusing to print his ads for "sexy grab bags" in the Murdoch newspapers (a crippling blow to Max's marital-aids business), and then, subsequently, by publishing his articles in *The Australian* and by bringing him to the *Post*.

In 1981, during a routine checkup, a polyp was discovered on Max's prostate gland: the polyp was diagnosed as malignant, and in April 1982 he was operated on at the Mayo Clinic. Having survived a brush with cancer and having moved so recently to the United States, a country he loves, Max has a special view of the world: "It's a wonderful time to be alive and be working and to be able to participate in the excitement," he says.*

SAGE OF TAMPA

July 28, 1986

One day in 1947 the front page of the old *Washington Daily News* carried a story about a child prodigy. WELL, CAN YOU READ THE BACKS OF DOMINOES? the headline inquired, and a photo showed a tyke in bow tie and bib overalls holding a large wooden domino up in the air with his left hand. The child's eyes glowed on the high-beam setting, as if a lollipop had just crossed into his line of vision. The story led off:

It nearly startled 2-year-old Marc Perkins' parents out of their skins.

"That's the wed dubble six," he said, pointing to an unpainted block of wood lying face down on the floor.

Proudly, he turned it over. Sure enough, on the other side, there was the double six of the domino set, colored red.

Marc's parents, Mr. and Mrs. Samuel Perkins, . . . bought him the set last Christmas. There were 28 blocks in all, each unpainted

* Max died on July 23, 1990.

except for the different colored dominos on one side. He had been
playing with them only two months before he began his magic.

It developed that the boy had learned to identify the dominoes
by the grain of the wood on their backs. It was further revealed
that his memory was like a sponge. "Give him a book by himself,
and he'll turn the pages, look at the pictures, and repeat the text."
the *Daily News* reported. "We think he's pretty remarkable," his
mother said. The story concluded, editorially, "He is."

Marc Irvin Perkins turned forty-one last week. He is chairman
of his own investment firm in Tampa and a financial thinker of
many attainments (and also, it should be declared, a subscriber to
Grant's). "Perkins" is not the name that his grandfather brought over
to this country from Russia before World War I but rather the name
that apparently struck the fancy of a U.S. immigration official. The
original was "Perchovsky" (or a name spelled very much like it).
Perkins stands five feet five inches tall in his stocking feet, is heavily
built, and can drive a golf ball 250 yards. In repose he has an extra
chin. He dresses the part of the investment banker and deal maker

he is, but his instinct is to dress down. He looks back with nostalgia on the sartorial enormities of his early career as an insurance company investment analyst—wearing the same wide, red polka dot tie for days on end, for instance, or obliviously attending a meeting in a pair of pants ripped all the way up the seam on the inner thigh to the crotch. He lives in a big house in Lutz, Florida, with his wife Margaret and a ménage including eight children from many marriages (both his and hers), four dogs, a horse, a cat, seven chickens, and a goose. He gets around in a maroon Jaguar XJ6.

To a reader of the child prodigy story in 1947, it must have seemed a foregone conclusion that such a wunderkind as Perkins was bound for the Ivy League and subsequently a post in the higher reaches of the American establishment. However, that was not the way things worked out.

The precocious child conceived an early disdain for authority. As an adolescent he decided that, while it was fun to learn, it was not necessarily fun to learn what he was supposed to learn. The study of French lost its fascination for him in the eleventh grade, and he methodically flunked the course. Two years later, in 1963, he matriculated into Ursinus College, Collegeville, Pennsylvania, instead of Harvard or the Sorbonne. He interrupted his studies after five semesters in order to start a company that painted the screens at drive-in movies. "When I say it was a company," Perkins explains, "it was me and another guy. I would add, by the way, that I was out of college for five years before I made as much money as I did on a day-to-day basis during those six months I painted drive-in movies." He was graduated with a degree in mathematics in January 1968, having earned the highest grade in his accounting class but attaining no other academic distinction. He says that John Belushi in the college farce *Animal House* might as well have been playing him.

Not even knowing what a business school was at that time, Perkins didn't apply to study at one. Asked now why he settled on the investment business, he replies that he needed a job. The father of a college friend was working at the Liberty Mutual Insurance Co., Boston, and Perkins sought work there as a junior investment analyst. He arrived for his interview in a noisy brown herringbone sports jacket of horse-blanket weight, a garment he had owned since high school. He was hired at $6,200 a year.

What has distinguished Perkins's investment career from that day to this is a flair for original thinking. This aloofness from the crowd has tended to make him an early seller but a wise and successful buyer. For instance, he turned forehandedly bullish on Florida banks in 1975, on Florida thrift institutions in 1982, and (although the jury is still out on this one) on farm banks, notably First Interstate Bank of Iowa, in 1986. He has won the plaudits of no less a financial family than the Tisches (they of Loews Corp.) for his bank stock analysis, and he has found incisive things to say on financial subjects ranging from the global debt predicament to thrift-institution accounting.

For instance, concerning debt, Perkins said recently: "When you have to rely on liquidation of assets to pay back debts, you've screwed up. Debt is designed to be serviced from income. It isn't supposed to be serviced by the value of assets because when assets are being liquidated to support debt, they call that a depression."

Concerning the art and mystery of thrift accounting, Perkins has devised a number of ingenious indicators. One of these, "The Cover," is a red flag to identify institutions that have saddled themselves with an uncomfortable burden of interest-bearing liabilities. The Cover has served Perkins well as a forecasting tool, for the higher The Cover, the deeper the hole a thrift is likely to find itself in.*

Perkins, though fluent in mathematics, is a two-plus-two person rather than a first-derivative person. He contends that higher mathematics have added no value to economic forecasting and that most of what one needs to know, mathematically, about investing can be found in the compound interest table. "The basic laws of arithmetic, common sense, and logic are immutable," he says without sounding pompous about it.

---

* "In the case of an institution that has an excess of interest-bearing liabilities over earning assets," Perkins explains, "The Cover tells us the number of basis points of spread that that institution must have between its yield and its cost to reach zero interest margin." Thus, The Cover amounts to a kind of bogey: For the institution that shows more interest-bearing liabilities than interest-bearing assets, The Cover would be a positive number. The higher The Cover, the greater would be an institution's temptation to reach for the yield to earn the money with which to pay its depositors and noteholders. The Cover can be calculated according to this formula:

$$\frac{(\text{Interest-bearing liabilities} - \text{earning assets}) \times 7\%}{\text{Earning assets}}$$

Seven percent is a proxy number for the cost of funds.

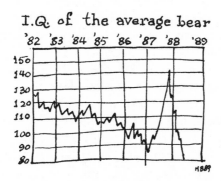

I.Q. of the average bear

Perkins got off to an unconventional start. Instead of suggesting a buy, which is what was expected of him and of every financial greenhorn, he suggested a sell. "I was in the business maybe three months," he recalls. "When I got there, Mobil was 42. Suddenly, it was 54. 'Hey, that's pretty good,' I said. 'Maybe we ought to sell that.' So we sold some. And it went to 60. And we sold some more. And then we discovered 1969–70, and the stock dropped like a rock, which, of course, made it different from every other stock. The lesson is that, as Bobby Spiegel said, 'Sell 'em when you can, not when you have to,' or 'Nobody ever went broke taking a profit.' "

By late 1969, Perkins had moved to John Hancock Mutual Life Insurance Co. to do much the same kind of analytical work he'd been doing at Liberty Mutual. He was assigned the oil, chemical, and photography industries. They were good industries, and his was a good job, but he was plagued by doubt. For instance: Did it really matter if Kodak earned a dime more or less than everyone expected of it? He decided it did not. Also, was it possible that the international monetary system was in the process of falling out of a penthouse window? His answer to that was yes, and he made a bullish case for gold stocks before the Hancock's august Committee of Finance in April 1971. When he finished, nobody said anything—at the time, to suggest a rise in the price of gold was tantamount to suggesting a decline in the creditworthiness of the U.S. government (which, of course, was just around the corner). At long last one of the directors said, "That was the most lucid description of gold I've ever heard." The remark was lost on Per-

kins, however, who at the time didn't know what "lucid" meant.
(Nowadays if he were caught out like that, he would waste no time
consulting the dictionary. He says that he is one of those people
who literally can't stand not to know.)

It is a testament to both Perkins's style and his substance that
people who knew him at the Hancock recall him being there much
longer than the year and a half he actually put in there. William
B. Budd, who hired him (and who now manages money at Favia,
Hill & Associates, a division of Chemical Bank), recalls a meeting
at the Ritz Carlton Hotel during the Perkins era. "The Ritz Carlton,
at that point, was the fanciest hotel in town," he says. "Pennzoil
and its new joint-venture drilling subsidiary were making a presentation, and all the oil analysts were invited to come and listen
and buy the stock. Toward the end of the meeting somebody asked
who was behind the subsidiary, and the answer was 'You shouldn't
have any question about that. Pennzoil is behind it.' From the back
of the room came the voice of Marc Perkins: 'And who's behind
Pennzoil?' "

Barry Good, now the chief oil analyst at Morgan Stanley and
then an analyst with Laird Inc., thought highly enough of Perkins
in those days to try to hire him away. "We were on the brink of
one of the greatest bull markets in the history of the oil business,"
recalls Good. "I think he grasped all of that." But Perkins was
already weighing an offer from Salomon Brothers. (A Salomon re-
cruiter, out to dinner with Perkins and the future first Mrs. Perkins,
employed the direct approach to persuasion. Waving an impressive-
looking W-2 form in the lady's face, he said, in effect, "Marc can
match this if he wants to.") Perkins had impressed Jonathan Bigel,
then a Salomon partner, by asking a characteristically blunt question
of the chairman of Phillips Petroleum at a conference in Chicago
at which Bigel was present. Bigel couldn't have missed Perkins
that day even if he'd wanted to. He was wearing a red shirt.

Perkins decided to take the Salomon offer and began to trade
over-the-counter bank stocks and convertible bonds in April 1971.
He lasted not quite two-and-a-half years, a stint that afforded him
a front-row seat on the collapse of Equity Funding, among other
financial adventures and misadventures. "I was fired from Salomon
Brothers," Perkins says. "I had a disagreement with a guy there.
His name was Salomon, so he won."

His boss at Salomon, Robert Spiegel, recalls of him: "He was short and ebullient."

Tampa is a city not universally associated with big financial goings-on. What it can and does boast about is having the world's longest continuous sidewalk, Bay Shore Boulevard, which fronts for six miles on the still, industrial waters of Hillsborough Bay. Tampa is a center of the phosphate export trade and the home of George Steinbrenner, the vocally active principal owner of the New York Yankees. Once, by chance, Perkins and Steinbrenner wound up together in a foursome at the Carrollwood Village Country Club in Tampa. What Perkins most clearly recalls about those eighteen holes was the life-and-death intensity of Steinbrenner's play. "He treated it like the World Series," Perkins remembers. A golfing partner of Perkins assesses Perkins's links deportment this way: "If he's playing well, he's very carefree and happy. He rides down the fairway singing. If he's not playing well, he barely talks to you."

Perkins has lived in Tampa for the past dozen years. Since leaving Salomon Brothers, his career has gradually moved in the direction of research and deal making and away from trading. Trading, or at least trading from the long side, was a calamitous line of work in 1974 when Perkins joined Jerry Williams, the Tampa brokerage firm. "The average stock in which we were making a market was down 80 percent in six months," Perkins says. "It was the toughest six months of my life." However, so well did Perkins's personal stock appreciate that by 1979 or 1980, when Tom Tisch sought out the leading authority on Florida banks, the man he was pointed to was Perkins. What Tisch says he likes best about Perkins's work is its depth: numbers supported by common sense and a knowledge of bankers and banking. "I find he has very good value sense when it comes to financial institutions," says Tisch. "He's very good at trying to sense out the inflection points." Not unfailingly, of course. And according to another longtime Perkins associate, David Hill, an Iowa banker, "Marc's got the ability to be wrong and not be devastated."

As Perkins chronically bites his nails, this seeming equanimity may be deceiving. After all, he didn't predict the spike in stock prices, and he doesn't pretend to enjoy it. "I really take pride in having one of the best bear market track records in the United States." Perkins says. "There are ways to measure undervaluation. And when you get undervalued, the lowest something can go is zero. But on the up side, I don't know how overvalued things can become. Since I thought it was patently absurd, Genentech has doubled." When the thrift industry was at death's door in March 1982, Perkins was prophetically bullish on it. Now the S & L stocks, or many of them, are grossly overvalued by Perkins's lights, and the Johnny-come-latelies fancy themselves geniuses. "Got to own a thrift," Perkins says, mocking them. "Can't do nothin' without a thrift."

Back in January, Perkins wrote a brief but searching piece on the significance of the debt predicament to the financial markets. He contended that the extraordinary expansion of debt in relation to the gross national product must ultimately be bearish for stock prices. If debt continued to grow at 15 percent as compared to 3 percent to 5 percent growth in GNP, then it would be only a matter of time before debt engulfed everything, like The Blob. The piece was a typical Perkins production, dismissive of expert opinion, reliant on the logic of compound interest, and grounded in the notion (a favorite Perkins aphorism) that "asset values are contingent but debt is forever. In other words, the value of the 100 shares of AT&T I own is contingent, but the value of my margin debt is steady." His piece said:

> We subscribe to the rather simplistic viewpoint that any time one of the major economic or financial aggregates gets out of line with the rest of the system, it warrants investigation. At this time, a dislocation that must stand out to even the most casual observer is that, over the last several years, we have undergone a credit boom of historic proportions. . . . In an economy that has historically maintained a ratio of credit to GNP of 150 percent, credit is now growing at 3½ times the rate of economic growth. Since 1981 the ratio of credit outstanding to GNP has increased from 144 percent to 167 percent, and the ratio of credit growth to GNP growth has increased from 114 percent to 335 percent. Two questions come to mind: "Why is this happening?" and "Why should anyone care?"

Perkins had a theory to advance on that point. Deregulated banks are under a kind of "compulsion" to lend: "The marginal deposit costs more than can be earned by marginal liquidity. . . . Because of deregulation, the banking system has been forced to lower its credit standards to earn a spread. We have seen the lunatic fringe of deregulated institutions already begin to self-destruct in the form of the more aggressive savings and loans. There is much more to come." He continued:

As to why should an investor care, simple arithmetic should give us the answer. If a dollar in economic activity is accompanied by $1.50 in debt, and the cost of money is 10 percent, then the cost of money to generate the $1 in economic activity is 15 cents. If $3.50 in debt accompanies the $1 in increased economic activity, the related cost of money would be 35 cents. Thirty-five percent of each dollar of increased economic activity goes to interest expense, hardly a sustainable rate. This may explain why this economic expansion continues to endure, befuddling the experts. We are pumping so much money, i.e., credit, into the economy that some increase in economic activity must result. Both common sense and history tell us that the culmination of this credit boom can come in two ways. The economy can reinflate to a level matching credit growth or credit growth can dry up, bringing about the long-awaited recession.

We wish that we were expert enough to be able to predict the exact moment that the backlash of this credit boom will begin to affect the economy and the financial markets. Unfortunately, only the experts are capable of such "forecasts." We do feel comfortable in asserting, however, that, during the next few quarters, the unexpected news is much more likely to be negative than positive.

That the news, at least on the market front, has been so oppressively positive this year has been a source of vexation to Perkins. Overvalued stocks have remained overvalued, and the nouveaux riches of the debt boom have bemused him. A few months ago the president of a speculative Florida thrift called him about a thrift institution that Perkins was offering for sale.

"He said he wanted to buy it," Perkins relates.

"I said, 'What are you going to pay for it with?'

"He said, 'I want to buy it.'

" 'With what?'

" 'I have the ability to raise unlimited capital,' he said.

"I told him to go raise the money, then call me back."

All the same, Perkins and his partner, Alen R. Smith, a laconic institutional salesman, have a firm to run. They have customers to deal with and employees to pay. They have just hired an over-the-counter stock trader, Gary Crooks, away from Morgan Stanley (he brings the Perkins-Smith work force to minimum double-digit strength, ten), and they have to pay him. It would be quixotic rather than profitable to suspend operations pending the return of value to the marketplace. "I'm very dull right here," Perkins admits. "We had a meeting the other day, and a salesman is screaming, 'We need more ideas, we need more ideas, we need more ideas,' and I'm screaming back, 'I don't have any ideas, I don't have any ideas, I don't have any ideas.' "

Perkins says that his guiding precept these days is not to capitulate, not to give in to what he has styled the "Compulsion to Play" or the "Law of Absurd Expectations." The "Compulsion to Play" is the impulse-buying trap, and the antidote for it, according to Perkins, is never to place an order while the market is open. The "Law of Absurd Expectations" is the conceit, most prevalent in the blow-off phase of a bull market, that 10 percent to 15 percent is an inferior rate of return. "We fully acknowledge that our business is really not going to be as good as others' in this kind of market," Perkins says. "But the first rule of making money is don't lose money. 'Don't confuse brains with a bull market.' You know, that stuff is really true, and there comes a time when you have to accept that as an investment philosophy."

Asked how Perkins-Smith intends to grow, the senior partner replies cheerfully, "By opportunity. We have no plan." Asked where the firm will be in three to five years, he answers, "We'll be a firm that will have established itself through a complete market cycle." Asked where the firm will be in ten years' time, Perkins replies, "It will have been sold to somebody else, and I will be talking to you from my portable telephone on the Riviera. No, I was never much on the Riviera. I'll be talking to you from Jackson Hole, Wyoming, or Crested Butte, Colorado."

DISASTERNIK

April 6, 1987

J oe Rosenberg is a connoisseur of extremes. His investment policy is to keep his head when all around him are losing theirs—and then to buy or sell the ears off the appropriate market. He has scored his biggest coups when the crowd was either gleeful or despairing, for, as he has said, "our greatest dreams and worst fears are never realized." His style is to foul off a few pitches but ulti-

Joe Rosenberg

mately to connect, and over the years he has hit for power and average alike.

"Mastery never comes, and one serves a lifelong apprenticeship," Anthony Burgess, in his new autobiography, wrote about writing. He might have written about investing. Rosenberg, who is fifty-four years old and who has plied his craft since 1961, continues to serve his apprenticeship (to declare an interest at the start, he happens to be a paid-up subscriber to *Grant's*). "I'm too early on buying, and I'm too early on selling" is his self-appraisal. "The too early on buying has never hurt me, but the too early on selling has." For instance, he caught the bottom of the U.S. government bond market in the spring of 1984 (everybody hated it) but sold too early in 1985 (everybody loved it, but it kept right on going up). Also, having been fundamentally bullish on the stock market as long ago as the fall of 1975, he has chosen to sit out the past couple of years of the greatest bull market in modern annals. "Your moment of discovery isn't the market's," he says. "We find again and again that investment committees come to decisions in three months that take us about three minutes. I should know better how the process works—I spent ten years of my life in a bank. Part of your job is to discover the facts, but part of it is to understand the institutional decision-making structure."

Characteristically, however, Rosenberg has survived this absence from the greatest-stock-market-ever with his self-confidence intact. He has been out of stocks but not short of them, and he has been profitably active in other financial theaters. Also, he has been around long enough to know that nothing lasts forever—or, as he once put it, "in every aspect of life, circumstances breed the seeds of their own reversal." He has a settled opinion on how the bull market will end. The dollar will break, the Japanese stock market will blow up, and the U.S. bond market will be put through the wringer. Rosenberg regards Japanese finance as a kind of supernova in the making, and he predicts a loud and gaudy end for it.

Rosenberg is the chief portfolio manager at Loews Corp., a company with interests in insurance, tobacco, wristwatches, hotels, shipping, and recently—to Dan Rather's distress—network television. Rosenberg's official title, for which he has no use, is president of Lawton General, a Loews investment subsidiary. There is no organization ladder at Loews, and investment decisions are taken collegially. Thomas J. Tisch and James S. Tisch, sons of the

chairman, Laurence A. Tisch, have offices down the hall from
Rosenberg's. Sometimes Rosenberg yells at Jim or Tom Tisch, and
sometimes Tom or Jim Tisch yells at Rosenberg. Sometimes the
father yells at the sons, and sometimes nobody yells at anybody.
"I like to say that this was a nice congenial family company till all
the children came here," says Rosenberg, deadpan.

Rosenberg does not look Wall Street. In the office he is partial
to sweaters, slacks, L. L. Bean–style shoes, and foul-weather-type
outerwear. He is bald. He stands five feet ten inches tall, weighs
a trim 175 pounds (he jogs and hikes), and wears large, rectangular
glasses. He has long ears and a broad, lined brow.

There are many things that most portfolio managers suffer that
Rosenberg does not or will not put up with. For instance, he does
not attend staff meetings because Loews doesn't have them. He
chooses not to have his name in the annual report, and he is not
mentioned in the proxy statement. He does not take the phone
calls of people who bore him. He is aloof from the relative-
performance derby.

If in a given quarter the market happened to be down by 10
percent and if the Loews portfolio happened to be down by only
8 percent, Rosenberg's interpretation of those results would be that
Loews was down by 8 percent. He would take no satisfaction from
the fact that others were down by more than he. He receives no
performance report card, and he is encouraged to do nothing when
inactivity seems the wisest course of action—"If it's in doubt," he
quotes the Loews credo, "don't do it." If sticking with an underwater position seems the advisable position, he is encouraged to
do that, too—as in the stock market in 1974 and the bond market
in 1981. Looking back on the bond episode, Rosenberg calls it a
kind of tulipomania in reverse and a wonderful money-making
opportunity (one earned 14 percent in coupon income while waiting
to be right). When bonds did turn, Loews reaped the rewards of
an $800 million position.

"I have respect for the market, but I don't throw in the towel
quickly," says Rosenberg. "We're stubborn, really. We make most
of our money, literally, in the things we first took losses in." Martin
T. Sosnoff, cofounder of Atlanta/Sosnoff Capital Corp., pays Rosenberg this compliment: "He's one of the few investment people
I know who knows how to stand alone."

Rosenberg may well stand alone in the straight-ahead style of business communications. Lisa Wolfson, who in the late 1970s and early 1980s was Rosenberg's bond salesman at Goldman Sachs, recalls some harrowing moments on the telephone with him—a common memory of Rosenberg's brokers. "I remember taking tremendous amounts of abuse. But he was the greatest customer a salesman could have had. I mean, you had to have your facts laid out, you had to have a strong argument. You had to have it well articulated, and you had to be able to present it in two minutes. You just had to get used to being hung up on in mid-word. You'd be going along, and you'd hear this click. Just click. ·

In reply to the stock question of how much money he has under management, Rosenberg offers the unique reply that he isn't sure. "I have huge sums here, but I've never found out exactly how much I have under management," he says. "What Larry's always said to me is, 'If you find something you like, we always have the money' "—Larry, of course, being Laurence A. Tisch. What Rosenberg currently likes are Australian-dollar bonds, which he began to accumulate last summer when the Aussie dollar was 10 cents lower than it is today and when unsold Aussie securities were a drug on the New York market. Judy, his younger daughter, had just returned from an Australian vacation with reports of the towering local yields, and Rosenberg, who had owned Australian bonds in 1985, decided to return to the market in force. He recalls it pleasantly as one campaign in which he wasn't early, and he estimates his total return over the past six months to be over 25 percent. "If I could have nothing but investments like that," he says, "I'd be happy as a clam—not dependent on analysts, not dependent on Wall Street. All I have to do is read *The Wall Street Journal* and the *Financial Times*, and I think I can do that. It gives me a secure feeling because I can rely on knowledge rather than information flow."

With the exception of silver and Aussie bonds and copper and ocean tankers and special situations like Tosco Corp. preferred, Rosenberg is not playing. He calls himself a long-term bull but a short-term bear on the U.S. bond market. He is out of step with bull stock markets from Mexico City to Tokyo. A bear these days might console himself with the company he keeps—Warren Buffett, for instance, who has stated that the U.S. stock market offers no value—and Rosenberg is certainly no more bearish than his astute employer, Larry Tisch. Nevertheless, nobody relishes a quarrel with the tape, and sometimes Rosenberg thinks about the good-natured ribbing he has taken from his bullish friend Barton Biggs, global portfolio strategist at Morgan Stanley. "I've told him," says Biggs, "he's a classic Middle-European Jew who can't stand prosperity. His tombstone's going to say 'Joe Rosenberg,' and the epitaph will read, 'I was early.' "

Rosenberg is prepared to concede the truth of some of this. He was six when his family fled Germany in April 1939, carrying memories of Hitler and the great inflation with them to New York. "They never really knew good times," says Rosenberg of his parents. "The whole period between the wars was horrible." (But not the war itself for the senior Rosenberg: "One of the great mysteries of my life is what my father did in Bialystock for four years—he was a quartermaster stationed on the Eastern front. He clearly enjoyed it.")

A newly landed New Yorker, Rosenberg attended public schools in Manhattan and the Bronx. He finished high school at night while working in the day. Two weeks after his graduation he left for Israel, where he spent two years on a kibbutz and a year behind the wheel of a green Ford dump truck for a rock-products company. He drove his Ford twelve hours a day and took it home for the weekends and out on dates. He dreamed of buying his own dump truck but was frustrated by a political strike that had nothing to do with what he regarded as his welfare. "A lot of my idealism was knocked out of me," he says, "but what I realized twenty years later was that this was part of the making of Joe Rosenberg. In a sense I went over to Israel as a scared refugee, and I came back as a confident person."

Rosenberg, twenty-one, returned to the United States. He entered the army, took basic training, completed radio operators' school, and served with the Second Armored Division in Bad Kreuznach, West Germany. He was a specialist third class who happened to love field maneuvers. "What happened in the army," says Rosenberg, "was that I realized that if I was going to stay in America there was a vast difference between educated and uneducated people. I realized I had to go to college."

Separated from the army in January 1957, Rosenberg enrolled in the night undergraduate program of New York University, holding down a daytime job in the accounting department of Columbia Pictures. "I reviewed producers' expense accounts. What that did, it convinced me I wasn't a detail man. At NYU I'd enrolled in something called international marketing, and I found out very quickly that international marketing meant I could be an import-export clerk." Gradually, his interests turned to Wall Street, and he began to wonder how he could major in the stock market. He married the former Aleza Goldstein.

"In 1961," says Rosenberg, "I got my B.S. in whatever it was —I couldn't get enough credits to major in finance—and I started to pound on doors on Wall Street. I would have taken anything, although I wanted to start in research. I didn't qualify for at least three reasons: I wasn't a WASP, I didn't go to the right college, and I didn't have an M.B.A. Even the firms that used to come to NYU to lecture on ethics wouldn't hire Jews in those days. Many of the major firms, from Morgan Stanley to Kidder Peabody to Goodbody, discriminated, and the Jewish firms were busy hiring 'Our Crowd' Jews. That left me with the option of going to Bache & Co., which I did."

His job was in Bache's information center, fielding brokers' questions over the telephone. "I thought it was a fabulous opportunity," says Rosenberg, "and when somebody asked me something, I didn't wing it. I made sure that I got the answers, and the brokers knew and appreciated it." Later on, as a junior analyst, when he was invited to tackle the airlines, he jumped at the chance. "Little did they know that giving me the airlines would light a fire under a rocket," Rosenberg recalls—and little did Rosenberg know that the airline stocks were going to quadruple. What he soon grasped, however, was the significance of the conversion from piston to jet power, and he became an early and prophetic bull on the industry.

Rosenberg's personal stock quickly followed the airlines'. "Joe was a terrific analyst," says the then head of research at Bache, Lawrence Bleiberg. "He was so terrific, in fact, that when I left Bache in 1964 to be head of research at Empire Trust Co., I took him with me."

Rosenberg, who had barely escaped the 1962 bear market with his job, flourished in the mid-1960s bull market. He began to write for *Barron's*, and a bullish piece on TWA under his byline in 1965—aptly headed WILD BLUE YONDER—produced a flood of buyers and a delayed opening in the Hughes-owned airline. But it was in this effervescent period that Rosenberg, characteristically, began to change his mind. He had never left NYU: After earning his B.S., he signed on for the four-year nighttime M.B.A. program. The topic he chose for his master's thesis was the economics of the supersonic jet, and his working hypothesis was bullish. But the more he delved, the more he doubted. His forehanded conclusion, well in advance of the airlines' top, was that the glory days were over.

Rosenberg was happy at Empire Trust, and he succeeded Larry Bleiberg (who had moved on to Kuhn Loeb) as head of research. But when Empire was merged with Bank of New York in 1966, cultures clashed. "The head of the trust division didn't like my new ideas, and he was annoyed with my style," is Rosenberg's recollection. "He would have been perfectly happy if I'd sat around and done nothing. His last comment to me was 'This bank was founded by Alexander Hamilton, and we got along without Rosenberg for two hundred years,' and I finished the sentence for him, 'and you're going to get along without Rosenberg from here on.'"

A year later, in 1968, Rosenberg was running hedge funds and directing research at J. Henry Schroder Bank & Trust Co. Five years later—the Nifty Fifty had come and had almost gone, and Rosenberg was pushing forty—he took stock of his life. He recalls: "I weighed 205 pounds. I wasn't exercising, I wasn't jogging, I wasn't hiking, I wasn't climbing mountains. I decided that that was crazy, that there was more to life than what I was doing."

Larry Tisch had asked him to run the Loews investment portfolio as early as 1971. "He was a unique thinker," says Tisch. When the invitation was renewed in the spring of 1973, Rosenberg accepted. He took a long vacation in Israel and started work for Tisch in August 1973.

Loews at the time was a $3 stock. "Remember," says Rosenberg, "this was before Loews had accumulated its full position in CNA Financial. This was before Jimmy and Tom Tisch were here. On the investment side it was Larry, myself, and another analyst. In 1973 we were running a huge stock portfolio. We thought stocks looked cheap, although by the end of 1974 they looked a lot cheaper. [In January 1973, the Dow peaked at 1,067; in December

1974, it bottomed, for the second time, at 570.] By the end of 1974, we were heavily under water in the stock market, but we owned a lot of very cheap stocks. There was a huge rally in January-February 1975, and we sold a lot of 'em. All you had to do was be there. We got out of 'em too early. We always do. That is the bane of our life." One position that was not liquidated, of course, was an investment position in CNA Financial, of which Loews today owns 80 percent. "We ended up owning it," says Rosenberg, only half facetiously, "because it wasn't a good investment."

Memo writing, along with staff meetings and long-range planning and in-house haute cuisine, is a low-priority item at Loews, and Rosenberg has produced a grand total of three memoranda in fourteen years. His first was dated October 1975, when the Dow had regained about half its sickening 1973–74 losses but before anything like a decade-length bull market was in sight. Rosenberg predicted a long pull on the up side, and he noted that crises, real or imagined, were nothing new in market history. He counseled Tisch:

> At this writing, the market is petrified by the prospect of a N.Y.C. default. No one knows its implications. Therefore, there will be sharp sell-offs in securities! But how lasting will the sell-offs be? The prospects at the time of the Cuban missile crisis were much worse and the outlook in 1970 was equally as bad as it is today. These moments of greatest fear have always been moments of great opportunity.

In the late 1970s, Loews played the stock market by sector, buying the oils, the utilities (especially American Telephone & Telegraph Co.) and—after the 1980 break—the retailers. Rosenberg recalls that his view of things was not so much macro as micro but that as the bond market quickened its slide, his attention turned to interest rates.

"When '81 came around," says Rosenberg, "there was nothing, to my mind, that could compare with bonds. What we did, we constructed 'what-if' tables, matrixes that showed what we would gain or lose if interest rates went up or down." The tables reinforced his bullishness, and Rosenberg and Loews stayed and stayed, buying as the market went against them. "I made the low tick in Fannie Mae stock at 6⅜ a share in September 1981," says Rosen-

berg, who was not a buyer recently at 48¼. He made another big
bond play in May 1984 (preceded by Rosenberg memo number
two), getting out too soon again, and reentered the interest rate
arena in the Australian dollar sector in late 1985 (memo number
three). He is there again.

Where he is not, of course, is the Japanese stock market, which
he regards as material for a new chapter of the old book, *Extraordinary Popular Delusions and the Madness of Crowds*, or in the U.S.
stock market, "because I haven't gotten used to paying eighteen
times earnings." He has other reasons, of course—among others,
"the substitution of financial guarantees for liquidity and portfolio
insurance which is really not insurance at all"—but the bulls so far
have paid him no heed. It was recently pointed out to Rosenberg
that he had made his money and reputation on the long side of
the market, not the short side. It was further noted that he had
scored his airline coup as a young man when he was relatively
unburdened by financial experience and market lore. The question
was put: At fifty-four, is he a back number? Is he perhaps missing
something in middle age that he had so clearly possessed in youth?

"I'll respond to that," Rosenberg said directly. "In the case of
specific industries, for instance in the airline industry, it's absolutely
true that a young analyst, looking at things fresh—if he is as hard-
working as I was and is really willing to dig in—has a tremendous
advantage over me. I'll always believe, by the way, that in hiring
analysts, the best guys are the ones with two or three years' experience, preferably from a poor background—hungry, cynical,
skeptical, taking nothing for granted. As concerns an industry, it's
absolutely true.

"However, as concerns the big issues—interest rates, what I call
the universal issues—I won't defer to anybody because a knowledge of history is so important. You have to be a historian, not a
'quant.' Really, in those issues, there's nothing new under the
sun."

EVERYONE IS NEVER BULLISH

July 13, 1987

O n July 8, 1932, *The Wall Street Journal* published a brief inspirational message from John D. Rockefeller, who that day turned ninety-three. Optimism from any reputable source was news in 1932, and the old capitalist's salutation got front-page treatment. It said, in part: "These are days when many are discouraged. In the ninety-three years of my life, depressions have come and gone. Prosperity has always returned, and will again."

Although there was no gainsaying Rockefeller's wealth, his reputation for market timing, starting with his immortal, mid-Crash boner, "My sons and I have been buying common stocks," had suffered a bear market of its own. His sons and he were at that moment building Rockefeller Center, but history's judgment—that the timing was merely perfect—was still to be written.

Thus, contrarians of the day might well have ignored the Rockefeller message. It is understood on Wall Street that nobody rings a bell; and—a corollary—if a bell *does* ring, it is probably the wrong

The surviving shorts map strategy

one. It is also axiomatic that everyone is bullish at the top of a market, and everyone is bearish at the bottom. Plainly, on July 8, 1932, not everyone was bearish. John D. Rockefeller was not bearish. Odd to relate, therefore, that the Rockefeller birthday call coincided exactly with the all-time low of the Dow Jones Industrial Average. On that date, on cue, the index bottomed at 41.88. A year later, it was over 100.

Market sentiment, that branch of investing concerned with words, not deeds, is a subject much in vogue nowadays. Our interest in this subject, or in one phase of it, is highly personal. We are, of course, bearish. We have, of course, been wrong on the big picture (or, as we like to say in-house, early). Having repeatedly heard that no major top is possible until every last bear has been exiled, shot, or converted to the long side, we've been moved to check the historical record. At the top, has every skeptic lost his tongue? At the bottom, is there even one optimist? How literally must one take this notion that, at inflection points, "everyone" must be on one side of the boat or the other?

Our investigation took us to the library. We checked a number of standard financial sources and read *The Wall Street Journal* for the month or so preceding major market turns. We checked up on the stock market in 1929, 1932, 1937, 1968, and 1973, and on the bond market in 1981 and 1984. In executive-summary form, our conclusion is that contrary opinion can be carried too far. By contrary opinion we mean the popular version of the credo that the majority, in financial affairs, is destined to lose. In its extreme form, the contrary opinion idea holds that the best financial company is none at all. It says that, at major market turning points, majority opinion is almost unanimously wrong.

Fortified by research, we would modify that idea. Although the consensus view is typically incorrect, a sizable minority can sometimes be right. When the chips are down, sentiment is typically lopsided but not invariably unanimous. For instance, on September 21, 1981, the eve of perhaps the greatest bond-buying opportunity ever, the *Journal*'s credit markets column was obligingly headed ANALYSTS SEE SOFT ECONOMY THROUGH 1981, ADDING TO PRESSURE FOR INTEREST RATE DROP. On that particular day the consensus was righter than rain.

Sentiment is a gossamer thing, and it is hard enough to measure day by day, let alone to reconstruct for times past. Thus, we make no claims to science, hoping only to show that contrary opinion is not exactly a branch of physics, either. Compounding the problems of definition and measurement is the evolution of *The Wall Street Journal*, our main source, from the insider's stock market paper of the 1920s to the general-interest business daily of recent years. From the 1890s until its World War II–era modernization, the *Journal* was written for the Street. The investment mood was faithfully reported, and if 1929 is the centerpiece of this study, it is because that episode was more elaborately chronicled than the others. Was there more caution in 1929 than in 1968? Or was it merely that the *Journal*'s antennae were keener in the 1920s than in the 1960s? We don't know, but the stock market claimed more of the *Journal*'s attention then than it does now. (By the way, we would hereby like to distance ourselves from the theory that the 1980s are merely a rerun of the 1920s or that 1987 is actually 1927 but with an extra zero tacked onto the end of the significant data. It will be different this time, whatever it is and however it ends.)

In any event, we can report that vocal minorities have prevailed at some market turns. As noted, the bond bulls were not completely annihilated in 1981, nor were they silenced at the bottom in 1984. Nor, as will be seen, were the equity bears wholly absent from the stock market in 1929.

What stands out most at market turns is not that nobody is right. Financial discussion is normally conducted in the tempered language of marginal change. Because fundamental change is rare and upsetting, people tend to project the present into the future. It is a convention appropriate for most markets in most times but not at turning points. What one almost never reads, on the eve of a major reversal, is that the current trend is over, whatever the trend was. There is a failure of financial imagination. Thus, in December 1972 and January 1973, as the Nifty Fifty bull stock market gasped its last, bears were little quoted in the *Journal*'s columns. What few there were spoke timidly about a correction, not a cataclysm. (That year *Barron's* fatefully headed its annual investment panel, "Not a Bear Among Them.") Ditto 1968; and ditto 1937.

Which brings us to 1929 and its wealth of market reporting. The striking feature about the *Journal*'s columns in the month or so preceding the peak of the Dow in early September is their tone of caution. We flatter ourselves, we electronic database moderns, if we imagine that the financial establishment of that day marched over the cliff in lockstep, chatting about the new era. Reading the old papers now, a contrary-minded trader might wonder that the high level of caution didn't preclude a top. Although nobody we read predicted collapse (Roger Babson, the most conspicuous doomsayer of the period, wasn't quoted), there was a chronic undertone of worry. "Abreast of the Market" on Wednesday, September 4 (the day after the Dow peaked at 381.17), summed up the mood:

> Although sentiment generally is quite optimistic, it is noted that a large number of commission houses are strongly advising customers to take profits during advances in the stocks being carried. Similar recommendations in the past resulted in clients losing their long positions and paying higher prices for their favorite shares, so that it is now admitted that many outsiders are not inclined to follow this advice at the moment. Many are looking for corrective technical reactions from time to time, but do not expect these to disturb the upward trend for any long period.

The old papers show the bears' travail but also their numbers. Not every skeptic was unemployed (a fact we noted with relief). From "Abreast of the Market," Tuesday, August 27:

> There is a growing feeling that technical conditions in the market are not as sound as they were a few weeks ago. The point is made that short covering has been on a large scale and that this has taken some of the buying power out of the market during reactions. This is true to a certain extent, but it is known that the higher prices again attracted a supply from the bears attempting to pick the top of the advance. Hence there is still quite a large sized short interest in the market.

Unfortunately, short interest is undocumented in this period, but "Abreast of the Market" suggests it was sizable—large enough, certainly, to furnish some sport for the bulls. On Friday, August 23:

Punishing the shorts has become a popular pastime with some of the traders who are optimistic. They seek stocks which had been targets for short selling and start an advance which usually results in urgent covering and sharp advances in quotations.

To be sure, it was a bullish time, and the *Journal* gave the new era its due. One of the favorite bull contentions was that "they" —the "big interests"—wouldn't permit a decline. "You hear that the big bankers do not care to see a declining market because they have too many big transactions on the carpet," said the "Broad Street Gossip" column of Friday, August 9. Another favorite was that the investment trusts—the mutual funds of the day—constituted an ever-bubbling brook of investable funds. On Saturday, August 24, the paper ventured, "Such powerful support underlying the general list is unprecedented in the history of the Stock Exchange and is the principal reason why the current market cannot be judged by the standards of the past." Merely substitute Japanese buying for investment trusts, and the "powerful support" theory is as fresh as a daisy.

In another familiar-sounding touch, the *Journal* noted a generational split in the market, with youth opting for the long side of the market and the old crocks for caution. From "Abreast of the Market," Monday, August 26:

A number of so-called old-time operators have been inclined to be increasingly cautious in the past few days on the theory that the technical position of the market is not as sound as it was some time ago. These traders have been taking profits whenever advances occurred.

On the other hand, most of the so-called younger element insists that there is no reason to look for any sharp reaction, because the upturns of the past have not weakened the technical situation. This group contends that most of the sharp gains have resulted from the smaller floating supply as a result of the large amount of stock taken out of the market for investment trusts [see new-era argument, above—Ed.].

As mentioned, the relative abundance of doubt at what proved an epochal market top was encouraging to us doubters. Richard Russell, editor of *Dow Theory Letters*, a longstanding bull on the stock market who recently has had his own doubts, was consulted on this matter of sentiment. He said, first off, that probably too much attention nowadays is given to what people are saying. "My experience is that every top is a fooler," he said, adding that the current divergence in the stock market between price and breadth is his candidate for the most ominous technical sign of the season. He noted also that the Dow currently yields less than 3 percent, a classic sign of overvaluation. He said that the one and only indicator that has held up at every market top has been value—or, more specifically, the lack of it. Russell, however, is still a bull. Some of our best friends are bulls.

LET'S BURY THE GOLD

September 21, 1987

A friend proposes to strike it rich in gold by giving the public what it wants. What the public wants is mining stock. We know that by the stupendous valuations accorded mining companies at a time of stable gold prices. People want mines—so let's give them mines, our friend proposes. Let's buy some gold, bury it, dig it up, and sell it.

Consider Echo Bay Mines, a large Canadian property with an enormous (sixty-seven times) ratio of price to earnings. Echo Bay has some 94.6 million shares outstanding on the American Stock Exchange with an aggregate capitalization (at 28½ a share) of some $2.7 billion. Its relatively modest debt is approximately balanced by its equally modest current assets.

Now then, our friend says, let's just go out and buy $2.7 billions' worth of gold (5,886,000 ounces at $458 an ounce) and bury it. We'll pull it back out of the ground and sell it in regular quantities over the next twelve years (490,500 ounces a year).

We quote from our friend's business plan:

To keep excavation costs down, I suggest loading the bars into inexpensive surplus railroad tunnels somewhere along the old anthracite routes at a capital cost of, say, $1 million. The use of potholes on New York City streets, while geologically feasible, would detract from the dignity of the enterprise and increase security costs. I suggest Golden Recycle as a possible corporate moniker.

Now then, what would our income statement look like?

At $458 an ounce, assuming $1 million in annual operating expenses and a twelve-year, straight-line depreciation of our mine site, you get: revenues of $221.5 million; operating expenses of $1 million, and operating cash flow of $220.5 million. Now then, subtract depletion of $221.5 million, depreciation of $80,000 and—presto—there's a loss of $1 million or thereabouts. The tax advantages of a reported loss have been obvious for years to Kohlberg, Kravis, Roberts.

The accompanying table presents a comparison of Echo Bay with Golden Recycle, with Golden Recycle, we submit, showing up to advantage.

THE CASE FOR RECYCLING		
	ECHO BAY (PRO FORMA)	GOLDEN RECYCLE
Market capitalization ($ millions)	$2,696	$2,696
Reserves (thousands of ounces)	5,550	5,886
Annual sales (thousands of ounces)	456	483.7
Cash production cost/ounce	$ 224	$ 2
Operating cash flow ($ millions)	59.8	220.5
Future operating cash flow of reserves at present prices ($ millions)	727.8	2,683
Annual after-tax earnings ($ millions)	31.6	(1.0)
Market capitalization/ounces of reserves ($)	486	458
Market capitalization/ounces of annual production ($)	5,912	5,574
Price/cash flow	45x	12.2x
Price/earnings	85x	N/A

Our friend elaborates:

In addition to being far more financially attractive, Golden Recycle
has a superior operating margin, lower costs, no environmental exposure, and fewer labor problems. Production rates can be accelerated at modest cost or slowed, with little adverse effect on
operating margins. Unlike other gold mines, it can be located, and
if necessary relocated, in the most politically stable and favorable
tax environments.

Several technical objections can be dealt with summarily. It is
true that Echo Bay Mines has an ongoing exploration effort. In the
first six months of 1987, exploration costs burned up cash at the
blazing rate of $4 million a year. It is our hope that Golden Recycle
might be able to devote some portion of its $161 million of excess
annual cash flow to remedy any problems of self perpetuation. To
the extent such expenditures are incremental expenses, since the
company has no taxable income, these costs might be partially re-
coverable through the creation of additional tax-loss carryforwards
to be offset against future income.

There is no provision in the Golden Recycle figures for promotional markup. I leave that to the fertile imaginations of the readers
of *Grant's* as to how such sums might be painlessly exacted.

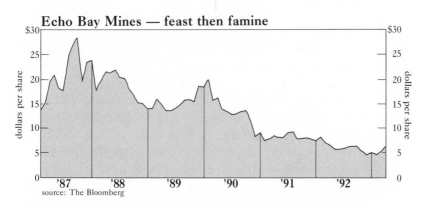

Echo Bay Mines — feast then famine

source: The Bloomberg

As desirable an investment as Golden Recycle may be, it is
arguably an even more lucrative investment banking project. Morgan Stanley, Goldman Sachs, First Boston, or any other reputable
applicant is invited to contact this office, day or night.

THE PARADOX OF PREFERRED

August 3, 1990

W hen a stock falls out of bed, the papers mention the selling, which is always "heavy." What they usually fail to mention is the buying. By definition it, too, is heavy. It is, in fact, just as heavy as the selling, down to the last share.

We mention this truism because of the recent heavy selling—not to mention the heavy buying—in American bank stocks. As every subscriber has read before, the tide of debt is going out. The decay in creditworthiness, long masked by strength in the economy, is now being exposed by weakness. It is, we think, no accident that the New York Stock Exchange new-low list is littered with the names of banks.

Everyone is entitled to his opinion about this predicament. Some (like us) expect it to be protracted. They will read the fall in bank stocks as part and parcel of the decline in credit generally—another scene in what is only the first act of a long play. Others will argue that the worst is over, that prosperity is around the corner, and that the sky is always darkest before the dawn.

We address this report on preferred stock to the bullish group. To judge by the heavy volume in certain falling bank stocks, there is no shortage of bulls. To judge by the lack of interest in the preferred stock of the same banks, however, not every last bull is discriminating.

We owe this flash to a reader who trades preferred, who has periodically watched his market sink almost out of sight, and who is struck now (as he has sometimes been in the past) by the presence of value. Our friend, who would rather go nameless, ventures no opinion about the future of American banking. He is not, in fact, bullish on the underlying bank issuers, taking his cue from the weakness in the stocks. He admits that if the common is doomed, the preferred might be, too. He is impressed, though, by the disparity between the yields on common and preferred, especially on adjustable-rate preferred.

Adjustable-rate preferred stock (ARPS) is a very unlucky security. Corporations buy it for tax advantages—dividends received are 70 percent exempt from federal income tax—only to have the tax advantages swamped by periodic capital losses. From time to time the market is jolted by rumors that the dividend-received deduction will be cut or eliminated (no such rumor is circulating now). And because so many ARPS issuers are banks, the market is tarred with the broad brush of credit. And if that weren't enough, the market is also illiquid.

But those tribulations, to the would-be buyer of a bank's common stock, may not be relevant. Let's take the case of Continental Bank, successor to unlucky Continental Illinois. When its common stock recently traded at a price to yield 7.6 percent, its adjustable-rate preferred stock traded at a price to yield 13.7 percent. The ARP came to market last year at 25; true to ARP form, it was quoted Monday at 18⅜. Now then, the Continental ARP pays a dividend of $2.52. It is structured to pay a dividend no lower than $2.25; even if Treasury rates revisit 7.90 percent or less, it will pay no less than $2.25. Taking the now-current dividend rate of $2.52 as a percentage of the 18⅜ purchase price produces the yield mentioned above: 13.7 percent.

You may say: Yes, preferred stock is a senior security, but it lacks the juice of the common. It doesn't have the up side, and that explains the price disparity. As it happens, that is not strictly accurate. Our anonymous source did some checking. In the case of Chrysler, for instance, the preferred did better than the common in the automaker's return from the dead between 1981 and 1983. Similarly, Consumers Power preferred outpaced the common during a two-year span of that company's recovery.

But to get back to the suspenseful bank-stock market of today: MNC Financial, parent to Maryland National Bank, has a well-known battered common stock and an unknown battered preferred. The preferred, an ARP, is quoted at 15½, to yield 23.2 percent. Whatever happens to the Treasury yield curve, the stock will pay no less than 14½ percent (assuming purchase at the current price, 15½). Mysteriously, the common, quoted at 9½, yields only 12.4 percent.

No doubt many bulls are buying the common stocks of money-center banks for their yields. If so, they are missing a bet because the preferreds frequently yield more. We have not checked every name, but Manufacturers Hanover is a case in point. At last report the common was priced to yield 10.70 percent. The series "B" preferred, on the other hand, was priced to yield 12.79 percent. If interest rates fell, the adjustable preferred dividend would be adjusted downward, but in no case (based on a purchase price of 34) would the yield be less than 11 percent. If interest rates rose, the yield could go as high as 22.8 percent.

Our anonymous friend reflected on these facts.* The buyers of common stock in troubled banks are placing a strange credit bet, he said. They're betting that a junior security will outperform a less-junior security. They are buying a lower yielding security when they might have a higher yielding one. They didn't even do that in the 1980s.

FLIGHT TO LEVERAGE

February 1, 1991

The stock market is the coldest fish in the sea. It doesn't say hello or goodbye, and it never looks back. It is no respecter of people or themes, and it does not subscribe to *Grant's* (although some of the people who work in it do).

---

* David Gale (now he may be named) was righter than rain. Bank preferreds excelled, in many cases outrunning the corresponding common stocks. MNC preferred, to pick an extreme example, rallied from 15½ on August 1, 1990, to 45½ at year-end 1992 (while the common, in the same period, appreciated from 9½ to 12⅞). The lesson I have taken away from this lucrative episode is always to ask, "What's cheap?"

We must remind ourselves of these hard truths for the day when the credit cycle turns. Come that time, it will behoove us to be looking forward to the next expansion, not backward to the last contraction. The past is an easier topic than the future, and a hobbyhorse is the most comfortable seat in the house. For years we have ridden the hobbyhorse of debt, and it's a cinch that the market will not ring a bell when it's time to dismount.

Is now the time? Nobody can deny that lots of bad news is already out in the open. ("Yes, there are terrible problems," an investor friend wrote to his clients recently, "but they're old news . . . the market's heard, digested, and absorbed enough melancholia to last a lifetime." Elaborating on the telephone, our friend said that the rush of purpose and patriotism is a new and irresistible force in the financial markets; he is very bullish indeed.) Citicorp, the largest banking organization in the country, is in deep trouble. Depositors in Providence, Rhode Island, have run for their insured deposits, the Bank Insurance Fund is nearing insolvency, state and local finances are going downhill, credit-card delinquencies are on the rise, and corporate bankruptcies are piling up. The Soviet Union has executed a reverse split of the ruble.

Yet the market has stopped reacting to the bad news. Last Friday's snap downgrade of Citicorp by Moody's, which to us seemed devastating, elicited a stifled yawn from the buyers and sellers of Citicorp common on Monday. In the broad market, as a reader notes, a "flight to leverage" has been under way for weeks. The worse the balance sheet, it's beginning to seem, the better the speculation.

One day, of course, the contraction will end and the cycle will turn. On that day, the market will sensibly consign the news of the latest default or bank run to the file marked "Irrelevant." The financial consequences of the contraction will have played themselves out, and investors will begin the lucrative work of discounting the next expansion.

Is now the time? It is not. Are we bearish out of habit or conviction? The latter, we like to think; we have our reasons. One is that the decade of the 1980s was decades in the making. The extremes of lending and borrowing were not the ordinary stuff of business cycles but something larger. It isn't every cycle in which Citicorp shoots itself in the balance sheet, in which something called "junk bonds" is invented, or in which the continued insurance of bank deposits by the federal government becomes financially unfeasible. These are momentous developments, and the reaction from them will probably be protracted and deep rather then short and sweet. Patience, we keep muttering to ourselves.

The consensus of forecasters, as we read it, expects a short war, a short recession, and a supine currency market. It does not acknowledge that the boom of the 1980s was any lustier (and therefore more potentially dangerous on the downside) than the boom of the 1960s. It does not expect a currency crisis, even given the remarkable yield premium that holders of deutsche marks and yen enjoy in comparison with the holders of dollars. It evidently seems to believe that foreign investors do not read the newspapers or that, if they do, they skip over the news about interest rates, monetary policy, the FDIC, and Citicorp,* proceeding directly to book reviews or Super Bowl commentary.

How will we know when the contraction is over? We will not know. We will guess. Our guess today is that a number of events will precede the end of the cycle. For example, the last perceived sure-fire class of banking asset—consumer loans—will show additional signs of wear and tear. The vast commercial-paper market, undergirded by promises to lend from questionable banks, will suffer new reverses. Perhaps the huge market in interest rate and currency swaps (which grew quickly in the dark, like a mushroom farm) will have a credit-related shock.† Our working theory is that the boom was so far outside the pale of conservative finance that the expectant majority now awaiting the start of the next expansion will almost certainly be disappointed. Probably, we think, the process of contraction will continue to work slowly. Rallies along the way will give heart to the bulls and scare the bears half to death.

As credit continues to shrink, we believe, so must business activity weaken. As to how the war might tilt the macro economy in the next weeks, months, or years, we have no guess. Perhaps (as

---

* Paradoxically, it was the very weakness of Citicorp that may have provoked the Federal Reserve to reduce its discount rate by one full point, from 4½ percent to 3½ percent, on December 20, 1991. On the same day Citicorp common hit a startling low price of 8⅝. On cue from the Fed, the stock market rallied. Even Citicorp went up.
† There was no such drama.

so many think) it will be bullish. But the shooting was not what stopped the lending, and it seems unlikely to us that peace will restore liquidity.*

YO, STOCK

March 13, 1992

I n the 1980s it was understood that private-market valuations were naturally higher than public-market valuations. Everybody knew that the collective judgment of the buyers of corporate equities was too conservative. Furthermore, everybody understood why. Owning a company outright bestowed the precious gift of control. Also, extreme financial leverage was a permanent good, because asset values and business activity both would rise perpetually. As times change, so do fashions in corporate finance. Nowadays, equity capital is cheap and abundant. It is lying on sidewalks, piling up in mailboxes, and falling out of pants pockets, and it is only a matter of time before the leading college finance professors explain why this condition, too, is normal and wholesome.

When Providential Corp., a new San Francisco–based mortgage company, needed financing to expand, it literally searched the globe. No capital was forthcoming from private sources because the company was (and is) cash-flow negative. Unable to grow, Providential temporarily stopped writing mortgages (its specialty are so-called reverse mortgages, debt obligations under which a

---

* To this day I do not pretend to understand why the great expansion of the 1980s produced such a comparatively mild contraction in the 1990s. Nobody who lost his job, his business, or his property in 1991 or 1992 would call the recession short or mild. However, in proportion to the offenses committed on Wall Street against safety and soundness, the aftermath of the boom might almost be counted a stroke of national luck. Rereading this piece, I am struck by how persuasive I was in making the wrong arguments. The lumpen consensus opinion—that the market was going to go up because everything was going to be better—proved to be the accurate one.

borrower may take the equity out of his home to supplement his income). "Bill Texido is a smart guy," says a man who was involved with the chairman of Providential during the long quest for money, "and if there was financing to be had, he would have found it. Scoured from Hong Kong to Paris. Lo and behold, an underwriter [two, in fact: Prudential Securities and PaineWebber] comes along and says, 'Let's go public.' " Priced at $16, the stock instantly traded in the low $20s. On Monday it topped $26.*

That is good news for the investment bankers, the entrepreneurs, and the customers. Is it also good news for the investors? In the 1980s countless companies raised billions of dollars, calling it debt. Now some of them are exchanging the debt for equity. Once again, taking the investor's side, one must ask whether the change constitutes progress. Is it possible that the characteristic investment-banking sin of the 1980s, even more than leverage, was overcapitalization? And isn't it also possible that the equity boom is only compounding that error, creating new seas of redundant capital (and junior capital at that) that our ancestors on Wall Street called "water"?

Here is a new law of market timing: Speculative excess isn't dangerous until it begins to seem reasonable. A case in point is Callaway Golf, manufacturer of the famous Big Bertha driver. Priced at $20 on February 27, the Callaway IPO instantly zoomed well into the 30s. (In a Florida hotel room on the morning the stock was launched, a dozen skeptical money managers rolled their eyes in disbelief over the valuation; then they began to compare notes about how much stock they had been allotted by the brokers. Not one admitted to turning down his allotment of stock on the grounds that it was an affront to the value-investing discipline.) The stock has since settled in around $28.75† a share for a market capitalization of $200 million, the equivalent of 4 times revenues, 18 times earnings before interest and taxes, 31 times net earnings, and 6.6 times book value.

Is the Callaway driver unique? Patent lawyers may argue the point, but Big Bertha was not alone at the recent annual merchandise show of the Professional Golfers' Association of America. It

* In mid-February 1993, it was quoted at 7¾.
† Now 44⅞.

competed with a number of other jumbo drivers, including Launcher, Whale, Wide Body, Fat Eddie, Big Z, Big Ben, Big Head, Mr. Big, Top Dawg, and The Judge. "The subjective preferences of golf club purchasers may also be subject to rapid and unanticipated changes," noted the Callaway prospectus. "There can be no assurances as to how long the company's golf clubs will maintain market acceptance." At thirty-one times net income, an investor must hit birdies and eagles and aces. Par is not good enough, and bogeys are disastrous.

Callaway does not take the cake this season, however. Radiation Care, which owns and operates outpatient radiation therapy centers for cancer patients, does. Radiation Care was organized in November 1990 and opened its first center in June 1991. Now it has eight facilities in operation and three under development. The Radiation Care IPO was self-underwritten (a so-called best efforts offering), and rumor has it that no investment bank in Atlanta, the company's home base, would go near it. At the current price of $14.75* the company boasts a market cap of $223 million, or 67.9 times annualized revenues.

The chairman is Thomas E. Haire, and his daughter, Christi K. Haire, is chief operating officer and chief financial officer. Thomas Haire, who also happens to be chairman and CEO of T^2 Medical, the home infusion therapy company, thought he could sell the stock himself, and he could. "To my friends in health care:" he wrote in December in a cover note attached to a preliminary prospectus,

> About a year ago, I started a new company to own and operate outpatient radiation therapy centers. We are pleased with its progress and have decided to proceed with a public offering of its stock. I thought you might be interested in making an investment and am enclosing a copy of the preliminary prospectus. . . .
>
> If, after reviewing this document, you wish to be contacted as the offering proceeds, please complete the attached form and fax it . . . or call . . . to indicate your level of interest. If you choose to call the office, please ask for Investor Relations. The offices of

---

* Now 3¹¹/₁₆.

Radiation Care only have eight incoming lines, so please bear with
us if the lines are busy.
  Very truly yours.

The Atlanta investment bankers could hardly believe their eyes.
A company that was little more than a business plan had managed
a market capitalization of more than $200 million over their barely
concealed guffaws. It succeeded despite the blunt disclosure that
"substantially all of the company's revenue to date has been derived
from cancer patients referred to the company's centers by physicians who are stockholders of the company, and loss of such referrals
would materially adversely effect [sic] the financial condition of the
company." The prospectus went on for three more paragraphs
about why the company's ability to do business in this way may
be outlawed in several states. As for the lack of an underwriter, it
said on page seven, "No independent due diligence has been performed by an underwriter, and this prospectus has not been reviewed by underwriter's counsel." If the prospectus was reviewed
by the investors, they sent money anyway. Eight incoming telephone lines turned out to be enough.
  Video Lottery Technologies, a designer, maker, and marketer
of gambling terminals, can thank its lucky stars that it didn't sell
out in 1990. A letter of intent was signed, and a price was set:
$13.6 million, representing approximately four times 1990 net in-
come, a little less than half of revenues and 1.9 times book. Then
happily—brilliantly—plans went awry, and the hoped-for merger
(with International Game Technology) was called off.
  That was on January 11, 1991. Seven months later, Video Lottery
itself won the lottery. It went public at $14 a share. Now its stock
changes hands at $31* a share for a market value of no less than
$318 million. For perspective, in the twelve months ended last
September 30, Video Lottery produced revenues of $24 million
and net income of $3.4 million. At $31 a share, it is valued at 9
times revenues, 49 times earnings before interest and taxes, 88
times net earnings, 7 times net asset value, and 7.5 times book
value.
  As for *Grant's*, we do not deplore these valuations so much as

* Now 11½.

covet them. Expect our preliminary equity prospectus in your mail, and please be patient. We have only five phone lines.

ONE-MAN FIRM

February 26, 1993

The Reichmann real estate enterprise had not yet run aground when, on March 30, 1992, the chief economist of Mabon Securities predicted that it would have to. "We believe Olympia & York will be a major unsettling influence on the markets over the next couple of months starting early next week," wrote Paul J. Isaac, who proceeded to describe the inevitable.

The O&Y essay, although one of the first by Isaac in his capacity as the chief economist of a firm that previously didn't have one, showed wide reading, keen deductive powers, technical competence, courage (Mabon is an O&Y tenant), and a formidable denseness of argument. "At $18 billion of debt net of the non–real estate assets," he wrote, a figure that proved to be $2 billion or $3 billion too high, "O&Y would owe about $400 per square foot in their portfolio. Let's put that in perspective." The next paragraph demonstrated another Isaac trait, the flattering assumption that his readers can keep up with him: "To cover a 10 percent debt service constant would require a free cash flow of $42 per foot with a 5 percent vacancy allowance. At an average of $15 per foot for operating expenses and taxes (certainly reasonable at these values in New York, London, and Toronto), this would imply average rents of $57 per foot," which, he added, the Reichmanns were almost certainly not getting. Not only does Isaac sometimes write that way, but also he sometimes talks that way. First-time reactions to the gale force winds of his mind range from "Wow!" to "Huh?"

Isaac, forty-two years old, is not a trained economist, a profes-

Isaac at his post. When dribbled, the rubber-band ball
in the foreground shakes the floor.

sional real estate authority, an *Institutional Investor* All-Star, or a
Chartered Financial Analyst. Before joining Mabon in 1976, he had
worked at a metal-fastener company, Allied International-American
Eagle Trading Corp. And before his stint in nuts and bolts, he had
traveled to Chile on a Watson Fellowship to study political problems
of foreign investment in developing countries. Although his LSAT
score of 779 was one of the highest, if not *the* highest, in the Williams
College class of 1972, Isaac did not go to law school. Nor, despite
a 780 business-board score, did he go to business school. He offers
two reflections on these feats: (a) a man on Wall Street has as much
use for academic distinction "as a fish does for a bicycle," and
(b) he is now, more than ever before, a dilettante.

He is, in fact, according to the people who know him, a kind of
one-man New York Stock Exchange member firm, a trading, investment, taxable bond, derivatives, municipal bond, research, due
diligence, and back-office department all in one pair of sleeves.
He manages his own money, looks out for some of his family's
money, conducts a brokerage business, chairs the Mabon credit

A paper ridge of average size

committee and its investment banking committee, and is called
upon to put out the still-raging merchant banking and real estate
fires that the Mabon partnership unintentionally lit under itself
during the boom years of the 1980s. He is the father of four children
who range in age from one to seven.

The one department of a one-man member firm that would not
be represented in the person of Paul Isaac is the custodial department. His office—situated on the southwest corner of the thirty-
second floor of One Liberty Plaza in lower Manhattan—is an indoor
ecological nightmare. Newspapers and periodicals are heaped not
only in piles, which might by themselves convey a specious illusion
of order, but also in berms and drifts. A hardened New Yorker
might assume that a burglar had broken in and that the police had
ordered that nothing be disturbed until fingerprints could be taken.
("He's looking at tons of ideas, and you can't throw them out
because you're never done with them," says Seth Klarman, the
Cambridge, Massachusetts, investor, concerning the general problem of materials management in an investment office. "So what
are you going to do? Put them in piles. At least then you might
see them again." It might be noted that Klarman's housekeeping
resembles Isaac's.)

One neat two-foot stack is devoted to regional business journals:
Isaac subscribes to fifty of them. Indeed, there isn't much he
doesn't subscribe to. He takes *Risk Magazine, Muniweek, Managing
Mortgages, Inside Mortgage Finance, American Demographics, Air Trans-
port World, Latin Finance, Mini-Storage Messenger, The Far Eastern
Economic Review, Partnership Profiles* and—does it need to be
said?—*Grant's Interest Rate Observer.* The annual cost of Isaac's
subscriptions, according to Patrick Maloney, his assistant, runs to

about $45,000, a sum that does not include the salaries of the two college students who clip and file for about forty hours a week. The spoor of Isaac's reading and study fills eighty legal-size file drawers.

"A lot goes in, but a lot goes out," says Maloney. "We are filling three or four large trash cans a day. People come in and say it's getting worse, but I think it's getting better. Paper seeks its own level. I've seen him in three different offices now, and the depth of the paper hasn't changed. We're taking it out as fast as we possibly can."

With practice, Maloney has devised what he believes is an ideal moving technique. "You just take a big plank, push on everything that's on his desk, take the plank to his new desk, and push it all back," he says. "I take boxes, put piles in and mark the box 'left-hand corner of the office,' or whatever, and empty the box." Maloney adds that Isaac "reads with a scissors and a pen, kind of like the chef on the Muppets show. . . . He reads *all* this stuff."

Certainly, Isaac writes as if he does. In the past month the topics covered in his "Economic Notes" and "Rough Cuts" have run from retail employment in America ("The old employment/real sales relationship is as dead as the Stassen campaign") to investment opportunities in the hated health care and pharmaceuticals stocks to the prospects for cost-push stagflation and estate taxes. He has proffered an inaccurate interest rate forecast, shaken his head at the success of Chrysler's recent equity sale, and remarked on the chronic overoptimism of sell-side equity analysts.

Another piece of circumstantial evidence to support the claim that Isaac actually turns the pages of the newspapers and magazines he gets in the mail is the experience of his friends. He communicates with them through newspaper clippings. For years envelopes have come to your editor from Isaac filled with information on subjects that fall within the vast orbit of Isaac's curiosity. Frequently, they are annotated; for instance, a regional business journal story on ostrich farming included skeptical comments by Isaac concerning the hopeful rate-of-return arithmetic claimed by the ostrich man. As Isaac has been writing more, he has been sending less; that he still sends anything may be regarded as a miracle of productivity, dedication, or compulsion, depending on one's attitude toward work, family, and leisure.

At the leading Wall Street institutions, a chief economist pronounces on the economy, makes himself available for the humiliating semiannual roundup of interest rate and GDP forecasts conducted by *The Wall Street Journal,* and (as if this needed to be said) avoids controversy that could impede the work of the sales force. Isaac pronounces on the economy but not in the accustomed ways. He is rarely quoted in the press and never in the *Journal*'s surveys (he says it's because he isn't asked). He is as likely to pass judgment on the investment merits of a company or an industry as on the GDP, and he is prone to season his financial arguments with sarcasm, a rhetorical breakthrough for the sell side of Wall Street. He might have pioneered it.

Isaac's investment views are conservative but imaginative, and he comes by them honestly. His uncle is the "value" investor Walter Schloss. His father, Irving Isaac, who died in 1984, was an arbitrageur and investor and an original director of Mutual Shares. After graduating from New York University, Irving Isaac went to work at the Bank of United States. In 1930, two years after he arrived, it made one of the Depression's historic bankruptcies. "He apparently came to the attention of his superiors because he could remember the closing prices of all the bonds in the portfolio when they were tallying up the market value each day," the son says, "a trick, by the way, I can't replicate. And he stayed with the bank until it closed in 1931, in the bond department. And then he went to work for a succession of Wall Street firms, mainly as a trader specializing in the securities of busted public utility holding companies and their subsidiaries and, to a lesser degree, railroads. He was involved in what today would be considered arbitrage activity, in reorganizations and workouts. Then, eventually, he became semiactive on the Street. He ran a small partnership that actually wound up taking over and liquidating a fairly complicated group of real estate companies in Brooklyn called Wood Harmon Corp. And taking over and running and then ultimately selling out a couple of small utility properties. He ran the Owego Waterworks in Owego, New York, from 1955 to 1980. He also ran the Cumberland Valley Electric Corp. for a while and a couple of smaller companies."

The second of three boys, Paul was born in Manhattan in 1950 and raised in Eastchester, New York, which is in Westchester

County. (Westchester is neither west nor east of Manhattan but north.) "When he was a young fellow, he was very knowledgeable on facts," Schloss recalls. As a first grader, young Paul was lecturing the fifth grade on dinosaurs. Later he was reading *The New York Times* in the morning and the *World Telegram* in the evening. Still later he was working for the election of Barry Goldwater, Mr. Conservative, and serving on the Eastchester High School audio-video aid squad. In his mid-teens he was writing away for information from the Calcutta Stock Exchange and corresponding with some of the British tea plantation companies in India and the Calcutta Light & Tramway Co. At the age of seventeen, he was an American Field Service exchange student in Chile.

As a Williams College undergraduate, Isaac advocated free-market, counterrevolutionary political views and majored in political economy. "Political economy meant you didn't know enough math to be an economics major, but you weren't quite shameless enough to major in political science," Isaac says, somewhat disingenuously, because he has a steel-trap quantitative mind. At Williams he won the Van Vechten Prize for the best delivery of a senior essay, which dealt with the negative income tax, and was elected to Phi Beta Kappa. In his freshman year, following a snowstorm, he jumped out of a second-story window while sober. Missing the snowbank at which his feet were aiming, he hit the asphalt sidewalk and was taken to the college infirmary with a concussion fracture. He says he finished the semester in a back brace.

(Isaac's mother, Marjory, danced professionally in the corps de ballet at Radio City Music Hall in New York. She was also treasurer of the Dance Notation Bureau, an organization that her husband sometimes called the "Dance Donation Bureau." Paul inherited more of the verbal genes than the dancing ones.)

Although not exactly a bear, Isaac has strong skeptical tendencies, and he ascribes them in part to a pair of formative experiences. The first was his coming to learn the history of Germany in the 1930s. "My father had a fair number of relatives in Germany and a fair number of his friends in the business were German refugees, and they didn't talk a lot about it, but there was a certain sense that the world can change very dramatically, not always for the better," he says. The second was the Chilean coup of 1973, which he witnessed in Santiago and which detained him in Chile for three weeks beyond his planned departure date. "It gave me a certain sense that the world didn't necessarily move by tenths of a percent," says Isaac.

More than most investors, certainly more than any known, living economist, Isaac is conversant with the business of Wall Street. He started out at Mabon in the back office, and to this day he is known by his former colleagues in the cashier and security clearance departments as a man who can settle trades as well as originate them. Furthermore, as a man who, when the situation required it, actually helped to make deliveries. In the late 1970s he made himself useful by helping to disengage the firm from a potential trading disaster in GNMAs. (Leon Pollack, now managing director and head of the taxable fixed-income department at Donaldson, Lufkin & Jenrette, oversaw the GNMA untangling, "What made him uniquely qualified to do this," he recalls of Isaac, "was his ability to grasp complex financial transactions and see through to the implications.")

Later, when the options department had a problem with reverse conversion strategies, Isaac lent assistance. Similarly, after the 1987 stock market crash, he was seconded to the junk bond department (where he was called, behind his back, "the prince of darkness"), and later he assisted in the attempted salvage of the firm's disaster-plagued investment in Global Motors, importers of the fragile yet unforgettable Yugo. Participating fully in the 1980s, Mabon also involved itself in several illiquid and unprofitable real estate investments, and Isaac says he has devoted approximately 10 percent to 20 percent of his time over a two-to-three-year period to helping sort *them* out. Notoriously, cleaning up mistakes is not the fastest route to the top on Wall Street, but Isaac says that he really had no choice. "I was a general partner and had general partnership liability, and there didn't seem to me to be a whole lot of alternatives to getting involved. I was going to get involved one way or the other." (Although Mabon is no longer a partnership—it is a subsidiary of IMI International, the Italian financial services giant—Isaac still has a residual partnership liability. He is still worried and therefore still deeply involved.)

Isaac, who lives in Larchmont, New York, frequently gets the 5:55 a.m. train. He reads *The New York Times* and *The Wall Street Journal*, gets off at Grand Central, descends to the Lexington Avenue subway, and gets into the office by about 7 a.m. He reads, circulates on the trading floor, and attends the morning meeting. From 9 a.m. to 5 p.m. he is "involved with people," according to Maloney. After 5 p.m., he resumes reading and writing. He takes his leave around 10 p.m. or 11 p.m. He often comes into the office on the weekend. He says that his ambition is to cut down to fifty to fifty-five hours of work a week, but no less.

From time to time Isaac has tried to lose some weight, but he has been no more successful at that than many other people would be at digesting some $45,000 worth of financial periodicals a year (not to mention innumerable annual reports, which are free). "We ought to make a video with Paul for the Executive Workout Plan," says Maloney when he is asked about his employer's approach to physical conditioning. "You have a bowling-ball-sized ball of rubber bands, you have to have a good, sturdy chair with arms, and you have to have stuff all over the floor. You juggle the ball to keep the upper-body strength up. You keep your phone away from the desk so that when it rings you have to hurdle over piles of stuff to get to the phone in under three rings. You then do press-ups in your chair. That's the workout. I know it will be great—you never have to leave the office."

In the time he does not squander by watching television or obsessively working out at the gym, Isaac has produced a startling body of work. Reading and thinking about as many things as he does, he is able to light up familiar topics from unexpected angles. When, recently, the Hong Kong market had a sinking spell because of the risk of forcible, early incorporation by the Chinese mainland, he had the presence of mind to ask why that should be bearish when the mainland new-issue market was so very bullish. "Something is wrong with this picture," he stated on December 24.

On February 10 he made a list of the principal themes of the Clinton economic program, from deficit reduction to fairness in executive compensation to government "investment" to a program of national service. If you eliminate national service, he wrote, "there is a country already far down the road to implementing this program almost point by point in a disciplined and technically competent fashion. It's called 'Japan,' and it also appears in real danger of slipping into a period of significant real economic contraction and incipient financial panic."

By temperament, Isaac is not so much bullish or bearish as disputatious, and he is at his best as a minority of one. *Grant's* has often been the better for this idiosyncratic turn of mind, as when, for example, in September 1987, an anonymous reader proposed to exploit the then-excessive valuations of public gold mines by buying some gold, burying it, and then—this is where the profit would come in—digging it up again. Golden Recycle, as the company would be called, could compete head-to-head with actual, working, overpriced mines, a model income statement showed. "To keep excavation costs down," our informant wrote, "I suggest loading the bars into inexpensive surplus railroad tunnels somewhere along the old anthracite routes at a capital cost of, say, $1 million." It is *Grant's* policy never to disclose the identity of a confidential source. However, it is hard to read this analysis—so subversive and, as it turned out, so profitable—without thinking of Isaac and wanting to ask him: Now what?

Isaac has no finely calibrated scenario. He calls the Clinton program "high-tech Huey Long," and contends that the stock market is not yet priced to reflect the risks of Southern populism. (Unfortunately, the one area in which Bill Clinton has already made a deep valuation gouge, health care and pharmaceuticals, is one sector on which Isaac has recently been bullish. He is still bullish, arguing that at eight to ten times earnings "with the best set of balance sheets in the world," with the "demographic wind at its back," it has discounted a lot of damage.) As for the bond market, he is anticipating a bout of stagflation and therefore, in time, higher interest rates.

"Regression to the mean" is one of the laws that Isaac lives by, and new-era talk never fails to put him out of sorts. "Betting 'this time it's different' (and therefore markets will not regress to, or through, reasonable historical standards) has about the worst overall track record we can recall of any conceptual proposition in the market," he wrote last month. One of Isaac's neatest feats of analytical exposition was a piece, dated December 24, that took to task the prevalent optimism on corporate earnings. (That, on the same day, he had also spoken his mind about Chinese equity valuations is itself an integral part of the Isaac phenomenon.) He approached the profits question from the point of view of return on historical book value. It has been running at 12 percent, he

Bond-market vigilantes
"in a meeting."

wrote, which is where it should be, where it has usually been at an 80 percent factory-capacity utilization rate. Two of his points were especially pretty. First, rebutting the idea that, because everybody has become "lean and mean," profitability should zoom: " 'Lean and mean' is like your spouse, compared to what? If everybody's leaner and meaner, that's an argument for low inflation, not high profits." Second, dispatching the claim that replacement book is necessarily higher than historical book: "If anyone believes those properties [that is, industrial structures] cannot in general be replaced at or below statement value, we have several score million square feet of space we'd like to sell them.

"In our opinion," Isaac went on, "the stock market seems to have implicitly accepted as a benchmark something like 18 percent of historical book, which we believe to be a generally unsustainable level of average corporate returns on equity. . . . Corporations are currently being rewarded for selling or closing businesses or facilities suffering from 'subnormal' profitability. By definition, *most* corporations cannot ensure that *most* of their operations *always* substantially exceed average corporate profitability, which average is itself below the market's implied benchmark."

Is some restructuring not beneficial? Of course it is, the chief economist allowed. However, he wrote, it is unlikely to be the boon that the market hopes. "We believe stable mediocrity acquired at a very low relative price will emerge over the next several years as a stock market approach likely to significantly outperform the averages," he wound up.

Stable mediocrity? For instance, says Isaac, Lincoln Electric, the largest manufacturer of welding equipment in the United States: "Losing money overseas, making money in the United States in a very difficult environment, one of these companies that dominates its market. It is largely employee-owned. There are about a million shares outstanding. It does close to about $900 million worth of business a year. It's got about $75 million worth of debt. It sells for about 200, so I'm buying it at a significant discount to book (even after restructuring charges) when you add back the over-funded pension plan and the LIFO reserve. It's a company that at one time earned 7 percent on sales and really, quite clearly, dominated its market. Its largest domestic competitor is still dealing with the consequences of an unsuccessful and still highly overleveraged (and restructured) LBO."

A somewhat less stable mediocre company is Texas–New Mexico Power. "They overpaid building a lignite power plant," Isaac says, speaking extemporaneously in his office, arms folded across his chest, chair tipped back. The words fairly gush: "They basically got into a fight with the commission. They're still trying to get rate relief. The company has a $1.63 dividend which is possibly in some jeopardy, although they've indicated they're going to keep it. The trailing book is around 21 bucks. The stock is around 19. In the long run I figured those guys should regress like every other crap utility to 100 percent to 150 percent of tangible book. And they're probably going to earn something close to two bucks next year. They've got a shot at getting that up to $2.50 to $2.75 if they get any decent rate relief. So if I can earn 8½ percent on the dividend and basically get some modest buildup of book value over the next three to four years, and have the thing regress to 150 percent of book from 90 percent of book, that's about a 20 percent rate of return."

Isaac has done some short-selling for his own account, and he has given some capital to professional short sellers. (One of them, William M. McGarr, relates that when the bull market is really pinning his ears back, Isaac will call him up, tell him how much he believes in what he's doing, and assure him that this, too, shall pass.) However, Isaac likes to say, the world must be net long— *he* must be net long—and he tries to find value in the market no matter what the macroeconomic situation. "A lot of my own investing is truly not macroeconomically motivated," he says. "In fact, most of it isn't."

A man who had worked in the front office of Mabon for a long time readily conceded Isaac's brilliance but said: "He holds his opinions very strongly, and he is the kind of person who is either very right or very wrong. And he does not take a lot of information back from the marketplace." To which Isaac pleads guilty but with extenuating circumstances. "I think some of that was a carryover from when I started," he says. "I tended to deal in very inactive securities or situations that I thought weren't followed much at all. Under those circumstances you really have to make a decision that you really have a point of view and that you think it's smart. I think, particularly when I became involved in more liquid securities or securities in which I had more and more intelligent competition, I had a tendency to fight the tape. It's something that I'm more cautious on now, and I'm more cautious on establishing positions."

In the back office where he started, Isaac is known as an odd duck, not a regular guy, but the kind who has been known to attend the funeral of a fellow employee's father in Staten Island when nobody expected him to. Discussing Isaac and his eccentricities, a pair of senior Mabon back office personnel recently agreed that he is more than bright.

"He comes off like—what's the word I'm looking for?—a geek," one ventured.

"A nerd!" the second corrected him.

"Yeah, a nerd!" the first agreed.

"I just like to hear him talk," the second said.

PART TWO

GOOD
BANKS
AND BAD

HOT ISSUE

February 24, 1986

The recent stock offering by the New Milford Savings Bank, New Milford, Connecticut, is one for the thrift industry record books. With less than $300 million in assets, the bank received subscriptions for $150 million worth of common stock.

The stock was priced on the offering at $16 a share. When trading began in the closing minutes of the St. Valentine's Day session, the first bid was $26.

Rarely has the conversion of a mutually owned institution to an investor-owned institution generated so much depositor interest and so much surplus money. Even before the offering, the bank's ratio of capital to assets was an ample 10.6 percent. The post-offering ratio of capital to assets, something on the order of 33 percent, is not so much ample as amazing. It is all the more astonishing because the bank hasn't any immediate plans for the proceeds (of which it accepted $59.2 million). It says it is taking that matter under advisement.*

The New Milford offering was noteworthy on several counts, but especially for its size. A year ago, according to Seth A. Klarman of the Baupost Group, investment advisers in Cambridge, Massachusetts, a bank like New Milford might have raised perhaps $25

---

* What it proceeded to do with the money was get into trouble, losing $17 million in one six-month period alone (ended December 31, 1990) in the stock and bond markets. Versatilely, it also lost money in lending and real estate development. Late in February 1993, its stock was quoted at 4, down from 24½ seven years earlier. In the 1980s and 1990s, many banks had too little capital. Some—New Milford, for instance—had too much.

*"Yo! You people still makin' those loans that the guy
don't have to pay you back?"*

million to $30 million. New Milford itself got twice that amount, and the offering, as noted, was massively oversubscribed. "The point," says Klarman, "is that, without an underwriter, that much money could be offered to an institution that doesn't need it." The underwriter, which was left with nothing to underwrite, was Keefe, Bruyette & Woods.

"Need," of course, is a subjective idea. The bank, according to Brian A. Arnold, executive vice president and treasurer, didn't "need" the money so much as it saw an enviable chance to raise it. It wanted to convert to stock ownership for competitive reasons and decided to sell stock while the selling was good. And the investors, knowing how well such converted thrifts have recently fared in the secondary market, might have felt that they "needed" a capital gain. In any case, last Tuesday, its first full day of trading, the stock closed at 24½ bid, down 3½ from Friday but up a mere 53 percent from the issue price. For those who missed the new-issue boom of the 1960s, New Milford Savings Bank common is what was known as a hot issue.

As for the bank itself, it is the largest bank or thrift in the prosperous western Connecticut county of Litchfield. It has eleven branch offices and sixty-three full-time employees. Its board of directors includes a chief of surgery, a retired retailer, a retired sand and gravel man, a retired postmaster, and three generations of Arnolds.

It's an unusual bank, distinguished not only by a concern for liquidity but also by a portfolio commitment to stocks and bonds. At last count, $138 million, or 51 percent of its assets, were consigned to securities, with notes and bonds (having an average maturity of two years) totaling $109 million.

The equity portfolio, while amounting to no more than 10 percent of overall assets, looms large in the earnings equation. To quote from the prospectus:

> The Bank actively manages its equity securities portfolio, having produced gains from the sale of these securities of approximately $2.8 million *or 51 percent of income* before income taxes and extraordinary items during the year ended June 30, 1985. In addition, the Bank engages in an ongoing program involving the sale of covered call options on its equity securities portfolio, which produced security option income of $516,000 for the 1985 fiscal year [emphasis added].

Thus, a small, stock-minded savings bank has raised a flood of money from its stock-minded depositors and neighbors. Thinking that this might be an early sign of the long-awaited public entry into the speculative arena, we told a bullish friend about it, hoping to worry him. But he laughed, shrugged, and said, sensibly enough, "To quote a famous New York philosopher, 'It ain't over till it's over.' "*

---

* Early in 1993, it still wasn't.

BANKING WITH TISCH

October 6, 1986

T homas J. Tisch, who is not to be confused with his father, Laurence A., the acting chairman of CBS (of whom he is the spitting image), nor with his uncle, Preston R., the new Postmaster General, nor with his brother, James S., the shipping magnate, has some tips for bank-stock investors:

"First, never buy a bank at twice book. Number two, don't trust any bank with a superior earnings record. Number three, you're buying a pig in a poke because the assets are inherently unanalyzable. So buy enough comfort and coverage. Number four, the exception to the rule, which I've often violated, is to buy Republic National Bank and never sell it."

Tisch is an investor and bank director (and also, for the record, a subscriber in good standing to *Grant's*). It was a year ago that a syndicate to which he belonged bought the Bowery Savings Bank from the Federal Deposit Insurance Corp., into whose lap it had lightly dropped. The other day, on the first anniversary of that transaction, Tisch reflected on what he had learned in the past year. He shared his ideas over the speaker connection to his telephone, characteristically punctuating his declarative sentences with a vocal question mark, as in, "It's harder to be a bank manager than a bank-stock investor?" He meant that it's much harder.

Tisch covered a range of banking subjects. He talked about credit risk, interest rate risk, deposit insurance, and bank stocks. He declared himself bullish on Norwest Financial (great finance sub), Republic National Bank (best managed bank, bar none), and the little First Interstate of Iowa. Putting in a kind word for junk bonds, he added that he was favorably disposed toward Columbia Savings

& Loan, Beverly Hills, California, which owns a ton of them. He said that junk bonds are better than junk real estate loans.

Before he got into details, Tisch enumerated some of the winning features of the banking business. "First off," he said, "you can grow as fast as your ingenuity will allow you to. Number two, you never have capital expenditures that far exceed your depreciation. Number three, I've never read about a strike against a bank. And number four, the Bank of New York and the Bank of Boston have paid cash dividends every year since you-can-look-it-up. [We did: The dates are 1784 and 1785, respectively.] So how bad a business can it be?

"Then there are the contra rules," he went on, such as the inability to earn exponential rates of return except through recklessness or fraud. "Also," said Tisch, "bankers don't own stock in their own banks. And banks put their customers on their boards of directors. I can't think of another business that does that. Another thing: A really smart person says to himself at a certain point—and this is part of the problem of it being so easy to enter the business—that your pricing is set by the stupidest person in the market." It is the marginal lender who makes the marginal loan at a bargain basement rate, and it is impossible to compete with that optimist. From the borrower's point of view, as Tisch noted, one bank's money is as good as another's.

Tisch, now warming to his subject, identified his choice for the number one problem in banking today. It is the complacency of bankers concerning the whereabouts of their principal. Preoccupied with interest rate risk, they play ducks and drakes with credit risk. They have relaxed their credit and amortization standards in return for the privilege of lending at floating rates. Everybody wants to be perfectly matched.

"In the old days," reflected Tisch, who at thirty-one doesn't remember them, "banks never thought about their mismatch"— although, he added, that was just the thing to have thought about in the years leading up to 1981. "Now they're obsessed with being perfectly matched. But the consequence of being perfectly matched is that they've competed away any chance of making a spread based on credit judgments."

Tisch was the recipient last year of an invitation to purchase a limited partnership interest in the Atlanta Marriott Marquis Hotel.

"Hey, let's make it a bank run!"

Scanning the offering memorandum, he was surprised to learn that a consortium of banks was prepared to lend $195 million against the collateral of the real estate in year one—and would still have an outstanding loan balance of $184.5 million on the due date in year ten. It was quite true that the banks would lend at a floating rate. However, the price of securing that interest rate feature was an amortization schedule like the one obtained by Mexico. One might wonder, as Tisch did: What if nobody wants to stay at the Atlanta Marriott Marquis in 1994? Where will the lenders be then?*

The striking thing about those terms, Tisch went on, is not how rare they are but how commonplace. Suppose, he said, that money is lent against a piece of commercial real estate at $100 a square foot, which happens to be 85 percent of its appraised value (it happens all the time). And say that the rate on the loan floats 100 basis points over the Treasury yield curve and that the term is thirty years. "A thirty-year amortization schedule means that you amortize, I think, only 10 percent of the loan in the first ten years," he went on. "So if you look at it that way, you're giving the person who owns the building a $90-a-foot put." For the privilege of which, as mentioned, the bank is earning the princely rate of 100 basis points over the Treasury rate.

---

* This particular real estate lending proposition ended well enough. The hotel paid off the $195 million loan in the summer of 1990 and replaced it with a seven-year bond. The FDIC insurance fund would be in better condition today if Tisch had been mistaken in his general real estate views. However, he was on the money.

We didn't quite get the put analogy, so we asked for an elaboration. If, after ten years, Tisch obliged, the real estate market is flat on its back, the owner can walk away from the building. In effect, he can "put" it back to the bank for the principal balance of the loan ($100 a square foot) minus the amortized balance ($10). That is, for $90.

Tisch contended that this is not an irresistible proposition for the lender. "I don't feel I'm being compensated for the inherent volatility of real estate when everyone is bullish on real estate and when I know that ten years ago real estate was worth $30 a square foot. My father is fond of saying that in the summer you always forget how cold it gets in the winter, and in the winter you always forget how hot it gets in the summer."

He blamed the boom in junk real estate lending on the suggestibility of appraisers and the gullibility of regulators. If one assumes that appraisals are usually too high, as Tisch does, then a great deal of commercial real estate is even more highly leveraged than it seems. "They tell you on the inside that they lend against 80 percent," he said, "but the reality of life is that you're lending against 100 percent."

Tisch contended that junk bonds are less junky than the run of commercial real estate loans. They are higher yielding and more salable ("but I'm allowed to make a junk real estate loan because I have an appraisal"). He cited, as a sign of the times, the recent decision by Lorimar-Telepictures to borrow more from banks and less in the junk bond market than it had originally planned in a feat of leverage that it announced it would undertake a few months back. Without letting it get around, according to Tisch, banks have become massive repositories of junk assets.

All of which steered the conversation in the direction of what to do. The banker's dilemma, as Tisch continued, is how to deploy the depositors' money. It can be lent at risk, or it can be parked in the money market without risk. But it can only be profitably parked when the yield on liquid assets (for example, Treasury bills) is higher than the cost of deposits, which it currently isn't. Echoing Marc Perkins, Tisch suggested that bankers are under a compulsion to lend. Liquidity—the alternative to lending—yields a bank no profit. Besides, deposit insurance premiums bear no relation to asset quality. (Apropos of risk-taking, Tisch has a pair of reforms to suggest. The first is that deposit insurance premiums be geared to the asset quality of each institution. The second is that the FDIC insure no deposit on which the yield is higher than the rate for the same maturity on the Treasury yield curve.)

Addressing his fellow bankers, Tisch said it is time to retrench. "If I were every bank in America," he went on, "I'd be raising capital and deleveraging myself." We asked him how a bank could expect to get ahead by doing that—how it could earn money and get itself written up in *Fortune*—and he pointed to the example of Republic, the balance sheet of which is a throwback to the Edwardian era. (Salomon Brothers last year ranked Republic the first of thirty-five bank holding companies in terms of liquidity and asset quality.) "I don't believe that banks trade on income statements," Tisch said, "because if they did, then Manufacturers Hanover wouldn't have traded at 23, which was three times earnings, in 1984. I believe that banks ultimately trade on people's perception of the quality of their assets minus the value of their liabilities."

McMORTGAGES

February 3, 1989

Someone has proposed the fifteen-minute mortgage decision, and that someone is Citicorp. As it is, the typical mortgage application is expeditiously processed in a month or less, down from two to three months in the refinancing glut of 1986. However, Robert D. Horner, chairman of Citicorp Mortgage, St. Louis, laid down the competitive gauntlet in a speech last month before a conference of the Mortgage Bankers Association of America: "In a society that features automatic teller machines on every corner and 'eyeglasses in about an hour,' fifteen days might as well be an eternity," he said. To compete in the mortgage market of the future, Horner went on, "we must stop living in the past."

Meanwhile at Moody's

"Hey, you know, I've never upgraded a bank. Have you ever upgraded a bank?
What the hell—let's upgrade a bank!"

So fixed was Horner's eye on the process of getting money out
the door that he failed to mention, even in passing, the banker's
ancient mission of getting it back in again. His speech contained
not a line about credit risk. Anyway, Citibank has been quietly
testing the fifteen-minute approval system with thirty of its so-
called Mortgage Power clients—real estate and mortgage brokers
with whom the bank does regular business—in New York and New
Jersey. It began to test "limited documentation" loan procedures
in 1980 and introduced them nationally in 1986. For instance,
instead of insisting on verification of an applicant's employment,
as it used to do, it settles for the stub of a paycheck. Instead of
ordering up-to-the-minute credit checks on its applicants, it makes
do with whatever relevant facts a credit bureau may have on file,
even if the facts are out of date. Loan-loss experience has been
acceptable so far, according to a spokeswoman.

The Citicorp challenge was front-page news in the *American Banker*, and the newspaper quoted a New York real estate broker who made a salient point. "Every other lender would have to match it or lose business," the broker, Theodore Z. Metalios, predicted. In other words, a Gresham's Law of lending may swing into operation. Easy credit may drive out stringent credit, just as bad money drives out good. As Citicorp has streamlined its mortgage application process—expediting appraisals and reducing documentation—to Citicorp will go the extra transaction. Let us suppose that there exists a bank that believes in thoroughness of documentation, even at the cost of a few weeks' delay in approval. And let us say that this retrograde institution is pitted against Citicorp Mortgage. Is there any question, at a given level of mortgage rates, which institution will do more business? "We can't let industry traditions lock us into a straitjacket," Horner said. "For progress to continue, we need a fundamentally different way of doing business. Not just improvements, but change."*

The last issue of *Grant's* cited chapter and verse on the long-running relaxation of automobile lending terms. Consider this modest report a down payment on the residential mortgage market. The basic financial issue facing lenders in the two markets is one and the same: Will the relaxation of lending terms yield enough extra income now to compensate for higher loan losses later? Bears will say "no" and bulls will say "yes," but each will be guessing. What can be said with assurance is that, in both vital consumer sectors, lenders are setting new twentieth-century records in underwriting liberality.

The Citicorp instant mortgage plan is portentously timed. Competition among mortgage lenders is intense, optimism about mortgage credit is widespread (on the Big Board, the Federal National Mortgage Association keeps making new highs), the forty-year mortgage is gaining a foothold, and concern about mortgage delinquencies is low—although the long-term picture, shown nearby, reveals higher highs in delinquencies after each recession since the 1960s. In this rarefied atmosphere, Wall Street has brought to market some $750 million in bonds secured by home-equity loans—

* There was change for the worse in 1991 when Citicorp, suffering distressingly high rates of mortgage delinquencies, disclosed that it was dismantling Citicorp Mortgage. The move left Horner, as the *St. Louis Business Journal* reported, "to seek another position within the banking giant's organization."

Home Equity Loan Asset Backed Certificates, Series 1988-1, if you
want to call your broker to place an order.

The Mortgage Bankers Association is heading up a drive to simplify and streamline mortgage-related paperwork, and anyone who
has ever had to fill out a form will wish it good luck. However, the
preoccupation of the market with speed and volume has given pause
to some credit-minded observers (with whom the readers of *Grant's*
will instantly sympathize). A month before the Horner speech,
M. Douglas Watson, Jr., at that time the director of structured
finance at Moody's, issued a warning about due diligence—or the
lack of it—in the mortgage-backed bond market:

> The competitive environment in the underwriting of residential
> mortgage pass-throughs and other consumer asset-backed structured
> financings is intensifying. The increasing competitive pressure on
> underwriters results from (1) new intermediaries, such as commercial
> banks, entering the field, and (2) the commoditization of the busi-
> ness created by an increase in volume and augmented by the ne-
> gotiating power of large, repeat issuers. The result is a squeeze on
> underwriting fees and intense pressure on underwriters to cut the
> expensive "due diligence" process.

A piece in January's *United States Banker* echoed those points,
noting, for instance, that "the greatly increased competition among
lenders scrambling for mortgage business in the past year has
spawned a new breed of deeply discounted loans—many with little
or none of the traditional documentation found with mortgage underwriting. And there are mounting concerns that many of these
questionable-quality loans are being unloaded in the secondary
market in security form."

As automobile lending terms have steadily been stretched, so
has the average maturity of a mortgage loan expanded. Before the
advent of federal housing guarantees in the 1930s—the government
created the flourishing secondary market in residential mortgages
—loans matured in eleven years or so. In 1935 the average maturity
on a mortgage on a new house was less than eighteen years. It
pushed through twenty years in 1938, twenty-five years in 1955
(the same wicked year in which three-year car loans caught hold),

and thirty years in 1962. It has been essentially unchanged ever since, but recently forty-year terms have been catching on.

THE 40-YEAR MORTGAGE IS HERE, BUT LENDERS ARE WARY OF RISKS, said a *Washington Post* headline the other day. The paper noted that although most local lenders had not moved beyond the customary three decades—for one thing, forty-year maturities aren't readily salable in the secondary mortgage market—the extra-long loan filled a need: "While still considered something of a gimmick at the moment, the loan is beginning to make more sense in this market, some local lenders said, as steadily rising home prices and upward-bound interest rates threaten to down-scale the home-buying aspirations of increasing numbers of Washington area purchasers." The ultra-mortgage comes with floating rates only, the story continued. And given the low starter rates prevailing on the adjustable type of loan, a family could lower its monthly mortgage payment significantly just by stretching an extra decade. In the case of a $100,000 loan priced, to start with, at 8¼ percent, the monthly payment on a forty-year mortgage would come to $714, compared to $751 on the same loan with a thirty-year term. Thus, a borrower could buy more house with less income and more debt: nirvana. To be sure, an ultra-mortgage, if amortized over the full four decades, would be costlier than a thirty-year model, and its appeal is therefore to the confirmed optimist: to the home buyer who, like a creator of leveraged buyouts, intends to sell an asset or refinance long before his debt falls due. "The 40-year mortgage makes the most sense for borrowers who won't need the loan for more than a few years because they plan to sell or refinance their home," the paper said.

It might not surprise you to learn where the forty-year mortgage originated. The *Post* continued:

The handful of Washington area lenders offering a 40-year option all appear to have some sort of link to California, where the loans have become popular because of the high cost of housing there. The parent companies of Ahmanson and Great Western Mortgage Co. have headquarters in California, while Seasons Mortgage Corp. offers the loan here on behalf of California-based lenders.

"That's where property values escalated the highest, the fastest, the soonest," says Seasons Mortgage's Michael Hubbard.

Thus, a distinct California flavor: rates adjustable to the Federal Home Loan Bank Board's 11th District Cost of Funds and the prospect of negative amortization if interest rates shoot up. Deferred interest payments are added back into the unpaid balance when changes in monthly payments lag the rise in yields.

A Fannie Mae executive noted, as some sobersided automobile lenders have been wont to point out, that longer amortization means greater risk for the lender. A home buyer's equity accretes ever so slowly in a forty-year loan, a circumstance that would heighten the temptation to abandon his property if worse should come to worst (it won't, according to most of the economists we read).

The first pass-through certificates secured by second mortgages were inevitable—if Merrill Lynch didn't invent them, the job would have fallen to *Grant's*—and a couple of weeks ago they materialized. Even if you don't plan to call your broker, the Home Equity Loan Asset Backed Certificates may appeal to your sense of financial history-in-the-making. To repeat, the certificates are backed up by a pool of home-equity revolving credit line loans; the loans, in turn, are secured by mortgages, most of which are seconds. Interest on the certificates is paid monthly at a floating rate: about 35 basis points over the AA-rated commercial paper rate.

The certificates are structured in three classes, according to seniority of claim on the pool's assets. The "A" class is rated AAA, and it has first call on principal payments the pool may throw off. The "B" class, which is next in line to receive principal payments, is rated AA−. Household Finance Corp., the originator of the loans, guarantees the "B" class debt, so the AA− rating is identical to HFC's long-term debt rating. The residual class, "C," is non-rated and, in fact, was not issued; HFC retains it. Underwriters are Merrill Lynch Capital Markets, Goldman, Sachs & Co., Morgan Stanley & Co., and Shearson Lehman Hutton.

To the credit prude, of course, the very words "second mortgage" smack of hellfire, notwithstanding a federal tax code that now encourages home-equity borrowing and a structure of consumer interest rates that makes home-equity loans a better buy than credit card debt even before taxes. Thus, we approached the prospectus skeptically. Turning first to the risk section, we noted that the home-equity loans are virtually balloon loans—borrowers generally pay the entire principal sum at maturity. The cautionary prose describing that fact, and the implications of it, sounded like the risk language in a junk bond prospectus:

> The ability of a borrower to make such a payment may be dependent on the ability to obtain refinancing of the balance due on the Mortgage Loan. An increase in interest rates over the Loan Rate . . . applicable at the time the Mortgage Loan was originated may have an adverse effect on the borrower's ability to pay the required monthly payment. In addition, such an increase in interest rates may reduce the borrower's ability to obtain refinancing and to pay the balance of the Mortgage Loan at its maturity.

In other words, the debtor, to repay his debt, may have to borrow or sell assets, and he might not be able to do either. Shades of Metromedia Broadcasting Corp.! To the deflation-minded investor, there is a gratifying note in the prospectus about the risk of falling property values: "An overall decline in the residential real estate market could adversely affect the values of the Mortgaged Properties such that the outstanding Loan Balances, together with any primary financing thereon, equals or exceeds the value of the Mortgaged Properties. Such a decline would adversely affect the position of a second mortgagee before having such an effect on that of the related first mortgagee."

However, as noted, Standard & Poor's rated the "A" and "B" classes top-drawer investment grade, and the recent experience in home-equity lending is more respectable than the foregoing passage implies. Although the stated maturity of the loans is fifteen years, for instance, the average life is more like three to four years.* Home-equity borrowers, who show the kind of demographic profile that magazine advertising departments like to boast about, tend to amortize their own loans.

A recent survey of the home-equity market by the American Financial Services Association found that 11 percent of homeowner households used some form of second-mortgage "product": 5 percent had traditional seconds and 6 percent had home-equity lines.

---

* As indeed it proved to be in this Household Finance Corp. issue. By August 1992 only about $100 million remained outstanding of the $656 million 1988-1 series. There was never a problem. Citicorp should have been so lucky.

Most home-equity debt was concentrated in the Northeast. The survey found that the average income of home-equity borrowers was higher than that of homeowners in general. According to the survey, home-equity debtors know what they have gotten themselves into, acknowledging the risks of foreclosure and of unwise extension of personal indebtedness.

Longer mortgages, faster mortgages, and a greater number of mortgages per household. The 1980s roar on.

ONE BANK CAN

February 16, 1990

Now that a credit crisis is knocking at the door, a look at the new annual report of Davenport Bank & Trust Co. may help to steady the nerves and improve the flow of oxygen to the vital regions. A reader sent us a copy, recalling our recent claim, "No bank is a safe-deposit box." Yet on page two of the annual report, V. O. Figge, the bank's ninety-year-old chairman, writes, "We can pay our entire deposit liability on demand, and our depositors can sleep at night with complete confidence during both good and bad economic weather."

Plainly, the Davenport, Iowa, institution is no ordinary post-Wriston-era outfit. Its equity capital amounts to 12 percent of its assets and 20 percent of its deposits. Its assets, which foot to $1.7 billion, consist mainly of federal agency securities, Treasuries, and tax-exempt bonds. These total $1.1 billion. The loan portfolio amounts to $356 million, although we are bound to report that the bank has chosen to make real estate loans in the sum of $114 million, as well as commercial and industrial loans amounting to $97 million. The allowance for possible loan losses is only $1.3 million. Ranked according to profitability, asset quality, liquidity, and capital adequacy (McCarthy, Crisanti & Maffei publishes a quarterly tabulation), Davenport turns up near the top of the heap.

Figge, who along with his three sons comes to the office every day, wrote the complete president's letter, touching upon events foreign and domestic and circumstances financial, economic, political, and moral. "In some of the media today," he wrote, taking off the gloves, "you will find the name of Keating prominently headlined. He is the one who was in charge of the largest savings and loan institution, Lincoln by name, where unbelievable things happened, and I might say, they come under the heading of just plain thievery."

In opening, the chairman had noted the accomplishments of Davenport Bank & Trust during its fifty-seven-year history—"extreme safety for depositors at all times, liquidity to the extreme, performance insofar as our obligations to this community and its institutions are concerned, and last but not least, may I say modestly, a reasonably good investment for our stockholders." Davenport Bank & Trust, incidentally, is not a stock for the milkman in Dayton. The low price in the fourth quarter was $1,110 a share, representing a 130 percent premium to book value and a multiple of a little more than eight times net income. There were only 240,000 shares outstanding.

Continuing, Figge took note of humble beginnings: "The bank was organized out of the wreckage of the old American Savings Bank & Trust Co. which closed, and the reorganization required the effort of the entire community." The date of organization was July 5, 1932, three days before the all-time low of the Dow Jones Industrial Average, 41.22. To start with, according to Figge, capital totaled $900,000 and assets, $8 million. Fifty-seven years later, the numbers became $205 million and $1.6 billion, respectively. "It may be interesting for you to know," the chairman advised, "that we have never had a year when we did not outperform the previous year, and I should like to tell you that we take great pride in having established this impregnable institution for the benefit of our entire community."

From great crack-ups, great institutions are sometimes born.

FORBEARANCE, AHOY!

December 21, 1990

On Monday, Citicorp, the nation's largest bank-holding company, paid the stunning rate of 12½ percent to place an issue of auction-rate preferred; investment bankers had expected a yield of only 10½ percent. On Tuesday, it cut its dividend. Also on Tuesday, it set aside a surprisingly small sum—$340 million—in additional loan-loss reserves. ("It's a joke," a reader remarked. "They pretend to reserve, and we pretend that they did.") Later on Tuesday, the Federal Reserve cut the discount rate.

The speed with which the Fed threw good news into the breach of Citi's bad news was impressive. It suggested, at a minimum, that the central bank was more concerned about the health of the number one bank, which it regulates, than about the international standing of the nation's currency, which it also regulates. Theorists may look for a pattern.

On December 4, you'll recall, banks were relieved of the obligation to set aside idle balances against certain kinds of deposit liabilities. Some $12 billion was thus released from monetary captivity for loans and investments. Within minutes of the Federal Reserve's action (not many noticed this), the Bank of Japan disclosed that it will expand the scope of its monetary operations. Henceforth, for example, it will deal in bonds and commercial bills denominated in foreign currencies—in dollars, for instance. In carrying out its policies, whatever they happen to be, the BOJ will rely less on lending, more on open-market operations. It was agreed that this, too, was bullish, and the Tokyo Stock Exchange surged.

"There are 725 basis points between the federal funds rate and zero," Edward Yardeni, chief economist at Prudential-Bache Se-

Lending officers' training class of the future

Blaustein '90

curities, likes to observe. So saying, he distills the bullish faith that the government is here to help.

The point deserves considered thought. What preceded the December 4 announcements was monetary stringency. What followed them was a rally in U.S. bank stocks, a rally in Japanese stocks, and a fall in Eurodollar deposit rates. Some risk rates—for example, the difference between Treasury bill yields and Eurodollar deposit yields—narrowed.

What was gratifying about that, to investors, was the familiar sequence of cause and effect: Central banks acted, markets reacted. The issue on the table of finance is the accuracy of that perception. Are "they" in charge or aren't they? Our conclusion, which we will take our own sweet time in reaching, is that they are not. Nevertheless, they will act as if they are. They will pull out every stop in the organ trying to show that they are.

What ails the country, we think, is a credit contraction, a kind of malady unseen since the 1930s. In a credit contraction, borrowers are denied. The principal rationing device for loans is not high interest rates but low creditworthiness, the credit of the borrower or the liquidity of the lending institution, or both.

This is not the government's doing but the market's. The government prosecuted Michael Milken, but it did not put Integrated Resources, Milken's client, into Chapter 11. It did not cause USG to borrow nor William Farley's bankers to lend. Although fostering the financial climate in which high-yield loans became necessary, it did not order Citibank into real estate lending. It did not send a Discover card to Zabau, a two-year-old Chinese Shar-Pei, in Earlysville, Virginia.

Because a severe contraction tends to follow a hell-bent expansion, the shrinkage in credit is jarring. It upsets calculations made in the boom and makes viable businesses (and solvent, job-holding individuals) seem uncreditworthy. The first to be squeezed are debtors at the fringe, but the process may carry to the investment-grade core. It began to do so in 1990: The investment-grade corporate bond market is illiquid, the debt of many high-grade bank holding companies trades at junk bond yields, and the credit of the government itself is under a cloud.

In the typical postwar recession, it was the Federal Reserve that took away the punch bowl. In the current slump, the precipitating monetary agent was a decline in lending capacity. Banks lacked capital, liquidity, and optimism. Bond buyers became risk-averse. Having overdone it, lenders decided that the time had come to stop. Whereas inflation ended the typical cycle, deflation has uniquely figured into the end of the current expansion.

The contraction is economywide, even international, because credit was broadly impaired. The balance sheets of industrial corporations, utilities, insurance companies, states and municipalities, and individuals all suffered. The more we think about the cycle, the more fatalistic we become about it. It is, we think, the legacy of the passage of generations (of grandchildren reliving the professional lives of their grandparents) and of a structure of socialized credit sixty years in the making. If one is fatalistic about the upside, one must also be resigned to the downside.

Some questions. First, we would like to know about the government's latitude to devise new stopgaps. It has almost no flexibility in fiscal policy; what could it cook up in credit policy? Second, for historical reference, we would like to know how the Hoover administration dealt with the credit contraction of sixty years ago, which was the last credit contraction in the American experience. What did it do, when did it do it, and what did it scruple not to do? Finally, borrowing from Yardeni, a semi-theoretical question: Why doesn't the Fed push the funds rate to zero? If a zero funds rate is bullish and if bullish is good, why should we settle for more than zero? We ask these things because the answers might help us to prepare for the federal policies of the future.

To start with banking and credit policy, we have drawn up a double-entry ledger, one side marked "easy" and the other side "tight." Under "easy" we have written: Federal funds rate reduced; discount rate reduction anticipated; reserve requirements cut; Bank of Japan committed (at least on paper) to monetize non-yen securities. On Monday a new accounting proposal came to light that, according to *The Wall Street Journal*, would enable "some banks to report lower amounts of nonperforming loans, smaller loss reserves, and higher profits."

Under "tight" we have written: Stiff new international capital rules still in force, the credit contraction notwithstanding; Comptroller of the Currency Robert Clarke, self-styled "regulator from hell," reappointed; Deutsche Bundesbank, the "central bank from hell," undaunted; the Bank of Japan, for all the hope surrounding its recent news release, still tight; FDIC assessments certain to rise* (smothering, as far as bank earnings are concerned, the cut in reserve requirements); proposal by the SEC to require banks to mark the value of some of their marketable securities to market; new SEC rule to restrict the exposure of money market mutual funds to commercial paper rated less than blue chip; speculation in *The Washington Post* that the "too-big-to-fail doctrine" might be scrapped, thereby greasing the skids for an arguably just, arguably salutary run on a money-center bank, but one that would not be construed as bullish by the stock market.

The net effect of these policies, we think, is more stringent than not. To conform to the evolving capital standards of the Bank for

---

* On January 1, 1991, they rose to 15½ cents (per $100 of deposits) from 12 cents; on July 1, 1991, they rose to 23 cents. On January 1, 1993, the riskiest banks were obliged to pay 31 cents, while the majority continued to pay 23 cents.

International Settlements, for instance, the big Japanese banks must raise new capital, shed assets, or both. This is not an American policy, but its consequences are universal. A lower federal funds rate may reduce the cost of a bank's capital, but higher capital standards may inhibit a bank's ability to lend. Falling asset values—stocks, junk bonds, real estate, etc.—similarly inhibit lenders and, for that matter, borrowers.

But none of this addresses the issue as it deserves to be addressed. The fundamental question is simplicity itself: Can an increase in the quantity of credit offset a deterioration in the quality of credit? In other words, are lower interest rates the antidote to credit contraction? In Hoover's time, at least, they were not. Rates fell and radical policies were enacted, but the liquidation proceeded unchecked. (Milton Friedman and Anna Schwartz have convinced nearly everybody that the Federal Reserve caused the Depression by being too tight for too long. We happen not to agree with their interpretation, but that is not today's problem.)

Times have changed, of course. It is no small thing, for instance, that investors have come to believe in the Federal Reserve System—not necessarily in its wisdom but always in its potency— or that the government's credit is thought to stand behind Citibank. On the other hand, some things never change. Crowd psychology, the cunning of frightened lawmakers, and the heartbreak of worthless options are American universals.

What the speculator-scholar will want to know about the early years of the Great Depression is how the government reacted to it. He will be interested in that period because (as Murray Rothbard notes) it was the first case of a managed liquidation in American history. The Bush administration is only now coming to understand that credit is actually contracting. The Hoover administration, too, was slow off the mark but inventive once it found its voice. In making comparisons, allowances must be made for the passage of time. Sixty years ago the financial system, in effect, wore a swallowtail coat, as opposed to a T-shirt. The government was subject to a run by foreign holders of dollars, and banks were subject to a run by their depositors. Dollars were convertible into gold, which the government could not print, and bank deposits were convertible into cash (there was no deposit insurance). With that understood, the bottom line of our historical research is as follows: Hoover tried anything and everything, stopping at almost nothing. Maybe Bush, in his turn (if current trends in credit persist), will amaze the market with radical measures.

Although no free-market purist, Herbert Hoover was a Republican in a more-or-less orthodox age. When faced with contracting credit, he put the government itself into the lending business. He tried to intimidate short sellers, urged insurance companies not to foreclose on overdue mortgages and signed the legislation that authorized the Federal Reserve System to monetize the public debt. In 1929–32, in short, the government threw its weight into resisting the liquidation of debt. In 1933–34 it did more: Private and public contracts made in gold dollars were abrogated by act of Congress, and the Federal Reserve System itself was put into the direct lending business. Under the so-called 13(b) powers, the Fed lent directly to industrial corporations, bypassing the banking system altogether. It is hard to imagine matters reaching that desperate pass now. If they did, however, John Sununu would have plenty of interventionist precedent to take to White House staff meetings.

One of the early creations of the first, or the Hoover, New Deal is especially telling of our plight. In October 1931 the National Credit Corp. was organized with $500 million in capital subscribed by the leading banks of the day. Two years into the Great Depression found them still notably solvent. From the official (and indispensable) Citibank history by Harold van B. Cleveland and Thomas F. Huertas:

> The crisis had pushed weak banks further toward insolvency. To meet depositors' withdrawals, they had sold their high-grade securities and were holding illiquid loans and lower-grade securities that were ineligible for rediscount at the Federal Reserve. Bank examiners made matters worse by adopting rules for valuing securities that helped relatively healthy banks but forced the weakest banks to reveal to the public just how weak they were.
>
> In contrast, National City [forerunner to Citibank] and other large banks had strengthened their liquidity as the depression deepened . . . Owen D. Young, chairman of the board of General Electric and a director of the Federal Reserve Bank of New York, commented that "if the rest of the country looks to New York [banks] for leadership in recovery . . . we shall not get anywhere, and banks will become no more than safe-deposit boxes."

The charge of the National Credit Corp. was to lend to banks with sound but—by the Federal Reserve's standards—ineligible collateral. Charles E. Mitchell, then chairman of Citibank, did not judge this a good idea, but his bank was in a position to mollify the authorities by subscribing $20 million for it. The comparison with today's Citicorp is too sad to need elaboration. When (as Mitchell expected) the venture failed, something bigger followed it: the government-owned Reconstruction Finance Corp. Now Washington entered the lending business on its own account.

There were more blows to laissez-faire. The Glass-Steagall Act of February 1932, an emergency measure, broadened the list of assets eligible for rediscount at the Federal Reserve banks and authorized the use of government securities as collateral for Federal Reserve notes (along with gold and commercial paper). Now the Federal Reserve entered the business of monetizing the government's debt. Reports of the bill caused a short, powerful stock market rally. In the month before its enactment, January 1932, government bonds made a Depression low in price and a high in yield: 4.32 percent. They, too, rallied, until 1946. Was the monetization of government debt really bullish for bond yields? For more than a decade the market entered no objection to it. In fact, it rallied its way through the entire Roosevelt inflation program.

The Hoover administration pursued other policies that might be dusted off next year if the contraction proceeds. In the fall of 1931, for instance, the Comptroller of the Currency allowed banks to value certain investment-grade bonds at "intrinsic value," instead of at market. "The action was seen as an effort by Washington to avoid further depression in this medium class of investments," *The New York Times* reported at the time. The concept of "intrinsic value" has obvious application to a broad range of bank assets in a time of deflation. The "intrinsic value" of downtown office buildings? One can imagine the trial balloon; one can visualize the headline.

If the past is a guide, the rhetorical volume of the government will soon be turned up. Thus, in the spring of 1932 (more than two years into the slump and only months away from the all-time stock market bottom), the chairman of the Reconstruction Finance Corp., Atlee Pomerene, addressed the banking industry: "Now . . . and I measure my words, the bank that is 75 percent liquid or more and refuses to make loans when proper security is offered, under present circumstances, is a parasite on the community."

In the Hoover contraction, the big banks were solvent, the gold standard was intact, and Washington was largely uninvolved in lending and borrowing. Government, therefore, could invent a new credit system to try to solve the problems of the old credit system. It could demonetize gold, guarantee bank deposits, and create federal agencies to lend and borrow. All that it proceeded to do. Today, on the other hand, the big banks are not quite solvent, the monetary unit is undefined, and Washington's credit has been pulled down with the banking system's. All of which raises the question: What is there left for the government to do? Given that no political party has ever won an election on a platform of debt liquidation, how will the government propose to stop it?

It might be, of course, that the contraction is stopping now. Maybe this recession is not so far out of the postwar mold as we think; perhaps we are overwrought and Citicorp is undervalued. If not, it behooves us all to try to anticipate the government's next move, although it will do no good to extrapolate current policy into the future. As Chairman Richard C. Breeden of the SEC proposes an accounting rule to force banks to mark their liquid securities and conforming mortgage loans to market, Comptroller Clarke proposes an accounting rule to permit the delayed recognition of problem loans. One idea would seem to fall under the hard, truth-telling category, the other under the lenient one. (John Britton asked top people at the SEC and OCC why they seemed to be working at cross-purposes. Each agency replied that it wasn't contradicting the other. However, for whatever it might be worth, the banking industry is lobbying furiously against the SEC proposal: Clarke opposes it, too.)

On reflection, the government is really trying to do two things at once. It is managing the costs of the credit system that was created in the midst of the last debt contraction. It is mopping up after deposit insurance and the consequences of the "too-big-to-fail" doctrine. Simultaneously, it is trying to extricate the economy from the current debt contraction. Hence, the so-called Danny Wall syndrome wars with the perpetual prosperity syndrome. In regulation, forbearance competes with resoluteness.

Several issues ago we ventured that the government would be

driven to extreme measures. We still think it will. Inasmuch as there are international constraints on domestic monetary policy, the federal funds rate will not reach zero.* However, if the contraction proceeds, legislative attention will certainly shift from avoiding a repetition of the S&L fiasco to avoiding a repetition of the Depression fiasco. In the 1930s the Hoover and Roosevelt administrations stopped at nothing, except the outright nationalization of the banks, to try to prime the pump of lending. These are not the 1930s, but the pump is wheezing.

What is an "extreme measure"? Postponement of the effective date of the international bank-capital rules (due to begin in 1992) would be one. The insinuation of the government into the ownership of a money-center bank would be another. The introduction of the concept of "intrinsic value" into the valuation of real estate assets would be a third. "Net worth" certificates—our own original contribution, which we recently offered to the government pro bono publico—would be a fourth.†

Government policy has been more stringent than the government knew. Our prediction is that policy eventually will become more desperate than most of us now imagine. In that case there are always deutsche marks (which, at the short end of the yield curve, offer a 175-basis-point advantage in yield over the dollar). There is always gold.‡

---

* Since this writing, the federal funds rate, at which a bank can float an overnight loan, has fallen to 3 percent from more than 7 percent. Yet the average dollar exchange rate has managed to hold its own. On February 18, 1993, the *Financial Times* reported that the dollar is the preferred paper money of Cambodia. In the wake of the Gulf War and the collapse of the former Soviet Union, the United States had an immense reservoir of international goodwill. It is unlikely that the Cambodians (or many other foreign investors, for that matter) would have thought any less of the dollar even at a 1 percent funds rate. Zero percent might have been pushing it, however.

† Acts of forbearance there were, though none so gross as I had imagined. For example, late in 1992 the Federal Reserve relaxed the rules that govern the size of the loans that one bank may make to another. In February 1993 the Office of Thrift Supervision reduced the amount of capital that a bank needs to carry a foreclosed asset. But perhaps the greatest federal contribution to the healing of the American banking system has been the long decline in short-term interest rates. The Federal Reserve, I think, did not cause this decline, but it has ratified and sustained it.

‡ And almost always in this period, a depreciating gold market.

SOLVENT IN MARYLAND

March 15, 1991

Maryland, like Texas and parts of Massachusetts, is known for other things besides prudent lending, but the crack-up of MNC Financial has obscured the quiet success of Mercantile Bankshares Corp., Baltimore. Mercantile is the holding company for eighteen little banks and one bigger bank. Mercantile Safe Deposit & Trust Co. is the bigger bank, and it constitutes a study in the dividends that prudence will pay if we only live long enough to see them.

We have no hot investment advice to impart on this note. Mercantile Bankshares was quoted on NASDAQ Tuesday at 23¼, a 42 percent premium to year-end book value. And the chairman of the executive committee, Edward K. Dunn, Jr., emphatically expressed the view on the telephone that every bank, even his own, is a blind pool, that is, *terra incognita*, to the investor peering at it from the outside. (Perhaps from the inside, too, considering the insider buying that preceded the break in Bank of New England, among others.)

What's so notable about Mercantile is the set of high-grade problems it has recently acquired. First off, it must deploy the new deposits that safety-conscious refugees from other institutions have brought it. It must decide how much to pay for them. It must make credit judgments on a raft of new loan applications and decide how many of its new depositors will stick around after the banking scare passes.

As for the first item, the Mercantile is buying Treasury notes. " 'Natural' loan demand in the Maryland area has been weak to off," says Dunn. "Natural" means the demand from existing customers, as distinct from newcomers. In fact, Dunn adds, many long-standing customers are paying down loans. Then, too, not every newcomer is creditworthy, and some of the applicants, not knowing any better, expect the Mercantile to do what Dunn says it never does, that is, lend below prime. Dunn, a former bank analyst, says the remarkable thing about the Mercantile for him is to see the influx of deposits yet not see top management clamoring for more loan production. "We wish we were making more loans," he says, but the bank does not wish that so fervently that it is willing to compromise its credit standards. "Credit is what drives this place," he says.

Credit and trust income. The Mercantile's charter dates from 1864 and the progenitor of the Reynolds tobacco fortune, R. J. Reynolds himself, brought his money to the Safe Deposit & Trust Co. after the Civil War, where it (or much of it) still resided at the time of the leveraged acquisition of RJR/Nabisco in 1988. The Mercantile has $7 billion under management and another $22 billion under custody, Dunn says.

At year-end 1990, Mercantile Bankshares, the holding company, showed equity capital equivalent to 10.6 percent of its $4.4 billion of assets. It earned 1.6 percent on average assets last year and returned 14.7 percent on equity. It also reported an 87 percent jump in nonperforming assets, but the new figure constituted only 1.18 percent of year-end loans and "other real estate owned." To put 1.18 percent in perspective, it was lower than the allowance for loan losses, which amounted to 1.64 percent of year-end loans.

To date, Mercantile is the exception that proves the rule about real estate lending. Its mortgage and construction loans last September 30 amounted to $1.3 billion, or 43 percent of total loans. Some 10 percent of the real estate lending book fell under the heading of "construction and land," according to Dunn; another 12 percent to 13 percent represented commercial real estate. Mercantile does not pretend that these credits are Treasury bills. On the other hand, according to Dunn, more than half of the commercial real estate against which it lends is destined to be owner-occupied. As for the other plagues of contemporary banking, Mercantile has no foreign loans and only one HLT* loan. It does not purchase loans from other syndicating banks. It does not like to lend against

---

* Highly leveraged transactions; leveraged buyouts, for instance.

collateral that is out of easy driving range. It does not give its junior lending officers allowances for travel or entertainment. "We do some relatively daring things," says Dunn, "but, goddamn it, we do it by looking the guy in the eye."

GUARDIAN AT BAY

February 15, 1991

Russell M. Jedinak, still the owner but no longer the president and chairman of the board of Guardian Savings & Loan Association, Huntington Beach, California, had a business motto. It was: "If they own a house, if the owner has a pulse, we'll give them a loan."

Jedinak stepped down the other day "to pursue other interests," in the words of the press release. It is possible to infer that not all was well at his thrift. Jedinak's successor, William J. Crawford, is a former California savings and loan commissioner. Also, the change in management was concurrent with an agreement that took the form of a "consensual cease and desist order." In it, the Office of Thrift Supervision obtained a promise that Guardian would lend more carefully and less frequently. In the Jedinak regime, the thrift had been lending at the hyperactive rate of seven times its capital every month. It sold a good part of that emission in the mortgage-backed securities market.

In general, flaming thrifts are yesterday's news, but the Guardian is a case for the future. In its heyday it lent to the marginal borrower. Now, under terms of the OTS agreement, it will do less of that (as banks from coast to coast are already doing, even without a government order). Guardian is not the typical shipwreck of savings and loan legend. Although it operated in an "unsafe and unsound manner," according to federal regulators, it is solvent. It has never suffered a loss on a loan. "Except for the reduction of volume of

[loan] originations," said the press release, "Guardian will now resume business operations as usual. . . ." It has had no truck with junk bonds, commercial mortgages, or construction and development lending. Its business is residential mortgages. Its chosen market niche was (and will remain) that of the less creditworthy home owner. "There's no place in the industry you can get thirty-year loans if you don't pay your bills on time," Jude Lopez, a Guardian vice president, told *The Orange County Register* recently, "We give people a second chance."

What commends Guardian to the readers of *Grant's* is, first and foremost, its credit philosophy. What makes a loan work, it believes, is not the borrower's pulse rate or employment history or TRW report. It is his collateral. Its operative belief is that California real estate appreciates. Lending no more than the equivalent of 80 percent of the appraised value of the borrower's house, it believed it could safely compete. With only slight modifications, it still believes it.

The bank, with assets of only $600 million, cuts a disproportionately tall figure in the mortgage world. In the past three years it has issued $1.7 billion worth of senior mortgage pass-through certificates—that is, securitized mortgages—to public investors in twenty-seven different issues. It has issued another $200 million in privately placed, subordinated mortgage pieces. The Guardian certificates have been rated by Standard & Poor's, reviewed by securities counsel, and cleared by the credit-review apparatus of Salomon Brothers, the illustrious underwriter. Now comes OTS with a list of woeful lapses at the thrift and also, by implication, on Wall Street. New questions come to mind: Do these infractions bear on the integrity of the Guardian securities or on the validity of the Guardian lending philosophy? If Guardian so easily slipped through the net of due diligence and full disclosure, why shouldn't others have, too?

Guardian was a three-shift loan factory. Before OTS lowered the boom, it would make fifteen hundred loans a month, or fifty a day. That worked out to twenty-five a day for each of the two loan-approval officers, Jedinak and Lopez, both of whom had other banking duties to attend to besides saying "yes." (A knowledgeable source explained: "When you commit yourself to a business that is experiencing a secular decline in margins, which Guardian has, you are forced to produce your way out of the margin squeeze.")

The Jedinak credit motto notwithstanding, Guardian did not literally ignore its applicants' financial resources. Loan-to-value ratios were adjusted according to an individual's creditworthiness. In many cases, the OTS found, Guardian would lend no more than the equivalent of 65 percent of the value of the house on a first mortgage. If a bigger loan were needed, it would make a second mortgage. Combining first and second liens, it would lend no more than 80 percent. (The regulators were critical of Guardian's tendency to discount its appraiser's reports, but at least it didn't fall into the typical lender's trap of inflating them.)

"While Guardian's first-lien loans are thirty-year amortizing ARMs with finance charges and fees that are within the parameters of what could be considered customary within the industry," OTS found, "its second-lien loans are five-year ARMs with balloon payments: these second-lien loans also have significantly higher finance charges and fees that are based on multiples of the fees being charged by Guardian on the concurrent first loan."

The government found one loan that Scrooge & Marley would have refused on humanitarian grounds. The borrower was a seventy-five-year-old widow and cancer patient, Odessa G. Howell, and the mortgage broker was Universal Capital Funding (UCF). From the OTS bill of particulars:

> On November 29, 1989, and on March 7, 1990, Guardian granted Ms. Howell two loans totaling $295,000 and $20,000, respectively.
> The documented purpose of these loans was for the payoff of an existing mortgage totaling $77,638 and for home improvements. Other than the payoff of the $77,638 existing mortgage and $50,000 to the borrower, the remaining payoffs did not match the stated purpose of the loan. Unexplained payoffs included amounts in excess of $100,000 disbursed to the principals of UCF, the loan broker on Ms. Howell's loan. The stated source of repayment for the loans was based upon a financial statement for a business that neither exists nor with which Ms. Howell is affiliated.

As for the fees collected by Guardian and the broker, they were almost worthy of the standards that ruled on boom-time Wall Street: 6.9 percent, or $20,411 on the first lien, and 22.5 percent, or $4,508, on the second. "OTS examiners have determined that the 'finance charge' on these two loans was understated by approximately $33,488.58," the document said.

Nor is that the end of it. From the investor's viewpoint, the most troubling details in the case concern the lack of public disclosure and the evident slackness in the Salomon Brothers due-diligence process. What Salomon didn't find, however, OTS did. It discovered a pattern of subterfuge in the thrift's reporting practices. Four employees had been cooking the books to improve the default and delinquency record. "In some instances," according to OTS, "these employees posted fictitious payments from unrelated Guardian accounts. In other instances the employees failed to timely reverse payments that were made by non-sufficient funds checks. After month-end delinquency reports were generated, the employees reversed the fictitious payments."

Jedinak found out about these abuses "on or about" May 15, according to OTS. He did not then blow the whistle. "[N]either Mr. Jedinak nor Guardian conducted a full investigation to determine the extent and scope of the problem and the nature or materiality of misrepresentations, if any, to the purchasers of Guardian's REMICs," said OTS. "Instead, a limited internal audit was conducted and was used by Guardian as a basis for wrongly concluding that such activity was an isolated incident."

The four employees were allowed to resign, and the bank said nothing to regulators or to the investors in its mortgage pass-through certificates. "There is no documented evidence that Guardian's board of directors was informed of this matter prior to October 1990," the complaint says, "when the delinquency rate manipulation was discovered by OTS examiners in the course of their regular on-site examination at Guardian."

Guardian continued to issue mortgage pass-through certificates. As usual, the prospectuses warned that Guardian's idiosyncratic approach to underwriting might cause higher delinquencies and foreclosures down the road. The actual delinquency and foreclosure record was, as noted, willfully distorted. "The actions taken by Guardian's employees, with at least some knowledge by senior management," said OTS, "may have resulted in a misrepresentation to investors who purchased Guardian's loans. Delinquency rates quoted by Guardian have a direct effect on the price received for the loans sold. Consequently, the manipulation understated Guardian's true delinquency rates and may have enriched Guardian at the expense of investors who purchased loans. No disclosure was made by Guardian to investors who purchased loans during the [relevant] period."

Not until December 6 did Salomon set the record straight in a three-page "prospectus supplement." The percentage of delinquent loans at year-end 1989 was not 3.96 percent after all. It was 4.56 percent. And the percentage delinquent on September 30, 1990, shot up to 5.22 percent. For all that, however, the world did not stop turning. On February 1, the same day Jedinak quit, Standard & Poor's affirmed its ratings (mostly AA) on $1.7 billion in Guardian's outstanding mortgage pass-through certificates. Acknowledging that the thrift had been through the administrative mill, S&P did not dwell on the past. It looked to the future and to promised reforms, for example, reducing the maximum loan-to-value ratio to 75 percent from 80 percent, reducing the maximum loan balance to $300,000 from $500,000, and halting the practice of offering secondary financing along with first-mortgage financing.

On Monday the Guardian mortgage issue that was the object of the December 6 "prospectus supplement" was quoted at 97½–98. It was therefore down by 2½ points from its par issue price last October, a major whack in a security that is subject to monthly interest rate adjustments.

As for the Greater Meaning, there is certainly room for improvement in the art of due diligence. Asking around about Guardian, what you are likely to hear is that it was a known high-risk lender. People say that they knew that, but Salomon Brothers, which also presumably knew it, undertook no rigorous investigation of its methods. Or, if it did investigate, it found out nothing useful. Or, if it did learn something, it neglected to put it into a prospectus. (The firm did not return phone calls.)

In the junk bond market, people used to say that the trouble would start when the recession began. As it developed, problems surfaced well before the recession. Similarly, Guardian got into trouble before the bear market in California house prices got up a head of steam. In 1988, Los Angeles house prices rose by 22 percent. In 1989 they were up by 19.7 percent. In 1990 they fell by 1 percent (all this according to the California Association of Realtors). Guardian believed that prices would continue to rise or, at least, not precipitously fall. In September 1989 a Guardian officer told *Grant's* that the thrift would continue to lend as it had in the past. There had been thirteen foreclosures in Guardian's brief history, and each had been turned to profit. Through last September, there had been forty-one foreclosures (counting the original thirteen), and still no losses. As of this writing, according to Lopez, there have been sixty-two foreclosures (and *still* no losses). To put sixty-two in perspective, it implies an additional twenty-one foreclosures over the past four and a half months. In the four years 1986–89, the grand total of foreclosures was twenty-two. The rate of decay in Guardian's portfolio is accelerating.

By the time the bear market in real estate is over, it seems to us, Guardian will have borne losses. By the same token, the buyers of mortgage-backed securities will have gotten into the habit of asking hard questions, such as: Do these people (underwriters, rating-agency personnel, interest-rate-swap counterparties, lawyers, trustees, and accountants) actually know what they're doing?

As for the regulators, who usually get no respect, *Grant's* hereby salutes them. "OTS is real strict these days," Lopez of Guardian told Jay Diamond of *Grant's*. Well, someone ought to be.

"C-SPAN—OVER HERE!"

July 31, 1992

Testimony by James Grant before the House Banking Committee on July 30, 1992.

Mr. Chairman and members of the committee,* I am honored to be here this afternoon to discuss the Olympia & York affair. My particular assignment is to try to put current events in perspective—to treat the financial collapse of the Canadian developer as

---

* Except for the presence of the Banking Committee chairman, Henry Gonzales, of my mother-in-law, Maria K. Kavanagh, and of my *Grant's* associate, Susan Egan, I would have testified in front of myself.

a symptom of the state of American banking rather than as an isolated multi-billion-dollar accident. I will try to explain how so much came to be lent against real estate collateral over the past decade and what, if anything, should be done about it today. Who is to blame for the losses? What are the consequences for the economy and the banking system, especially that aspect of the banking system given over to the process of credit creation?

First of all, if only for the sake of our generational self-esteem, we should all bear in mind that misconceived real estate lending is an American staple. Overbuilding brought on by overlending is a recurring phenomenon, and the first bad real estate loan no doubt occurred along about the opening of the first bank. So checkered was the American experience with land speculation that real estate lending was virtually prohibited under the enabling legislation of the national banking system, the National Bank Act of 1864.

It is equally important to acknowledge that excessive real estate lending in the 1980s was a global error. It blighted Australia, Britain, Scandinavia, and Japan as well as the United States. Whatever colossal delusions American lenders might have entertained about real estate were therefore not the unique by-products of the American regulatory system. They were as common in Stockholm and London as they were in Dallas and New York.

It would be easier and tidier for Congress if the financial failure of O&Y could be attributed to one specific public policy—for instance, the removal of loan-to-value limits in real estate lending by the Garn–St. Germain Act of 1982. I don't think it can be. Real estate crises are recurrent, and no monetary or regulatory system in America has yet prevented them. We have had O&Y-like episodes with and without deposit insurance, with and without the federal securities laws, with and without the Farm Credit System, with and without a gold standard, and with and without so-called double liability on the common equity of failed national banks. I do not mean to sound a note of pure fatalism, but the truth is that people with money, acting in crowds, periodically go off the deep end. There are times when they believe (or seem to believe) almost anything. Every banker is taught to secure adequate collateral and obtain current financial information about a borrower before lending. Bedazzled by the Reichmann's stature and reputation, however, many lenders forgot to ask. This absentmindedness was a hallmark of the boom.

What makes O&Y so relevant is that it illuminates the real estate dilemma; and what is so interesting about real estate is that it illuminates the banking dilemma. Bankers have favored the wrong class of asset before, many times, from ships to oil rigs to Third World governments. Now, by the way, for whatever it might imply about the outlook for interest rates, they are piling into Treasury notes. However, they have rarely overlent so extensively and for so long as they did against land and commercial buildings in the 1980s. Mistakes and misjudgments are inevitable in any economy and any social system. The preeminent appeal of capitalism is that mistakes tend to be cut short. What I still cannot explain is why this rolling real estate depression continued to roll along for so many years: from Texas to New England and the mid-Atlantic states to California. Astoundingly, New England seemed to learn nothing from Texas, and California stayed in the dark about New England. Considering the gullibility of the great New York banks toward Paul Reichmann, you might have supposed that *The Wall Street Journal* had no Dallas correspondent. Bankers operating in the so-called information age absorbed surprisingly little information.

The condemning truth about lending practices in the 1980s is that bankers kept lending as the number of empty offices (and stores and warehouses) kept increasing. From 1985 through 1990, the national office vacancy rate and the year-to-year growth in real estate loans each registered in the mid to upper teens. In the same six-year period the rate of return on office-building investments steadily fell. In 1985 commercial banks became the biggest lenders for real estate development, and they held that dubious distinction through at least 1990.

The sheer persistence of error is what makes this financial episode so troubling. It is what leads me to believe that the longstanding bipartisan policy of socializing the risk of bank failure should be reexamined and overhauled. I mean not only deposit insurance but also the "too big to fail" doctrine and miscellaneous federal assurances to the customers and owners of banks and thrifts. Humanely intended, these policies have succeeded in selectively forestalling the myriad runs on illiquid banks that the lending practices of the 1980s otherwise would have provoked. On the other hand, except for federal subsidy, actual and implied, would lenders have been quite this reckless? Would they have remained this reckless for so long? I doubt it.

If our greatest regulatory achievement is the absence of a calamitous run, that must also be counted as our costliest regulatory indulgence. Runs cut short unsound booms. In the process, to be sure, they also rob a certain number of innocent savers, disturb the peace, alarm investors, enrich speculators, and penalize production. Taking one thing with another, our forebears chose to dispense with them. Still, I have often wondered how it would have been if the real estate bubble had burst in 1985 or 1986 with runs on the big Texas banks. No one can be sure, but I am inclined to believe that it would have been a blessing. As it was, without a run (the Continental Illinois affair of 1984 was harrowing but localized), the nation built itself a 19 percent national office vacancy rate and canyons of empty warehouses, shopping centers and hotel rooms. It bore—and continues to bear—years of subpar economic growth and the virtual stagnation of M-2, M-3, and bank credit. Today, for the first time in twenty-seven years, according to the Federal Reserve Board, bank balance sheets show more government securities than business loans. The exact origin of these deflationary trends is unknowable, but the impairment of banks through the lending practices of the 1980s—in particular, the overextension of credit against real estate collateral—must bear a round share of the blame.

The trouble with real estate depressions is that they go on and on because a new crop of expiring leases comes up for renewal and downward adjustment every year. As long as rents are falling, a landlord's prospective income stream is shrinking. In New York, for instance, rents are still falling, and the prospects for real estate values (and loans against real estate values) are therefore still guarded. The slow growth of the economy of the early 1990s is certainly preferable to the economic collapse of the early 1930s, but in one respect, at least, the New York real estate market must be judged worse off today than it was then. In the 1920s no New York Clearing House member bank made real estate loans. In the 1980s almost every one did. Probably, then, the Manhattan office market is more overbuilt and vulnerable today that it was even in the 1930s.

"So I said, hey, we'll just take the rumor and run with it."

Thus, I urge the committee to scrutinize the recent vogue in "stakeout" transactions, investments in weak banks made by stronger banks with the understanding that the stronger bank does not have to serve as a "source of strength" for the weaker. The investment amounts to a kind of option: If the death's-door bank grows out of its problems, the stronger bank buys control of it. If not, the stronger bank loses only the par value of its investment. The taxpayers then play their accustomed role of cleaning up the mess. My question is whether the taxpayers should not share in the upside in case things do work out. In other words, is the initial investment made (for instance) in MNC Financial by NationsBank large enough? Is the government getting its money's worth? I am skeptical. . . .

With the advent of chronic inflation in the 1960s, real estate came to be viewed as a privileged class of collateral: an inflation hedge. It did not matter if a building or a parcel of land failed to flow cash to the prospective buyer. Developers and their lenders looked beyond the P&L. They were in the "asset-appreciation business," not the "cash-flow business." Shopping malls, office parks, industrial parks, festival marketplaces, and multiuse retail projects were all in need of financing, and commercial banks furnished more and more of the money.

Not every bank was (or is) nationally chartered, of course, and not every national bank observed the letter of the real estate lending law. Thus, the country many years ago developed extensive experience with the consequences of speculating in buildings with borrowed money. In Chicago in the late 1920s, for instance, first mortgages worth 100 percent of the cost of a property were commonly available, and another 20 percent could be borrowed in the form of a second mortgage. Also in the 1920s, "Straus bonds," forerunners to the junk bonds of the 1980s, were issued to finance commercial real estate construction, often on precarious terms. In general, such speculative credit performed badly in the Depression, but the Banking Act of 1935 moderated the longstanding discrimination against real estate collateral that was contained in the National Bank Act. The sponsors of the reform contended that the banks needed help to compete with the government (which itself had gotten into real estate finance) and that the economy needed help to recover. It is interesting to record the objections of one contemporary witness to this far-reaching legislation. "To the real estate speculator, easier credit terms would no doubt be advantageous, but to the lending bank, they might well prove the reverse." So said Winthrop W. Aldrich, chairman of the Chase National Bank, forerunner to the real estate–freighted Chase Manhattan.

In a sense, therefore, we have come full circle. In reaction to a series of perceived credit inequities and historic financial upheavals—the alleged discrimination against agricultural borrowers after the turn of the century, the Panic of 1907, and the Great Depression itself—the banking laws were overhauled. Deposits were insured, systemic failures guarded against, and real estate collateral admitted into the lending mainstream. In return for these measures of support, however, the nation's bankers were subjected to an ever-widening net of control. No doubt the complaints of any trade group concerning the regulatory burden of its members should be divided by two, at least, to arrive at an objective estimate of the cost of compliance. Even applying the standard trade-group discount, however, bankers do seem to be genuinely put upon. (Last month the American Bankers Association contended that its members spent $10.7 billion complying with federal regulations in 1991, a sum representing 59 percent of their total earnings. Even 29.5 percent would be a lot.) Agreeing that something went wrong with the art of lending in the 1980s, we must ask what to do about it in the 1990s.

As directed by Congress last December, the FDIC recently circulated a proposal that would, in effect, render commercial real estate a second-class form of bank collateral again. The rules would reimpose loan-to-value ratios on real estate loans a decade after Garn–St. Germain abolished them. For instance, a bank could lend no more than 60 percent of the value of raw land and a maximum of 75 percent of the value of improved property.

What is one to think of this proposal (of which I have given only the barest bones)? To start with, of course, that it is approximately ten years too late; the damage has been done, and banks are pulling back from commercial real estate lending anyway. Also, that the limits might be too high, too low, or just right, but we will not find out until another ten years have passed. (By then, incidentally, we will also find out if the government unwittingly has promoted another real estate lending crisis by creating so many incentives for banks to make residential mortgage loans.)

One must return—at least, I return—to this paradox of error. How did so many capable people blunder so badly for so long? Is the answer to tell them exactly what to do in the future? Or is it to let them decide what to do themselves, settling more directly on them the consequences of their own actions? Everything I know and believe leads me to favor the second alternative.

Because the future is always unfathomable, there are always buyers and sellers in every market. If the socialists were right—if the future could be accurately divined—markets would disband because nobody would ever take the losing side of a trade.

What none of us knows about real estate is whether it will prove to be a worthy class of collateral in the future. (Does anyone know where interest rates are going? If so, would that person please legislate appropriate ceilings for bank investments in Treasury notes. It might be, as the traditionalists would argue, that real estate is an inherently unsuitable asset for a commercial bank, securitization and all the other financial advances of the day notwithstanding. I have my opinions, and the chairman of Citicorp has his, but not even the FDIC can know which of us is going to be right. Surely, in these circumstances, more flexibility—the application of judgment by people with specific knowledge—is better than less. It follows that less regulation is better than more. Or it would follow, if the people making the decisions were allowed to bear the consequences of them.

What I would propose, therefore, is a policy of enlightened federal retreat. What makes enterprise work is, first and foremost, the recognition that information is often lodged with people far removed from the nation's capital. On the other hand, what makes banks susceptible to regulation is the recognition that innocent depositors are sometimes caught up in guilty institutions or that in a fractional-reserve banking system, one bad bank can cause a chain reaction of failure. How can we know whether the proper loan-to-value ratio of a hundred acres of Texas prairie should be 60 percent, 62 percent, or 0 percent? If it should be 62 percent in 1992, might it not be something entirely different in 1993? The first step in regulatory wisdom is the recognition of what we don't know—can't begin to know.

Perhaps a system of uninsured (or privately insured) banks might coexist with a system of banks designed purely for the safekeeping of the risk-averse depositor's money. The uninsured system would pay a higher deposit rate than the risk-averse system. If an uninsured bank became illiquid, it would suffer the risk of a run. Perhaps, if the uninsured system became overextended, it would suffer the risk of a systemwide run, but the threat of such an event would surely impose a saner standard of lending and a higher standard of liquidity. It would do more to assure clear thinking among bankers than anything stipulated in the FDIC Improvement Act. My suggestion, in short, is that banking be restored to the capitalist system, not so much for the bankers' sake as the country's.

PART THREE

———

IT'S A
NEW
ERA

LOW FINANCE

May 21, 1984

Multivest Securities, municipal-bond brokers to the people, is in liquidation, but the slogan on the bulletin board in its empty office at the foot of Broadway is inspirational: TOUGH TIMES DON'T LAST—TOUGH PEOPLE DO!

To look around the place, a corner suite on the seventeenth floor of No. 11, the motto seems out of place. Taped to the glass front doors is a court order (in which it is hereby "ORDERED ADJUDGED and DECREED that the customers of MV Securities Inc., a/k/a Multivest Securities, Inc. . . . are in need of the protection afforded by the Securities Investor Protection Act"). The salesmen, two dozen strong, are gone, and the president, James R. Stephens, is being sued by the Securities and Exchange Commission for alleged colorful and brazen violations of the securities laws. Hanging in the president's office are framed portraits of the president's yacht. But whether the yacht lawfully belongs to Stephens or the firm, or even to the customers, is one of the questions that the court-appointed liquidator, Lee J. Richards III, and his staff are in the midst of tackling. (In the interests of full disclosure, Richards is a partner in the Wall Street law firm of Grais & Richards, of which *Grant's* is a client.)

If nothing else, the saga of Multivest proves just how hard it is to make money in the bond market through any known technique. According to charges filed by the SEC, the firm marked up bonds for resale by as many as 13 points, employed unregistered salesmen, baited and switched, cooked up phony selling stories, and pushed the securities of the Washington Public Power Supply System on anyone and everyone. Richards reports that, at the end, the firm had 1,001 accounts and some $18.4 million worth of securities on hand. It specialized in the small and unknowing customer. One such financial innocent, a thirty-eight-year-old Russian immigrant now living in Brooklyn, subsequently explained in broken English how he came to buy WPPSS: "I wanted something to invest—to keep my money in a very safe, security place. This guaranteed interest."

According to the SEC, there was a lot of loose talk around Multivest about interest. The Commission alleges that, last August, a salesman named Gary Falber called a customer to sell him an issue of Chattanooga (Tennessee) zero-coupon bonds at a price to yield 11 percent. But they didn't yield 11 percent. They yielded 8 percent. Falber, incidentally, was Multivest's "Account Executive of the Month" in August and also in January, May, and September 1983. His name is engraved on the plaque that still hangs in the empty boardroom. (Reached for comment last week, Falber said: "I can't talk to you now. I'm working." The firm at which he works is McLaughlin, Piven, Vogel Inc., which in *The Wall Street Journal* last Wednesday advertised "17% Tax Free Income—Obligations of a Federal Agency. . . ." The bonds turned out to be—WPPSS, Nos. 1–3.*)

Selling bonds at an unconscionable markup, a firm might at least be expected to keep its head above water. Yet no: The reason that Multivest was closed was for deficient capital. (An ameliorating fact was that its impairment occurred after a two-week spell in which its salesmen were enjoined from soliciting orders.) What went wrong? For one thing, of course, according to the SEC, it broke the law. And for another, it hurt its customers, buying WPPSS for them all the way down. There is an irony in this. On March 14, the day the court order was served and taped to Multivest's door, the WPPSS 10⅞s of 2015 changed hands at 12. But then, as the Treasury market fell to pieces, WPPSS rallied; and last week the bonds were quoted at 18½.† Moral: In the bond market, crime doesn't pay, but on most days neither does anything else.

---

* Everyone should have bought some. By early 1993, the price of one such WPPSS issue had risen to 100 cents on the dollar from approximately 35 cents on the dollar.
† Now at 9½.

BLIND POOL

February 10, 1986

The launching last week of ML Media Partners for the purpose of investing a quarter billion dollars or so in TV and radio stations, *the identities of which the managing partners don't happen to know at the moment*, is a news story of possible historic interest.

As *The Wall Street Journal* reported, Merrill Lynch Capital Markets will sell the partnership units, and Elton H. Rule, former president of ABC, and I. Martin Pompadur, another former ABC executive, will manage the media acquisitions, whatever and wherever they are. They will manage them for five to eight years, then sell them and distribute the profits, if any. We called an actual hands-on broadcast executive we know to ask him about this scheme, and he asked us, in turn, "Now how are they going to hire good people to run those stations if they're going to turn around and sell them five years later? If it wasn't so much money, it would be a joke."

In any event, the "blind pool"—so-called because the investor can't be sure exactly what he's getting into—is an ancient and portentous investment medium. It proliferated before the Crash, and it has been turning up in the debt markets recently, for example, last summer, when Goldman, Sachs & Co. raised $200 million for Chicago Pacific Corp. to finance undisclosed takeovers. To invest in anything without knowing exactly what it is reveals the kind of faith that makes market tops.*

Perhaps the oldest and purest blind pool on record was the "company for carrying out an undertaking of great advantage, but nobody to know what it is" during the South Sea Bubble of the early

---

* I might have written, "that *eventually* makes market tops."

eighteenth century. Probably Rule and Pompadur could do no better for themselves than could the unnamed founder of this imaginative enterprise. For their benefit, and for the benefit of the partners of Goldman, Sachs & Co., we quote a bit of Charles Mackay's famous account of this ultimate blind pool in his *Memoirs of Extraordinary Popular Delusions and the Madness of Crowds:*

> The man of genius who essayed this bold and successful inroad upon public credulity, merely stated in his prospectus that the required capital was half a million, in five thousand shares of 100£ each, deposit 2£ per share. Each subscriber, paying his deposit, would be entitled to 100£ per annum per share. How this immense profit was to be obtained, he did not condescend to inform them at that time, but promised that in a month full particulars should be duly announced, and a call made for the remaining 98£ of the subscription. Next morning, at nine o'clock, this great man opened an office in Cornhill. Crowds of people beset his door, and when he shut up at three o'clock, he found that no less than one thousand shares had been subscribed for, and the deposits paid. He was thus, in five hours, the winner of 2,000£. He was philosopher enough to be contented with his venture, and set off the same evening for the Continent. He was never heard of again.

CAPITULATION ROUNDUP

April 7, 1986

"**M**arkets make opinions," John W. Schultz, the estimable analyst at Brean Murray, Foster Securities Inc., reminds us.

And why not? In trading, after all, pride of opinion precedes a margin call. Still, it is a fine line between adapting to a market trend and capitulating to it—between bending to circumstance and surrendering to it.

"Don't worry, dumpling. I just know that something terrible is going to happen."

In the past few months, it strikes us, a number of institutions have surrendered, have yielded to what they believed to be an irresistible market force. We have identified three such cases, each to be filed away under the heading "Signs of the Times."

I. CHEMICAL BANK

Saul P. Steinberg was 29 years old and his company, Leasco Data Processing Equipment Corp., was eight years old when Steinberg appeared out of left field to bid for Chemical Bank, then 145 years old. It was a minnow-and-whale deal ahead of its time: Chemical had assets of $9 billion, Leasco $400 million. But it was early in 1969, the stock market was still up, and anything seemed possible.

It was Steinberg's contention (also ahead of its time) that Chemical should offer an array of financial services, not just the conventional banker's menu. That contention Chemical accepted. But Steinberg himself it rejected, and it marshaled the legal, political, and financial establishment against him.

John Brooks described the uneven fight in his book, *The Go-Go Years*:

"They"—the Chemical Bank, most of the banking business, the Cravath law firm, a cross section of Wall Street power and influence, the leading proxy solicitors, the governor and legislature of New York State, the members of the Federal Reserve Board and the Senate Banking and Currency Committee, and sundry more or less related forces—had combined to beat Saul Steinberg of Leasco, and apparently to cause him to lose his nerve at the last moment.

Twenty years later, another great bull market is under way, and conservative finance is on the defensive again. As before, the establishment is beset by bright young men with fast ideas about leverage.

But the position of Chemical Bank this time around is ironically different. To be sure, over the past five years, the bank has rebuilt its capital base, borrowing heavily in the process, and has boosted profit margins.*

But it has also made revealing concessions to the leveraged times. Though its chairman, Walter V. Shipley, has inveighed against junk bonds, greenmailers, and corporate raiders, the bank has done more than its share of lending to such acquisitive customers as Pantry Pride. (The contrast between Shipley's remarks and the lending of Shipley's bank was the subject of a biting story in the *American Banker* early this year.)

And just recently Chemical hired a thirty-two-year-old merger and acquisition whiz, reportedly paying him as much as $2.5 million a year (or three times the chairman's salary), to head up a new risk arbitrage department. Such a thing is a first for a commercial bank, and it remains to be seen if this pioneering activity will be profitable for Chemical.†

What is clear is that the establishment isn't as square as it used to be. In 1986 where are the fuddy-duddies?

---

* In 1985, Chemical reported a ratio of net income to stockholders' equity of 15 percent. In 1969, it could report only 10.3 percent. On the other hand, its equity amounted to 6.1 percent of its assets in 1969. The ratio was less than 5 percent in 1985.

In 1969—that distant unregulated day!—the bank could report a ratio of loans to deposits of only 73 percent. Last year the loan-to-deposit ratio was 150 percent, surely an unimaginable state of affairs to the Chemical team that beat away Steinberg.

† By the middle of 1987, the young man had moved on to Merrill Lynch.

II. BANK REGULATORS

It's no longer front-page news that federal bank regulators, in a stunning reversal, have disclosed a kind of capital amnesty program for banks that lend significantly to farmers and oil and gas companies.

Until just now every federally insured bank was required to maintain a minimum 6 percent ratio of primary capital to assets. At a regulatory stroke that ratio, in the special cases of worthy farm and energy lenders, is reduced to 4 percent. In certain hard-luck cases it is reduced to 3 percent. Afflicted banks may be unlucky or unable. They may be neither crooked nor grossly inept (average ineptness, however, the kind that would lead an institution to bet the bank on $30 oil or $600-per-acre Iowa farmland, is allowable).

Reading a recent Federal Deposit Insurance Corp. policy statement, we have decided that forbearance is the wave of the future. Perhaps this regulatory capitulation is an important banking watershed. We quote:

> There may be banks which do not meet the . . . definition of an agricultural/oil and gas bank, but nevertheless believe they are suffering capital pressures caused by problems in these economic sectors. *The FDIC will consider extending their capital forbearance policy to these banks on a case-by-case basis upon written request and explanation submitted to the appropriate regional office* [our italics].

If farm and energy lenders deserve special treatment, then why not steel lenders, airline lenders, shoe lenders, technology lenders? Surely the farm and oil slump, in a direct or indirect way, affects nearly everybody? And if, as the regulators also propose, loans of all types can be restructured but not charged off (if certain Financial Accounting Standards Board conventions are complied with), then why should there not be more and more restructurings?

Where this leads us, nobody can say, but it is not where old-time doctrine says it should lead. It is not to the prompt and orderly liquidation of bad debts from the banking system.

III. ITALY

Compared to Milan, New York is a financial disaster area. In the past year Italian stocks have tripled. On a single March day, the Milan list (featuring the likes of Fiat and Olivetti) surged by 5 percent, the equivalent of 90 Dow points. And now *L'Unità*, the official newspaper of the Italian Communist Party, has decided to publish stock quotations.*

It's one thing for Chemical Bank to set up shop in risk arbitrage or for the Comptroller of the Currency to play ducks and drakes with bank accounting standards. But it is something else again for the Communist Party of Italy to lend its temporal authority to stock speculation. Here we have capitulation of the highest historical order.

We report on Italian finance with our eyes wide open. We are under no misconception that the average American investor cares more about the Milan Bourse than President Richard Nixon, some years ago, cared about "the [expletive deleted] lira." On the other hand, there is nothing average about the readers of *Grant's*, and there is nothing dull, pedestrian, or uninstructive about the Italian stock market in this bullish spring.

We've tackled Italy because (first and foremost) it seems a kind of bull-market laboratory. It represents, to us, an almost controlled experiment in the laws of financial gravity and in the proposition that every great bull market reaches a stage in which speculation becomes an end in itself. Italian banks have created credit by the carload, the Italian economy has been turned around (after a fashion), the Italian people have been bitten by the investment bug, and Italian stocks have gone into orbit. The question is, What lies at the end of the rainbow? Has the Milan Bourse, in its zeal, discounted a new Roman Empire? More generally, in this global bull market, how high is high?

The Milan bull market might furnish a clue to the answers, might provide the scene for a bearish dress rehearsal. If any stock market on the face of the earth is overbought, it would seem to us, then Milan is. If any populace has thrown itself headlong into the white waters of speculation, then the Italians have. If the rules of contrary

---

* It still publishes quotations today, although they are lower.

opinion still apply anywhere, then they should rule in Italy. By degrees the Milan bull market has progressed from conviction to exuberance to zaniness. Compared to Milan, which has been the second strongest stock market in the world recently (behind Spain), New York remains a study in sobriety. "In Milan recently," the *Financial Times* reported the other day,

> white collar workers at RAR, the country's largest insurance company, blocked the streets for part of a·day as they went on strike demanding the right to stock options. . . . Stockbrokers say they are working until midnight and weekends to keep up with the orders, while the bureaucratic backlog at banks which act as clearers with the Bank of Italy's Milan branch is becoming a logistical nightmare. As a result, banks are issuing investors a type of promissory note instead of share certificates, which can take months to be processed.

Thus, if they serve no other purpose, the goings-on in Italy will help American observers to redefine speculative excess, to remind them (we're addressing ourselves) of the truism that bull markets almost always run longer than anybody had dreamed possible. Nor is this wholly an abstract issue. Now that Shearson Lehman Brothers has produced The Italy Fund, a blind pool dedicated to the Milan market, American investors have a ready-made (and New York Stock Exchange–listed) vehicle for Italian investment. Should the fund be bought, sold, or sold short?

And what of the Italian fundamentals? An interesting question. It seems that not many people are current on them. The Italy Fund prospectus, for instance, though dated February 26, 1986, contains Italian macroeconomic data of mainly 1984 vintage. Owing to the importance of the "parallel" economy (as the prospectus diplomatically describes the Italian underground economy), the official data are not only behind the times but also highly questionable. Ditto Italian financial reporting, a new and impressionistic art.

The latest Italian monetary data appear to be vintage September 1985 (though none of them made the prospectus). At that time, bank credit was tripping along at an annual rate of 16.3 percent, and M-1 and M-2 at a 14½ percent annual rate.

Strategic Research International, a division of Carl Marks & Co., forecasts that real GNP will grow by 3 percent this year and that

"Herbert, did you hear that? Bush is bullish and Clinton is bullish.
Low interest rates are bullish and high interest rates are bullish.
We're in clover, the man says."

inflation will amount to no more than 7.6 percent, the best price performance in a decade and a half.

The Italian discount rate stands at 15 percent (it was cut from 15½ percent last November). The average Italian price-earnings ratio stood at 33 in February when the market was 21 percent lower than it was at the end of March.

The basic bull case is kindly furnished by Strategic Research:

> Behind this [Italian share] advance is a growing savings pool in the form of mutual funds, which reached $19 billion at month-end February, about double the level of only four months ago. . . . In combination with huge domestic money flows, there are the additional demand forces coming from foreign institutions and domestic financial powerhouses (e.g., deBenedetti), adding fuel to the already raging fire.

Furthermore, to lean again on the excellent Strategic Research, Italy enjoys a composite national ranking—a grade based on such factors as the current account and foreign exchange reserves—of thirteen among nineteen major industrialized countries. Thirteenth may be an unprepossessing rank, but the United States finished fourteenth.

All of which—strong flow of funds, lower inflation, surging bank credit—suggests that Italy is prospering and that the Milan bull market may continue its run. Weighed against these considerations are the facts that the brokers can hardly settle trades, that the country has gone stock mad, and that the Italian Communist Party has thrown in the towel. ("Who's left to buy," a friend muses, "the anarchists?")

And The Italy Fund at last report changed hands at a price that represented a 20 percent premium-to-net-asset value. If the Milan market triples again, then we'll apply for Italian citizenship.*

ALGER'S CHAUFFEUR

July 28, 1986

F red Alger, the money manager, was recently surprised to receive the resignation of his chauffeur. Asked by Alger what he was going to do with himself and how he intended to eat, the chauffeur replied that he didn't have to worry about that anymore. He explained that he had overheard Alger talk enthusiastically about Genentech on the car telephone. He said that he'd taken a flyer on the calls, had won, and now was cashing out. He said he would never have to work another day in his life. The driver, a young man whose first name is Albert, is a poet.

---

* The market peaked a month later; almost seven years afterward, it was 43 percent lower than the 1986 top.

HOUSTON ANTIQUES SALE

November 17, 1986

W hat made the 1970s the 1970s was inflation, and the place where inflation settled down to make its home was Houston. What Boston is now to financial assets—Boom Town, U.S.A.—Houston was then to tangible assets. It was an era decked out as a city.

It's no front-page news that collectibles and real estate have had their day or that Houston is on the downslide—at the latest monthly foreclosure sale, for instance, 2,738 houses were hammered down in Harris County, a record. All that has gotten its share of notoriety. What has escaped public attention so far are the newfound opportunities in Houston for collectors of fine objects. The nation's energy capital has gone into liquidation.

When people need cash, of course, they sell the good things first (as Thomas Jefferson's estate did at Monticello) because those are the things most readily salable. A sign of the times is that dealers in Houston have recently suspended the prosperity-era practice of guaranteeing their consignors a minimum price. Items are put out for the bid, whatever that might happen to be. And the supply of better-than-average pieces is building.

Like so many barrels of petroleum, collectibles have come down in the world. Over the past eighteen months, according to Wynonne Hart (Hart Galleries, 2301 South Voss, Houston, Texas 77057; 713-266-3500), there's been a 30 percent decline in the prices for art, furniture, and rugs, and a considerable increase in the volume of merchandise put on the market. For instance, she reported that paintings by the artist Robert Wood (whose work has enjoyed an audience in the Southwest) had fetched $12,000 in 1981, $25,000 in 1984—and only $10,000 in 1986.

If the art market were the bond market, of course, there would be no regional price disparities, but there are no arbitrageurs in collectibles. Mrs. Hart says that she recently sold an 1820 Queen Anne–style chinoiserie double-dome secretary-bookcase for $10,000, a piece that, she estimates, would have fetched $15,000 to $17,500 in New York. She says she expects the supply of fine pieces to increase slowly but steadily in coming months.

Carolyn Foxworth, the Texas representative of the auction house Christie's (214-239-0098), notes that there's been no flood of pieces from bankruptcy cases if only because the courts are so backed up (although jewelry offerings have doubled this year). "Gradually, however," she says, "we should be handling materials from bankruptcies as they are resolved."

A lady we spoke to in Houston the other day reports a buyers' market in rugs and antiques. A Serapai rug, for instance, an early one, that "should have" sold for $18,000, recently fetched $9,000; and a Heriz rug went for $2,000 as opposed to (she estimates) $3,000 or $4,000 in New York. "I bought an American Federal secretary, 1824, for less than $2,000." In New York, she went on, that would be "out of sight." (Sotheby's, in fact, we discovered, recently auctioned pieces of that description for $4,500, $8,250, and $19,000.)

An old-line Houston rug dealer recently ran a telling newspaper ad: "forced out of business, final auction, no minimum, no reserve." Boston, please copy.

BROKER CAN'T VOTE

June 29, 1987

The youngest stockbroker in the country drives a 1959 Corvette. He is about to install a car telephone to facilitate mobile, two-way communication with his clients whom he was recently obliged to call from a public phone in the hallways of Greenwich (Connecticut) High School.

Daniel Stein, seventeen, graduated in June. He passed his Series 7 examination in April and received his broker's license in May. He works for Hamilton Grant & Co. and expects to enter Cornell early next year.

Stein—he calls himself Danny—eschews long-term investment in favor of hot stocks. He has no opinion on interest rates but says that the stock market is going to keep rising. "I do not foresee, contrary to popular Wall Street opinion, any major correction in 1987," he says. "The market should stay strong throughout the year." It has been strong since he was twelve.*

---

* Graduated from Cornell in 1992, Stein went to work as a management trainee at Lechter's Houseware Co. Asked for a stock market prediction, he declined. However, he did volunteer a comment on the chairman of Lechter's, Donald Jonas: "An unbelievable leader with great vision and great management skills who has attracted a first-rate management team that will lead the company through the nineties into the next millennium."

MIDDLE AGE TRIUMPHANT

November 30, 1987

The Monday after the crash, *The Wall Street Journal* ran a front-page story about irrepressible youth. MARKETS MAY SINK BUT FOR THE YUPPIES IT'S FULL SPEED AHEAD, the headline said, and an anonymous young person elaborated at length:

> "This is kind of mean," says a twenty-four-year-old analyst with Merrill Lynch & Co., speaking from his limousine phone outside Boston, "but for some of us the real problem [was] the fleshy middle layer. The odds of sprinting up the corporate ladder were fairly small. Now a lot of these forty-year-old managing directors have been fired, so the people who survive feel this is an opportunity."

Reading that, a ranking middle-aged Merrill Lynch executive went off like a rocket. He sent out the word: Get me the name of that twerp.

Presently, the word came back. "The good news is, we've found the guy," he heard in just about those words. "The bad news is, he's your assistant."

The middle-aged executive confronted the young man and gave him a choice. It was dismissal or the mailroom. The young man chose the mailroom. He is understood to be carrying out his junior-executive duties at night.

Youth will be served—but not without an occasional slap on the back of the head.

BELLS PEAL IN BROOKLYN

February 8, 1988

A t a dinner party in Westport, Connecticut, on a pretty summer night in 1985, the conversation turned to the problems of the rich. A well-tanned, middle-aged woman spoke up. If one's husband commutes to work by helicopter, she said, the helicopter must land on one's lawn. And if one's lawn has been freshly cut, the cuttings are bound to be scattered into one's swimming pool. Can nothing be done about this nuisance? A financial journalist in attendance made the mental note that the problem would probably be self-correcting. The bull market, however, lasted for another two years.*

One hears what one wants to hear, as the Westport lady might put it, and *Grant's* has been hearing bells toll for financial leverage, and for leveraged investments, for years. With that said, however, we must report a number of new soundings. For instance, a blind pool, based in Brooklyn, has done a leveraged buyout with a loan provided by a savings and loan association. A new publication called *Corporate Restructuring*, "the authoritative newsletter on the re-shaping of American business," is soliciting subscriptions. *Trump: The Art of the Deal*, by the great Donald J. Trump, has topped *The New York Times* nonfiction bestseller list for the past three weeks. And Bruce Wasserstein and Joseph Perella, formerly the Ruth and Gehrig of the First Boston Corp. investment banking department, have left their old employer to found Wasserstein, Perella & Co.

Reading about these marvels, we asked ourselves, "Is this the run of news commonly associated with a bear market bottom?" Plainly, no. At the bottom of the cycle in stocks and debt, as we

---

* A hasty, post-crash assessment. Stocks and bonds only went higher.

well knew, the *New York Post* will not be featuring inspirational pieces about successful blind pools. Yet a recent *Post* story led off:

> Who says you need a fancy Wall Street address to do a corporate takeover deal?
> Not Alan Weisberger, who works out of his Flatbush apartment.
> The twenty-five-year-old entrepreneur says he's trying to take some of the risk out of "blind pools" by going after dull—but solid—companies rather than glamour firms that are more sizzle than substance.
> He's just taken over Compton Press of Morris Plains, New Jersey, one of the state's biggest and most profitable printing plants, with sales of $25 million and a few dozen Fortune 100 companies among its customers.
> He did it with his Equity Finance Group, Inc., a blind pool he operates out of his apartment on Avenue O in Flatbush, and a $13.5 million leveraged buyout.*

According to the story (we couldn't reach Weisberger to check the details), there were seven hundred investors. They put up an average of $500 each, for a total of $350,000. The balance of the purchase price, about $13 million, was lent by Glendale Federal Savings & Loan. The price worked out to just three times pretax earnings. Could Wasserstein, Perella & Co. have done any better?

However, we wondered: Would seven hundred Brooklyn investors have invested in a blind pool at the bottom of the market? We *have* had a global stock market crash, have we not? Yes? Well, then, why doesn't the world act a little more frightened?

We had no answer but resumed our internal monologue. Consider Trump, for instance: "Warner Books will pay more than $500,000 for the paperback rights to the best-selling *Trump: The Art of the Deal*, *The Wall Street Journal* reported last week. Trump's book, whatever else it isn't, is not your standard bear market fare. At the bottom of the market, surely, the public will not pay $19.95 to read such lines as "The point is, you can't be too greedy" (*op. cit.*, page 34).

Concerning Wasserstein, Perella & Co., we wondered, why

---

* The transaction ended in litigation, Weisberger and his partner suing to get their money back. Compton Press, which once employed 120 people, went into bankruptcy.

wasn't the firm founded last year or the year before? Why now, after the crash? A friend of Wasserstein's told the *Journal*: "[Bruce] sees guys going out there and doing exciting and interesting things. He wants to go out and make some real money." Real money? At the bottom of the market, any old money will do.

A "THRIFT" FOR OUR TIME

May 13, 1988

Countless man-years have been devoted to the search for the perfect investment. It is a universal occupation. However, the hunt for the least perfect investment has attracted relatively little interest. Where is this grail-in-reverse? What would it look like if one came across it?

The worst investment would be badly secured and illiquid, of course. It would offer a yield—but, ultimately, would fail to pay it. It would look substantial but would furnish no substance.

It would be presumptuous to hold up the one-year 9½ percent debentures or the two-year 10½ percent debentures of American Continental Corp. as *the* worst securities available. That is up to the financial jury, which is out. At the least, however, the bonds are instructive, for they lead the student of markets to their issuer, American Continental, and then to the issuer's thrift subsidiary, Lincoln Savings & Loan. These are emblematic institutions—companies for our debt-laden, shot-taking time.

You probably have read about Lincoln, a $4.7 billion California thrift that has been fighting with the Federal Home Loan Bank Board. Lincoln is said to have undergone the longest audit in the Bank Board's history, and matters raised in the FHLBB examination report have prompted an order of investigation by the SEC. Charles H. Keating, Jr., chairman of American Continental, the holding company, is noted for financial innovation, strong views, and survivability. At Lincoln he chose to make money with credit risk rather than with interest rate risk, and he transformed a conventional thrift into a space-age model. In high places he counts friends and enemies alike. The *National Thrift News* has disclosed that no fewer than five U.S. senators intervened with federal regulators last spring on behalf of Lincoln, "pressing for more liberal appraisals on the thrift's real estate investments." In Phoenix, according to a local businessman, Keating has shown "incredible ability to convert assets into cash." He is going to need it (there's talk of a sale of Lincoln itself to a group led by the thrift's newly resigned chairman, but so far no action).

Lincoln is a thrift only in name. Instead of conventional home mortgages, it has stocked up on commercial real estate, real estate loans, and junk bonds. These assets it finances with federally insured deposits, thereby sharing its risk (but not its profits or the handsome salaries of its officers or the handy privileges of its insiders) with the insurance-assessment-paying members of the thrift industry. Ultimately, if the federal deposit insurance system keeps going downhill, Lincoln will share its risk with the taxpayers, who have not been consulted on the composition of its investment portfolio.

The margin for error is tight. For instance, the real estate assets of the holding company totaled $821 million at year-end. Of this total, "land acquired for development" was $591 million, "land held for resale" was $170 million, and real estate acquired through foreclosure was $78 million. Allowance for possible losses was $19 million. It is a number that, although double the 1986 reserve, suggests an optimistic reading of the Southwest market (the company's real estate activities are concentrated in the nonboom states of Arizona, Colorado, Georgia, and Texas). To put the $821 million real estate portfolio in perspective, consolidated year-end equity was $137 million. The junk bond portfolio is a little smaller than the land portfolio: $622 million at year-end, up from $561 million in 1986 but a large multiple of net worth.

One consequence of the company's emphasis on real estate investment, or speculation, is that its selling, general, and administrative expenses handily exceed its net interest income. Unlike the typical thrift, its income is dependent on the sale of securities and real estate, that is, on sources of revenue usually deemed irregular, or nonrecurring. American Continental is a kind of real estate development and junk bond enterprise subsidized in good measure by the Federal Savings & Loan Insurance Corp., which is broke.

Since 1984, the year American Continental acquired Lincoln, the holding company's leverage has risen and its return on assets has fallen. Ratio of equity to assets over the past several years has trended this way: 6.36 percent, 1984; 3.47 percent, 1985; 2.88 percent, 1986; and 2.75 percent, 1987. In 1984 return on average assets was 1.02 percent; in 1987 it was 0.4 percent. With all that leverage, you might have expected big gains in return on equity, but they didn't happen. ROE was 14.6 percent last year, a shade lower than in 1984.

With the approval of the Bank Board, American Continental has begun to offer its debentures—the subordinated one- and two-year securities nominated above for consideration as worst investments —in Lincoln's twenty-nine branch offices in southern California. A five-year bond is also available at 12 percent. The bonds are meant to be held to maturity or to the holder's death, whichever comes first. The selling literature serves fair warning on the lack of liquidity: "These bonds are not traded in the secondary market, but they can be transferred to another individual. It is the responsibility of the debenture holder to determine a suitable price and locate the buyer." That may or may not be easy, as the field of potential investors, possibly, is limited to people who don't read or who can't understand the American Continental prospectus.

The document is a pip, describing a perfect miniature of new-era finance. For instance: "Virtually all loans made since the acquisition of Lincoln Savings require 'balloon' payments of principal at various points up to, and including, final maturity of the loan . . . The risk of loss on all loans depends upon the accuracy of appraisals. However, the risk of loss from an inadequate appraisal for any particular loan is greater with larger loans." And so forth. The document cautions that debenture holders have no claim against American Continental's subsidiaries, notably the thrift subsidiary. In point of fact, as an interested reader points out, the holding company, ex-Lincoln, suffers a deep negative net worth. How, then, can the bondholders expect to get paid? Absent divi-

*"And I'm telling you that the Delaware Trust Company does not
'have it all over' the U.S. Trust Company."*

dends from subsidiaries (the payment of which depends on approval
from Lincoln's friends at the Bank Board), the company means to
borrow the money—or tap the subs for miscellaneous advances and
"tax sharing agreements."

Some months back, Roderick MacIver & Co., Basking Ridge,
New Jersey, issued a blistering report on American Continental,
citing, among other unflattering things, a series of property transactions with insiders. "Over the last three years," said MacIver,
"the company has sold $92 million of its properties to entities
affiliated with insiders. In one instance the company provided $3
million in secondary financing to the purchasers, who put none of
their own money down."

The 1988 proxy statement disclosed the purchase of 417,000
shares of American Continental stock from the insiders, including

117,000 shares from Keating himself on November 5 and 6. It was a timely accommodation for Keating, inasmuch as the total volume of American Continental traded on NASDAQ that day was just 16,300 shares. It can be imagined that a block of 117,000 shares would have weighed heavily in the marketplace just three weeks after the crash.

The public should be reminded that no such instant liquidity is available to the holders of the American Continental debentures. You must wait out the maturity date or die. The prospectus contains the details. Read it carefully before you invest or send money.*

HAIL, 1990s!

January 6, 1989

T he zany 1980s aren't over yet. New debt securities backed by recreational-vehicle loans (call First Boston Corp.) and time-share mortgages (Merrill Lynch) have been created, and the "Visa Our Treat Sweepstakes" offers hope to millions of overextended consumers. There is a very small chance that you can win the equivalent of last month's credit card bill. The *National Enquirer* put this on its front page: DONALD TRUMP GETS $10 MILLION HOME AND $2 MILLION CASH—FOR $2,812 DOWN. West Virginia lost $200 million in what was supposed to be a money market fund, but employees of Drexel Burnham stood to make $400 million on a long-shot investment in a leveraged chemical company, Rexene. There was apparently no connection.

Deals Are Us, a pint-size, $150,000 blind pool underwritten by Westminster Securities, New York, was successfully sold. Preced-

* American Continental Corp. entered bankruptcy on April 13, 1989. Lincoln failed a day later. Keating, who faces up to 525 years in federal prison, at least $17 million in fines, and forfeiture of $265 million in assets, was working in February 1993 as a prison busboy at the California men's colony at San Luis Obispo.

ing it (from the same sponsor) were Big Mergers, Bigger Mergers, and Biggest Merger; expected to follow are Deals Are Good and Deals Are American. Patricia Kluge, wife of John, the midas man of Metromedia, said of their newly finished ten thousand-acre estate near Charlottesville, Virginia: "Now that it's complete, what gives me the most pleasure is that I'm able to leave a bit of John and myself to our descendants. This house is a statement to the generations of what we stood for."*

On the face of things, then, all is well. But just beneath the surface the rumble of change can be heard. Drexel Burnham Lambert has settled with the government, RJR Nabisco has encountered resistance, Michael Milken is on the griddle, and credit problems have welled up at a number of Drexel clients, including I.C.H. Corp., an insurance holding company with an appetite for other Drexel clients.

In an oddball transaction proposed four days before Christmas, I.C.H. agreed to buy 7.5 million common shares—new and unissued—of Integrated Resources, the cash-eating financial services company. That would constitute control of Integrated, the real estate syndicator that, under the lash of tax reform, branched out into non–real estate investment products. More oddly, I.C.H. disclosed that it had agreed to buy 900,000 Integrated shares from Selig Zises, chairman of Integrated, and from his brothers, Jay and Seymour. The price to be paid is $21. The price available to the public in the open market on the day of the announcement was $13.50. A SPECIAL PRICE FOR BOSSES' STOCK, was the headline in *The New York Times*.

It was a classic 1980s moment—the insiders getting theirs but the public not getting its; or, better, *some* of the insiders getting theirs, for the Zises cut the deal for themselves alone. Both companies, Integrated and I.C.H., promptly landed on the Moody's watch list for possible downgrade, their stocks having suffered a long-running downgrade in the open market (Integrated's preferred has also been featured regularly on the New York Stock Exchange new-low list). Thus, I.C.H., which has invested in Southmark, the monumentally fouled-up Dallas real estate com-

---

* In the divorce settlement, she got the forty-five-room house, Albemarle Farm; he got another house on the same ten thousand acres. "From a distance," *The Los Angeles Times* has reported, "Albemarle Farm looks like a neo-Georgian theme park painted against the Blue Ridge Mountains."

pany, among other leveraged entities, now wants to control Integrated, even as the Ziseses seem to want out. It's the 1980s but with a difference.

In and out of the Drexel circle, arguably, sentiment has turned. Preceding Integrated and I.C.H. on the Moody's watch list by a day were Salomon Inc. and Shearson Lehman Holdings. "Moody's cited both firms' 'risk appetite in the merchant banking area,' " *The Wall Street Journal* reported, "and said the review is part of the rating service's overall look at the implications of the expanding risks in the field."

GEE WHIZ! GUY

March 17, 1989

D avid Martin Darst is a renaissance man who happens to work on Broad Street. He reads, writes, lectures, runs, teaches, thinks, travels—and sells stocks for Goldman, Sachs & Co. Darst is a bond man's stock man, a student of the compound interest tables and of the earning power of interest piled on interest. He is the author of *The Complete Bond Book* and *The Handbook of the Money and Bond Markets*, and the mentor of dozens of students who have taken his course on new securities at the Harvard Graduate School of Business Administration.

Darst is a connoisseur of weird, complex, and improbable debt instruments, for example, "subordinated primary capital perpetual floating rate notes." He contends that a subordinated perpetual note is a contradiction in terms, "like jumbo shrimp or temporary eternal flame," and that Wall Street is pulling the legs of investors more often than investors may know. Darst is the father of two, the husband of the former Diane Wassman of Larchmont, New York, a resident of Greenwich, Connecticut, and the living inspi-

David Martin Darst

ration for the David M. Darst Hustle Cup, a prize awarded annually at Yale to the freshman "who has made the greatest contribution to the baseball team through desire, enthusiasm, and hustle."

At the age of forty-one, Darst continues to demonstrate desire, enthusiasm, and hustle in astonishing measure. He lectured for five hours straight last Sunday at a meeting of the Association of International Bond Dealers in Montreux, Switzerland, and ran the 1987 New York City Marathon in two hours, fifty minutes, and twenty-two seconds. Once he compiled a list of his personal interests: "America, languages, physics, astronomy, computers and artificial intelligence, Japan, mathematics, architecture, music, art, outdoor sports (running, swimming, surfing, skiing), dance, people, reading, writing, and thinking." Manuela Hoelterhoff, the Pulitzer Prize–winning critic for *The Wall Street Journal*, remembers the day she met Darst for lunch: "He talked about Pakistan, Los Angeles, and Italo Calvino [the late Italian author]—that was in the first five minutes."

Darst may be the only active stockbroker in New York who would rather not talk about stocks. Except during business hours, he rarely

Darst's telephone sculpture: "Watson, come here. I need you."

mentions them. If he does bring them up conversationally, it will probably be all of them—"the market"—rather than a specific company in which he might happen to have a rooting interest. In fact, throughout the great bull market and its aftermath, according to Darst, he has invested in Treasury bills. Furthermore, he has kept his bills at the Federal Reserve Bank of New York, a depository with many of the same advantages and disadvantages of Fort Knox. (As Darst knows better than most people, stocks have excelled in the past century—have left bills and bonds in the dust. "Stocks are human endeavor," he says, summing up the long-term bullish case in four words. But he steadfastly refuses to buy them.) Nor does he own any of the exotic securities that constitute the syllabus of his course at Harvard: payment-in-kind preferreds, bonds with embedded options, junk bonds, currency exchange warrants, variable coupon renewable notes or collateralized mortgage obligation residuals. He is, in short, the type of financial person who will be glad to see the back of the 1980s. "I am not risk averse," Darst says, "I am loss averse."

Darst joined Goldman Sachs in 1971, went to its Zurich office in 1975, returned to the home office in 1981, and currently directs the international equity sales group in New York. He began a second career, college teaching, in September 1981—a month that, as is clear now, might have been better spent buying long-dated

15 percent Treasuries on margin. He has a modest, vice presidential–size office on the twenty-eighth floor of the new Goldman Sachs building at 85 Broad Street.

"All of these guys on Wall Street have offices furnished with advertisements for themselves," says Darst, showing a visitor around. "There's a lot of me in this room, but it's not too territorial, I hope." On the walls are a Phillips' Commercial Map of the World, the Dymaxion Airocean World map (designed by Buckminster Fuller and favored by Darst for the appreciation it shows of the mass of Antarctica), and a National Geographic map of the universe. The cosmic map, says Darst, helps him to keep day-to-day vexations, such as reproaching telephone calls from the back office, in perspective. There are no framed stock certificates, investment-banking trophies, diplomas, letters of commendation, or photographs of the occupant shaking hands with the president of the United States. There is an advertisement of the Dewars' Profile variety, featuring a former student of Darst's, a young venture capitalist and saxophonist, Jon V. Diamond. "David was one of the people overseeing the summer training program," recalls Diamond of his mentor. "Once we went out to lunch together at noon—pizza and diet Cokes. We talked about music, architecture, life, the investment business, and a book we both enjoyed, Douglas Hofstadter's *Gödel, Escher, Bach: An Eternal Golden Braid.* We got back at six in the evening." In a corner of the office is a sculpture by Darst—a telephone set bursting with the colorful wire that, before the sculptor disemboweled it, was hidden in the bland beige box. "What this symbolizes for me," explains Darst, "is that every human being has beauty and complexity. Not just every human being—every*thing.* In the name of your building. In the name of a street, 'Garden Place,' 'Sidney Place'—why? And technology. We in this century are missing a big bet by not relating to the beauty of technology as we do to the beauty of flowers."

Darst is not ill-disposed toward money—he has earned and saved a fair amount of it and written and spoken about it extensively—but the subject does not obsess him, and he is not what Wall Street calls a money-maker. When his contemporary Michael Milken had one idea in the mid-1970s, Darst had hundreds. The result was that Milken created the contemporary junk bond market. Darst wrote *The Complete Bond Book.* In 1981, Darst published his *Hand-*

book, an advanced sequel to his *Complete Bond Book* (a title that had seemed to imply no sequel). It was a formidable survey of the fixed-income landscape, but it neglected to mention Mount Milken, and it was without a distinct investment point of view. In retrospect, of course, the early 1980s were just the years to have locked in high investment-grade yields, but Darst's book was not the work of a broker who wanted to sell you something. It was the work of a broker, or scholar-broker, who wanted to teach.

Darst is the third of five sons born to Susan McGinnis Darst and the late Guy Bewley Darst, a business executive who retired from DuPont in 1979 and died in 1987. Guy Darst was the president of the class of 1935 at the University of Tennessee, and Susan Darst was the homecoming queen. David was born in Knoxville, grew up in Nashville, attended Father Ryan High School, and graduated in 1965 from Phillips Exeter Academy. It has been one blue-chip institution after another from that day to this: Yale (class of 1969), Harvard Business School (class of 1971), Goldman Sachs—and then, in teaching, Yale and Harvard all over again.

The author pictured on the dust jacket of Darst's two bond books would not be served a drink by a conscientious bartender. The middle-age Darst has a fleshier face than the youth in the picture but has lost no hustle or hair. He continues to distribute copies of his favorite Shakespeare sonnets to Goldman trainees ("I figure that if Sir Siegmund Warburg, this century's greatest investment banker, said 'Study Shakespeare,' we should all study Shake-speare—a little bit"), to order a TV set from the audiovisual de-partment for the day of a televised space launch, and to set personal objectives: this year, for instance, to learn the names of stars and constellations. Coming across a dumpster full of discarded personal computers recently, Darst took one home with the idea of turning it into another electronic sculpture. (Once, at Yale, Darst brought a girl to his room to watch some television. He had purchased three expendable secondhand sets for the occasion. The first had poor reception, as Darst had anticipated. "I can't stand this anymore," he said finally, getting up from his seat, lugging the set out into the hall, and throwing a billiard ball through the screen. Set number two got the same rough handling. "That girl positively shivered through the program on the third set," Darst remembers. " 'How's the reception?' I'd ask her. 'Fine, fine, fine,' she'd say.")

"Higgins from The Wall Street Journal, *General. So many of the financial analysts are bullish on the war, sir, I was wondering—do you feel bullish on the stock market?"*

In his eighteenth year at Goldman Sachs, Darst is not a partner, and his chances of being tapped seem somewhat distant. "My mother says this and my wife says this," Darst genially reports, "that 'a little of you goes a long way.' " (Some insight into what it must be like to be Mrs. Darst was furnished by the *Yale Daily News* in 1982. "On nights after his seminar, Darst arrives home at about midnight, 'recharged' by his contact with the students, he says, and wakes his wife Diane up to tell her about it.")

"Some people really like him, and other people really don't like him," reflects a friend on Darst's position at Goldman. "That is not the way to do it. The way to become a partner is to have somebody really like you and everybody else not care." There is almost nothing that Darst doesn't care about, up to and including the art on the walls. In the twenty-eighth-floor reception area is a sketch by Christo. Taped to the inside of the coat closet is a not-altogether-flattering review of Christo's work by Manuela Hoelterhoff. Who taped it there? Who else?

Once in a blue moon Darst will turn to his longtime friend and partner, Michael K. Parekh, or Parekh will turn to Darst, and one will inquire of the other, "Jennifer Bartlett?" Bartlett is a contemporary painter whose work Darst and Parekh saw and reveled in at a 1985 show at the Brooklyn Museum. The success of that lunchtime expedition has led to other intramural outings, including one to Brooklyn Heights (for the architecture) and another to Iceland (for the volcanoes).

A subversive sense of irony is not the characteristic most commonly identified with Goldman Sachs partners. A partner must have coveted partnership, almost single-mindedly, before becoming a partner, and Darst's list of long-term objectives doesn't even mention it. Otherwise, the list runs the gamut, with the exception of sleep:

— Visit every U.S. state.
— Visit every Canadian province and spend some time traveling the country by car.
— Sail to (a) the Elizabeth Islands, (b) Block Island, and circumnavigate Long Island [Darst has done little sailing; he just thinks he would like to].
— Read every single plaque in the Metropolitan Museum of Art.
— Write a play and have it performed at the Cherry Lane Theatre.
— Write a book that moves large numbers of people.
— Have the president of the United States want to have dinner with me.
— Earn an honorary degree.
— Give a building to Phillips Exeter Academy.
— Have a book turned into a movie.
— Cook a banquet for fifty people.
— Meet Stevie Wonder.
— Build up a company that has an impact over a huge area.
— Own a farm in middle Tennessee.
— Read every word that Shakespeare wrote.
— Read the Feynman lectures on physics, all three volumes.

Richard P. Feynman, whose lectures Darst proposes to read, was "arguably the most brilliant, iconoclastic, and influential of the postwar generation of theoretical physicists" (*The New York Times* said that), and he is one of Darst's heroes. Another is Stevie Wonder, the rock musician, whom Darst calls a modern-day Shakespeare. Still another is the late Sir Siegmund George Warburg, the eccentric and learned banker. "Compare him," says Darst, "to the talent we take in and clone and *de*individualize in our business. One day my mom was waiting for me outside the building. She said, 'You know, everybody who walks out the door looks the same.' *And it's true.*"

Darst says that his greatest hero was his father: "He was an enormously strong human being of immense energy and intellectual curiosity. So many of my father's letters would begin 'I had no idea that . . .' and he would go on to tell me about something he'd just learned. During World War II, Dad served in the Army Engineers, in a black unit, and one rainy day they were training in Mobile, Alabama. (I didn't get this from him—he never talked about the war.) Four officers, including Dad, were in the running for command of this outfit, and a general was coming by to decide which one it would be. When the general got to the tent, in this pouring rain, he saw only three of the officers. 'Where's Guy Darst?' he asked. 'Oh,' somebody said, 'he's down there in the mud with the niggers.' The general went nuts. 'Well, he's your commanding officer now. Now get down there with him!' There are two types of people in this world—'so what?' and 'gee whiz!'—and Dad was the ultimate 'gee whiz!' guy."

For all his interest in painting, literature, Antarctica, Iceland, physics, and other non-commission-generating topics, Darst is a natural salesman. He shakes hands as if he were running for president and yours was the deciding vote. He pours himself into your eyes, laces your name into his conversation, and shows off his memory by recalling miscellaneous details about your life. He talks to cab drivers, and they talk to him. "It was marvelous seeing you on the elevator the other day," he was recently overheard to boom into the telephone to a colleague at Goldman. He delivered the line with aplomb. He remembers middle names. "He knows my middle name," one of his former students, David Byrd Singer, says. "And he knows every one of my family's middle names."

Darst talks on the phone with customers, visits customers around the world, and recruits for Goldman at Harvard. But he makes his greatest impression as a public speaker, performing for hours on end, darting from Shakespeare to collateralized fixed-rate multi-tranche tap notes, pacing the floor and changing subjects in mid-clause. "It's like being at a wonderful, sophisticated circus," says Singer. "You don't know what's going to happen next, but you know you're going to enjoy it."

Darst distributes a thick handout to an audience and warms them up with some questions: "What can I tell you that you don't already know? Will it make a difference? Can *I* make a difference?" He contends that the financial markets resemble a supernova—"energetic, bright, mystical, attractive, spectral, astral, celestial, rare, fleeting, unearthly, puzzling." Which leads him, naturally, to a plaintive question: "How do you explain about Ben Johnson to a ten-year-old watching the Olympics?" Which (flipping to the second page of the handout) leads him to J. Paul Getty. "Getty had five wives and died with $2 billion," he says. "Anybody who did that is somebody we can learn from." Next, he quotes Getty: "A sense of thrift is essential. Make your money first—then think about spending it." Similar advice is quoted from Baron Rothschild and the late nineteenth-century bestseller, *The Business Guide: Or Safe Methods for Business* by J. L. Nichols. There are inspirational quotations from former basketball coach John Wooden and former baseball manager Earl Weaver. There are readings from a selection of famous love letters, including one from Napoleon to Josephine that leads off, "I love you no longer; on the contrary, I detest you."

PR Week reviewed a performance of Darst's last fall before the

Market extremes
yet unreached

Investment-banker
trading cards

National Investor Relations Institute. The critic was impressed, if puzzled: "He was critical of everything from the deindividualizing of talent in the financial services industry to the high turnover of stocks on Wall Street, the percentage of bank profits coming from leveraged buyouts to ridiculous tombstone ads. He compared last year's British channel ferry disaster with the stock market crash, noting that 'there is an insufficient understanding of the risks,' observing the ironic parallel that the ferry was named 'Herald of Free Enterprise.' You had to be there."

Darst, whose father was once out of work for a year, has the demographic profile of a yuppie but the heart and soul of a Depression child. He worries about debt, distrusts financial innovation, and is chronically bearish on the stock market. He says that he refused to read Tom Wolfe's novel *The Bonfire of the Vanities* because "the first three guys who asked me about it on this floor, in the bathroom, were wearing suspenders." He is, arguably, the most ebullient, positive, and life-giving bear on Wall Street, but he is as pessimistic as the worst sorehead. Asked to explain that anomaly, he says, "I would like us to scale new heights based on solid foundations. There is this parable in the New Testament about not building your house on sand."

Sand, for Darst, encompasses debt, hyperactive finance, and the all-around decline of standards (specifically, his standards). Concerning debt, the readers of *Grant's* probably don't need to be

"Gee, Dad, thanks! Warrants!"

reminded. As for financial activity, Darst fingers, in particular, the decade-long rise in the rate of turnover of common stocks on the New York Stock Exchange. "Can it go on like this?" he asks. "How about a week with quill pens?" he suggests. The investment-banking analogue to frenzied trading, he continues, is the out-pouring of new and exotic debt securities. No Darst presentation is complete without a recitation of some of the least plausible debt securities of the bull market years. The list includes variable spread floating rate notes (*"everything* floats!"), floating rate sterling notes convertible at the option of the holders into U.S. dollar–denominated floating rate notes, guaranteed floating rate notes with warrants to purchase ECU-denominated guaranteed retract-able bonds, cumulative redeemable commodity-indexed preferred shares, duet bonds, synthetic floating rate notes, and retractable facsimile bonds. Almost without exception, he says, his students and he, upon examining such wild specimens, reach the conclusion that the investment bankers have done better than the issuers or customers.

Among Darst's favorite tombstones is one heralding an $80 million credit facility for the Iowa Student Loan Liquidity Corp. Funds were provided by ten banks, of which nine were foreign—"And that's Iowa," Darst marvels. As for the decline of standards, Darst holds up a full-page advertisement announcing that Jackpot Enterprises, newly listed on the New York Stock Exchange, inherited the ticker symbol "J." The date of the ad is October 19, 1987, and Darst is beside himself with the timing and symbolism. *"J,"* he

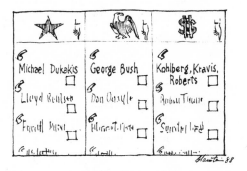

says. "Before Exxon was XON, it was J—Standard Oil of New Jersey. Now what does that once-proud symbol stand for? A company that operates gambling machines in Nevada. Does this summarize it all? What would John Davison Rockefeller say if he saw this page . . . his symbol?"

Darst has responded with a personal boycott of equities. He confesses he did not buy stocks at the bottom of the 1973–74 bear market nor at the bottom of the 1982 bear market, but he is not ruling out the next opportunity. "I want to buy stocks when they are being given away. Maybe I'll never get the chance. I want to borrow money when they're giving *it* away. When nobody else has the will."

Come that day (if it ever does come), Darst can refer to pages 47, 48, 48A, and 48B of his current handout, which deal with compound interest. It is information for all time but especially for ours. To start with, Darst notes, the total return to the holder of a $1,000, 10 percent bond, held for thirty years, is no less than $18,679. The components of that number are interesting. Repayment of principal counts for $1,000, or just 5.4 percent. It is always nice to get your money back, but that is the least of it. Coupon income counts for $3,000, or 16.1 percent. Interest on interest—income received by the reinvestment of coupon income—counts for $14,679, or 78.5 percent. That is assuming, of course, that the money can be reinvested at 10 percent, which, except in the special case of zero-coupon securities, is a fanciful assumption.

The mathematics apply equally to the stock market, Darst con-

tinues. Total return on equities—capital appreciation plus reinvested dividend income—amounted to 9.9 percent per annum,
compounded, in the sixty-two-year span from 1925 to 1987. However, capital appreciation alone in the same period provided an
annual rate of return of just 4.9 percent. The moral is that one's
grandchildren will be more grateful upon one's death if one conscientiously reinvests one's coupon and dividend income rather
than frittering it away on oneself in one's lifetime. Incidentally,
Darst predicts that reinvestment opportunities will improve in the
near term as the yield curve flattens and long-term interest rates
rise by 100 to 150 basis points.

Darst this week begins another spring term for his "New Financial Instruments" course at Harvard. If last year's curriculum
is any guide, the enthusiastic professor will begin by reminding his
students to pay attention to details. He will stress punctuation and
tell them the story of a proofreading mistake that last year cost
Prudential Insurance some $8 million. Not everyone within earshot
of Darst will pay attention, of course. On inquiry, a spokeswoman
for the Business School said that she knew nothing about a course
called "New Financial Instruments," had never heard of Durst or
Darst—she hadn't quite gotten his name—and could find no record
of his ever having taught there. She added that Dean John Mc
Arthur could not spare the time to talk about Darst, whoever he
was. Apprised of this arrogant confusion, Darst roared with laughter. "Don't you love it?" He will, on the first day, rip apart a
prospectus for something called "Collateralized Real Yield Securities" issued by Franklin Savings Association. He will remark on
the irony of invoking Franklin's name to sell this piece of work to
the investing public.

Finally, Darst will try to impress upon his students his personal
motto: "There are no little people."

NIP AND A TUCK

May 12, 1989

Pardon us, but is your nose straight? Are your thighs firm, your stomach flat, and your face everything it used to be (before the accident)? Not exactly? An effective and financially accessible solution has become available.

Profiles and Contours, which bills itself as New York's "leading plastic surgery center," last week advertised liposuction and breast enlargement for as little as $85 a month—"when financed." An alert reader called to note this curiosity. He said he had two questions: Are the loans collateralized? Will they be securitized?

For our reader's information, quoted terms are one-third down and 12 percent interest expense (perhaps the effective annual percentage rate is higher—he can ask in his personal consultation). A credit check is performed in advance, and a customer's checking account is automatically debited until the loan is extinguished. The loan, however, is technically unsecured. There is no collateral, whatever the procedure selected. There are no immediate plans for securitization, but never say never. These are the 1980s.

"Dreams of Wealth"

1987: Closing that big deal

1988: Hitting the lottery

ALFRED CHECCHI, LEADING INDICATOR

June 7, 1991

N WA, parent of Northwest Airlines, has debt on its wings, but Alfred Checchi, its *Bartlett's*-quoting co-chairman, is lighter than air. In a speech to the Detroit Chamber of Commerce the other day, Checchi rebuked the leverage artists of the 1980s, not naming himself. He praised goodness, jobs, craftsmanship, excellence, permanence, quality, and "giving back." Understandably, he applauded the state of Minnesota for agreeing to lend $740 million to his loss-making, cash-seeping airline at low, subsidized interest rates and for contemplating a $200 million "investment." (The yield on his own holding company debentures was recently quoted at a high, condemning 18 percent.) He quoted William James, Keri Hulme, and the late Lee Atwater. What is missing from American life, he contended, is "a little heart, a lot of brotherhood" (he said that he borrowed that line from Atwater). He implied that there is no better means of promoting social cohesion than by mounting a raid on a nearby public treasury, in his case, Minnesota's.

Checchi drove there on May 1 in a new burgundy Cadillac, according to David Phelps of the Minneapolis *Star Tribune*. He dropped in at the office of Governor Arne Carlson and presented his case. Two and a half weeks of lobbying ensued, involving Checchi and his directors and lobbyists, including Walter Mondale. "It was a case of 'Who's Who' versus 'Who's He,' " a defeated legislator wearily told *Grant's*. The enabling legislation was passed in each house by a majority of close to 70 percent.* Here is what the legislation enabled: $350 million in state revenue bonds to

---

* Despite a toll-free telephone number set up by the Citizens Committee to Stop the NWA Loan. Easy to remember, it was: 1-800-NO-WAY-AL.

"You know what the old fool said? He said that $300,000 a year is a lot of money."

finance a pair of aircraft-maintenance facilities at Duluth and Hibbing, Minnesota, and up to $390 million in Metropolitan Airport Commission revenue bonds, not to build anything but to recapitalize NWA, which, as the readers of *Grant's* well know, could use it. The $350 million in maintenance bonds will be backed, in part, by general-obligation pledges by the state and by the county of St. Louis and by a pledge of utility revenues by Duluth. In all, the credit support will add up to 71 cents on the dollar. The $390 million issue will be backed by the ability of the AAA-rated Metropolitan Airport Commission to levy property taxes on the citizens of seven surrounding counties.

In 1989, when Checchi borrowed more than anybody except Bankers Trust, his fee-hungry lender, deemed wise or even plausible, he conspicuously did not consult with the legislature of Minnesota or with the people who elected it. He did not offer them a share in the upside in case everything went according to plan. Now that everything is not working out, he's taken up the political doctrine of burden-sharing.

The NWA affair would be noteworthy if only for the injustice of it, but there are other reasons for paying attention. One is the new light it sheds on the finances of the Checchi holding companies. Gene Merriam, chairman of the Minnesota Senate Finance Committee, is (according to Merriam himself) one of only two persons in the legislature who were allowed to see the complete NWA financials, including those of the super holding company, Wings Holdings. He was sworn to secrecy about them, and he refused to so much as clear his throat over the telephone to confirm our suspicion that the picture is bleak.* He did say, however, that he is against the transaction. "If I had it in my power to halt the proceedings, I would have," he said. "Not because of anything I saw or didn't see, but because the benefits were not commensurate with the risks."

Which risks?

"It's what we were talking about—just who's going to pay the bills and the chance of NWA not paying is not remote." (During the lobbying effort, Checchi insisted that all was well financially. "If we had to today," he said, "we could write a $500 million check." At year-end 1990, NWA showed cash and securities of only $200 million. In fairness to Checchi, however, he did not say how he would date the check or whether it would clear.)

Another point of relevance to NWA is the future of national politics. If Checchi's statism finds favor in other parts of the country, that would be a straw in the wind. One would want to be prepared for the centralizing, inflationary financial consequences. (The risk is not so much in the financing itself—Checchi did not invent the game of playing state against state for tax benefits—but in the explicit political philosophy of Checchism. It is the philosophy of making the trains run on time through comprehensive state action.) Another point of interest is credit. If junk-caliber debtors

---

* Very bleak. NWA would show a net loss of $316.7 million in 1991 and $405.1 million in 1992. Its management would spend more and more of its time contriving means and devices to avoid bankruptcy, the prospects of which were not improved when KLM–Royal Dutch Airlines, the owner of 20 percent of NWA's parent company, chose to write off its investment rather than contribute more cash. In January 1993, Checchi, who never moved his home from Los Angeles while running Minneapolis-based NWA, announced that he would be scaling back his management role.

"Of course I'm over 21. I'm a managing director of Morgan Stanley."

can sell equity, thereby liquefying themselves, and if Checchi can slip his hand into the taxpayers' pockets, in the name of "jobs," the credit cycle may play out differently from the way it otherwise would. Perhaps (though we happen to doubt it) the rejuvenation of balance sheets will proceed painlessly and Checchi will be elected our next president on a platform of caring.

What Checchi told the Detroit Chamber of Commerce bears close reading: "We recoil from the notion of 'industrial policy' because it conjures up visions of a controlled and planned economy dominated by Washington bureaucrats," he said. "Instead, we have a controlled economy dominated by Washington bureaucrats—it just doesn't have even the pretense of planning or coordination.

"We need to stop deluding ourselves. In a modern state, the public and private sectors are inextricably linked. Neither is going to go away. The actions of one affect the other. In a capitalist system such as ours, the private sector is the ultimate instrument of public policy. We should appreciate this."

When in February, Checchi begged for relief from the 10 percent federal ticket tax, we read no editorial that took him to task for his own crash-prone balance sheet. It was Checchi's idea to leverage a cyclical business, not the federal taxpayers'. Similarly, in Minnesota this spring, the debate centered on the jobs to be kept and created, not on the financial dice that Checchi had been gaily rolling for himself and his partners.

The key feature, to us, in the assistance package negotiated by Checchi is the source of the ultimate credit. It is not the airline but the state. It is the taxpayers of the state and of the counties surrounding the Minneapolis–St. Paul International Airport. "I haven't seen an issue lobbied like this for a long time," said another state senator, Charles Berg. "They act like we're the Bank of Last Resort."

In creating an ultraleveraged airline, Checchi personified the finance of the 1980s. What an investor will want to know is whether he now typifies the politics of the 1990s. Two things are impressive about the dealmaker's political campaigns this year. First, their success to date; second, their lack of effective opposition. "With moxie and muscle seldom seen in Minnesota politics," the *Star Tribune* reported, "the Northwest gang performed the remarkable, pushing through a huge financing package through a cost-conscious legislature in less than three weeks." Now more than ever, it seems to us, Checchi is a man to watch.

WHY NOT PLATINUM?

May 8, 1992

"**D**ear Ms. Grant," the letter started out. "There's a lot more to traveling than just packing a suitcase. You know that more than most people. But then, we don't invite most people to apply for the American Express Card. We are inviting you."

Emily Grant, the addressee, is eleven years old, going on twelve, but she is highly responsible and almost ready for nighttime baby-sitting. She is tall for her age and does her homework without being prompted, except, now and then, for her French. Even so, she is no "seasoned traveler," as the American Express solicitation letter flatteringly put it, and she has no job, no salary, and no alimony income. She could swing the $55 annual fee, but it would run down her savings account into the low double-digits, leaving her unable to finance that exotic vacation American Express seems to think she is leaving for any minute.

Gift Ideas from Grant's *for 24-hour Trading*

Aqua-Quote pontoon system

Retrieve-a-Rate mono-dog harness

Motorized Lazy Susan mount

Financial cinema, New York style

Osmosis-Scope sleep monitor

Quote-Run athletic pack

The mighty financial services conglomerate must be feeling the competitive heat because it also, in the same week, invited Philip Grant to apply for an American Express Gold Card. "Charges are approved based on your ability to pay, as demonstrated by your past spending and payment patterns, and by your personal resources," said the letter, which is over the signature of one Lewis M. Taffer, "senior vice president." About Taffer only one thing can be known for certain, and that is that he has never visited Philip's room. Although tidy at particular times and on given days, it is almost certainly not the room of the median Gold Card holder. Philip is not quite ten, and his allowance, at $1.50 a week, is $1 less than Emily's. After a largish investment in raffle tickets for a school fair last week, Philip's savings have been run down to the zero mark, so that even if he had a driver's license, he could not afford to rent a car on *his* next vacation (are American Express cardholders ever *not* on vacation?). There is one feature of the Gold Card that must appeal to the parents of any nine-and-a-half-year-old boy, and that is the "Purchase Protection Plan." He does like to limber up his pitching arm indoors.

It will be noted that, despite his lower allowance, lower net worth, and more distant prospect for gainful employment, Philip was invited to apply for the Gold Card, whereas Emily was invited to apply for the green card. Would a competent litigator accept the green card in satisfaction of the fees for a potentially lucrative sexual discrimination suit? As soon as Emily gets back from the Caribbean (or was it Hawaii?), we'll investigate.

PART FOUR

FOREIGNERS IN DEBT

NIPPONOMANIA

February 9, 1987

Japan is the international graveyard of bears. It is the nation of the housewife speculator and of the sure-thing stock at fifty times last year's lackluster earnings. It is home to *zaiteku*, meaning high-tech investing, and of institutional traders of the bull-market-genius class, celebrated by the name of Shinjinrui, meaning new men. It is the land that Graham and Dodd forgot.

This small essay on the Japanese financial scene is written in a spirit of bilious awe. Skeptical, we have tried to imagine the skeptic's lot in Tokyo. We have tried to imagine a Doubting Thomas who must reconcile wholesale price deflation, stagnant corporate earnings, and a near recession with one of the greatest bull markets in stocks and real estate in modern times. We have tried but failed. Mercifully for the bears, there is no short selling on the Tokyo Stock Exchange. (If you like, you may sell short the Japan Fund, which changes hands on the New York Stock Exchange at a 20 percent discount from net asset value.) It is said that foreign investors, with their un-Japanese notions of price-earnings valuation, gave up on the Tokyo bourse as long ago as 1984 when the Nikkei index was less than half its current level. Since 1974, as Morgan Stanley notes, the Japanese market has declined in absolute terms only once (in 1977, by 7 percent), and it has excelled, in comparison with the rest of the world, for the past twenty years. It was up 47 percent in 1986.

What roused our interest in Japan was a report that the big Japanese banks have been loading up on U.S. bonds. Reading that, we naturally wanted to know more about the banks. Are they the kind of banks that one would want to keep investment company with? (Answer: Assuredly not.) One thing led to another, and we found ourselves reading up on the Japanese stock market, the second largest bourse in the world. And that, at last, got us wondering, How high is up? If the Japanese market took a header, what would be the international repercussions? (Answer: Unknown. However, when the Japanese banks recently closed for a local holiday, transactions volume on CHIPS, the international bank clearing wire, dropped about 25 percent.) Which is the more immediate threat to world financial stability, we asked ourselves, Mexican debt at 50 cents on the dollar or Japanese stocks at 50 times earnings? (Answer: Unknown, but we lean to the Japanese alternative. It would be an interesting bolt from the blue if the problem country of the late 1980s were Japan, not Mexico or Brazil.)

We also considered the bullish possibilities—for instance, the chance that Japanese investors will bid for American assets as if the Republic itself were a corporate takeover candidate. Perhaps, as financial deregulation proceeds, the world will become more perfectly arbitraged. Will Citicorp fetch 40 times earnings (instead of eight), while Sumitomo commands a mere 60 times earnings (down from 110)? To redefine the problem: Which is the more powerful Far Eastern financial force, Japanese market psychology (which must be counted as manic, and therefore negative) or stupendous hoards of investable yen (bullish)?

Grant's, admittedly a nonexpert on Japan, will venture the view that the frenzied tone of the Japanese stock market is a negative force to be reckoned with. Japan, it's true, is a nation dripping with excess liquidity. Interest rates are down (the next half-point reduction by the Bank of Japan would drop the discount rate to a mere 2½ percent), and bank credit is ample. In these circumstances, the question is always asked: Where else can the money go but into the stock market? The answer is that it can be lost. Money can always be lost because markets can always go down. To the objection that what is overvalued and manic can always become more overvalued and more manic, we have nothing to say, for it is true. Before proceeding, and in order to set the proper psychological stage, we quote from an item in the *Financial Times* last September:

Janome, Japan's second largest sewing machine maker, made an operating loss this year and is expected to show another next year. Moreover, it has no tantalizing assets tucked away. Some brokers believe Janome was a pure speculative play, pushed by stock market clubs of dentists and accountants. Others suggest it was a "political stock," ramped by supporters of a politician needing funds.

At that writing (which was just before the market's autumn pull-back), Janome Sewing Machine was quoted at about 1,900 yen a share. Last week it fetched 2,800. Clearly, it is important to keep an open mind on the subject of Japanese valuation. "The Japanese stock market always looks too high, just about always," observes Sam Nakagama, the American economist who also knows Japan.

As we say, what initially caught our eye was a report that Japanese banks had bet heavily on a fall in U.S. interest rates. According to the Bank for International Settlements, the wagers were placed last fall, and the banks, in the time-honored tradition of U.S. thrifts, borrowed short and invested long. (Bears on the bond market can only hope that the Japanese banks are still invested; if Eurodeposit rates continue to move up, they may be forced to sell.)

Reading on, we saw that the big Japanese banks last year consolidated their position as the world's largest and most powerful financial institutions. Sumitomo made overtures to Goldman Sachs & Co., and Dai-Ichi Kangyo Bank evidently displaced Citicorp as the owner of the world's biggest bank balance sheet. As the *Financial Times* noted:

> By one definition—that of foreign currency lending by banks within Japan—Tokyo took over London's role as the world's leading Euro-currency center. BIS figures also show that Japanese banks have taken over from their U.S. counterparts as the world's largest lenders, commanding a 32 percent share of the market compared with 19 percent for U.S. banks. Two years ago their respective shares were 23 percent and 26 percent.

As we say, all this inspired a crash course in Japanese banking and equities. The topics turned out to be intimately related because the banks are allowed to count a portion of their unrealized securities gains as capital for regulatory purposes.

The foreigner will not know exactly what to make of that ac-

YOU MEAN THEY TRADE THE DOLLAR?

counting convention, just as he may be baffled by the interwoven interests of the banks and their corporate customers. There is an undercurrent of rigging in Japanese markets that leaves the outsider with the distinct impression that not every price moves by accident. The bulls will say, "I don't think they'll let this market break until after the big privatization deals are done," and the bears can only nod sagely. A new report by Salomon Brothers, *The Japanese Banks: Positioning for Competitive Advantage*, reviews the financial positives and negatives for each of seven big banks and adds this intriguing postscript: "One of the specific concerns of an overseas investor should be the possibility that corporate holders of bank equities, particularly those with earnings problems, may distribute holdings that no longer play a functional role in the marketplace." We suppose that means the holders might dump. (Until a couple of years ago, the Japanese bank stocks were rigged by common understanding; they all moved together, like a marching band.)

In their financial analysis, the Salomon analysts struck an attitude of reserved approval. They noted that the big Japanese banks have suffered relatively few bad loans and have held their expenses in check. In 1980–85, the banks reported strong earnings, although in a number of cases profits were produced by the sale of stocks instead of by traditional operations. In three cases out of seven, operating income actually peaked in 1983. The study concluded (this was mid-October): "In view of the sharp price advance in Japanese bank stocks and the difficult short-term earnings outlook set against an unsettled deregulatory backdrop, we do not currently recommend purchase of Japanese bank stocks at prevailing prices."

The joke, of course, as it so often is in Japan, was on the analysts because prices today are miles higher than they were even last fall. In the new year's surge, banks and financial stocks have led (until last week, when the AIDS-related stocks enjoyed a vogue). Admittedly, at 1,900 yen, or sixty-five times 1986 earnings, Sumitomo Bank might have looked rich. At last week's price of 3,200 yen, it looked even richer.

The Salomon study doesn't begin to suggest that Japanese bankers work miracles. The banks' return on assets is low, and their reported capital is meager. Furthermore, an American observer must scratch his head at the determination with which the Japanese have bought market share in the U.S. financial guarantee business, writing standby letters of credit in support of municipal bonds at spreads that U.S. institutions deem uneconomic. In any case, to quote Salomon: "On a reported basis, the Japanese bank composite's 0.27 percent return on assets ratio in 1985 and 11.1 percent return on equity are below international standards." The comparable U.S. money-center composite numbers were 0.78 percent and 13.9 percent, respectively.

The interpretation of Japanese bank capital requires some art. As stated, the numbers—ratios of equity to assets—are among the lowest in the world. If adjusted for so-called hidden assets and unrealized stock market profits, however, the stated numbers would double. According to the February edition of Standard & Poor's *International Creditweek*: "When credit is given for the undervalued securities adjusted for stock market volatility and tax effects, Japanese banks are capitalized as well as most British and American money center banks. They are below the best of the Swiss and German banks when their internal reserves are considered." (By the way, late last year when the big seven Japanese banks fetched something on the order of forty-nine times earnings, Swiss banks were valued at twenty-eight times earnings and German banks at only eighteen times earnings.) Perhaps we're missing something, but it would seem that bank capital in the form of common stocks would be plentiful when a bank didn't need it and scarce when it did.* It would be depleted at the only time the depositers really care about capital, which is during a bear market.†

An interesting case in Japanese bank valuation is that of the Bank of Tokyo Ltd., the country's traditional overseas lender and the institution that perhaps most closely shares the LDC loan baggage of U.S. institutions. As of last March 31, the Bank of Tokyo showed a portfolio of loans to distressed countries, notably Mexico, of 725.8 billion yen ($4.3 billion). The exposure represented 128 percent of its equity and loan loss reserves, according to Salomon Brothers, which is more than twice the Japanese norm.

After a fashion, the bank has paid for its mistakes on the Tokyo bourse. When the Salomon analysts wrote, Bank of Tokyo common fetched 870 yen, a mere thirty-one times estimated 1986 earnings, the lowest multiple of all the big Japanese banks. Whether the Bank of Tokyo continues to bring up the rear in valuation, we don't know. But at last week's price of 1,400 yen, or forty-five times earnings, its stock is 61 percent higher than it was late last year. (J. P. Morgan, by the way, changes hands at ten times earnings.) By Salomon's reckoning, the bank shows an adjusted ratio of equity to assets on the order of 5 percent, or "somewhat below Ministry of Finance guidelines for international banks." Without so-called hidden assets, for example, unrealized stock market gains, its ratio of equity to assets last March would have amounted to 2.47 percent.

---

* In March 1991 the big Japanese commercial banks were sitting on unrealized stock market gains of 24.8 trillion yen, the equivalent of $176 billion. By the end of September 1992, the number had dwindled to 9.2 trillion yen.

† On the subject of bear markets, the Japanese did have one. Their experience in the 1920s was searing and instructive. Burdened by price deflation and bad debts—the residue of wartime inflation and the 1923 Yokohama earthquake—the banking system was plunged into panic in 1927 by the failure of the semiofficial Bank of Taiwan.

"The Bank of Taiwan," wrote historian Hugh T. Patrick, "was an extreme case of a highly growth-oriented financial institution willing to incur high risks in gambling on the continued prosperity of the Japanese economy and especially its major borrowers." A three-week bank moratorium was declared on April 27, 1927, six years before Washington got around to declaring *its* bank holiday. Patrick, writing in 1971, commented: "The extent of the financial crisis of 1927 severely frightened the monetary authorities; they haven't gotten over it yet." To this day, Japanese banks remain among the most closely regulated and protected institutions in the world.

It can be seen that the Japanese market is inclined to take the sunny view of things. No sooner had the export sector slid under the waves than the Shinjinrui began to discount the coming domestic prosperity. Asset plays enjoyed a vogue: Speculators bought loss-making steel companies for the value of the land underneath the mills. Consumer stocks rose. The latest Salomon Brothers monthly Japanese Stock Review recommends a department store chain, Mitsukoshi, at a price of 230 times last year's consolidated earnings (a fluke even in this bull market; the Morgan Stanley model Japanese portfolio, which is 24 percent in cash, shows few stocks with multiples over forty).

As might be expected in the twelfth year of the rise, a certain frothiness has entered the market. For instance, as *The Wall Street Journal* reports, there is a boom in thievery:

> Last year more than twenty-two thousand Japanese were swindled out of a total of $608 million, at current exchange rates, according to the National Police Agency. . . .
>
> Although ordinary Japanese once shunned the stock market because it smacked of gambling and corruption, individual investors are now plunging into more glamorous—but riskier—markets, drawn by the promise of easy profits.
>
> "The feeling is that you're stupid unless you're playing money games," says Hiroyuki Ota, assistant director of the police agency's financial fraud unit. "Japanese may have an inherent fear of securities and commodities, but when they hear about places like the Chicago Mercantile, they're intrigued."

SWINDLERS SNARE SMALL JAPANESE INVESTORS, the *Journal's* headline said. BROKERS EXPLOIT CRAZE FOR FINANCIAL FUTURES. No swindlers were asked for their side of the story, but a philosophical thief might reflect on the difficulty of bamboozling an honest, or even a conservative, investor.

On the corporate level, the urge to play is apparently just as intense as it is among postal workers and housewives. In Japan, of course, interest rates are down, liquidity is high, and profits are scarce, which has driven more and more nonfinancial companies to a sideline business in trading and arbitrage. For instance, a Japanese company might sell low-coupon warrant-based bonds in London and relend the proceeds at a spread, hedging itself against currency and interest rate risk along the way. It is believed that such financial game-playing is on the rise.

Euromoney recently told the story of a medium-size Osaka trading house, languishing in the steel bar and wire trade but taking up the slack with arbitrage and currency trading. Hanwa, the Osaka firm, has earned itself the sobriquet "Gnome of the Orient" for these non-steel-bar-and-wire exploits:

> Since 1983, Hanwa has issued ten overseas bonds, raising 118.1 billion yen. Its 1983 issue of Swfr80 million convertibles was intended to finance the construction of the Keiyo steel distribution center. That project was postponed indefinitely because of the recession in the steel industry.
>
> The proceeds from the bonds, which had a coupon of 3.4 percent, were used in part for high-yield dollar deposits, and in part to prepay bank loans with a higher interest rate.*

Zaiteku, or paper trading, has its detractors among conservative Japanese businessmen, and the Ministry of Finance is reportedly worried about it, too. *Euromoney* quoted an anonymous banker to the effect that industrial companies increasingly borrow in order to lend to inferior credits, bearing the risks (and also, of course, enjoying the opportunities) that traditionally have been the province of insurance companies. In any event, the Japanese public has been smitten by the urge to play.

Morgan Stanley's latest piece on Japan recommends a few familiar-sounding stocks at modest multiples, for example, Honda Motor at 10.6 times earnings. Nevertheless, Morgan Stanley economist David E. Gerstenhaber concedes that the risk of a Japanese recession "remains high" and Morgan Stanley equity analysts Timothy Schilt and Jonathan Allum allow for the possibility of a nasty spill in the Tokyo real estate market. "It is worth noting," they write, "that the current strength in demand is very narrowly based,

---

* In 1991, Hanwa became one of the first Japanese companies to admit receiving compensation for investment losses, a dubious (though not explicitly illegal) practice that inflamed the resentment of the many Japanese who bore their losses themselves, without their brokers' subsidy. A 52 percent drop in 1992 profits was put down to losses on securities investments as well as to the more prosaic cause of sagging steel prices. "Money is just a commodity," said Shigeru Kita, Hanwa's president, in September 1989, before the roof fell in on the stock market. "We trade it for a profit." Sometimes, however, for a loss.

coming entirely from the financial and overseas sectors, and that the returns on new developments have fallen to the point where Mikui Real Estate is claiming that such projects are no longer economic."

The significance of real estate in the Japanese financial equation is that a number of equity asset plays are based on the presumptive value of land, while the land is valued on the presumptive growth of financial activity. Sam Nakagama quotes a series of price indices for land in the most desirable sections of major Japanese cities: In 1986, prices were up 60 percent in Yokohama, 67 percent in Osaka, and 79 percent in Tokyo (which compares with the trifling 47 percent gain in stock prices). This surge in land prices has created an enormous "corporate wealth effect," Nakagama says. Investors are marking to market assets that corporations are carrying at cost. Add this wealth effect to lower interest rates, superabundant liquidity, and proposed tax reform (interest on certain deposits would be made taxable for the first time), and the bull market becomes more intelligible.*

What can never be known about market moves, until they end, is what was behind them. The bulls will contend that the Tokyo bourse is driven by the prospect of a healthy change in the Japanese economy from export demand to finance and domestic demand. The bears will counter that each and every omen of a blowoff is already in place and that what is driving the market is nothing more than excess liquidity and sheer habit. The bulls, clearly, have local precedent on their side (for the past dozen years Japanese stocks have hardly corrected, much less crashed), and they also have a point of timing. The *Financial Times* reported of last summer's excesses:

> Buy orders for large capital issues such as steel and shipbuilding, which were considered certain to become non-dividend-paying due to the yen's appreciation, were placed with securities firms en block with 10 million shares worth 3 billion to 4 billion yen.
>
> Trust banks with huge funds under management and investment advisory firms had to appoint inexperienced young employees as fund managers in the face of mounting orders. Those raw young players took part in the money game, earning large capital gains.

---

* Also the current bear market. Real estate values and financial values have fallen in tandem.

The point, a bull would say, is that *that* sounded like the top, too. The market, in fact, pulled back from the summer peak (by 17 percent), but it is all the way back up again and making new highs. And if, as expected, Nippon Telegraph & Telephone is assigned a market multiple in excess of IBM's when it comes to market this week, that does not foreclose the possibility of its going even higher. To that, a bear can make no objection because none is possible. He must bide his time in the knowledge that every boom goes boom.*

YASUDA TRUST & BANKING

June 1, 1987

In terms of valuation, we find Yasuda Trust's prospective [price-earnings ratio] to be comparatively low, both in relationship to the banking sector as a whole and to the market. While the FY 88 prospective market average multiple is now 73.4X, and that for major city and long-term banks 99.5X, that for the trusts sector is 63.9X. Yasuda's prospective multiple is about average for the trusts, at 63.2X.
—*From a Merrill Lynch report dated May 6.*

A global oddity: U.S. Trust Co. is the Rolex watch of the American trust business. Last year it earned 18.3 percent on its equity. Yasuda Trust & Banking, a kind of Japanese Timex, earned only 13.5 percent on its equity.

However, while U.S. Trust fetches only 10 times last year's earnings on the New York Stock Exchange, Yasuda commands 133 times earnings on the Tokyo and Osaka exchanges. To put it another way, U.S. Trust is a 2-times-book institution, while Yasuda is a 17-times-book institution. U.S. Trust common yields 2.7 per-

---

* The market peaked at almost 39,000 on the Nikkei 225 stock index on December 31, 1989, not quite double the level at which *Grant's* first became incredulous. The elapsed time was nearly three years.

cent, while Yasuda common yields less than 0.2 percent (after giving effect to a 15 percent withholding tax on foreign dividends, the yield is even closer to zero).

Granted, this kind of disparity has lost its power to shock people. The Japanese stock market is high and ours, by Japanese lights, is low. Also, Yasuda is a big bank (some $40 billion of banking account assets), while U.S. Trust is little ($3 billion of assets). For another thing, Yasuda does its business in yen, while U.S. Trust deals in dollars. Perhaps one should leave it at that, but we can't because the facts and figures are so mesmerizing. We've tried to imagine a similar valuation disparity within the confines of one market (New York, for instance), but the picture won't come into focus. Perhaps, if all the arbitrageurs went to jail, a 10-times-earnings bank could coexist with a 133-times-earnings bank, but it is hard to see the discrepancy lasting for very long (especially when, as in this case, the 10-times-earnings bank is evidently the better institution). For that matter, it is hard to imagine the discrepancy persisting for any length of time in world markets, although in this case and hundreds like it, the discrepancy has persisted. At what point does the world, coming to its senses, simply buy the cheap stock or sell the dear one, or do both simultaneously?

We don't know, but we're intrigued by Yasuda, the epitome of bull market enthusiasm. Yasuda is the subject of a brand-new encyclopedic Merrill Lynch report and of a recent commercial-paper rating by Moody's. Each document is passably upbeat, although the Merrill study is bullish only in conclusion. Pages 2 through 16 read like death.

Yasuda, the fourth largest of seven Japanese trust institutions, does a combination commercial and trust business. It was founded in 1925 under the wing of the Yasuda *zaibatsu*, one of the prewar corporate combines that continue to cast their shadows in Japanese affairs. Nowadays, Yasuda is associated with the Fuyo group, which numbers among its member companies a number of the industrial walking wounded. Unhappily, Yasuda has lent to them and to the Third World, and its asset quality, according to Merrill Lynch, is subpar. Moody's, in assigning the bank its top-flight Prime-1 rating, described Yasuda's asset quality as "respectable," which to us, however, is not the first triple-A adjective that comes to mind. We like Merrill's analysis of the asset issue, especially the last sentence:

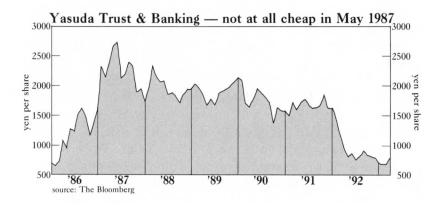

Yasuda Trust & Banking — not at all cheap in May 1987

source: The Bloomberg

Yasuda Trust's domestic loan portfolio is considered the shakiest of the four larger trusts, chiefly as a consequence of disproportionately large exposure to steel and shipbuilding companies and to the Yasuda group's shipping company, Showa Steamship. This orphan [that is, Yasuda] will need more than just street smarts to realize its ambition of catching up with Mitsubishi and Sumitomo's level of diversification and secure profitablility. *It will also have to be very lucky, in our opinion* [italics added].

Unluckily, Yasuda has had a history of low-margin lending and high-intensity interest rate betting. It has bet heavily on falling interest rates. It has accumulated a book of Third World loans equivalent to 100 percent of its estimated equity, and it owns a book of "poor or nonperforming" loans, both domestic and foreign, equivalent to four times its estimated equity. (U.S. Trust, by the way, has had some of these problems.) Luckily, however, the bank has survived these policies, recently earning the kudo from Merrill of "most dynamic profit growth over the past two terms."

Not surprisingly, if only in view of asset problems, Merrill has conferred a "speculative" investment rating on Yasuda's shares. However, it has deemed intermediate-term prospects "above average" and the technical prognosis bullish. The Merrill technical view is easily condensable: "Near-Term Trend: UP, consolidating; Medium-Term Trend: UP, overbought; Long-Term Trend: UP."

Up, up, up—and away?

WING AND A PRAYER

June 29, 1987

Until First Boston put its finger on the investment-theme pulse of the Tokyo stock market recently, Japanese finance was a mystery to us. There was nothing unfathomable about the price trend—up is the theme in that department—but the cause of the movement was baffling. Japanese companies (many of them) are struggling, yet the prices of their common stocks (most of them) are rising. First Boston, however, has played the part of an analytical Commodore Perry, opening what was previously closed, and we quote from the report—"Theme Chasing: The Engine of the Tokyo Stock Market"—gratefully, "Historically," the firm relates,

> the Tokyo stock market was characterized by individual investors who relied on brokers for hot tips. The lax enforcement of insider trading regulations and the concentration of trading in the hands of four major stock market players makes the Tokyo market susceptible to ramping or talking a stock up. Failure to react quickly left one in the dust, buying shares at appreciated prices.

In the dust, of course, is where the bears have been, underestimating the importance of themes. A theme is an investment concept, and concepts are the stock in trade of the Japanese broker. In Wall Street it is correct to disparage themes. In Kabutocho it is correct to push them. "Fighting a tide is a battle not won," as First Boston explains, "and a herd instinct is a sound survival instinct in an environment of excess liquidity."

"Buy substance, not fluff," the firm adjures, going on to suggest ten "current or developing themes" for your money, or your clients' money, including fiscal stimulus, financial stocks, superconductivity, AIDS, latent assets, and privatization, among others. The privatization theme especially caught our eye, as we'd just put down a new report on Japanese Air Lines by Hoare Govett, the eminent British broker (and no Johnny-come-lately to the Japanese scene).

From a fundamental angle, as the report wastes no time in acknowledging, JAL, the government-controlled carrier, is flying low. The line "faces continuing problems with cost competitiveness. Increasing international competition will probably force JAL to cut fares further. Combined with the company's high operating costs, margins are expected to decline."

However, as it will stun nobody to learn at this late date, mere second-rate fundamentals are not the end of the investment story but the beginning. (Second-rate is perhaps charitable. The report mentions labor troubles, looming excess capacity on trans-Pacific routes, increased competition and—not least—a 1987 net loss.) What the airline boasts is the imminent sale of a tranche of its shares by the Japanese government, "privatization," of course, being one of the ten hot concepts enumerated by First Boston. "We expect the market to continue to ignore JAL's poor fundamentals in favor of the privatization theme," writes Hoare Govett. "The company remains a speculative buy."

The Hoare Govett investment conclusion is so pure a bull market specimen that we reprint it whole:

> In terms of fundamentals, JAL remains unattractive. However, fundamentals have historically proved irrelevant to JAL's share price movement. Investors have consistently shown a remarkable ability to shrug off bad news about the company because JAL is a "political" stock. Furthermore, following the success of the NTT issue [Nippon Telegraph & Telephone], there is now the additional attraction of the privatization theme. With privatization having been postponed to September at the earliest, JAL's share price declined from the Y17,000 range it reached in March and has now consolidated around the Y15,000 level. We remain confident that July will signal renewed interest in JAL's privatization and are looking for the share price to climb to the 20,000 level by September.

Anything is possible, of course, although JAL a week ago fetched not Y15,000, around which price it was said to be "consolidating," but Y14,000. The good news, perhaps, is that Y14,000 indicates a

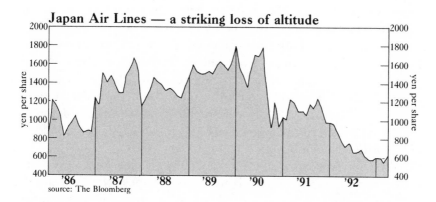

Japan Air Lines — a striking loss of altitude

source: The Bloomberg

multiple of only 406 times estimated 1988 earnings, not the 435 times associated with the Y15,000 "consolidation" price. (No meaningful price-earnings ratio is available for 1987 owing to the detail that there are no earnings.) The other good news is that cash has not yet entered the brokers' lists as a bona fide Japanese investment theme. When it does, look out.

SHOUTING MATCH

January 11, 1988

A New York brokerage firm that was short of Japan Air Lines was surprised to receive an indignant telephone call last month from the general counsel of the New York office of Nomura Securities. The Nomura man, an American, had deduced that the New York firm (name withheld) was short. The Nomura caller proceeded to berate the firm for a delivery problem (which, in the firm's opinion, was not its problem at all) and more generally for having had the temerity to be short of JAL in the first place. According to the recipient of the call, the Nomura lawyer was profane, agitated, misinformed, and loud. An American, to be sure.

In Japan short selling is discouraged, if not prohibited outright. In America short selling is also, usually, discouraged, although not prohibited. The reasons for selling JAL were laid out in *Grant's* last June 29. The problem with the trade has been borrowing the American Depository Receipts. For those who could find them, though, the experience was gratifying (to $200 a share from $250 or so in mid-November).

Asked for Nomura's side of this strange encounter, a Nomura spokesman (also an American) would only repeat the phrase: "It was a domestic discussion that was resolved to everybody's satisfaction." Well, yes, in a way; JAL was down again last week.

UNDERGROUND ECONOMY

July 8, 1988

So hot is the Tokyo real estate market that speculation has moved underground. So, at least, reports the *Japan Economic Journal*, describing a trend toward subterranean development:

> The projects now being discussed range from the mundane—dropping elevated trains and highways underground—to the exotic—creating entire cities underground. But unlike the existing subways or the numerous shopping arcades that already fill the basement levels of scores of office buildings, the latest plans call for development at fifty to one hundred meters below the surface—depths largely unexplored.

And unowned, according to the Ministry of Construction, which is moving to restrict the right of property owners at the fifty-meter-to-one hundred-meter level. If the boom proceeds—no small "if," of course—construction may be approved without the say-so of the surface owners.

What the shortage-of-stock idea is to the stock market, the shortage-of-land idea may be to the real estate market: a top maker. One of the leading subsurface developers, Shimizu Corp., has been going nowhere on the Tokyo Stock Exchange recently, we note. On the other hand, it has a lot of company in aimlessness. The Tokyo-listed financial companies peaked in April 1987.

All hands can agree that the advance of the Tokyo property market has grown ragged, but not everyone concedes that land prices have broken. Goldman Sachs, in a May 30 report, was un-flustered, writing, "In general, prices are declining slightly," and adding, "Although present prices are extremely high, they can still rise further in the long run.

Watching from New York, we can only report what others see, and so we pass along a report in the current *Euromoney* about a broad-based slump in land prices in and around Tokyo. Interest-ingly, the magazine said, "The outlook for liquidity in the Tokyo real estate market continues to worsen as the Japanese banks strug-gle to comply with the Bank for International Settlements' pro-posals for stronger capital ratios. Most banks have slammed the brakes on asset growth, and many are actively pruning their loan portfolios." Maybe they won't have to dig after all.*

---

* It is a good thing that subterranean development never caught on because aboveground property has suddenly come into surplus. "Residential land prices are diving at double-digit percentage rates in Osaka, Toyko, and Nagoya, while the slide in commercial land prices nationwide is also speeding up," the *Nikkei Weekly* reported on February 15, 1993. "For the period covered by the current survey, October 1, 1992, to January 1, 1993, the majority of districts in Osaka, Nagoya, and Tokyo reported annualized price declines in residential land of over 20 percent—with the steepest drops concentrated in the three urban centers."

SINGAPORE FLING

March 31, 1989

W estward winged the jet across the wide Pacific. Eastward lagged the body. The destination was Singapore, that Switzerland by the equator, mecca of thrift and orchids and humidity, a city-state even less accessible than Fargo. The flight from New York took twenty-two hours, or rather the flight of the aircraft took twenty-two hours. The body, unkempt and feeling sorry for itself, straggled in later.

The purpose of the trip was to deliver a lecture on finance, but a glance at the local papers suggested that the visitor had more to learn than to teach. The interest rate situation, for starters, seemed just about perfect. Prime rate: 5½ percent; thirty-year mortgage rate, 5¾ percent; five-year auto loan rate, 4 percent; five-year "business loan" rate, 7 percent. The ninety-day Treasury bill was quoted as 3¼ percent, and the five-year government note yielded 5½ percent. Stocks changed hands at about twenty times earnings.

Other economic vital signs appeared in order. The warehouse occupancy rate last year was 93 percent. The consumer price index rose by less than 2 percent, and economic growth was a steamy 11 percent, up from 8.8 percent in 1987. A little less growth and a little more inflation are expected in 1989—perhaps inevitably, as continued real growth at 11 percent would imply that Singapore, with a $23 billion GNP, would inevitably overhaul the United States, with a $5 trillion GNP. Perhaps the Singaporeans were seeking the Americans' advice on how to achieve high inflation, low P/E multiples, and an 11½ percent prime.

Singapore, a former British colony bordering Malaysia (which is south of Burma, which is in the Pacific Ocean, which washes up on California), has 2.6 million people and a land mass of only 239 square miles. The people speak English, various Chinese dialects, Tamil, and Malay. For years the country has had the highest savings rate and the fastest rate of economic growth in the world. It has had an exceptionally low rate of inflation coexisting with exceptionally brisk monetary growth. It has had capitalism comingling with socialism. Under the all-wise, all-seeing rule of Prime Minister Lee Kuan Yew and the People's Action Party, the national program is to work and save.* Littering, spitting on the sidewalk, eating on the subway, pornography, and untoward criticism of the government are prohibited. There is no tipping and no deposit insurance. The work week is Monday through Saturday morning. Crime is discouraged, especially at night, as a little story in the *Straits Times* illustrated:

6 YEARS, 36 STROKES
FOR STRIKE-AT-NIGHT ROBBER

A twenty-year-old robber who struck only after dark was sentenced to six years in jail and thirty-six strokes of the cane yesterday. . . .

Robberies committed between 7 p.m. and 7 a.m. carry a higher sentence than those committed in daylight—a minimum of three years in jail and six strokes of the cane.

Just the same, it is better to rob, even after hours, than to deal in drugs. The automatic penalty for that transgression is death.

To a New Yorker, Singapore may resemble Co-Op City in the Bronx, but with hibiscus, mangoes, and palm trees instead of chain-link fence. Most Singaporeans live in high-rise public housing, which gleams white in the tropical sun. The government encourages the people to buy their own apartments. It exhorts families to bear children ("four or more," since the population is aging) and children to study. Early in their lives, pupils are routed to the appropriate learning track, bright or dim. Miraculously, in this matter, too, the government is all-knowing, and the children selected for higher education are put to work on languages, math, and science.

---

* Now the government is worried that the economy is so very nearly perfect that the people are turning soft. Lee Kuan Yew, today the *former* prime minister, has bade his countrymen to pack their bags, venture out into Asia, and compete.

Despite the PAP's unstinting efforts, however, not every adult is grateful. "I have friends and neighbors whose children spend almost the whole day in school, taking lessons and activities, which leave them exhausted when they return home," wrote a citizen, signed "Concerned," to the editor of the *Straits Times* recently. On the same page and the same day, "BC" wrote to applaud the letter of a certain Loh Hock Seng. The Loh letter had been plaintively headed, TOO TIRED AND TOO LITTLE TIME TO GET HITCHED. "I agree with Mr. Loh," wrote "BC," sounding a very tentative note of labor militancy, "that most people will not mind working another half or one hour each weekday so that their Saturdays can be more at their leisure and disposal."

For the time being, however, there seems as much chance of Singaporeans not working on Saturday as of Americans not taking the day off. For another thing, Singapore saves as hard as it works. The national savings rate was estimated at 40 percent in 1987, and that represented a downtick. The peak was 46 percent in 1984. Savings are compulsory. The Central Provident Fund collects 24 percent of an employee's paycheck, to which the employer is required to contribute another 12 percent. The proceeds are invested mainly abroad.

It goes without saying that, if the government wishes to undertake a certain course of action, that policy is necessarily wise and just, whatever it may be, but the ambition to create a local government bond market seemed a mystery. In pamphlets and television commercials, Singaporeans are exhorted to buy the government's notes and bonds, even though the government doesn't need the money. The budget is in surplus. (One big difference between the public finances of Singapore and the United States is that the People's Action Party allocates next to nothing for welfare assistance. The stated welfare policy of the government is that everybody should work.) The Monetary Authority of Singapore (MAS), the national central bank, contends that the market will serve as a useful benchmark for pricing public corporate debt. It will provide a safe and handy investment for Singapore's banks and savers and "a means of hedging interest rate risk." It will help to propel the city-state into the first ranks of world financial centers. The Singapore Stock Exchange has completed the automation of its trading floor, and the Singapore Futures Exchange has begun to trade options on futures. A two-way market in the public debt is thought to be in harmony with the modern trend.

But Singapore's version of a government bond market is different from America's. The government has established a sinking fund to retire its debt in an orderly way, and the tombstone for a forthcoming issue of two-year notes would strike any American visitor as unheard of: "Annual contribution to the sinking fund of not less than 20 percent of the total principal monies in respect of this issue will be made."

However, perhaps the most un-American aspect of Singapore's finance is the balance sheet of the central bank. The MAS does not monetize government debt. Its principal asset is gold and foreign exchange. There is hardly a trace of domestic government securities on its books. By way of contrast, the principal asset of the Federal Reserve is U.S. Treasuries. Thus, the Fed is a study in circularity: Its assets comprise debt, that is, government securities. Its liabilities comprise Federal Reserve notes, that is, currency. The Federal Reserve's promises to pay—that is, its "notes"—are secured by the Treasury's promises to pay, that is, *its* notes (and bills and bonds). One promise offsets the other, although what the Fed is promising its noteholders, even tacitly, is not very clear. Under the gold standard, a dollar bill was convertible into gold. Under the current free-form standard, a dollar is convertible into nothing; nowadays, everyone may run his own gold standard as he sees fit. Singapore, too, is on a paper standard, but the assets of the central bank are qualitatively better than those of the Fed. They are the assets of a central bank that has somehow not gotten the word that anything goes in the 1980s. The city-state's finances must be viewed in composite form, the visitor was advised. Lumping together MAS with the Board of Currency Commissioners and other official financial bodies reveals roughly the following: gold and foreign securities (the state's assets) offsetting pension and savings commitments to the citizenry (the liabilities).

Yet there is an element of circularity even in the affairs of the MAS. A good deal of the bank's foreign exchange is surely denominated in dollars—how much is a state secret. This fact presents the Singaporeans (and the Taiwanese, who run a similarly tight ship) with a dilemma. Dollars are the liabilities of a central bank that has recently agreed to accept as good collateral the notes of the Federal

Savings and Loan Insurance Corp.—the FSLIC, of course, being broke. That fact, for now, is of symbolic more than tangible import, but it symbolizes what Singapore has so signally been able to avoid. Will Singapore, then, continue to accumulate dollars? As usual, the People's Action Party keeps its own counsel. However, so vast is the gap between the safety and soundness of central banking practices in Singapore, on the one hand, and those in the United States, on the other, that gold (or deutsche marks or some other nondollar asset) may yet stand to gain by it. To put this anxiety in tangible perspective, the MAS showed assets of the equivalent of $14 billion on the last public reporting date, a year ago. To put *that* into perspective, the Federal Reserve's assets total almost $300 billion. Thus, although sound, Singapore is tiny.

The city-state is perhaps the most open economy in the world, and the central bank's monetary target is therefore not the local money supply but the Singapore dollar exchange rate. And because the local dollar has tended to appreciate against other currencies, inflation has been held in check—notwithstanding double-digit growth in money supply and bank credit. The latest MAS annual remarked of the Singapore dollar: "Its appreciation over the 1980s has allowed domestic price inflation to be held at a comparatively low rate of 3 percent, or little over half the average recorded amongst Singapore's trading partners." Also, it is a pretty piece of paper, engraved with a likeness of a coasting vessel, a fish, or a feat of engineering, for example, on the ten spot, "public housing."
     Probably not every Singaporean will rush out to lock in 5½ percent in government bonds. Cab drivers play the stock market, and DBS Land recently changed hands at 109 times earnings. SPK-Sentosa Corp., another property company, is listed in the Singapore Stock Exchange *Journal* at 1,554 times earnings (short selling, incidentally, is almost impossible to carry off). Also, it must be stated for the record that the Singaporeans put their pants on one leg at a time. There was a recession as recently as 1985–86—a salutary reminder that, even in a land that has apparently attained nirvana, cycles turn. There was the spectacular flameout of Pan-Electric Industries in November 1985, a failure that precipitated a three-day closing of the Singapore Stock Exchange, a bailout of the local brokerage industry and a spate of regulatory reform. When straight arrows stray, they often stray far.

"Young Winters, I think, has something to tell us about his long–Hong Kong, short–New York spread, don't you, Winters?"

The plane ride afforded the opportunity to read what proved a fascinating and pertinent new book, *The Third Century: America's Resurgence in the Asian Era* by Joel Kotkin and Yoriko Kishimoto (Crown Publishers, $19.95). Far from facing a day of reckoning, the authors contend, the United States stands at the threshold of a great opportunity. The theme is a tonic at a time of so much anxiety about Japan and "competitiveness." Kotkin and Kishimoto agree that the center of economic gravity is shifting west, but they hold that this country is uniquely equipped to participate in the "Asian era." It is, to start with, an open society, like Singapore, and its immigrants routinely become its entrepreneurs. "The rising numbers and impact of new Americans, particularly from Asia and Latin America, are changing the United States from a European offshoot to a multiracial world nation," they write. For another thing, America tolerates failure—bankrupts are given a second chance. Not so in the two most admired economies in the world,

Germany and Japan. (The other day Japan reported that business failures plunged to a sixteen-year low. Readers of *The Third Century* will ask themselves if that is good news or bad news. Nothing ventured, nothing gained.) The authors argue that, in any contest between Japanese planning and untidy American entrepreneurs, the entrepreneurs will out. Thus, the more open American society, the more hospitable it is to capitalism and change, the truer it is to its ideals, the better it will be able to compete. "In the coming economic competition," they write,

> the edge will belong to those nations and organizations strong enough to nurture individual initiative, creativity, and quick decision-making. With the explosion of entrepreneurial vitality in the last decade, the United States—which provided the role model for the mass-production methods and giant organizations in the past—could again force the next economic paradigm. Similarly, this trend will also likely increase the importance of the highly entrepreneurial family networks within the Chinese diaspora. Dominated by fast-moving and highly flexible small firms, Taiwan and Hong Kong—not Japan and Korea—may provide the key Asian role models and the most potent competitors in the coming decades.

Most impressive and potentially very bullish, we thought—after some intervening financial and economic adjustments not unexpected by the readers of *Grant's*. Another book gave pleasure on the long flights, Boswell's *Tour to the Hebrides with Dr. Johnson*, the chronicle of a trip to Scotland that was taken, without jet lag, in 1773. Samuel Johnson—learned, wise, pious, above all human—shook his head at the sight of so many Scotsmen setting sail for America. It was folly, he told his companion, since the colonies "for ages" would be a wilderness unfit for civilized beings. He regretted, too, the rise in trade and nonagricultural pursuits, which he took to be a kind of zero-sum game. "Depend upon it," Johnson told Boswell, "this rage of trade will destroy itself. You and I will not see it; but the time will come when there will be an end of it. . . . Then the proprietors of land only will be the great men."

In calling the big turns, keep watching and keep calling. And never write anything down.

NIKKEI PUT WARRANTS

July 7, 1989

The wonderful Herbert Stein remark about patience—"If something can't go on forever, it won't"—has been as good a motto as any to lose money by in this epic bull market. In general, things that can't go on forever have kept right on going. Donald Trump, "trophy" hotel prices, leveraged cable-TV companies, Wasserstein Perella & Co., and the Japanese stock market all come annoyingly to mind.

However, the inevitable can happen, even in the roaring '80s—the break in Integrated Resources is proof—and the Japanese market may yet have its well-deserved comeuppance. If so, you will want to be prepared. Ahead of time, you will want to investigate a little-known series of put warrants on the Nikkei Stock Average. The warrants were issued by Salomon Brothers International. They are relatively liquid (an advantage over the so-called European-style puts issued by some New York brokerage firms) and offer impressive leverage if worse should ever come to worst. By the way, Salomon has also issued a number of Nikkei call warrants. We report this fact for the sake of journalistic balance.

One potential legal obstacle: The warrants were not registered with the Securities and Exchange Commission, and a prospectus states flatly that they "may not be offered, sold, or delivered directly or indirectly in the United States . . . or to United States persons." This language may not be the last word, though. Warrants were issued as long ago as June 1988, and your lawyer may opine that they are "seasoned" and eligible for purchase by a United States person like you. For any American so bearish on the Nikkei that he or she is contemplating a change in citizenship to accommodate a leveraged investment program, the most desirable destination would seem to be Luxembourg. Some of the warrants are listed on the Luxembourg Stock Exchange.

Every faithful reader of *Grant's* can recite the basic bearish case for Japanese stocks in his sleep. The arguments are familiar, even shopworn, but they may yet carry the day. We note, for instance, that whereas the Nikkei 225-stock average has been going up, many individual stocks have been going down. Then, too, the Japanese political establishment is losing its grip on events, and the Ministry of Finance has made it harder for the big four brokerage firms to manipulate stocks (no one firm is allowed to generate more than 30 percent of the trading volume in any one stock on any one day). And Japanese interest rates have turned higher—in late June, the prime vaulted to 4⅞ percent from 4¼ percent. A short, sad item from *The Japan Economic Journal* caught the spirit of the times:

> The option of allowing foreigners to hold shares of Nippon Telegraph and Telephone should be examined when considering Japan's communications policy and NTT's future, Prime Minister Sousuke Uno said June 9 at the Lower House plenary session. Foreigners have not been allowed to buy the share. However, since it has fallen to a low level, the government might possibly allow foreigners to buy the share.

Alternatively, foreigners may choose to buy the Salomon. Let's look at the 28,000 strike-price series. It's the oldest of the three —issued on June 22, 1988, to expire on June 19, 1991—and has, naturally, the lowest strike price. We say "naturally" because the Nikkei does tend to go up, demoralizing the bears and taking their money. The offering price of this first Salomon issue was 28¼. It was quoted the other day—some 5,000 Nikkei points higher—at 4½. It is the put-holder's conviction that the bullish spell will break within the next two years.

The arithmetic of the speculation is easy. Break-even is 28,000 (actually, 28,139) on the Nikkei average on the 1991 expiration day. Let's say that that expiration day finds the Nikkei average at 14,000. That is a big assumption, but it is perhaps no more unreasonable than 33,000, the current level. What would the warrants be worth? Just subtract 14,000 from the strike price, 28,000. Result:

14,000. Divide by the exchange rate—let's take 140. Result: 100. That happens to be the price—*in dollars*—of each warrant. So if the Nikkei were to plunge to 14,000, one's $4.50 investment would produce $100. That is without considering any time value that the warrant might have.

The other two Salomon warrants have somewhat higher strike prices. They are the 31,000 series (expiring August 7, 1990) and the 33,000 series (expiring April 24, 1992). As you will see if you work through the arithmetic, however, neither offers as gaudy a return if the bottom falls out. Let's examine the same hypothetical case with the 33,000 series. The strike price minus a 14,000 Nikkei average would yield a price per warrant of about $136. That is a nice-sounding price except in comparison with the current price of the warrant—about $14.20. A collapse to 14,000 would therefore fetch a return of 9.6 times one's money. In the case of the 28,000 series, the leverage would be on the order of 22 times one's money.

William Fleckenstein, a Seattle money manager (and paid-up subscriber to *Grant's*, by the way), says that, after thoroughly checking the field, he bought the 28,000 series. "I give up the first 9 percent," he says, comparing them to the 33,000 models, "but when [the Nikkei] starts rolling on the downside, I have almost three times as much leverage." The question is: "What is your premise going in?" Fleckenstein goes on. "The idea either works—and the market trades on reality—or they keep it going forever," he says. Thus, he contends that the extra year of time value isn't worth the cost. Yes, we said, but we could just have easily have been bearish in 1988, 1987, or 1986. In fact, we were. Yes, Fleckenstein replied, but the Japanese market is palpably closer to a fall than it was three years ago. Courage, he advised.*

* Superb advice. The 28,000 series warrants, quoted at $4.50 each in July 1989, expired in June 1991 at a price of $29.50. The 33,000 series, quoted at $14.20 each in July 1989, expired in April 1992 at a price of $115. By chance, on the day in February 1993 when Fleckenstein was pleasurably reminiscing about his warrant trades, the Japanese government was stepping up its efforts to support the Tokyo market. Now a bear on American stocks, Fleckenstein said it was inspiring to remember that the Nikkei index was once believed to be impregnable.

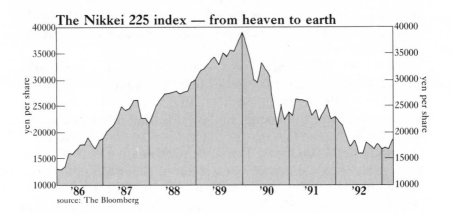

The Nikkei 225 index — from heaven to earth

source: The Bloomberg

PHANTOM COLLATERAL

September 13, 1991

Nui Onoue, sixty-one-year-old Osaka restaurateur, spiritualist, mah-jongg parlor operator, and ten-figure debtor, is the Meryl Streep of the summertime financial scandals. By pale comparison, John Gutfreund is a stagehand and BCCI a kind of prop. Ms. Onoue (oh-NO-way), as you have no doubt read, was able to borrow far and wide on the collateral of forged certificates of deposit allegedly issued by a regional credit union, the Toyo Shinkin Bank. Specifically, according to news reports, she was able to raise Y342 billion ($2.51 billion), or very nearly the entire Y360 billion that comprised the bank's deposits. With these proceeds she became the toast of the Tokyo Stock Exchange and the largest individual stockholder of such top Japanese institutions as Dai-Ichi Kangyo Bank. As the astounding details came to light last month, the *Financial Times* asked the incisive question: "The facts of the case appear so bizarre, and the alleged fraud so blatant, that it begs the question of whether there is not a deeper rot at the heart of the Japanese financial system. Highly reputable banks accepted huge amounts of phony paper from a small bank apparently without question."

Americans may marvel at this news, but they must not gloat. In its latest issue, *National Mortgage News* reports on the case of the "rented" registration numbers, a racket distressingly similar to the Japanese CD scandals. "According to law enforcement officers," the paper said, "a high-tech ring of alleged con artists has obtained the registration or CUSIP numbers of GNMAs, sometimes renting those numbers to borrowers who got millions in loans."

To be sure, the word is "millions," not "billions" (and "$50 million" at that), but the scandal is national, not regional, and is apparently growing. "Investigators note that stolen GNMA numbers also are being used by ailing insurance companies, and perhaps by thrifts and banks, to prop up their sagging capital base . . . ," the story continued. "Investigators for the Federal Bureau of Investigation are trying to determine why some banks would lend money to borrowers who would only post the CUSIP number without posting the actual security as collateral."

We think that we can shed some light on that mystery. Lenders did not demand the actual securities for the same reason that they chose to finance Robert Campeau. It was because it seemed that all the risk lay in saying "No," not "Yes."

"Law enforcement and insurance investigators seem most concerned about insurance companies that rent GNMA numbers and post them as capital on their books," the story said. "Also of concern is the renting of other types of securities that insurance companies, and even banks and thrifts, can use to boost their stated capital positions. Investigators said some individuals under investigation also are the subject of bank and thrift fraud probes. 'We're up to our necks in these kinds of cases: bank fraud, securities fraud, insurance companies,' said [U.S. Attorney Joe Cage of Shreveport, Louisiana]. 'We haven't seen anything like this since the S&L crisis hit us.' "

PART FIVE

HAVE MONEY, WILL BUILD

MARGINAL STREET

July 29, 1985

In 1913 the Woolworth Building, the first of the great skyscrapers, was completed for $13.5 million, the price including gold mosaic, spectacular vaulted ceilings, and gargoyles.

In 1986 the American Express world headquarters, now under construction in lower Manhattan, is expected to be finished at a cost of $690 million. That is without the gargoyles.

The Woolworth Building was built for cash. The American Express building is being financed, in part, with zero-coupon notes. The collateral supporting the notes is the building itself.

The American Express tower—fifty-one stories rising on landfill evocatively bounded by Marginal Street—may constitute the outer limit of late twentieth-century financial ingenuity. The investors put down $84.9 million in return for the promise of $450 million in the year 2000. The issue was sold, and sold successfully, in the Euromarket a few weeks ago. It was the first such "building-specific" zero-coupon security ever done.

Standard & Poor's, rating the notes AA, stated that there are no imaginable circumstances in which the building would fetch less than $450 million on the open market when the securities fall due in fifteen years.* The agency noted that American Express itself would be occupying the tower but that the notes are secured by the building alone.

Sam Kirshenbaum, an S&P analyst on the case, agrees that office

* Now a half rating notch lower, AA –.

space is in surplus at the moment (the national metropolitan area vacancy rate climbed to 18.6 percent in June, according to Coldwell Banker, up from 17.6 percent in March). He reports that six or seven new "building-specific" financings are currently under review and relates that painstaking credit precautions are being taken with each one. He says that S&P is testing the relevant financial projections against a set of very pessimistic assumptions. "Believe me," he says, "I don't think anybody in his right mind would dream up the scenario we did." Frank W. Woolworth, roll over.

TULIP BUILDINGS

November 4, 1985

Trammell Crow, age seventy-one, the legendary industrial property developer, is selling real estate, not to a partnership (his customary outlet) but to the public. Mack Pogue, fifty-one, chairman of Lincoln Property Co., and the Rockefellers, variously aged, are also lightening up. In the past few months has come a succession of offerings of real estate securities by developers and syndicators who presumably know their business. They have been selling— and the public buying.

There is always the outside chance that the public knows more about buying real estate than Messrs. Pogue and Crow do about selling it. Perhaps the Rockefellers, who executed the real estate masterstroke of the century by buying a dozen non-petroleum-bearing acres of midtown Manhattan at the bottom of the Great Depression, have sold too soon. Perhaps the heirs of John D. Rockefeller have absentmindedly left the lion's share of appreciation of that great property for all the thousands of retail customers of Goldman, Sachs & Co. and Shearson Lehman Brothers who bought the shares of Rockefeller Center Properties a few weeks ago.

Improbable. More likely is that this change in the character of ownership of real estate marks a turning point. Property values, arguably, have peaked, and the risks associated with the new real estate securities in general outweigh the potential rewards. We notice that real estate advertising linage in *The New York Times* has just set an all-time record. National office vacancy rates have made new highs, and second-mortgage lending continues to soar. And the "securitization" of real estate continues to win adherents on Wall Street.

We talked about real estate the other day with a distinguished investor who happens to know property (and who prefers to speak anonymously). He ventured the opinion that hotels, office buildings, and shopping malls are grossly in surplus and that bankers and insurance companies have lent too much against them. He had no quarrel with the recent and prospective sellers of real estate securities, Crow and Pogue and the Rockefellers. "These are the best people in the field," he said. "They know the market better than the buyer. They see a great price, and they take it. It's an opportunity for them to get liquid." What he questioned was the wisdom of the buyers.

What can the buyers expect? What do they stand to gain if all goes according to plan? The numbers are not the ones that got the Rockefellers where they are today. In the Rockefeller Center prospectus, for instance, a series of "growth" or inflation assumptions are presented along with the projected annual rates of return that they would yield. Here they are. If property values, rents, and lease rates increase by 6 percent a year, then the stockholders would enjoy an average annual return of 13.08 percent. At 4 percent inflation, the return would be 11.42 percent. At 8 percent inflation, the return would be 15.07 percent. A comparable set of returns is presented by Goldman Sachs in the Trammell Crow prospectus.

The numbers raise some provocative questions. In the first place, is 13 percent to 13½ percent (to take the rates of return associated with a 6 percent inflation assumption) enough? Do they compensate an investor for his risks? Are the inflation assumptions realistic? Then, too, there are the secular or cosmic questions: Why should property values increase? Why can't they decrease?

Furthermore, even if inflation does return, maybe real estate, in which everybody seems to have positioned himself already, won't go up. Maybe the market has already discounted the next inflation.

That is surmise. But the fact is that even in the aftermath of last week's rally, 13 percent yields were still available in the better grades of junk bond.

Perusing the Rockefeller Center prospectus, we hit on a sentence that seemed to distill the bullish case. The sentence described a "risk factor" (the Rockefeller common stock has some interesting risks). The specific risk that the sentence addressed is the dilution of the stockholders' interest by the holders of a pair of convertible bond issues. The passage read: "Unless the Property appreciates significantly in value by the Equity Option Exercise Date, little or no value will remain for holders of Common Stock after paying off the claims of the holders of Convertible Debentures." In other words, it's appreciate—or else.

The "or else" contingency appears in another prospectus passage. This will require a short word of explanation. Buyers of the common shares of Rockefeller Center Properties in effect are lenders to the Rockefellers. They own no equity interest in the property, and they will own none until the year 2000 when they can exercise an option to acquire 71.5 percent of it. Meanwhile, in prospectus lingo, the family partnership is the "Borrower." The lenders—the public shareholders—are the "Company." The passage reads as follows:

> During the years 1985 through 1992 and again in 1994, it is not expected that the Borrower will be able to service the Base Interest . . . payable on the Loan out of cash flow while at the same time making required capital expenditures. This shortfall . . . is forecasted during these nine years to aggregate approximately $251 million. The Borrower's ability to service the interest payable on the Loan in 1995 and thereafter is in large measure dependent upon whether market conditions permit increases in rental rates as leases turn over. The Company understands that RGI [Rockefeller Group Inc., another family entity] intends to make capital contributions to the Borrower to permit it to service the Loan and make required capital expenditures, but RGI is not obligated to do so. RGI will obtain for the Company's benefit the Letter of Credit in the amount of $400 million which will exceed the forecasted cash flow deficit. If the Borrower does not receive additional capital from RGI and the Base Interest shortfall and any other amounts which may be drawn by the Company under the Letter of Credit for permitted purposes

exceed the amount then available under the Letter of Credit, the Borrower would likely default on the loan.

It is hard to think of the Rockefeller descendants as the "Borrower." It is hard to imagine them welshing. Furthermore, according to bulls on the stock, the odds are strong that lease and rental rates will rise from the current (and below-market) Rockefeller Center average of $26.75* per square foot in coming decades. That, of course, is a bet. It is a bet on the midtown property market, and it is no less a bet on the monetary system. Real estate investors need a little inflation. What they positively do not need is deflation. "It is expected that inflation would generally benefit the Projects and increase the rate of return to the Bondholders . . . ," states the prospectus for a new issue of bonds of Lincoln Property Associates Ltd. It almost goes without saying (and the prospectus didn't say it) that deflation would do the commercial real estate market no good. An even more practical investment question is this one: In the best of circumstances and under the best assumptions, what's in it for me?

---

* The asking rent at this writing is $35 a square foot, 10 percent lower than in 1992. As for Rockefeller Center Properties, the common stock was quoted at 9⅝ late in February 1993, down from 20 in September 1985.

GREENWICH ROUNDS THE BEND

January 25, 1988

As lovely lanes as any in Devonshire, as beautiful chateaux as many in France, a seashore lined with villas like Italy—such is Greenwich on the Sound, crowning the undulating ridges of the foothills of the Catskills or the Berkshires.
—Greenwich: Old and New *by Lydia Holland and Margaret Leaf; Greenwich, Connecticut, 1935.*

Following the 1929 stock market crash, Paul A. Dahlgreen, an alert Greenwich real estate broker, appealed to his neighbors to invest in the lovely lanes, villa-lined seashores, and undulating ridges directly underneath their own feet. Even then it was hard to imagine Greenwich poor, and Dahlgreen evidently could envision no circumstances in which an acre of Greenwich land would ever command a smaller price than it had in 1929. He was wrong about that. According to Thomas B. Gorin, a contemporary broker who has looked through the old records, some estates that fetched $1 million at the top of the market in 1929 changed hands for as little as $75,000 in the 1930s. (According to *Greenwich: Old and New*, incidentally, the town itself sailed through the Depression, running budget surpluses, financing capital expenditures out of income, and generously filling the Community Chest.) Not anticipating the slump, however, Dahlgreen advertised in the *Greenwich News & Graphic* on January 3, 1930, "Invest in Greenwich Real Estate Instead of Stocks":

> The Town of Greenwich "market" never hits the toboggan. In fifty years there has never been a decrease in value, but in fifty years total assessed valuation has increased fifty-fold.

One Round Hill Road: four bedrooms for only $5.5 million

The name of the broker who first said that Greenwich real estate never falls is unknown, but it was surely not Dahlgreen in 1930. Jeremiah Atwater, a real estate speculator from New York, was on record with a bullish opinion as early as 1865 (if Dahlgreen's figures were right, they imply a fifty-year compounded rate of return in Greenwich property of 8.14 percent; it was therefore correct to have been bullish in 1865, if not in 1930). The only recorded calamitous setback to Greenwich property values, besides the Great Depression, was the burning of houses by British troops during the Revolutionary War.

Rebuilt nicely since the 1770s, Greenwich is situated twenty-eight miles northeast of New York City just over the Connecticut line. It is the richest suburb in the Northeast, and it is the Connecticut town closest to New York. It has excellent shopping, polo facilities, convenient transportation, and a civic-minded population. It votes Republican and is 50.6 square miles in size. According to the Bureau of the Census, there were 59,578 Greenwichites in 1980 but only 58,270 in 1986. The town denies that there has been a decline, and certainly the real estate sales population has boomed. The Greenwich Board of Realtors has almost 700 members, including a contingent from neighboring Stamford, representing 1.2 percent of the Census Bureau's version of the 1986 Greenwich population. To put 700 brokers in perspective, there were only 649 residential real estate transactions last year. However, to judge by the undiminished bullishness of the brokers toward the Greenwich market and the 5 percent to 6 percent commissions paid on each brokered sale, one should probably not squander much sympathy on the local sales force yet. (Asked for advice on how to proceed in what has become a difficult market, one realtor helpfully suggested, "don't price your home more than 10 percent higher than last year. Also, put your house on at a 6 percent commission rather than 5 percent to cover more advertising costs and to make the broker's commission more palatable to the selling broker.") Greenwich is not the most intensely brokered community in the United States, although it may be close. Aspen, Colorado, musters 285 brokers out of a year-round population of 8,000, for a ratio of brokers to populace three times greater than Greenwich's. However, by any standard, Greenwich is a case study in the happy confluence of financial bull markets, abundant credit, and low tax rates. It may also be a bellwether for what is to follow.

Greenwich is bounded on the south by the Long Island Sound —in the sunshine, the Manhattan skyline gleams—and to the north by what is known as the back country. In a testimonial advertisement for Conyers Farm, a one-thousand-acre development being offered in lots of ten to twenty-three acres at prices of $1.3 million per lot and up (that is for the land only), a satisfied customer stated, "Conyers Farm is perfect for the polo-playing businessman." It is the type of marketing line that is thought to play well in Greenwich. In 1987 the average price of a Greenwich house was $706,150.* That was only slightly less than the town's outstanding general

---

* In 1990 and 1991, according to Stanley Klein of Empire Realty Corp., the average price of a Greenwich house declined by 2 percent and 3.2 percent, respectively, from the prior year, the first such consecutive percentage declines since 1952 and 1953. Still, the 1992 average price, almost $820,000, was 3.2 percent higher than the 1988 average price, at about $795,000. Greenwich has survived.

obligation debt, $830,000, to which Moody's has assigned the fully warranted rating of Aaa.

According to *Greenwich*, a publication of the Greenwich Board of Realtors, "Greenwich's homes range from reasonably priced colonials and ranches to impressive estates and waterfront properties." These are elastic terms. To a Greenwich broker, "reasonable" can denote anything up to and including a four-bedroom, brick-and-shingle, not-much-to-look-at, 1961-vintage colonial on 2.09 acres for $910,000. Recently, a woman from Larchmont, New York, was shown what her broker described as the cheapest house in Greenwich. It was in the Glenville section and was offered for $243,000; opinions are subjective, but the would-be buyer called it a wreck. At the baronial end of the market, a 60-odd-acre estate on Old Mill Road, complete with manor house, stables, and outbuildings and a sign at the entrance warning BEWARE OF THE LIONS went unsold last year. The asking price was $21 million, a figure so high, even for Greenwich, that it was thought to reveal an unexpressed preference by the owner to stay put.

People want to live in Greenwich. Tom Seaver, Barton Biggs, Diana Ross, John Reed, Harry Helmsley, Donald Trump, Ivan Lendl, and David Stockman own houses there. People have always wanted to live in Greenwich, and during most of the postwar period they have been willing to pay ever more fabulous prices for the privilege. Since 1945, house prices have registered annual declines in only six calendar years, according to *The Greenwich Record of Real Estate Sales*. The years were 1952, 1953, 1956, 1958, 1962, and 1972. Generations of Greenwich brokers and homeowners have come to view a strong financial return on their homes as another Greenwich amenity, like the public library.

In 1986 the price of the average Greenwich house broke all annual price-appreciation records by jumping 43 percent, to $656,000 from $458,000 in 1985. Nothing quite like it had been seen before, or at least not in the postwar period; in the runner-up percentage-gain year, what had been a $32,460 house in 1956 became a $40,068 house in 1957, representing a rise of 23.4 percent. Probably, therefore, at least in relative terms, 1987 was bound to be a disappointment. It was.

Last year the average house rose by just 7.7 percent (to $706,150), the average elapsed time from listing to sale stretched out (to about three or four months from one or two months in 1986), and the volume of transactions dried up. Late in the year, real estate advertising linage in the *Greenwich Time* dropped off. Condominium sales softened. The Revenue Act of 1987, which effectively limits a taxpayer's mortgage-interest deductions to a mortgage no greater than $1 million (for primary and secondary homes combined), was passed—a knock at the baronial end of the market. And on October 19, the stock market crashed, discommoding local investors just as it had done in 1929 and furnishing local realtors with another opportunity to compare a substantial investment in Greenwich property with a flyer in an untrustworthy common stock.*

Going up, of course, is what Greenwich property values are supposed to do—have almost been warranted to do. Nothing like a bear market has started yet, but nobody who has worked on Wall Street will deny the theoretical possibility of one. For ourselves, we expect there will be less bull market money with which to buy houses. In any event, a bear market in Greenwich property would fly in the face of a number of received truths—for instance: *Low interest rates are good for property values, and the lower the rates, the better.* However, the decline last year in thirty-year, fixed-rate mortgages to 8½ percent, an eight-year low, sparked no new surge in prices, and it is a matter of historical record that the rock-bottom interest rates of the late 1930s were associated with the Dark Ages of Greenwich house prices. Thus, if interest rates drop for deflationary reasons, house prices will not rally. Or, another axiom: *A weak dollar delivers strong foreign buying, especially at the top end of the property market.* However, no dramatic influx of foreign money has been seen in Belle Haven, Rock Ridge, or out on Round Hill Road, where a $5.5 million house built on speculation awaits a buyer. If, in view of accessible mortgage rates and the still-weak dollar, Greenwich property continues to languish, that would be worth

---

* The *Greenwich News & Graphic*'s coverage of the crash, November 1, 1929, might have been reprinted, with only minor editing, on October 20, 1987:

> A steady stream was noticed calling at the local broker's office, representing people from every walk of life. Even women were among the clientele. A reporter for the *News & Graphic* visited the office, but the manager and employees were too busy to discuss the matter.
>
> One employee was heard to comment that there was such a rush it was sometimes impossible to get an order through to New York City over the phone and that when connections were finally established, the price would be different than when the call was started.

knowing about. It would suggest that the value of cash is rising and that $1 million is on its way to becoming real money again.

Here and there recently, hot real estate markets *have* cooled down. According to The Tokyo Land and Housing Dealers' Association, for example, land prices in Tokyo have fallen by 15 percent from last year's peaks. (According to Thursday's *Financial Times*, some Tokyo properties have fallen 30 percent to 50 percent from the high. "Despite this heavy discounting," the paper reported, "much of the market is now frozen, with buyers sitting on the sidelines waiting for prices to stabilize.") Cushman & Wakefield recently disclosed a rise in midtown-Manhattan office vacancy rates, to 10.2 percent in the fourth quarter from 9.1 percent in the third quarter. And the Manhattan residential market has lost its bounce. Each week, the broker L. B. Kaye advertises apartments, mainly expensive ones, in the "Luxury Homes and Estates" section of the *New York Times Sunday Magazine*. Since December the headlines over the ads have suggested a rise in the anxiety level of the owner-sellers, for example, from last Sunday's layout, PRICE CRASH! ("Owner must sell now!") and SACRIFICE ON PARK. Land in Tokyo and apartments in Manhattan and houses in Greenwich may have nothing much in common. On the other hand, it is a truism that major moves in markets are international in scope (witness stocks and bonds in 1985–87). If Tokyo land prices can go down, is it unthinkable that Greenwich can follow?

Unthinkable? Perhaps. Impossible? No. In the wake of the crash, some buyers retreated and a handful of deals have been broken. However, no across-the-board decline in house prices has been reported. One reason, perhaps, is that sellers have chosen to hold fast at the old high prices rather than do business at new and lower ones. Also, perhaps, in the eyes of the lenders, the crash has changed nothing fundamentally. Joseph D. Gioffre, president and chief executive officer of Greenwich Financial Corp., holding company of Greenwich Federal Savings & Loan, related that in his institution the creditworthiness of a Wall Street loan applicant is assessed by taking an average of three years' salary and bonus. When a man observed that the bonuses of the past three years have been spectacular and possibly nonrecurring, Gioffre replied that things have not gotten really bad yet—"The bonus decreases I've been reading about have been 20 percent or so."

In a real bear market, of course, a number of people who commute from Greenwich will be lucky to have a salary, let alone a bonus (Gioffre did add, by the way, that corporate executives handily outnumber financial people in Greenwich and that, in any event, buyers of the Taj Mahal–type of property are relatively unleveraged). In January 1987 the number of unsold houses in the Greenwich Multiple Listing Service stood at 345. The inventory reached 561 in April, and all hands braced for the inevitable rush of springtime buyers. However, the buyers kept their distance—monthly sales volume peaked in June—and the house inventory has not significantly receded. It stands at 473. Sales are predictably weak between the Army-Navy game and the Super Bowl, brokers will tell you, but the seasonal weakness was much more pronounced in 1987. You have to go back all the way to 1981 to find a duller fourth quarter than last year's. Sales in the period from October to December 1987 (115) stacked up badly not only against the tax-bloated 1986 fourth quarter (244) but also against the fourth quarters of 1980 and 1982 (175 and 132, respectively), years of punitively high mortgage rates. "You better see a hot market from February to mid-March—that's before they go away on spring vacation—or you'll know that something happened," Louis D. Duff, a Greenwich broker, said.

"When you are buying a house in excess of a million dollars, you are buying a fantasy," another Greenwich broker remarked. Passage of the Revenue Act of 1987, which caps a taxpayer's deductible mortgage debt at $1 million, starting last October 12, has heightened the element of fantasy in the seven-figure neighborhood. Odd to report, therefore, that the year of the crash and of the million-dollar tax bill saw a little boomlet in luxury "spec" houses. According to a report by Douglas Stevens, sales manager of the real estate brokerage firm of William Pitt, about thirty-six such speculative properties are on the market, of which about two dozen have price tags of $2 million or more. To put those two dozen in perspective, only nine $2 million-and-up spec houses were sold between January 1986 and June 1987, a period that encompassed neither a stock market crash nor passage of a disadvantageous tax bill.

The thirteenth annual real estate issue of *The Nutmegger*, a Greenwich monthly magazine, was devoted to the theme, "The Challenge of Selling a Big Estate," and it featured a handful of properties that could not appropriately be described, even in broker talk, by the expandable phrase "reasonably priced." The first such estate happened to be the $5.5 million spec house, "One Round Hill Road," situated at the intersection of Round Hill Road and Lake Avenue, a Greenwich address equivalent to Park Avenue in the 70s. "While Black Monday on the stock market altered the prospects of estate owners to a degree as yet unknown," the magazine commented in introducing the house, "the positive aspect is that Greenwich real estate remains intrinsically a good long-term investment comparing favorably with the ownership of stocks and bonds."

In view of the stock market, of course, that might not seem an unreserved expression of civic confidence. However, Round Hill's owners—John Crowley, a retired executive vice president of Xerox, his wife Carol, and a builder, Brad Carlson—are, or were when they began the project, brimming over with optimism. Carlson had had his eye on the site, "and when he heard rumors of its being developed, he stepped in fast to acquire it before it went formally on the market," the magazine related. The house is almost finished. It is a massive Georgian-style structure (the big houses in Greenwich loom up above the tree lines the way the aircraft carrier *Intrepid* does over the West Side Highway in Manhattan) with clapboard exterior, six fireplaces, custom millwork, an English pine custom kitchen, servants' quarters, and four bedrooms. "Mr. Crowley, a venture-capital entrepreneur," said *The Nutmegger*, "appreciates that it will be a special sale but remains confident that the buyer is out there waiting to be found, whether it be an Arabian oilman, a Texas tycoon, a Japanese electronics giant, or a solvent yuppie. The magnetism of Greenwich is universal." The price, $5.5 million, includes 4.85 acres. It works out to $1,375,000 per bedroom.*

Thumbing through *The Nutmegger*, a professional investor can't help but be struck by a sense of foreboding. For instance, there is the condominium problem. Last November, 204 Greenwich condominiums were up for sale. This year it is estimated that over 300 new units will be built and brought to market. Inventory plus new supply—204 plus 300, or 504—"represents a figure nearly 20 per

---

* The actual sales price was considerably lower: $3,235,000, not even $1 million a bedroom. The Connecticut Bank & Trust Co. foreclosed on the Crowleys and on Brad Carlson in November 1989, and the complaint mentioned debt of almost $3.5 million. When, in April 1990, a judgment was delivered against the unlucky developers, the debt had grown to almost $3.8 million. The sale took place two months later. On paper, someone—the developers, the bank, the contractors, the subcontractors—bore a loss of more than $500,000.

cent greater than the combined sales of all condominiums in 1986 and 1987," wrote the broker Douglas Stevens, who wound up, dryly, "It should prove interesting to see if the demand for condominiums in the year ahead is proportionate to the generous supply that is anticipated."

There is also the sentiment problem. In financial markets a preponderance of bullish sentiment is taken to be a bad omen because it suggests that a market has already discounted the good news. For decades, in the case of Greenwich, being bullish has paid, and brokers have made a handsome living by preaching the destiny of rising prices. However, the times probably have changed, and what used to be congenital bullishness may already have become a form of denial.

For decades after the Crash, the giant homes of the 1920s bull market were viewed as white elephants. Nowadays, in Greenwich (and, no doubt, outside it), grand is in vogue once more, and no elephant is thought to be too big or too white for the carriage trade. In the 1930s and 1940s, according to the broker Tom Gorin, people would rent their houses to people who couldn't think of buying them. Maybe that is the strategy for 1988. Rent until the ratio of real estate brokers to $5.5 million speculative houses falls more reasonably into line.

D. TRUMP: ROLE MODEL

June 10, 1988

At the age of nineteen, according to *The New York Times*, Abe Betesh may be the youngest licensed real estate agent in New York State. He may be the most enterprising, too. The *Times* rode uptown with Betesh in a red sports car and listened patiently as the young man reflected on Donald Trump, the inventor of real estate and noted author:

"Wasn't that book of his great?" Mr. Betesh said. "He really knows how to put a deal together. That Trump is one great dealmaker. And I'm doing deals, too. I've done a dozen deals—no, not a dozen. Today my thirteenth deal goes to contract."

Onward and upward!

O&Y UNDER THE GLASS

July 6, 1990

To sell short the Reichmann family of Toronto would seem to be, in almost equal measure, unprofitable and impertinent. The Reichmanns have built one of the world's great real estate fortunes. They are the number one landlord in New York City. They have accumulated sizable assets in energy, newsprint, and retailing. They are, at this very minute, building the largest commercial real estate project in the world: the Canary Wharf complex in east London on a New Jersey–style industrial tract known as the Isle of Dogs. What Sam Walton is to retailing or Nolan Ryan is to pitching, the Reichmanns are to building.*

So when Jack A. Sullivan, a paid-up subscriber in San Francisco, mentioned that he was accumulating a short position in some of the Eurobonds of the Reichmann's flagship company, Olympia & York Developments Ltd., we paused to reflect on the state of the world. "One thing leads to another," ventured Sullivan, a salesman and money manager at Van Kasper & Co. and a bear on California real estate. "I think it's all interconnected."

Sullivan said that he has begun to notice the Reichmann name

---

* Before very long they became just another debt-afflicted real estate family. In the United Kingdom, Olympia & York is operating under court administration. In Canada it is trying to emerge from bankruptcy proceedings. In the United States it is trying to avoid them. None of this seemed plausible, let alone inevitable, in the summer of 1990.

turning up in the unfamiliar context of trouble. For instance, Landmark Land of Carmel, California, has failed to dispose of some real estate that federal regulators have ordered it to sell. O&Y owns a 24 percent interest in Landmark. Also, CalFed, the big California thrift-holding company, recently disclosed that its principal subsidiary holds a $160 million mortgage secured by a New York office building. During the first quarter, said CalFed, "the principal tenant in the building sought protection from creditors under the federal bankruptcy laws. However, the borrower (which is unrelated to the tenant) has continued to make all required loan payments and has expressed its intent to do so in the future." It turns out that the building is 60 Broad Street, the tenant is Drexel Burnham Lambert, and the borrower is O&Y. Finally, noted Sullivan, no sooner did one new tenant recently sign up for the mega–Canary Wharf development than another one, formerly committed, backed out.

Visiting London last month, Sullivan went on, he was struck by the weakness in the real estate market. While Paul Reichmann is certainly no Donald Trump, Sullivan suggested, negative cash flow is negative cash flow.

This is a speculative piece on the Reichmann enterprise and its significance in the unfolding credit drama. Speculate we must, for O&Y is closely held, and the details of the family's finances are guarded. But enough is known to convey a sense of the magnitude of the family's achievement and to prompt a debt-minded observer to ask, in this time of real estate peril, "Now what?"

If, as we think, the world is taking a deflationary turn, the evidence is bound to show up in even the Reichmann's finances. In a true deflation—a general decline in asset prices—adjustments would be forced on everyone. It wouldn't matter whether the leveraged owner of land or buildings or natural resources was soft-spoken and retiring (the O&Y style) or loud and boastful (The Donald style). The only thing that would matter would be the burden of compound interest, which is punitive.

Probably the Reichmanns would not put it just this way, but they have invested in inflation. They own controlling interests in Gulf Canada Resources, Canada's largest oil and gas company, Abitibi-Price, the world's biggest newsprint maker, and Consumers' Gas Co., Canada's largest natural-gas distribution utility.

Similarly, they are long financial activity: They own real estate in the money centers of New York, Toronto, and London. Also, in effect, they are long financial leverage. They have invested in Campeau Corp. and Landmark Land, both of which are highly leveraged (you've heard about Campeau). Gulf Canada Resources, their largest portfolio investment, showed a ratio of earnings to fixed charges in the March quarter of 2 to 1. In April, Moody's cut its commercial-paper rating to P-2 from P-1, and in the same month Standard & Poor's put the company's senior debt under surveillance for a possible downgrade. Moody's rates the senior debts Baa1, or low investment grade.

In sum, the Reichmanns have cast their lot with the world of the 1970s and 1980s, a fabulously profitable world but one that is changing fast. They have bet that asset values will continue to rise and that the structure of debt will remain intact.

O&Y is accustomed to winning its bets. In 1977, when New York seemed a goner, the Reichmanns purchased eight Manhattan office buildings for $320 million. At the peak a decade later, the market value of the same properties was estimated to have risen tenfold. In the early 1980s, the company stepped in to take charge of what was then called Battery Park City. Now it's the World Financial Center. "At the time the state-run project, built on Hudson River landfill that was a by-product of the construction of the World Trade Center, was in financial trouble," *The Wall Street Journal* reported. "Other developers were wary and were willing only to build one office building at a time in the project. But O&Y committed itself to building four mammoth office towers almost simultaneously. . . . O&Y's decision to move ahead on construction all at once paid off when the 1987 stock market crash took Wall Street real estate prices down with it. For O&Y had the development almost fully leased by that time, at pre-crash prices."

Although the Reichmanns don't disclose a consolidated balance sheet, they make no secret of their m.o. They are bull market operators. They bought New York when it was cheap and the Isle of Dogs when *it* was cheap, or at least undeveloped. They are long-term investors who believe that London is destined to become the financial capital of a wealthy new Europe. Some of the things that they do *not* believe may also be surmised. They do not seem to believe that financial activity is peaking, that credit is contracting (even at the margin, much less at the center), or that real estate has entered a worldwide bear market. They are, in the admiring old Wall Street expression, "upbuilders."

Canary Wharf may be the world's most sincere expression of optimism. Situated two and a half miles east of the Bank of England in London's own North Dakota, the project aims for 10 million square feet of office space on twenty-four separate building sites spread over seventy-one acres. The projected cost is some £4 billion, or the equivalent of $7 billion. "To understand Canary Wharf is to understand Olympia & York," Paul Reichmann, the first among three equal Reichmann brothers, has said. "O&Y has always been an innovator." Reichmann also said that this huge undertaking may not yield positive cash flow—cash "to exceed the cost of money," as he put it—for "ten or fifteen years." Reichmann added, though he hardly needed to, that O&Y is in it for the long run.

So far Canary Wharf's unique appeal is to a handful of American tenants. American Express has just signed on, but Merrill Lynch has just dropped out. Morgan Stanley, Texaco, and Manufacturers Hanover have signed on. Only one-fifth of the project's space has been spoken for, and not a single British company has committed to rent. "Although O&Y's publicity refers to 'amount of space taken,'" the *Financial Times* reported, "some of the companies have only signed letters of intent which do not bind them to take up a tenancy contract."

A little like Eurotunnel, Canary Wharf is calculated to worry a nonbeliever. Visiting London nowadays, a skeptic will see construction cranes stabbing into the sky. He will be told that the construction is necessary to salvage the city's office stock from obsolescence: Three-quarters of it was put up before 1980 and is therefore wanting in electronic amenities, like floor plates and heavy-duty air conditioning, and windows that you can't open. Furthermore, he will be told, rents in the City of London are still exorbitant. He will hear that Canary Wharf, though inaccessible now, will satisfy the inevitable demand for ultramodern space at reasonable rates. By 1996, the planners promise, an underground will link it to urban civilization.

Being who he is, however, a skeptic will worry. He may not

necessarily doubt that, in time, the demand for office space will absorb the prospective supply. However, he will question the timing of cash flows. Watching the cranes at work, he will remember Dallas in 1986 or 1987, when everybody knew that the jig was up but the redundant projects still went forward because the money to build them hadn't run out. (The analogy is imperfect because building activity in London is a lagging indicator. Almost half of the city's biggest construction projects are significantly behind schedule, some by as many as two years.) The thought will strike him that the real estate bear market is international, not domestic, and that London may still be far from the bottom. He will have eagerly read a bearish item in the June 15 *Financial Times:*

> Indigestion is crippling the City of London. Hunger for space has not abated as much as might be expected when the economy is going through one of its regular bouts of illness, but the setback has piled more space on the City's plate than can comfortably be consumed.
>
> Like stubborn children, tenants are having to be tempted to eat. Prime rents have fallen away from the heady days when £65 to £70 a square foot was confidently predicted. Smaller spaces in the old City core may still bound into the sixties, but larger blocks are more likely to be valued at £45 to £55.
>
> Lower rents are not enough, however. Bribes are commonplace in the form of rent-free periods and reverse premiums—particularly on the least palatable buildings.

If this sounds like a composite of Boston, New York, and Dallas, the comparison ripens: "More than twenty-five buildings larger than 150,000 square feet are due to be completed in the next eighteen months, so the immediate future looks gloomy for landlords—if not for tenants," the story goes on. ". . . In the meantime, the discomfort could be acute. With 12 million square feet on the market by December, some 14 percent of the City's offices could be standing empty. Top rents may hold steady, but the problem of letting secondhand offices could drag down average values by another 5 percent this year."

What no outsider can know is the significance of the office building slump to the Reichmann's finances. In New York a deep bear market is under way downtown, and midtown seems headed in the same direction. No. 59 Maiden Lane was nearly full when O&Y issued $200 million in Eurobonds to finance it in 1985 but is no longer. The Reichmanns' tolerance for vacant space must depend on their financial strength: by how much they have mortgaged low-cost assets to finance the acquisition of high-cost assets. If O&Y is suffering a bout of negative carry (that is, if the cost of its assets is greater than the cash yield of its assets), how long can that go on?

Longer than the average married man could begin to imagine, Paul Reichmann seemed to suggest in a *Financial Times* interview last January. "Early years with low income do not disturb us," said Reichmann concerning Canary Wharf. The headline over the piece beckoned optimistically: THE DEVELOPER WHO LOOKS A DECADE AHEAD.

Everybody would like to extend his investment horizon. It is the bankers and margin clerks and institutional investors who refuse to allow it. Under what financial constraints do the Reichmanns operate? How leveraged are they? How leveraged—if markets take their expected, deflationary turn—might they become?

Dominion Bond Rating Service in March published a bullish overview of O&Y's finances. It prefaced this analysis with the pertinent disclaimer that it has not been privy to the company's financial statements. The agency made these summary points:

—The real estate portfolio of O&Y in North America is one of the most attractive of any real estate company known to DBRS.
—The company has an investment portfolio worth $6 billion–$7 billion at present market values, and could possibly be worth $8 billion–$9 billion if "control block" premiums are considered.
—The company is one of the biggest manufacturers of building products in Canada.
—Debt levels against this large portfolio of assets have not been publicly disclosed, but we believe that there is substantial net worth (equity) above and beyond direct outstanding debt. The revenue generated by the stock portfolio on a tax-adjusted basis is sufficient to support about $2 billion of debt on a tax-adjusted basis, based on the $163 million dividend that it generates. The portfolio is worth about $6.6 billion at today's market prices. Thus, supportable debt levels equal about one-third of the portfolio's present market value.

Dominion also listed some "areas of concern," including Gulf Canada, Canary Wharf, and Abitibi-Price. "The drop in newsprint prices, the growing newspaper surplus, the high Canadian dollar, environmental issues, and labor negotiations are the main problems," said the agency, "and we expect weak industry conditions to 1993." Concerning O&Y's dicey investment in Campeau, the maximum estimated loss was put at $150 million, "which is insignificant in relation to the size of the investment portfolio."

On the other hand, to paraphrase the politician, a few hundred million dollars here and a few hundred million dollars there, and pretty soon you're talking about real money. Paul Reichmann is no Donald Trump, but Reichmann, too, is in the asset-appreciation business.

BETTING THE STORE

December 20, 1991

M all of America, which is opening next August in Bloomington, Minnesota, has an American investor, Teachers Insurance and Annuity Association, and a Japanese construction lender, Mitsubishi Bank. It has both an American developer, Melvin Simon & Associates, and a Canadian developer, Triple Five Corp., Ltd. It has the space for twelve thousand automobiles, four department stores, four hundred specialty stores, and fourteen movie theaters. It is the site for Knott's Camp Snoopy, a seven-acre enclosed theme park featuring America's favorite beagle. It is expected to feature Golf Mountain, Underwater World, LEGO Imagination Center, and America's Original Sports Bar. The bar will have a boxing ring. Neil W. Peterson, the mayor of Bloomington (population: 86,335), has called Mall of America "the last deal of the decade." It is, in fact, the 1980s distilled into 4.2 million square feet.

It is America's mall and America's newest financial laboratory. The promoters have provided for all known contingencies, but they have not provided (any more than the Bush administration or the Federal Reserve have provided) for economic growth. The "nation's largest, fully enclosed, combination retail and family entertainment complex" is nearing completion at a time when more and more Americans are staying home to eat macaroni and cheese. No doubt eventually the public will visit Mall of America, but questions present themselves in the meantime. When will they come?* In what numbers? And at what cost to competing regions and retailers? Must the success of the mall come out of the hides of its far-flung competitors?

Mayor Peterson is dry-eyed concerning the possibility that downtown Minneapolis retailers might suffer on account of the biggest construction project in Bloomington history. A downtown Minneapolis retail developer returns those sentiments with interest. "If Knott's Berry Farm is the customer that this mall is looking to draw from this region, understand: That person is not a Bloomingdale's or Nordstrom customer," he says. "Minneapolis is very cosmopolitan, but twenty miles outside of town, you're in pasture. Those people don't understand Bloomingdale's or Nordstrom." In the past several years, Gaviidae Common (Saks Fifth Avenue, Neiman Marcus), the Conservatory (FAO Schwarz, Sharper Image), and Nicollet Centre (Gussini Shoes, Hit or Miss) have opened, but there has been no massive, or even moderate, influx from the provinces. Southdale Mall, the nation's first enclosed mall, now thirty-five years old, received a face-lift last summer. It looks great. However, its parking lot had plenty of room at 5 p.m. on a Monday two weeks before Christmas.

It is physically impossible to walk the grounds of Mall of America without standing in awe of the national wealth. The premises will house a cornucopia, and they stand as a symbol of the durability of the American economy. Despite business cycles, credit cycles, the U.S. Congress, the chairman of the Council of Economic Advisers, and other scourges, natural and man-made, the United

---

* An estimated 16 million in the first six months of operation, through February 11, 1993. By then, management said, 80 percent of the mall's leasable space had been leased, the updated vendor roster including (among others) Bows Bows Bows, Everything but Water, The Leftorium, Wild Pitch, Original Corn Dog, *and* Corn Dog Plus. Visits to Knott's Camp Snoopy "are about 30 percent ahead of original estimates" (whatever they might have been), a Mall of America press release said. So far, so good.

States only becomes richer. It does not become richer every single day, however, and lending capacity sometimes outstrips earning capacity. When the bankers get ahead of themselves, surpluses develop, as they did in real estate in the 1980s. Thus, one must pause to ask if the mall is a monument to the last cycle or a shrewd investment in the next one.

Inclined to answer "the last cycle," we are therefore also inclined to ask additional questions. For instance: Has the project's principal American investor, TIAA, correctly taken the measure of the deflationary times? Will R. H. Macy & Co., one of the mall's four anchor department stores, stay out of bankruptcy court? And is this or is this not the "destination" shopping mall that the promoters hope it will be? Will it attract shoppers from Fargo and Tokyo as well as from Burnsville, Minnesota?

It follows that the conscientious student of Mall of America must also be a student of the national economy. Reflecting on the state of mind of the mall's promoters, c. 1987, he or she must also consider the morale of the mall's would-be customers, c. 1991. They are wholly different. In December 1987, when Melvin Simon & Associates, the famous Indianapolis developers, teamed up with Triple Five Corp., builders of the even bigger, more stupendous West Edmonton Mall in Alberta, Canada, the stock market had crashed but business activity had not. Corporate profits were on the rise. Nowadays, the stock market is up but consumers are down. The retail climate resembles the Minnesota winter or even the Minnesota autumn, which has produced sub-zero temperatures and sixty inches of snow. Bulls on the project will tell you that the timing is heaven-sent: better to open at what almost certainly will be the end of the recession (so they say) than at the beginning of one. What they do not dwell on is the possibility that recession-like symptoms may persist. They do not speculate on the likelihood of a modern debt deflation. They do not believe that the megamall, as it's locally known, might merely leech the profit margins from countless surrounding retailers, creating a long-running, region-wide retail funk.

They do not discuss these things, arguably, because they have learned that it is not even profitable to think about them. Trammell Crow used to say that in America "the buyers have been right and the sellers have been wrong," and Mall of America is as pure an expression of optimism as the banking, architectural, retailing, and development professions have yet produced. "The Mall of America," reflects Thomas Crowley, the local mortgage banker who brokered the deal among Simon, TIAA, and Triple Five, "is like nothing you've ever seen. Sincerely, I think it'll be a phenomenon. I'm probably a minority of one up here, but I think it'll be a sensation. I think what's underestimated is the power of the Twin Cities. We've got two and a half million people in the metropolitan area that outmakes, outfinances, outdances, outproduces, outsaves, and outperforms any two and a half million people in the United States. We read more, we spend more, we buy more, we do more, we travel more than any other group in the United States. Period."

Crowley drew a breath, then continued: "Secondly, we're in an area where we got half of Wisconsin, half of Iowa, all of the Dakotas that depend on the Twin Cities. We're in a service center for essentially a four-and-a-half state area. It's a very important area for all those little territories.

"We're in an area that's starved for atmosphere. Nothing grows up here for six months of the year. This is all going to be indoors. In the summer, it's so hot you gotta be indoors. In the winter, it's so cold you've got to be indoors. It's perfect. We've got three department stores saying, 'This is Norman Rockwell territory.' It's the most boring population I've ever seen, but they make a lot of money."

The mall is built on the site of the old Metropolitan Stadium, former home of the then non–World Championship Minnesota Twins (a site abandoned after a 5–2 loss to the Kansas City Royals on September 30, 1981, which was also, incidentally, the day the long-bond yield peaked at nearly 15 percent). More than $100 million of the cost was financed by the city of Bloomington, which had thought about building an office complex but settled instead on the mall (for which Mayor Peterson says he thanks his lucky stars). The city used about $25 million to buy the one-hundred-acre site and $75 million to build the parking garage. Furthermore, it issued $80 million in bonds to finance the accelerated construction of highway repairs and improvements. Ground-breaking took place on June 14, which is Flag Day, in 1989. Two and a half years later, construction is nearly complete. Depending on one's frame of reference, the looming structure suggests the state of Texas, the cross–Channel Tunnel, or the U.S.S. *Nimitz*.

Our John Britton toured the construction site last week with

Dennis McLauchlin, the Mall of America project manager. Britton wrote as follows:

> Entering unobtrusively through a side door, the casual visitor will quickly notice that the interior walls and staircases are intact—all that is missing in many places is a paint job. But this is only the first corridor, and such scrutiny of detail is quickly blown up when the visitor rounds the corner and the Big Picture comes into view —the seven acres that will soon be Knott's Camp Snoopy. The news accounts say that the room is immense—it is that and then some. Standing on the second of four levels looking out over men on tractors, the men laying pipe and yet more men on other substantial machines, the visitor will momentarily forget that he is indoors. With seven acres of skylights, the sun streams in, and it seems like a busy outdoor building site on a beautiful spring day.
>
> All told there will be roughly four miles of storefront, but that counts three levels—the tour is only one level. At every corner there is a different skylight and architectural theme for the anchor located in that niche, and between each of the four anchors are different decorative styles, meant to reflect the panache of the retailing rank and file that will be sandwiched in between.
>
> There are twelve hundred workers in the building now, says McLauchlin, and there will be three thousand to four thousand each day when the retailers start moving in. None has yet. It is hard to imagine three times as many workers. Every corridor, overhang, back alley, side door yields at least one worker diligently going about the business of completing megamall.

Sooner or later someone may float an election year proposal to build one Mall of America in every state or important regional hub. To sustain business activity after completion, each community would be required to shop in the mall of some distant community, thereby enlarging the GNP through travel-related expenditures and validating the recent advance in the Dow Jones Transportation Average. In any case, Britton went on:

> "Here is where we're going to put the $17,000 chandeliers," said McLauchlin.
>
> "This is South Street [still in the mall, of course], which will be done in 1919 grand hotel look." Then there is the East Village, which "has an Art Deco feel" and where "there's more attention to detail than in most state capitals." Then we're in Nordstrom's Court,

where the fifty-foot palm trees will sway, or would sway anyway if there were a breeze.

We tromp through the Knott's Camp Snoopy construction site to admire the fake rock going up in the corner. Even at a distance of two feet it looks and feels real, which causes McLauchlin to beam. He doesn't bother to stop at Golf Mountain, which will house a two-level, eighteen-hole miniature golf course, and we also skip LEGO Imagination Center, the five-thousand-square-foot LEGO theme park.

McLauchlin makes a point to stop and look down at the aquarium under construction. When finished, it will be a massive walk-through affair with multiple micro-ecosystems to surround the curious shopper. There has been some discussion over whether the financing for the aquarium is secure (like the financing for a possible Michael Jackson interactive music museum, which is also apparently problematical), but McLauchlin thinks it is, and we move on.

The financial facts are interesting, as far as they go. For one thing, local Minnesota banks are conspicuous by their absence, just as Dayton Hudson, the big local department store chain, is conspicuous by *its* absence. The main construction lenders are Japanese. Mitsubishi and the banks in its consortium lent $400 million, and TIAA advanced another $225 million. When construction is finished and the anchors are up and running and about 50 percent of the tenant space (excluding the anchors) is leased and occupied, TIAA will begin to take over the Japanese loan. Teachers' resulting $625 million commitment (that will be its maximum exposure) is to become an equity investment. It will be the largest real estate investment on Teachers' balance sheet, which last December 31 footed to $50 billion. When all is said and done, TIAA will own 55 percent of the mall, and Simon and Triple Five will each own 22.5 percent. At the beginning, TIAA will receive a "preferred cumulative return." If the cash flow falls short of an undisclosed guaranteed rate, the unpaid balance will accumulate as an IOU. At an undisclosed date, the cumulative feature will lapse, leaving TIAA with a plain preferred return.

If R. H. Macy's business has fallen half as precipitously as the prices of its junk bonds this month, the construction lenders must be wondering if the store is going to show up on opening day. At 275,000 square feet, Macy's is the largest of the four anchors, and its absence would be hard to disguise with even the finest new fake-rock technology. Arthur W. Spellmeyer, senior vice president at Melvin Simon & Associates, says he has no doubts about Macy's. "They're building right now," he tells *Grant's*, "and we have every confidence that they will be there."* (A man at TIAA adds, with some heat: "They've just got a leverage problem—they're just overleveraged. But we've seen others in their position, and we would assume that it would continue to operate under any scenario." What nobody can know, of course, is whether the trade creditors would continue to ship to Macy's under "any scenario.")

Spellmeyer might very well be right, and for this interesting reason: When Federated Department Stores filed for bankruptcy protection, the terms of the Bloomingdale's lease with Mall of America came into the public domain. In the words of the court documents, the contract afforded Bloomingdale's "virtually no economic downside." In September 1990, Sally Apgar of the *Minneapolis Star Tribune* reported that the Simon organization, through Mall of America, had offered to reimburse Federated for its construction costs "and to supply an additional $8 million to stock the store and cover any nonconstruction expenses related to the opening." Small wonder that the Federated creditors raised no objection to Mall of America or that the other anchors are said to enjoy "very favorable" leases themselves. (So far is Bloomingdale's from abandoning ship that it has accelerated the pace of construction, including a knockout, eighteen-foot, pyramidal skylight.)

For some time, the Simon people have said that 70 percent of the retail space in the mall is "spoken for," meaning that leases are signed or negotiations for leasing are complete. Godiva Chocolatier is on the list of "committed" prospective tenants. However, it is under the subheading of merchants for which negotiations are incomplete. "Nothing is firm until the lease is signed," Bud Sell, Godiva's director of real estate, notes. "Nothing is firm beforehand." Even when the lease is signed, he says, there frequently are co-tenancy clauses that stipulate other tenants have to be in the building as well to make the lease valid. On the other hand, Susan Schulte, leasing director of the Coffee Beanery, Flushing,

---

* They came and they stayed, despite the January 1992 Macy's bankruptcy filing.

Michigan, reports that business is strong (sales growth in double-digits, the calamity howling of the national press notwithstanding), and that Coffee Beanery is indeed committed to the lease that is pending in the corporate "in" box.

Given that the Simon organization gave sweet leases to the anchors and that the City of Bloomington issued tax-exempt debt to help finance the infrastructure, a capitalist must wonder why Mall of America was built in the first place. Was it to satisfy the customers, the developers, or the lenders? Was it because of the need of the City of Bloomington to stick one in the ear of the city that shoplifted its professional sports teams? (Simon's Spellmeyer ventured last summer: "It's a moot point now. We *are* doing this. The loan cleared, and we are focusing on how to be successful.") The impetus, according to a man at TIAA, is that "the economics were good." Was it also because the credit was available? Specifically, did the superavailability of credit in the 1980s create a business and financial climate in which all things seemed possible? In which people would mistake peak results for a long-term trend? Did the country operate on the principle: "Borrow it and they will build"? Thomas M. Crosby, Jr., a leading Minneapolis real estate lawyer, sheds some light on that possibility with a one-sentence description of the local office-building market: "The problem with the downtown office market is that there was a study done which said there's room for one office building, and that building got built four times." Result: net rents in older but still serviceable Minneapolis buildings are quoted in the neighborhood of $2 a square foot, or about the level plumbed a few years back in Dallas.

Office buildings are not shopping malls, of course, but real estate development is real estate development. John R. Borchert, a Regents Professor emeritus in geography at the University of Minnesota, has studied the mall and its feasibility and is not a believer. "The numbers just don't add up," he contends. "They're going to cannibalize 15 percent to 25 percent of the volume of the neighboring shopping centers, plus 6 percent to 9 percent of downtown, but that still doesn't add up to their projections. So you go a little farther out and soak up 3 percent to 5 percent, and then you go to the upper Midwest and take another 3 percent, and then you say the rest will be tourism. But you're talking about the profit margins for a lot of these places."

Borchert relates a conversation that he says he had with a man from TIAA. "They had a problem of where to put money," Borchert told Britton. "One of these guys called me up a few years ago, and he said that they had 'money lying on the floor.' And they all had money lying on the floor. So they did what they've always done—they built a shopping mall. For forty years you keep on doing what you know how to do, until even a fool can see you've got to quit." (A source at TIAA denies that the availability of funds was as important as that. "The transaction wouldn't have been entered into unless the economics were good," he says.)

Of course, almost nobody predicted the current slump in retail sales. Susan M. Sterne, the Stowe (Vermont)-based consulting economist who *did* predict it, notes that growth in nationwide consumer spending this year is running at just 3.9 percent. "It's the lowest increase in nominal consumer spending since 1961," she says. "And remember, those are the retailers' revenues." Government data show that Minneapolis is not now the retailing mecca that Melvin Simon & Associates must hope it will imminently become. Minnesota employment growth peaked three years ago. Growth in Minneapolis department store sales has lagged behind the national and regional averages. To these facts Simon's Spellmeyer replies that Minneapolis is a "significantly understored market" and that "there are 5 million people in a 150-mile radius." To which Sterne replies that Minneapolis is not so much "understored" as other markets are "overstored." Or possibly, she adds, Minneapolis is underpopulated. The population of the Twin Cities in 1990 was 2.3 million. In 1970 it was 1.9 million. Growth over those twenty years took place at a slow walk of 1 percent per annum. Growth for the next twenty years is forecast by the Metropolitan Council at the identical 1 percent rate. "It's not going to grow like the Sunbelt has grown," said a Minneapolis retail developer who is not involved with Mall of America except as an unhappy prospective competitor.

One must sympathize with the promoters, Sterne goes on. "If I were sitting there with 1985 or 1986 data and extrapolating it out into the future, maybe it would have made sense. Or, at least financially, it might have looked like a viable idea." But the 1980s have given way to the 1990s. Economists, journalists, and urban planners can and do change their minds. Not so a long-term investor. "It is a viable long-term investment for a pension fund," says our source at TIAA. "This is a pioneer project. . . . And don't forget, this is an equity investment, and it's for the long term. Our commitment was made with the knowledge that it's a long-term investment. I challenge anyone to tell me what the retail environment will be like in the year 2000. We're building for the future, not yesterday."

Fair enough. If, however, the boom was as big and distended as we think it was, its consequences will reverberate longer than people now imagine. Great things may well light up the prairie before the year 2000. For many years before the millennium, however, the retailing years of the mid-1980s will probably seem like a long lost Golden Age.

THE SLOWEST ASSET

April 24, 1992

In Houston, office rents are falling again, fully a decade after the Texas energy business stopped inflating and began deflating. Rents continue to fall in New York, too, and Citibank is reportedly trying to sell the mortgage it holds on 40 Wall Street at a distress price. The amount that Citi is owed on the seventy-story building, once a holding of the late, great Ferdinand Marcos, is $80 million. The amount that it is willing to accept in payment, according to *Crain's New York Business*, is $20 million, or $20 a square foot. A source of ours relates that the offered side of the market is, in fact, lower: a spokeswoman for Citicorp declines to provide a number. If the cost of refurbishing the building to attract an institutional clientele is anything like $100 million (as *Crain's* reports), the building's true economic value might well be less than zero. It would certainly be low enough to rattle the downtown real estate community.

The lobby of the Equitable Building. If only beauty could be capitalized.

Real estate is an admittedly slow and illiquid asset, but it isn't in every postwar cycle that tall buildings collapse on the heads of the billionaires who own them. Recently, David Shulman of Salomon Brothers predicted that the slump in commercial real estate may last, in some regions, until the end of the decade and that it will be twelve years before the national office vacancy rate returns to 5 percent from about 20 percent today. To equity investors who have become accustomed to measuring bear markets in terms of days, weeks, or months, such a thing is almost beyond imagining.

Precedent is on Shulman's side, however, and the documentary evidence is available at the New York Public Library. One instructive story is that of the Equitable Building, 120 Broadway, a still-magnificent Wall Street skyscraper built in 1914–15. We've been reading up on the Equitable's past to try to reach a clearer understanding of the future. What we want to know is whether the real-estate-related credit cycle is over or ending, or, as Shulman and others suggest, still unfolding. The answer to that question is easy: It is still unfolding. H. Dale Hemmerdinger, a reader and New York City property owner, contends that years of misery lie ahead as long-term leases are replaced by new, lower-cost leases. "Costs are front-end loaded," Hemmerdinger says. "Even if the market turns tomorrow (which it won't), it will take me a long time to get rid of my free rent, of my $30 to $50 work letters, and I've got to get my rents up. In the meantime, my costs are still going up. . . . What Olympia & York is looking for is a short-term solution. I don't know how that works."

The period selected for this investigation was the last glacial, deflationary bear market in New York City real estate, that of the 1930s. We skipped the 1970s bear market because it was an inflationary downturn, one that featured rising commodity prices and expanding bank credit. In the Depression era, occupancy rates and interest rates fell, and chastened lenders hung back from committing new funds. It has been a little like that in the 1990s, too. What is most interesting about the Equitable story, however, is what happened in the long succession of disinflationary years between the alleged return of prosperity in 1933 and the United States entry into World War II in 1941. The company stumped through the Depression only to seek bankruptcy protection at a time of relative prosperity. For those who like to use the stock market as a leading indicator of business activity, the failure occurred some nine years after the Dow Jones Industrial Average made its all-time low.

We are relating this story because it helps to convey a sense of the rhythm of a deflationary liquidation. It is slow motion, like a family reunion. If past is prologue, lessons from the 1930s may also apply to the 1990s (with certain modifications, of course, allowing for the mature welfare state, the full paper monetary standard, and the possibility that the federal government may yet engineer a new inflation). For instance, construction activity will not make the hoped-for contribution to the next business expansion, real estate losses will continue to weigh on banks and life insurance companies, and the patience of newspaper readers will be sorely tested. Like the man who came to dinner, Paul Reichmann might move onto the pages of *The Wall Street Journal* indefinitely. He and his lenders and their lawyers may carp and cavil and negotiate into the next millennium (but—to strike a bullish note—not into the one after that).

The best reason to study the Equitable Building is that the Equitable Office Building Corp. was once an investor-owned company, and its financial history is available in *Moody's Banks & Fi-*

nance. The original Equitable Building burned to the ground in 1912 on the same Broadway site, and Coleman DuPont came up from Delaware to organize a corporation to put up a bigger and better successor building. No visitor to 120 Broadway is likely to quibble with management's appraisal (c. 1915) that the building, originally housing 1.2 million square feet, is "among the great business structures of this hemisphere." It was so great, in fact—forty stories rising straight up from the building line without a single setback—that the shadows it cast on lower Manhattan galvanized a political movement to restrict the construction of anything so overpowering in the future. The Equitable Life Assurance Society of the United States gave DuPont a long-term, $20.5 million mortgage, one of the largest ever written up until that time. The interest rate was 4½ percent.

It is impossible to appreciate the Equitable story without a proper respect for the building's gleaming place in the Wall Street skyline. "Emphatically and unequivocally," said the original sales brochure, perhaps reflecting market conditions as well as management's sense of decency, "we will not make to one tenant, regardless of his size or his importance or his desirability, any concession which is denied to others." The capitalization of the Equitable Office Building Corp. was conservative, and the tenants were grade A. The fact that 4½ percent eventually became an unmanageable rate of interest is a useful lesson in the relativity of nominal yields and the changeableness of rents. What seems low may later appear high, even oppressive; and, of course, vice versa.

The moral of the Equitable story is that a decline and fall takes time. In the roiled credit markets of 1930 and 1931, the Equitable Office Building Corp. 5s of 1952 were still quoted in the low 90s and mid 80s. In the nightmare year of 1931—marked not only by a global liquidity crisis but also by a rash of real estate foreclosures by New York savings banks and life insurance companies—the company showed a profit and comfortably covered its fixed charges; rental income was almost $6 million, or $5 a rentable square foot. After expenses, depreciation, and taxes, net earnings totaled $2.4 million. Cash on hand totaled $1.5 million. Altogether it must have seemed to the Equitable's creditors as if the Depression were happening to somebody else.

In 1932, rental income dropped by less than 5 percent, earnings per share by a little more than 10 percent. The common dividend was cut to $2.50 a share from the old $3 rate, but at least there was a dividend. So far, so good.

If the phrase "world coming to an end" has ever pertained to the resilient American economy, it was descriptive in 1933. Rental incomes plummeted, and 25 percent of the mortgage investments of the major U.S. life insurance companies wound up in default. In that harrowing year, the Equitable Office Building Corp. was able to earn $1.4 million, or $1.54 a share, a testament to the quality of the tenancy and the long terms of the leases.

Inevitably, of course, leases came up for renewal. Some tenants did renew (others moved out, and still others went bankrupt), and the new leases were signed at low, Depression-era rates. In 1933, rentals fell to an average of $4.16 a square foot. In 1934 they averaged $3.66 a square foot. Operating expenses and real estate taxes happened to drop in 1934, but the capital expenditure program went on. Hoping to save on energy costs—the price of oil had vaulted by 71 percent in the first year of the Roosevelt recovery—management converted the building's oil-fired steam generating plant to anthracite coal power. Earnings in 1934 just topped the $1 million mark, or $1.25 a share, representing less than half of the 1931 rate. In the summer of 1934, the common dividend was omitted. It was reinstated at a lower rate in 1936: a false harbinger of recovery, it turned out.

The worst of the Depression was over, but rental income continued to fall as high-cost 1920s leases were annually converted into low-cost 1930s leases. (For 1920s and 1930s, of course, read 1980s and 1990s, respectively.) By 1936 the building's rental income amounted to just $2.68 a square foot, down by 46 percent from the levels prevailing in 1930. The Equitable Building's vacancy rate in the mid 1930s hovered around 15 percent. For perspective, the 1992 vacancy rate stands at 15.8 percent. Counting space available for sublease, it would amount to 20.5 percent. (We leave it to the real estate scholars to determine the underlying cause of the decline of rents in lower Manhattan in the 1930s. Was it the still-weak national economy or overbuilding in the boom? Our bet is on the first hypothesis. In the 1920s, no self-respecting New York bank made real estate loans.)

Periodically, but without great success, management petitioned the city for tax relief. The corporation paid $807,533 in real estate taxes in 1935. It paid $788,800 in 1937 but $846,800 in 1939. War broke out in Europe in September 1939, and America became a haven for frightened money. It might have seemed to the average Wall Street investment strategist that a rally in rental income was imminent. But the building realized only $2.41 a square foot, on average, in 1939 and reported a net loss of $14,685, or two cents a share, its first annual deficit of the decade. It just barely covered fixed charges.

The company fell short in 1940 and again in 1941; management gave up the ghost eight months before Pearl Harbor. "The [bankruptcy] petition said that, although the company would not be able to meet its current obligations as they fall due, it has an income and assets sufficient to make possible an equitable reorganization," Moody's reported.

The same slow, dreamlike pace of activity continued during the reorganization proceedings—another cautionary precedent for today's lenders. Committees were formed, plans submitted, and meetings held. Paul J. Isaac, the reader who inspired this piece, tells a story about one such proceeding. He says that he got the anecdote from his father. An arbitrageur named Lou Green, of the firm of Stryker & Brown, was questioned by an SEC examiner, Isaac relates. Asked what class of security holder he represented, Green did not reply "the debenture holders," "the senior mortgage holder," or "the preferred." What he said was, "the short interest in the common."

Wartime prosperity notwithstanding, the vacancy rate in early 1942 was almost 14 percent. On July 10, 1942, Federal Judge J. C. Knox approved the purchase of a $16 million war and bombardment insurance policy for $16,000 a year. Rents and margins were down: The net loss grew.

As for the Equitable reorganization proceeding, it was conducted without undue haste. Competing plans of reorganization were submitted, and at least once the U.S. Circuit Court of Appeals reversed Judge Knox. By the time the final plan was confirmed, in October 1948, fees and allowances to the trustees and attorneys had piled up to $792,521. In November 1947, the building got a new, twenty-five year mortgage from the John Hancock Mutual Life Insurance Co. In place of the overbearing 4½ percent interest rate was a reasonable 3.7 percent interest rate (which would later increase to 3¾ percent). The downward adjustment was just in time for the start of the long postwar rise in interest rates and also, of course, in rental rates. Still, the rent roll in December 1948 returned only to an average of $3.47 a square foot, lower than the average for 1934.

Scrolling ahead a half century, to 1992, the Equitable Building is owned and managed by Silverstein Properties. A fund managed by J. P. Morgan Investment Management holds a participating mortgage on the property (entitling the creditors to a share of the cash flow). The lobby is still splendid, and the rentable area of the building is now put at 1.9 million square feet, an increase of 58 percent since the 1930s. According to a broker, the reasons for this miraculous growth relate, first, to the expandable definition of a square foot under New York law and, second, to the general tendency of potato chip bags to hold fewer chips every year. He implied that space inflation was in the air. As noted, the vacancy rate, not counting available sublease space, is 15 percent. One big tenant nowadays is the office of the New York State Attorney General; another is the law firm of Lester Schwab, Katz & Dwyer. The defunct Crossland Savings Bank occupies ground-floor space. Brokers say that deals can be struck at an effective rent of less than $22 a square foot over a ten-year lease for a 10,000-square-foot space. The number includes a work letter to finance construction and a certain amount of free rent. Neither Morgan nor Silverstein would comment on the economics of the building, but the numbers can only be bleak and—in view of the weakness of rents and the long-term nature of big-city leases—getting bleaker.

At a meeting of the New York Real Estate Board the other day, Larry A. Silverstein, head of Silverstein Properties, explained the real estate profit-and-loss dilemma, and the April 15 *Real Estate Weekly* gave this account:

> Silverstein said the real problem is that commercial rents are so low—the deals are not economically viable for the owners. He said operating expenses amount to $7 and $8 per square foot, real estate taxes are running from $7 to $11 per square foot, tenant work letters are at $5 per square foot, and $1 is going for leasing expenses. This adds up to $21 per square foot before debt service, he said.

Postwar building debt service averages $25 per square foot, so Silverstein said owners need to see $46 per square foot just to break even. "In a $30 market," he said, "it's hard to see a profit and impossible not to incur a loss." In fact, he added, "There is no profit, and the question is the magnitude of the loss."

In other words, losses loom indefinitely. If $21 per square foot is the average operating cost of a building before interest expense, it's a cinch that the owner of the Equitable Building is showing no profit after paying its lenders. "Quality projects in the end will become profitable," a vice president of Olympia & York Properties (Oregon) assured the Portland *Business Journal* recently. "It's just a matter of time." Based on the history of the Equitable Building, we would amend that claim. In a deflation, even quality projects will become unprofitable. It's just a matter of time.*

TRUMP FOR THE BID

February 2, 1990

A coincidence in the latest *Playboy:* Donald J. Trump, the subject of the *Playboy* interview, and Miss March, Deborah Driggs, share the same basic philosophy of life. Says Miss March ("from sunny Southern California"): "I'm daring. I'm outgoing, edgy—an explorer. There's not a lot I haven't done, but if you have any ideas, try me." Says Trump: "As long as I enjoy what I'm doing without getting bored or tired . . . the sky's the limit."

So, then, go for it! But Trump's remarks contain an undercurrent of caution. Do you regret having gloated about missing the 1987 stock market panic? *Playboy* asks. Trump replies, "No," but adds,

* Silverstein lost the building to his creditors in November 1992.

Trump Princess -282 feet
(leveraged)

Tugboat -110 feet
(unleveraged)

Taj Mahal (leveraged)

Taj Mahal (unleveraged)

surprisingly: "I think the cash market is the great one right now —cash is king, and that's one of the beauties of the casino business."

Cash is king? In the principality of real estate, debt has always ruled. True to real estate custom, Trump says he prefers to use other people's money, and the division of his risk and his lenders' is rarely disclosed. Boston Co., for instance, according to a report in *The Boston Herald*, "was involved" in the 1988 purchase of his famous yacht, the *Trump Princess*. No innocent, Trump tells *Playboy*, "My attitude is to focus on the downside because the upside will always take care of itself." Also, he intimates that he is holding reserves for some future downturn. He says that he will build his long-delayed, often-criticized Trump City, a new Rockefeller Center–type undertaking on the upper West Side, when New York hits a rough patch, and not before—"because every city in every nation has its ups and downs."

The *Playboy* Trump is thus a calculating operator with a sense of the impermanence of things. He may read his own press, but he doesn't necessarily believe it. Another exchange:

> *Playboy*: Then what does all this—the yacht, the bronze tower, the casinos—really mean to you?
> **Trump**: Props for the show.
> *Playboy*: And what is the show?
> **Trump**: The show is "Trump" and it is sold-out performances everywhere. I've had fun doing it and will continue to have fun, and I think most people enjoy it.

This is the sequel to a piece of more than two years ago. In "Sell Donald Trump," we ventured that the builder was making a major personal top. The owner of the Trump Shuttle, the Plaza Hotel (for which he paid the equivalent of $483,000 a room), and the author of *Trump: The Art of the Deal* was then worth $850 million, according to *Forbes*. Trump's net worth today, also according to *Forbes*, is $1.7 billion. Trump himself has derided that number as low and suggested that Malcolm Forbes, whose own yacht, comparatively, is a rubber ducky, is jealous of him. In response to a question from *Fortune*, Trump recently produced a letter from Arthur Andersen & Co. warranting that his cash and marketable securities totaled $700 million at the end of 1988. Trump stated that nothing much has changed in the intervening twelve months. To *Time*, which asked about his net worth, Trump replied, disarmingly: "Who the f—— knows? I mean, really, who knows how much the Japs will pay for Manhattan property these days?"

The answer to that rhetorical question would seem to be: They will pay less than they used to pay. Credit has begun to contract around the world. In New York City, the locus of Trump's operations, big banks are pulling back from real estate lending. Interest rates are rising (here and abroad), and bids, in general, are falling. Risk rates of interest are rising faster than government rates. Two years ago, Trump's Atlantic City mortgage bonds were quoted in the neighborhood of 13 percent to 14 percent. On Tuesday, the Taj Mahal 14s were quoted at 76 bid, to yield almost 20 percent.

The Trump's Castle 13¾s fetched 87, to yield almost 16 percent. Either Trump has become less secure or his creditors are imagining things.*

Let's say that his public creditors are not imagining anything. Something has changed, plainly. In last Friday's *New York Times*, Rita Reif disclosed that a presumptive Japanese moneybags had failed to pay for a pair of paintings for which he bid astounding, record prices. The solution to this embarrassment was that Shigeki Kameyama, the fellow without the money, "consigned a number of pictures, more than ten of which are valued at more than $1 million each. All are to be auctioned in Sotheby's art sales in April in London and in May in New York." It develops, therefore, that the art market is two-tiered. There is a big tier and a settlement tier. Owing to a lack of liquidity, the settlement price is sometimes lower than the bid. Because the art market is emblematic of the 1980s in general, and of new wealth in particular, the Kameyama revelation gives pause. It recalls Trump's own aborted $120-a-share bid for AMR last fall. It is hard to pay record prices in a credit contraction, even if you want to, which Trump allegedly did, briefly. ("Donald wants to own the airline," Jack H. Nusbaum, one of his lawyers, said on the eve of the October 1989 collapse. "He's a pretty determined guy when he wants something done.")

We approached the Trump problem mainly by deduction, starting with a set of syllogisms: All real estate operators are leveraged. Trump is a real estate operator. Therefore, Trump is leveraged.

Then: Trump is leveraged. Leverage magnifies volatility. Therefore, Trump's affairs are volatile.

Finally: Trump's affairs are volatile. In a contraction, the direction of volatile change is down. Therefore, Trump's affairs are likely to worsen.

Just as a credit expansion lifted Trump's net worth, so should a contraction reduce it, sharply. In New York City, residential real estate is making heavy weather of it, and even the Hero of Wollman Rink may not emerge unscathed. The new issue of *Crain's New York Business* contains a skeptical piece about the Plaza (to which Trump did not affix his name). The article pays tribute to the lavish

---

* They weren't: Trump defaulted on both the Taj Mahal 14s and the Trump's Castle Funding 13¾s. In the course of separate bankruptcy proceedings, bondholders received new securities with lower coupons and longer maturities as well as 50 percent equity interests in the respective issuing companies.

care with which the old landmark was restored—"Suites house such trappings as a nineteenth-century, $40,000 Biedermeier chest and Italian silk tablecloths. All rooms now have Frette linens." And on and on. Everything is just right, that is, except for the income statement. The piece speculates that no profit will be turned unless and until the average room rate is bumped to $350 a night, up about $100 from last year's average. In a bear market?

According to the Trump Organization, Trump Tower, Trump Parc, and Trump Palace are under the ownership of Donald Trump. (There is some confusion as to whether Trump Plaza is also owned by Trump. One spokesperson insisted that it is, but others—a clear majority—told *Grant's* that it isn't.) At Trump Parc, 106 Central Park South, fewer than 10 percent of the windows are lit of an evening. Perhaps, as the Trump Organization contends, most of the apartments have been sold to foreigners, and the foreigners are in Tokyo or Paris or Ho Chi Minh City. "The building is almost fully sold," says Toni Redford, a Trump Parc sales representative, "so as far as we're concerned, we don't know why it's dark." It's a mystery.

Trump, undaunted, is building the upper East Side's tallest apartment building at Third Avenue and Sixty-ninth Street. This may well be, as the promotional literature promises, "a palace for the twenty-first century," but the cost of carry until the millennium could become burdensome. (Suggestion: Eliminate electrical connections in apartments designated for sale to absentee foreigners.) Completion is slated for spring 1991, and offering prices range from $350,000 for a studio apartment to $6 million for the fifty-fifth-floor grand penthouse. (Storage rooms start at $21,200.) The sales material has bull market heft and gloss, and the prose has an almost antebellum flavor: "As with every palace, your Trump Palace home has its loyal retinue of attendants who, each day, ease the round of your chores and smooth the way of life for you. The concierge staff, the doormen, the hallmen, even the availability of daily maid and housekeeping services and a twenty-four-hour attended garage are all part of the acclaimed Trump lifestyle."

An integral part of the Trump lifestyle is income, and a bear market may deplete even the prospective Trump resident's. So when word got out that Trump's ultrafabulous, world-wowing motor yacht, the 282-foot *Trump Princess*, was up for sale, we thought

"It's only money? It's only money?
What the hell do you mean,
it's only money?"

we smelled a liquidation. *USA Today* gave the story the bull market gee-whiz treatment: "Real estate super magnate Donald Trump finds his 282-foot motor yacht somewhat limiting. He's trading up to a $200 million, 420-foot flagship that will feature a Roman bath, an amphitheater, and a crew of forty-six. . . . The old yacht is cruising the South Pacific in search of a buyer. Price tag: $115 million. Trump bought it for what he called 'a song'—$30 million—from the Sultan of Brunei in 1987, then spent $10 million refitting it." The craft's original owner was the formerly rich, formerly unindicted Saudi arms dealer, Adnan Khashoggi.

There are price tags and then there are checks. As the illiquid Kameyama could attest, it is easier to ask a price than to get one. On the evidence to date, the most sought-after craft of the early 1990s will be lifeboats, not yachts. For us, we will believe the $115 million when we see it.

In his 1987 autobiographical masterwork, *The Art of the Deal*, Trump wrote, "I've never been tempted to take any of my companies public. Making choices is a lot easier when you have to answer only to yourself." In a December 1989 interview with *Fortune*, however, he said (to quote *Fortune* paraphrasing him) "he might think about taking part of his empire public to raise cash."

One of the beauties of the casino business, Trump told *Playboy*, is that it produces cash. To judge by the action in his publicly traded bonds, however, Trump's Atlantic City gambling emporia are not producing it fast enough. On the evidence of the junk market, of course, every creditor of every public debt issuer is sweating nowadays. Nevertheless, Trump has fallen under suspicion for special reasons. First is his exposure to real estate in general. The second is his exposure to Atlantic City in particular. In December, a month of arctic cold, gross revenues in Atlantic City fell by 7 percent from December 1988; for the full twelve months, eleven casinos registered a gain of just 2.6 percent. In a new report, Salomon Brothers has questioned the security of the mortgage debt of Trump's Castle Funding Inc. (which is the bond-issuing entity of the casino of Trump Castle, the old Atlantic City Hilton). For one thing, said the report, coverages are falling. As against 1.32 times interest expense in 1988, earnings before interest, taxes, depreciation, and amortization will suffice to cover the interest bill by just 1.17 times in 1990. For another thing, the casino this year must begin to set aside large sums of cash to satisfy the first of an annual series of sinking-fund payments. Probably, Salomon notes, the Trump partnership will draw down $24 million in an available credit line. Even so, the report projected a 1990 cash deficit of more than $13 million. It cited, last but not least, the competitive menace of the Trump Taj Mahal, slated to open April 2. Trump may eat his own lunch. ("Anyone who bought the [Trump's Castle] bonds is earning an exceptionally good return, and the bonds are now selling at a premium."—*Art of the Deal*, page 162.)

The Atlantic City Taj is three times bigger than the Indian original. It will have more employees (sixty-five hundred), more slots (three thousand), and—we are guessing—more junk bond debt than the one in Agra. By itself it will expand Atlantic City's gaming and cavorting capacity by 20 percent. But it may not stimulate a proportionate increase in the clientele, high rolling or low.

Speaking of high rollers, the Treasury Department in 1988 proposed to tighten the cash-reporting requirements of casinos under the Bank Secrecy Act. If enacted, the new rule would tend to burden the casinos with reporting requirements and to inhibit their free-spending customers. A decision is expected shortly.

Including interruptions, the project has been under way for eight years. Finished, it will encompass 4 million square feet on 17.3 acres and accommodate fifty thousand visitors, who, Trump expects, will lose (or otherwise deposit on the premises) at least $1 million a day. Although lacking the fake volcano and live sharks of Golden Nugget's Mirage, the Taj will boast nine seven-foot-tall elephants in sculpture. "The ersatz-Indian architecture has $20 million worth of ornamentation," *Engineering News Record* recently reported. "There are forty brilliantly colored exterior domes up to thirty feet in diameter, plus minarets, pinnacles, and other trimmings with various interior support masts designed by the structural engineer." In a Trumpian touch, more than one hundred chandeliers, each weighing four to five tons, have been added at a cost of $20 million. "As such," *ENR* added, "their required support frames, which hang from the structural steel, had to be engineered to avoid ductwork already installed in the space above the hung ceilings." Without exactly understanding, the layman gains the sense of vanishing money.

Atlantic City is bullish on the Taj—John Britton of this staff polled a number of visitors on site. "Anything with Trump is great," said Larry and Alice Precker, of North Babylon, Long Island, New York, who identified themselves as frequent visitors to resort hotels. "The Castle and Plaza [each a Trump establishment] are fabulous, and the Taj will be A-1." Britton asked them what they particularly liked about Trump's operations. "Everyone is more courteous, and the whole place is nicer. The drinks are also freer."

Extra-free drinks will not surprise the student of Trump. In the *Playboy* interview, for instance, the master offered his philosophy of building design and management—spare no expense, cut no corners on materials, obtain the best location. The best costs money, of course, and Trump has borrowed lots. In November 1988, Trump Taj Mahal funding sold $675 million in 14 percent first mortgage bonds. The 14 percent is payable in cash, not paper, and the security of the third coupon payment, due May 15, was in

The United States in 1992

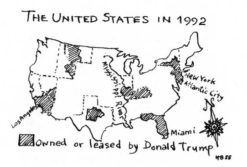

Owned or leased by Donald Trump

doubt on the day the bonds were issued. The element of suspense was introduced by two unknowns. First, would the casino open on time, then defined as February 15 and now as April 2? Second, would business boom from the start? "The Taj Mahal," the document said,

> will be the largest casino/hotel complex in Atlantic City, with approximately twice the room capacity and casino space of many of the existing casino/hotels in Atlantic City. Neither the Partnership [that is, Trump] nor any other casino/hotel operator has had experience operating a complex the size of the Taj Mahal in Atlantic City. Consequently, no assurance can be given that, once opened, the Taj Mahal will be profitable or that it will generate cash flow sufficient to provide for the payment of the debt service on the Note and/or on any future borrowings by the Partnership.
>
> If the Taj Mahal does not generate sufficient cash flow to pay the debt service on the Note or other indebtedness of the Partnership, the Partnership may have to borrow additional monies to provide for such payment. The ability of the Partnership to obtain additional financing will be restricted by the terms of the Indenture.

Thus, the course for a creditor of the Taj Mahal or of Donald Trump is clear. He should round up all available customers and ship them (by bus, if necessary) to the Taj on opening day in April. He should lobby the Treasury Department against any further tightening of cash-reporting rules for casinos (although it appears that on this question the die is already cast). He should call the attention of the fiscal and monetary authorities to the nascent credit

contraction, demanding relief. He should insist on a resumption of
the global bull market in equities (the better to furnish the Plaza
with guests and the Trump Parc with residents who can afford to
pay their electricity bills). He should discreetly arrange for someone
of means to buy the Trump Princess—perhaps a Third World
country in need of a well-appointed minesweeper.*

Trump claims to be a man of the people, and John Britton,
touring Atlantic City, found no evidence to the contrary. "All cab
drivers love him," said Patrick Gilroy, an Atlantic City hack. "He
brings a lot of jobs and class to the city." In that case the significance
of some future cancellation of "Trump," the show, might be more
far-reaching than people imagine. Five full points off the Michigan
survey of consumer confidence is our best guess—Trump, we
think, would insist on nothing less.†

---

* The Boston Co. acquired the yacht in what *Business Week* reported to be a repossession but what Trump
described as a friendly sale. "I was unable to find the time to use it," the busy developer explained.
† Like Brazil, Trump owed enough. In February 1993, *The Wall Street Journal* reported that he had "cut
a deal with his bankers that he hoped will get him out of personal debt within two years and effectively
end bank supervision of his business activities." The Michigan survey of consumer confidence showed
no immediate gains in response to the news.

PART SIX

ADVENTURES IN LEVERAGE

JUNK DEBUNKED

September 24, 1984

Payment of interest on a bond is fixed, and if not paid when due, failure is precipitated. Most corporation directors, no matter how successful the enterprise may be, hesitate to burden it with fixed charges, even if the future gives promise of earnings that exceed the charges many times over. And even in those instances when there seems no reasonable doubt but that the new money obtained from the sale of bonds will be invested so as to earn immediately, through new or improved equipment, more than sufficient to pay the charges, there is no assurance that this increased earning capacity will continue through the life of the bonds.
—Arthur S. Dewing, *The Financial Policy of Corporations.*
Volume IV, 1920

In the bond market this is a day of high hopes and low interest-coverage ratios. It is a day of the near extinction of the triple-A corporate credit and the rise to investment respectability of the sub-Baa credit. It is a time that has nurtured the junk bond movement and has taken to heart the junk bond investment philosophy. As recently as a decade ago, only three "high-yield" corporate bond funds existed; their combined assets were $400 million. At last count there were thirty-two such funds with assets running to $6 billion. In the mid-1970s, it was a rare speculative-grade new issue that was admitted to the public debt market; nowadays, it's a rare triple-A issue that sees the light of day. (In fact, according to Salomon Brothers, no triple-A debt security has been sold this year, while the average monthly volume of Ba-or-lower merchandise is running just below the record pace set last year.) Merrill Lynch, describing the growth of the "high-yield" market, notes that there

now are junk-minded insurance companies (it counts a dozen or
so with a "major" commitment to speculative bonds), junk investment advisers, and junk savings and loan associations. Not
coincidentally, Drexel Burnham Lambert, the principal force in
the junk market, is the fastest-growing investment banking house
in Wall Street.

To junk proponents, of course, all this is as it should be. Better
to own the low-rated debt of an up-and-coming business, they say,
than the investment-grade debt of the next International Harvester.
They invoke Michael Milken, dean of junk at Drexel Burnham,
who says: "Risk is a function of knowledge." In general, they say
that the rating agencies are backward-looking while markets exist
to discount the future ("I'm much more interested in the
future"—Milken). In credit analysis they emphasize the significance of prospective growth in earnings and downplay the importance of historical balance sheet ratios. They observe that the rate
of default on corporate debt is vanishingly low, and they say that
diversification will reduce such risks as may exist in one given
portfolio. They recite the excellent junk investment record. "The
total return to investors in high-yield securities has been very impressive," writes the corporate-bond research unit at Merrill. "An
investment of $100 in high-yield securities made in 1935 would
have grown to $4,056 at the end of 1983, while a $100 investment
in high-grade securities would have grown to $713 in the same
period. Using more recent data, a $100 investment in high-yield
securities in 1965 would have grown to $446.73 by the end of 1983,
while a $100 investment in high-grade securities would have grown
to $271.25."

So apparently airtight is the case for junk, so much of it has been
sold, and so great is the institutional appetite for it that one is
obliged to doff one's hat to the junk pioneers. Standing there hat-
less, however, one also must scratch one's head and ask if this Wall
Street concept will go the way of all fads. The question must
concern everyone in and out of the bond market. For one thing,
the junk phenomenon reflects the chronic weakness in insurance
company operating results; as underwriters lose money in price
wars or through wind damage and asbestos settlements, they are
increasingly obliged to reach for yield in their investment portfolios.
More basically, the rise of speculative bonds is a symptom of the
piling-up of debt and of the long-running deterioration of corporate

finances. In that sense, the gentrification of junk amounts to the making of virtue out of unpleasant necessity.

Grant's is anti-junk.* While conceding the extraordinary record of high-yield bonds, we would observe, to start with, that the present-day world is very long on debt and very short on equity. It is long on debt that may well be repudiated. According to an old investment adage, one should own the thing in short supply and shun the thing in surplus. What an illiquid world needs is cash, what it owns (or owes) in superabundance is debt. In the circumstances, the type of income-producing security to own is probably the one that affords the greatest margin of safety—that is, the one that offers the highest ratio of cash flow to interest expense. By definition, junk bonds of any description are claims on companies without much financial leeway. (Moody's defines Ba, the highest junk grade, this way: "Bonds which are rated Ba are judged to have speculative elements; their future cannot be considered as well assured. Often the protection of interest and principal payments may be very moderate and thereby not well safeguarded during both good and bad times over the future. Uncertainty of position characterizes bonds of this class.") Needless to say, the averages conceal both good and bad, and as far as the BB and B rating categories are concerned, the numbers vary enormously within each class. For instance, in 1982, while the bottom of the pile of the BB sample reported a ratio of cash flow to long-term debt of 15 percent, the best of the class reported a ratio of 36 percent. However, as a general rule, the headroom in speculative issues is short.

We have two more anti-junk declarations. The first is that the holdings of certain speculative bonds are concentrated in a handful of financial institutions and that that fact tends to rob the safety-through-diversification argument of some of its force. The second is that the junk idea has been carried too far. The signs (to us) are clear that a faddish consensus has formed around the person of Mike Milken and around the firm of Drexel Burnham. There is, we think, an unspoken faith that Drexel *is* the market and that it

---

* A moralistic and unprofitable judgment. A better, if less stirring, declaration would have been, "*Grant's* is anti-junk at the prices now prevailing but is keeping an open mind."

won't let anything happen to it. ("We get up at 4 a.m.," a Drexel bond salesman told the *Los Angeles Times* earlier this year, "and we don't go out to lunch, we don't take personal phone calls, we don't tell jokes, don't talk about the ball game. No one in America works as hard as we do.") The truth is that markets are bigger than market makers and that nearly every investment enthusiasm has an unhappy ending.

Junk bonds have recently underperformed. Since the rally began in June, low-rated debt has trailed not only the Treasury market but even an average of nuclear-fired electric utility bonds. (The numbers are striking. On May 31, the Merrill Lynch low-grade index yielded 194 basis points more than the Merrill high-grade index did: on August 31, the difference was 298 basis points.) Paul H. Ross, director of corporate-bond research at Salomon Brothers, puts down the laggardliness to the specific woes of airline and oil-drilling issuers. He says that, as a matter of trading history, junk has tended to bring up the rear of bond market rallies—it lagged governments by five months in 1982. Barring a recession, he adds, spreads between junk and Treasuries should close; however, if there is a slump in the offing, credit-quality concerns will heighten, and junk will suffer.

For ourselves, our hunch is that this time things will be different, that, in some basic way, junk has had its day.

JUNK SUPREME

December 3, 1984

The idea that an issuer of bonds should actually be able to meet its interest and principal payments is a notion so puritanical that sooner or later it was bound to be junked. Now Metromedia Broadcasting Corp., in a pioneering $1.3 billion debt financing, has served notice on prospective investors that it may not be able to pay them their interest. It states in plain English that it may not be able to redeem their principal. Notwithstanding such stunningly clear notification, investors last week lined up (mostly with other people's money) to buy.

Metromedia Inc., parent of the issuing concern, is no stranger to debt. It's the company that went private last June in what was ranked then, and what still remains, as the biggest leveraged buyout transaction ever. It's the company that in 1982 structured a private placement for the purpose of selling its outdoor advertising business. This was the esoteric tax deal that, at least by the lights of Abraham Briloff, the accounting critic, writing in *Barron's* at the time, was too clever by half. Bear, Stearns & Co., its broker in both the billboard and the going-private affairs, is co-manager of the new bond offering. It almost goes without saying that Drexel Burnham Lambert, the R.H. Macy of junk, is Bear's underwriting partner.

The issuing company, Metromedia Broadcasting Corp., was specifically created by the parent, Metromedia Inc., in order to sell bonds. As the prospectus notes, the birthing entailed a change of ownership of the Metromedia broadcast properties: "Metromedia Broadcasting Corp. is a newly organized, wholly owned subsidiary of Metromedia Inc., formed by Metromedia to conduct substantially all of its broadcasting operations. The Company's [that is, the subsidiary's] business will consist of the ownership and operation of seven television stations and nine radio stations."

Grand design of the offering is for the investing public to relieve the banks that financed the leveraged buyout. The new issue consists of $300 million worth of "serial zero-coupon senior notes," $550 million worth of "senior exchangeable variable-rate debentures," $200 million worth of "adjustable-rate participating subordinated debentures," and $200 million worth of "senior subordinated debentures"—in all, $1.25 billion worth. The parent's going-private bank debt amounts to approximately $1.2 billion.

As the parent must pay the banks, the sub won't keep the proceeds of the offering for long. Again, to quote from the prospectus: "All but $50 million of the aggregate net proceeds will be dividended or advanced to Metromedia. Metromedia will use the funds received by it to repay senior bank indebtedness. . . ." Thus, assuredly, the banks will get paid. Can the bondholders hope for as much?"*

The answer reads very much like "No":

> Required payment of interest on the Debt Securities (other than the Serial Senior Notes) will consume a substantial portion or all of the anticipated cash flow of the Company. Based on current levels of operations, the Company's cash flow would be insufficient to make interest payment on the Debt Securities (other than the Serial Senior Notes), and it would have to use other funds, to the extent available, to make such interest payments.

Any extravagant hopes of the holders of Serial Senior Notes, however, are promptly deflated in the next paragraph:

> In addition, based on current levels of operations and anticipated growth, the Company does not expect to be able to generate sufficient cash flow to make all of the principal payments due on the Serial Senior Notes without taking action to refinance a portion of its indebtedness. No assurance can be given that such a refinancing can be successfully accomplished.

Perhaps the buyers of the companion Metromedia Broadcasting exotica (that is, of the participating subordinated debentures, which, if the broadcast companies make enough money, may yield a return above and beyond the coupon rate) know something or have reason to hope for something. For that matter, perhaps cash flow will more than satisfy the needs of the holders of the straight debt. However, the pro forma results have not been encouraging.

The other day the postman walked into this office, paused after dropping off the mail, and announced that he'd just plunked down $325 for a real estate seminar. He said that he was buying real estate books for $16 and $18 a crack. He said that he was trying to learn how to get rich by buying property with no money down. Surely there's a place for this visionary man in the burgeoning world of high-yield debt.

---

* They were paid, although not so well as the acquisitive John Kluge was able to pay himself.

PEOPLE EXPRESS

May 5, 1986

In the airline industry, debt flies first class, business class, coach, or standby, depending on the carrier. A surprise standby entrant: the 17½ percent secured equipment trust certificates of Eastern Airlines, which changed hands 10 points above par the other day, despite a huge first-quarter loss. This is the same Eastern that was flirting with bankruptcy last year and that (if all goes according to plan) will be merged with Texas Air this year.

And now People Express, the ninth-largest U.S. carrier, is offering $115 million worth of ten-year secured equipment trust certificates to yield 14⅜ percent.* People has, in fact, already sold them—Morgan Stanley and Hambrecht & Quist shared the underwriting honors late last month. The proceeds of the sale will go mainly to redeem bank debt. As the cost of the bank debt to the airline was 11.8 percent and the cost of the note issue will be 14⅜ percent, we asked People what the idea was.

The answer was that the bank debt contained "certain restrictive covenants." What covenants? Covenants to limit debt as a percentage of net worth. Oh.

In any case, a pertinent fact: The People notes are secured, not unsecured, obligations. The collateral that supports them is a fleet of fourteen Boeing 737–100s and seven Boeing 727–200s, the value of which has been estimated to be $146 million. That is $31 million more than the par value of the notes. None of these planes is exactly a spring chicken—the average age of the 737s, for instance, is eighteen years—but the useful lives of the aircraft are supposed to exceed the ten-year life of the notes.

* Now in default.

A second and equally pertinent fact: The People notes are secured by collateral that, in bankruptcy, may not be available for the protection of the noteholders. The prospectus is frank about this possibility:

> Because of the . . . broad discretionary powers of a bankruptcy court, it is impossible to predict how long payments under the Equipment Certificates could be delayed following commencement of a bankruptcy proceeding, whether or when the Trustee could repossess or dispose of the Aircraft or whether or to what extent holders of the Equipment Certificates could be compensated for any delay in payment or loss of value of the Aircraft through the requirement of "adequate protection."

We asked around about this last week and came up with a number of opinions, some reassuring, others not. John Mattis, an airline analyst with Morgan Stanley & Co., is one of the skeptics. He contends that the People noteholders are ineligible for protection under Section 1110 of the Bankruptcy Code. To understand the significance of this chink in the credit armor, consider what protection the Eastern noteholders (for instance) do enjoy. To quote Mattis:

> If Eastern were to file a Chapter 11 petition and continue operations, certificate holders would continue to receive scheduled payments. If the certificate trustees chose to seize the aircraft, the planes could be sold or released early in the bankruptcy proceedings. This is a distinct advantage over other secured and unsecured debt, [for example, the brand-new secured equipment certificates of People Express] which would be tied up in the bankruptcy court.

Thus, to simplify only slightly, the People notes are wholly secured as long as the company is solvent, but questionably secured if it ever went broke. The premier credit consideration, therefore, is not so much the collateral as the company. What goes on at People Express?

The company showed a loss of $20 million in 1985. It expects to report a $30 million to $35 million loss in the first quarter of 1986, almost double the loss in the year-earlier period. It is leveraged to the tune of 2.5 to 1, and it is in the process of digesting the recent acquisitions of Frontier Airlines and Britt Airways (a Midwest commuter line that itself is about to sell public debt). And in a major strategy shift, it has just decided to seek out business travelers.

Mattis of Morgan Stanley forecasts an improvement in People's creditworthiness. He expects that, although 1986 will show no better than break-even results, 1987 will yield a profit. Standard & Poor's hasn't rated People's debt, but the S&P analyst we spoke to, T. S. Hyland, had his doubts about the company. Speaking of the Frontier and Britt Airways acquisitions, he said, "I don't know how all that's going to cut and meld together given a free-wheeling management style where the chief financial officer can't attend a meeting because he's up there at thirty-seven thousand feet, serving coffee."

Here is what we would like to know: How can a company afford to pay 14⅜ percent for capital when it very probably cannot earn 14⅜ percent on that capital?* That is our universal junk question, and it would seem to apply as well to People as to anybody else.

THE ANNOTATED HARCOURT

October 5, 1987

Harcourt Brace Jovanovich is out with a 132-page paperback titled *Prospectus*. It is written in the fiduciary style and distributed by The First Boston Corp. It gives chapter and verse on a $1 billion offering of junk-grade subordinated debentures,† which came to

---

* People Express, at least, could not afford it. Nor could Texas Air, which bought People later in 1986. Continental Airlines, the successor to Texas Air, filed for bankruptcy protection in 1990.
† The senior subordinated 13¼s of 1999, the subordinated discount 14¼ of 2002, and the subordinated pay-in-kind 14¼s of 2002.

market two weeks ago. Critical judgment, as expressed in the bid side of the bond market, is lukewarm.

HBJ, the Orlando-based textbook publisher, amusement park operator, and insurance company, could use a best-seller. Generally, it is in need of low interest rates, prosperity, and good luck. It specifically requires visitors to Sea World, strong demand for its elementary and high school textbooks, and the continued inclination of investors to focus on the sunny side of leverage.

You'll recall that Robert Maxwell, the imperial British publisher, made a pass at Harcourt last spring. Fending him off, William Jovanovich, who is the "J" in HBJ, led a leveraged management recapitalization, which resulted in stock repurchases, a one-time dividend to the public holders, and massive borrowings. (Fees paid to lawyers, investment bankers, and accountants in connection with the recapitalization amounted to $67,256,000, a sum of money greater than net profits earned in the twelve months ended June 30, 1986.) All at once the HBJ balance sheet was transformed from conventional to surreal. Management, as if it had just discovered the idea, pledged unstinting attention to cost control and the bottom line. At least the prospectus reflects the zeal of the newly converted (management and the company's ESOP acquired 25 percent of the common):

> The Company intends to reduce corporate overhead and generate cash by disposing of certain non-revenue-producing assets, including the sale of the Company's airplanes, sale of apartments, houses, and condominiums used by transient or newly hired employees, elimination of Company-owned or leased cars (except those needed in sales), and the sale of certain undeveloped land.
>
> Other measures to reduce costs are under way, including the reduction of staff by 5 percent to 10 percent (partly through attrition) over the next twelve months; the cancellation of philanthropic contributions at least until the end of 1988; and the postponement of wage and salary increases where possible and practicable.

A reader of *Grant's*, who happened to be present at a Harcourt Brace/First Boston road show, stuck up his hand when talk turned to the sale of corporate planes. "If you need them, why are you selling them," he asked, "and if you don't need them, why did you buy them?" Management replied with a rhetorical wink, saying it is committed to both the symbol and substance of cost control. Whereupon our reader wondered (this time to himself) what the management was doing with the public shareholder's money before Robert Maxwell knocked on the door. If all the redundant condominiums, charitable donations, cars, aircraft, and employees were "non-revenue-producing," and therefore wasteful, he wondered, what were the directors of the company thinking about when they authorized their acquisition? Wondering those things, one is gratified to read that the company is embroiled in litigation with stockholders over the equity of the transaction, but that is the subject for an angry editorial.

Harcourt is a new-era showcase. Its capitalization comprises long-term debt of $2.8 billion and stockholders' equity, as reported, of *negative* $1.6 billion (and market-value equity of about $500 million). The equity account was depleted by the recapitalization scheme. The current ratio, on June 30, was a nearly invisible 0.26 to 1. Moreover, $1 billion or so of bank debt carries a floating interest rate. It is hoped that most of that debt will be repaid with the proceeds of asset sales. However, for the time being, as the prospectus notes, "The Company will be significantly more sensitive to prevailing interest rates than in the past." Also in keeping with the new age, Harcourt was the recipient of a $1 billion bridge loan from the merchant-banking arm of a brokerage firm. "So," said First Boston, the firm in question, in a full-page ad the other day, "we loaned them the money. Immediately." Immediately. Of course. (Salomon Brothers, another brokerage house, has defended the Harcourt balance sheet, contending, in effect, that it is no uglier than the average recapitalized company's.)

As a kind of new-era composite, Harcourt ought to interest students and speculators alike. We know both bulls and bears on the situation. The substantive bull case (which we got from an analyst who is not selling anything) is approximately this: Under Jovanovich, HBJ was run for prestige and growth. Now, stripped, it is run for cash flow. With the 1986 acquisition of CBS Publishing, HBJ stacks up as the number one elementary and high school publisher and the number two college publisher. Educational publishing is a solid, all-weather business, and book publishing, nowadays, is a hot business. The CBS amalgamation creates the opportunity for higher publishing margins and lower costs. The recreational park business is lucrative as long as the public has money to spend. Assets must be sold, of course, and the prospectus lists five expendable divisions, including trade magazines and the History Book Club. Real estate is being sold. If all goes according to bullish script, the sales will succeed, operating margins will expand, costs will be cut, and leverage will magnify the bottom line.

Probably the best bullish play, our friend advises, is the 12 percent payment-in-kind preferred. The stock pays dividends in additional stock for the first six years, and then must pay in cash. "Once HBJ becomes profitable," Salomon Brothers has opined, "which we expect to be sooner rather than later, the equivalent pretax cost of the preferred is effectively 18 percent, assuming a 33 percent marginal tax rate. This is HBJ's most expensive financing." Redemption of the stock by a profitable HBJ is therefore a good bet. If the stock, now 10, were called at the 13½ redemption price in, say, three years' time, one's all-in return would amount to 23 percent. If one had to wait six years, our bullish friend notes, the total return would shrink to something like 16 percent, which is better than T-bills.

We have read no bearish commentary on HBJ but have heard (and egged on) a couple of negative oral presentations. To start with, the bears say, the balance sheet is intrinsically absurd. Capitalization, at market values, is in excess of $3 billion, compared with pro forma annual sales of $1.2 billion. Could the company, precariously capitalized even at current levels of interest rates, survive a bout of higher rates? Or a recession? Sea World would not be insensitive to a drop in disposable incomes. Will the bonds pay? If they do, is a speculator not better off in the common stock or preferred? Broadly, can the assets be sold quickly enough, and advantageously enough, to keep the creditors at bay? Can the cash flow cover fixed charges? A doubter we know points out that HBJ's publishing and parks businesses are made or broken in the third quarter. "You have a window," he said. "We'll all see pretty soon how it's working." Through June, and after charging to income almost $100 million in recapitalization expenses, Harcourt suffered a net loss of $70.8 million, or $1.70 a share, against net income of $10.9 million, or 31 cents a share, the year before. Revenues, bolstered by the CBS acquisition and by good park results, were up by 31 percent, to $409 million.

Anyway, Harcourt is taking a chance, and the more we thought about the odds, the more we thought about a financial textbook that HBJ didn't have the good luck to publish. *Security Analysis: Principles and Techniques* by Benjamin Graham and David L. Dodd was a McGraw-Hill title, and it first appeared in 1934. It has been through four editions, will soon have a fifth, and has sold a grand total of 750,000 copies. If there were anything like scriptural authority in the financial markets (there isn't, of course, which is what makes markets), the Good Book would be Graham and Dodd's.

As long ago as 1962, the co-authors inveighed against the tendency toward heightened corporate leverage, and it is unlikely that they would have approved of Harcourt. Appearing as it did so soon after the 1929–32 bear market, *Security Analysis* propounded safety and value. Of course, fortunes have been made by selectively ignoring the Graham and Dodd strictures on leverage (or for that matter, we suppose, by not subscribing to *Grant's*). However, as Graham and Dodd, citing Horace, also adjured, "Many shall be restored that are fallen, and many shall fall that now are in honor."

The Graham and Dodd approach is that certain investment principles are permanent. On the specific subject of credit, they wrote that more than half the corporate bonds in a 4,500-bond universe were selling for less than 50 cents on the dollar. That was in 1932, which briefly saw a mid-Depression spurt in interest rates. Investors wanted cash, and they wouldn't take paper or promises. If credit nowadays is a nonissue in the investment world, there is reason enough to suppose that that will change.

Graham and Dodd, though little inclined to junk, were not indifferent to the opportunities created by investment fashion. Thus, the fourth edition contains an important concession to what has become the fundamental plank of the bullish case for high-yield securities. People don't like junk, the authors observed, and this unpopularity tends to depress the prices of speculative-grade debt relative to the prices of common stock:

> From the standpoint of the intelligent buyer, this undervaluation must be considered a point in their favor. With respect to their intrinsic position, speculative bonds—and, to a lesser degree, preferred stocks—derive important advantages from their contractual rights. The fixed obligation to pay bond interest will usually result

in the continuation of such payments as long as they are in any way possible. If we assume that a fairly large proportion of a group of carefully selected low-priced bonds will escape default, the income received on the group as a whole over a period of time will undoubtedly far exceed the dividend return on similarly priced common stocks.

Junk bond partisans take that argument one step further nowadays, of course, contending that returns on a diversified portfolio of high-yield debt will reliably outstrip those of a lower-yielding portfolio of investment-grade debt. The theoretical argument, which has been propounded by a number of professors and which is based solely on the experience of the 1980s, is that the risk premium of junk to investment-grade yields is, if anything, too high. We don't know what Graham and Dodd would have said to that one, but on page 645 they sounded a cautionary note:

> The soundness of straight bond investment can be demonstrated only by its performance under unfavorable business conditions; if the bondholders needed prosperity to keep them whole, they would have been smarter to have bought the company's stock and made the profits that flow from prosperity.

Against that passage might be set a line from the HBJ prospectus: "The company's highly leveraged capital structure could significantly limit its ability to withstand competitive pressure or adverse economic conditions." The modern-day junk market is a fairweather market, with most of the original-issue supply coming since the 1982 bottom in business. In general, the masters wrote, the bond is an inherently unattractive form of investment, a security with a limited return. "Since the chief emphasis must be placed on avoidance of loss, bond selection is primarily a *negative art*. It is a process of exclusion and rejection rather than search and acceptance."

Graham and Dodd were not dogmatic about leverage. They understood what it can do for you as well as to you, but their emphasis on the risks may strike a contemporary reader as quaint or irrelevant. A friend points out that junk bonds—deal-related junk, in particular—are viewed not so much as straight debt as a kind of participating preferred stock. Nobody intends to hold them for very long. On the other hand, Graham and Dodd:

> It is clear that leverage is an inherently speculative factor and one that intensifies the possibilities of both gain and loss. Abstractly considered, leverage would seem to be more favorable than unfavorable, on balance, to common stocks—first, because in the average case it tends to increase the percentage earned on the common; and second, because the amount of possible profit from future changes is always a bad thing for the senior securities since it means that the common holders are exploiting the senior capital without offering an adequate "cushion" or margin of safety.

Graham and Dodd weren't talking about 14 percent, 15 percent, or 16 percent yields, and maybe the mere power of compound interest at those levels would have impressed them. On the other hand, maybe not. The authors favored a ratio of after-tax earnings to fixed charges of 2.9 times for industrial companies, a level hard to achieve for companies that, like Harcourt, show no after-tax earnings at all. *Security Analysis* contains a memorable passage on the entropy of credit, or how the rich get richer:

> Allowance must be made for the fact that the rate of interest tends to vary inversely with the ability of the company to pay it. A strong company borrows at a low rate, although it could afford to pay more than could a weak company. This means that "good credit" itself produces "better credit" through its own saving of interest charges, whereas the opposite is equally true. Although this may seem paradoxical and unfair, it must be accepted as a fact in security analysis.

There are profitable facts and unprofitable facts, and what might be styled Graham and Dodd's First Law of Credit has not recently been a money marker. Although the junk market has suffered rising rates of default in the past few prosperous years, one has been better advised, so far, to have participated in it than to have knocked it. When will that change? It will change when the stock market breaks or when corporate assets can no longer be sold at the drop of a hat in order to service a debt. How long can companies borrow at 14 percent pretax while earning less than 14 percent pretax? Not forever, surely?

BALL FOUR

April 1, 1988

I f you collect baseball cards or chew bubble gum (the brand is Bazooka) or read the hot-stove-league baseball guides or buy Garbage Pail Kids stickers, you already know about Topps. You may have seen the name in the financial pages, too. Until 1984, Topps was a public company with shares on the American Stock Exchange. Then it was taken private in a leveraged buyout with Forstmann Little. Then some 10 percent of its shares were reoffered in the public market.

A secondary offering was planned last September, but along came you-know-what. An alternative financing scheme was hit upon: a $10-a-share special dividend, to be financed with bank debt. The lead lender: Manufacturers Hanover.

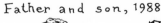

Father and son, 1988

E. Harold Benton, rainmaker;
E. Harold Benton, Jr., baseball
card collector.

Topps just might be the ultimate fad company, with a balance sheet as up to the minute as Thumb Fun. No financials have been released since the latest recapitalization, but long-term debt is about $140 million. Stockholders' equity is a negative $90 million.

Last November, before the special dividend was paid, the Topps balance sheet stood as testimony to the success of the 1984 recapitalization. Net worth was $49 million, and long-term debt was $3.5 million. Then the company levered up all over again.

Curious (incredulous, actually), we called up Topps to ask some questions. Why double the bet now? Since when do toys and debt mix? In general, is everyone else crazy, or is it us?

Louis Walker, the chief financial officer, patiently explained what, as he said, seemed almost obvious. Topps paid a special dividend as a way of realizing shareholder value (for the public and inside holders alike). Taking account of the $10 dividend, of dividends paid along the way, and of appreciation of the shares in over-the-counter trading, Walker noted, "The stockholders have made out like gangbusters." He said that Topps's proclivity to borrow has afforded the public holders what ordinarily is reserved for the big fellows only: a chance to participate in a highly leveraged investment (and in a liquid investment, at that).

When the first leveraged buyout was proposed in 1984, Walker went on, he was suspicious. "I told the bankers, 'You're crazy. If I were a bank, I wouldn't lend to us.' " He added, however, that Topps, even then, had the requisite management and cash flow to make the deal work. It still does, he said. "Doing the new leveraged deal in January," he continued, "was a piece of cake—no sweat."

When his caller confessed doubts, Walker replied, "I think maybe some companies are setting themselves up for trouble. But I'm not so sure that a lot are." He added, in Topps's case, that the interest rate on the bank loan starts at just 1 percent over prime and gradually works lower. There are no junk bonds.

Hearing that, we called Manny Hanny to ask how it justified the risks in view of the thin margins—its own borrowing costs have been going up recently, of course. It was close to deadline, however, and we received no answer. Probably the up-front fees figured prominently in the risk-reward calculation. The rewards are booked sooner, whereas the risks are borne later.

In a research comment on Topps, Goldman Sachs noted, "The company plans to increase baseball card capacity another 40 percent by April. Although there are many factors contributing to the surge in baseball card sales . . . we are unable to determine their respective impact on demand or on the longevity of this increased demand."

Exactly. To judge by the overwrought sales literature, the baseball card market is even hotter than the stub-stock market.* "Dear *Sport Magazine* reader," an advertorial led off recently:

> Did you know that the long-term performance of baseball cards beats the pants off of stocks, T-bills, and rare coins?
> One hundred dollars invested in baseball cards in 1980 is worth $2,449 today . . . (and the future performance looks even better.)
> Baseball card collecting is not just a fun sports-based hobby any longer. It has become an extremely profitable field in which to be involved.

The ad claimed that, on the Friday following Black Monday, a set of baseball cards changed hands "for the highest price on record. The market seems to keep growing and demand gets stronger and stronger while supplies of the best players diminish." Maybe, although we like to believe that supply sooner or later will catch up to demand. James S. Chanos, a hedge-fund manager, said that Topps reminds him of the indebted toy companies: "What I used to say about Coleco holds for Topps. Anytime you leverage up a company and are dependent on the whims of twelve-year-old boys, you are in trouble."

Also, as the *Sport Magazine* ad eventually got around to admitting, "Just bear in mind that nothing goes up forever."†

---

* A "stub stock" is the equity of a highly leveraged company. In April 1988 the stub-stock market was going up.
† On March 1, 1993, Topps was quoted at a little over 7, which is approximately where it had been in April 1988. In August 1989, however, it was quoted at 17½, which shows that betting on the inevitable, although reasonable, is not always profitable.

NAPOLEON ADVANCES ON MOSCOW

June 24, 1988

Campeau intends to retain control of the preeminent department store divisions of Allied and Federated, together with . . . the Ann Taylor specialty retail stores.
—Campeau Corp., 1987 annual report

CAMPEAU PLANS TO SELL ALLIED'S ANN TAYLOR UNIT
—The Wall Street Journal, *June 16, 1988*

Although opulent, the 1987 Campeau Corp. annual report is dated. On April 1, two months after the close of the Campeau fiscal year, Federated Department Stores entered the corporate world. The $6.7 billion merger was treated on page 56 of the annual, in the "subsequent event" department, but the Campeau consolidated financials are Federated-less. That is the way of Campeau: Nothing is the same for very long. Last month the brand-new annual report promised that Ann Taylor, the hundred-store specialty chain, would not be sold. (You may recall that Campeau bought Allied Stores, Ann Taylor included, in 1986.) On June 15, the annual moved deeper into obsolescence when Campeau reversed itself, disclosing plans to sell the division after all. The news rattled the Allied debt holders, sending the 11½s of 1997 to the mid 80s, to yield 14.3 percent or so, from the high 80s, and serving notice to the watchers of Campeau Corp. that they know less than they think (which was little enough anyway).

Campeau, the Toronto-based real estate and retailing giant, is as inconspicuous as a great debtor can be. In the words of the Canadian analysts who try to keep up with it, the company "is a moving target." When Robert Campeau, the unpredictable chief-

"What did you do in the '80s, Daddy?"

tain, says he won't sell this or that division, he may or may not sell it; when he says he won't sell junk bonds to the public, he may sell them anyway—about $1 billion in Campeau paper is expected around Labor Day. By that time, perhaps, the major debt-rating agencies will have formed an opinion of the issuer. As of last week, Campeau was (from the agencies' point of view and most of Wall Street's) *terra incognita*.

So for now, pending receipt of new financials, the Campeau annual will have to do. Creditors will worry about its lavishly thick paper, oddball statistical contents (for example, a drop in cash to $19 million on January 31, 1988, from $302 million on December 31, 1986) and pseudo-Churchillian prose. "In retailing and real estate," it says on page 4, "industries that have become predictably conservative over the years, Campeau is a company that is prepared to take calculated risks. Campeau Corp. has the visionary qualities to see what others do not, to act while others hesitate, and to create value in innovative ways."

Although $1.7 billion of secured debt was paid down last year, it can't be said that Campeau's creditors have had a value-laden time of it. When Campeau bought Federated Department Stores this spring, Federated's debt rating (covering about $980 million worth) plunged to B2, which is junk, from Aa2, which is not. The magazine *Corporate Finance* has revealed "How Campeau pulled off an equity-free acquisition: His $6.6 billion takeover of Federated tested the outer limits of leverage." The monthly found that the only true equity involved in the purchase was $195 million (less than 3 percent of the price) raised by Campeau through the sale of another Allied division, Brooks Brothers—"and it isn't even enough to cover the front-end fees on the bank debt." On Tuesday, following release of lackluster retailing results by Allied and Federated, Allied's $3.3125 cumulative exchangeable preferred was quoted at 16¾–17¾, evidently a post-crash low. It was issued in March 1987 at 25.

What is so striking is the vast asymmetry between the creditors' upside and Campeau's. If his dream (whatever it may be) is realized, Campeau will take his rightful place among the world's moguls. In that happy event, the creditors will get their money back, which, by the way, they had before Campeau borrowed it. "Campeau is a company that is prepared to take calculated risks" is an understatement that ought to focus the bondholders' attention on the topic of risk and reward. It is late in the business cycle, arguably, for a debtor to be acting out his self-image as a cross between Frank W. Woolworth and Napoleon. It is a stunning personal ambition, and we envy Campeau's future biographer. However, nothing is forcing the investors of hard-earned capital to finance the equivalent of the emperor's invasion of Russia.*

QUANTUM'S LEAP

January 6, 1989

Quantum Chemical Corp.'s $1.14 billion recapitalization plan promises a $50 special dividend to the stockholders and a mouthful of ashes to the bondholders, and it was to the stockholders that John Hoyt Stookey, Quantum's chairman, addressed a hopeful New Year's message: "We hope that it will be perceived as a recapitalization that sets a new standard for how the tools of leverage can be used in a responsible way."

---

* Campeau Corp. filed for bankruptcy protection on January 15, 1990.

Certainly, the chairman is half right. The Quantum scheme—a plan to raise the value of the common stock through borrowing and the sale of assets without a sacrifice in either the common dividend or capital spending—sets a new standard in coincidence.

Press accounts of the restructuring emphasized management's frustration over the low price of the stock, and Quantum began to repurchase shares, in the open market on the day of the crash. From October 19, 1987, through last August, the nation's leading polyethylene producer bought back 7.7 million shares, or 23 percent of the shares outstanding on Black Monday.

The company also sold bonds, which at the time of sale were rated BBB − (the new rating is lower: BB −). Three well-spaced offerings of twenty-year debentures raised $700 million in 1988: $300 million in January, $200 million in June, and $200 million in September. It cannot be said that the ink on the September prospectuses was still wet when Quantum disclosed its plan to restructure, but the point survives the exaggeration.

News accounts of the restructuring are noticeably short of moral indignation, and perhaps the ill-used bondholders felt more sheepish than outraged. The September prospectus contained a bland description of the use of proceeds: "general corporate purposes, which may include capital expenditures, repayment of indebtedness, repurchases of Quantum Common Stock, acquisitions or working capital requirements." Unmentioned was the possibility that in fact materialized—payment of a massive special dividend —although a frank warning about financial leverage would not have helped to sell the bonds at investment-grade yields.

We put the question to Chairman Stookey himself: When did management contemplate the recapitalization? "In October," he answered. Not September? we asked—the latest Quantum debt prospectus was dated September 15. "Absolutely not," Stookey replied. He said that one decisive event was the stock market's ho-hum reaction to a 382 percent gain in third-quarter earnings. We suggested that the holders of the new Quantum 10⅞s of October 1, 2018, are nursing a grudge anyway. "We have a contractual relationship with our bondholders, which is intact," the chairman said.

Calls were placed to the underwriters of the Quantum debentures, Dillon, Read & Co. and First Boston Corp., for price information. Each declined to respond, citing involvement in the recapitalization. Clearly, selling corporate bonds these days is a better business than buying them.

Back on the telephone, Stookey pressed his case. He said that a company must balance the interests of its several constituencies—stockholders, employees, and what he called "the corporation itself"—and that Quantum had done this carefully. He said that in the past four years investment in the chemical and propane businesses had doubled, to $2 billion, and that another $1.3 billion will be invested in the next three years.

Stookey insisted that this is a unique transaction. "First and foremost, this massive investment in the future takes precedence," he said. Also, "The incentives applying in this recapitalization are noteworthy for their moderation. . . . The thing is to be the cleanest and highest-plane deal we can construct."

Finally, he said that Quantum would repay its debt in five years, even assuming a recession.* In the not-too-distant future, he said, the bondholders will actually be glad that things worked out the way they did. Our guess is that most investors right now would be grateful for a bid.

59 WALL STREET RINGS A BELL

January 20, 1989

The 1818 Fund is a new investment partnership with an old sponsor. Its name is Brown Brothers Harriman & Co., the oldest and largest private bank in the country. You can guess the year of Brown Brothers' founding because it matches the last four digits of Brown Brothers' telephone number and the name of the new Brown Brothers' fund. The telephone number, incidentally, 483-1818, is an

---

* Quantum's long-term debt was $1.3 billion at year-end 1988. It was $2.5 billion at year-end 1992.

uncharacteristic touch of public display. The firm never advertises except to publish its balance sheet, which is liquid.

The more credit-minded the observer, the higher his opinion of Brown Brothers is likely to be. For one thing, the firm is a real partnership, the principals sharing unlimited liability in case of disaster. For another, its banking business is uninsured, so no big money has been lent to Brazil and no undignified petitions for help have been addressed to the Treasury (hello, Morgan Guaranty). *The New York Times* recently reported on the voluntary closing of a pair of private banks in Texas, noting that each institution, though solvent, was out of step with the times. "Today," another solvent Texas banker reflected, "financial institutions are looked upon as a box you put your money in and think, 'It's okay; the government will take care of it.' That's why banks are in such trouble."

Thus the appeal of Brown Brothers. When *Forbes* put the firm through the wringer last summer, a reader was inclined to side with the victim. If an Edwardian-style balance sheet is a sign of obsolescence, so much the worse for the roaring 1980s.

Enter now the 1818 Fund. Frankly "nontraditional," it is not an ordinary Brown Brothers investment vehicle. Its purpose is to buy shares of newly issued convertible preferred stock after friendly negotiations with corporate issuers. Receiving the proceeds from such an investment, a corporation could retire common stock, pay a special dividend, restructure, recapitalize, or otherwise "enhance shareholder value." It could leverage its balance sheet or stiff-arm a corporate raider. The fund proposes to acquire what will represent the largest single block of an issuer's voting securities. In a phrase, the fund is a blocking-preferred investment partnership.

Kohlberg, Kravis, Roberts & Co., Drexel Burnham Lambert, Wasserstein, Perella & Co., Brown Brothers Harriman & Co.— which name does not belong? Hearing the news that Brown Brothers had entered the twentieth century, a sadness came over us. Presently, however, there was a sense of exhilaration. If 59 Wall Street has capitulated, we thought, maybe the tide is really turning.

A call was placed to Lawrence C. Tucker, one of the Brown Brothers partners in charge of the fund. How's business? we asked. Fine, said Tucker. The fund—up to $500 million—is expected to close by the end of March. Getting to the point, we asked what the hell was going on: Why is *Brown Brothers* dabbling in leverage?

He answered, to start with, that Brown Brothers, contra *Forbes*, has never been out of the corporate-finance swim. It does a brisk advisory business, especially with family-owned companies, and is a niche-type participant in the merger-and-acquisition business. It has no ideological position on debt. Thus, Tucker went on, the fund signifies no capitulation and no paradox.

Furthermore, said Tucker, 1818 is different from the ordinary LBO fund, of which there are many. Notably, Brown Brothers itself will serve as the general partner, meaning that the partners, jointly and severally, will be on the hook if something goes wrong. (That is the full extent of the general partner's commitment, however; no cash will be contributed.) Also, most of the general partner's compensation will come in the form of profit sharing, and no investment-banking fees will be charged the limited partners up front. As for potential conflicts of interest with the Brown Brothers advisory business, Tucker noted, they are fully disclosed in the offering circular.

The 1818 is a small fund, as Brown Brothers is a small bank. The partners' year-end capital totaled $97 million, which supported banking assets of $1.1 billion. To put $97 million in perspective, it was almost four times the size of the 1988 bonus of James Dahl, the government informant and Drexel Burnham junk bond salesman. However, it was not quite half of Michael Milken's reported (and unpaid) bonus. Plainly, Brown Brothers has missed the boat of financial leverage, as not a few of us have. If the partners are not vexed by their relative impoverishment these past few years, they are even more ossified than *Forbes* implied.

The most telling sentence in the 1818 circular, it seems to us, is one on investment timing: "Because of the current and expected equity market valuations in the United States, accompanied by continued high levels of corporate restructuring and change of control activity, the General Partner believes that the present time may prove to be especially advantageous to organize a special-purpose investing pool such as the Fund to make investments designed to permit investors to benefit from these recent market conditions and corporate activities."

Note this well: Future market valuations are expected to be as high or higher than those prevailing now. High levels of corporate restructuring and change-of-control activity (read "debt") will continue. Now, therefore, is an "especially advantageous" time to proceed. Never mind that there was a crash, that anti-merger agitation is building in Washington, and that Kohlberg, Kravis, Roberts & Co. proposes to do a $25 billion deal. If now is an "especially advantageous" time to do what Brown Brothers proposes to do, we'll eat our hat (again).*

SPARRING PARTNER FALLS ILL

June 23, 1989

O n the day before Integrated Resources admitted that it had run out of borrowed money, a buyout rumor circulated. The grapevine had it that Integrated, the diversified financial services company, junk bond consumer, and longtime investment banking client of Drexel Burnham Lambert, would be the recipient of a $21-per-share bid. The stock jumped—what takeover candidate, real or imagined, doesn't these days?—and closed above the $15 mark.

That was on June 13. On the morning of the fourteenth, the broad tape clarified the situation: The alleged takeover candidate was, in fact, unable to fund itself. It could not roll over its commercial paper or induce its bankers to lend. On the fifteenth, a halt in the company's debt-service payments was announced. On this cue, the entire Integrated capitalization—bonds, preferred and common—collapsed. On the twentieth, the common stock closed at $4.25. An issue of senior subordinated notes—the 10¾s of 1996—fetched 23.

The story of Integrated Resources is a 1980s miniature. It is the story of illiquidity, debt, and credulity. It is also the story of inev-

---

* Although the UAL acquisition blew up nine months later, thereby ringing down the curtain on the opera buffa of extreme corporate leverage, investors in the 1818 Fund earned a 24 percent annual rate of return, net of fees and expenses, through year-end 1992. I prefer my hat baked.

itability. In the roaring '80s, the inevitable eventually happens, but it takes its own sweet time. For instance, illiquid balance sheets cause debt crises. Also, negative cash flow is less desirable than positive cash flow. In the end, Integrated Resources did run out of willing lenders, but the end came five years after some of us began to count the days.

To a credit-minded investor, the details of the Integrated story are not as important as the outline of the plot. Suffice it to say that the company was once the premier vendor of syndicated real estate partnerships, that tax reform and the bear market in commercial real estate did it no good and that it set about diversifying into insurance, money management, and other so-called financial services. Its accounting is controversial. Its cash flow is negative. Its operating income peaked as long ago as 1984. Its capitalization—heavily tilted toward debt and preferred stock and totaling almost $2 billion—has ballooned. Its insurance companies have invested heavily in junk bonds. In sum, the company is almost a perfect high-yield specimen, and its embarrassment may prove a financial landmark.

One of the most telling comments of Integrated's officers in their hour of crisis was, in effect, that they didn't know what hit them. "As far as we're concerned, nothing changed" in the company's capitalization to account for its troubles, said Philip Cohen, Integrated's chief financial officer. Said the president and chief executive officer, Arthur H. Goldberg: "The capital structure requires some type of continued confidence. In retrospect, it was a fragile capital structure." Remarked an anonymous Integrated salesman: "Mike Milken used to arrange credit in two seconds. Now that he's gone, the new management is playing games." (As for Selig Zises, the Integrated chairman who forehandedly sold a block of stock last December, investors were told at this year's High Yield Bond Conference in Beverly Hills that he wanted a change in "lifestyle.")

Seen in retrospect, Integrated's long career in the credit markets was a miracle of faith. "Integrated believes that it will continue to require additional funds from sources other than operations in order to finance its operations," said the company in 1984. In other words, cash flow was negative and was expected to remain negative. But the company thought none the worse of itself for that fact. *"Due to its strong financial position,* Integrated believes it will not, over the near to intermediate term, experience any difficulties in obtaining financing to meet the requirements of its investment program activities and for working capital needs," it also said in 1984 (our italics). In the newspeak of leveraged finance, there was nothing incompatible about negative cash flow and a "strong financial position." Access to borrowed money was the same as cash—until suddenly it wasn't.

In truth, the high-yield bond market has been conditioned to ignore plain English. Even the strongest junk issuers routinely serve notice that, barring future asset sales or refinancings, they won't be able to service their debts. Nowadays, it takes a powerful imagination to conceive of any circumstances in which assets could not be sold or the markets would be closed, even to a bankrupt. So the smart money long ago stopped reading prospectuses, or at least stopped believing the risk language that the lawyers put in them. (Those who worry have been worrying for years, and their predictive stock has fallen accordingly. We could name names. . . .) During Michael Milken's rule, a Drexel client could be plausibly led to believe that the money would never stop. But Milken's number, as you know, was retired recently (he resigned, in fact, on the very day that Integrated hit the wall), and Integrated Resources borrowed one dollar too many.

Integrated's balance sheet did not become "fragile" overnight. From 1984 to 1988, revenues tripled (to $1.7 billion) and assets climbed by almost fivefold (to $7.9 billion). But operating income fell—to $52 million from $62 million—and indebtedness rose. Clearly, "earnings" were not the kind of money that one could take to the bank; they were the kind of money that one borrowed against. In 1984, capitalization consisted of $359 million of long-term debt, $341 million of preferred stock, and $109 million of common. In 1988, capitalization consisted of $917 million of long-term debt, $351 million of preferred, and $188 million of common. What tipped the company's hand to the bears was the relentless rise in borrowing, both short-term and long. At year-end 1984, bank debt and commercial paper totaled $240 million. By year-end 1988, they amounted to $563 million. At a meeting with its creditors on Monday, Integrated estimated its current short-term borrowing to be $957 million, a stunning rise since year-end. And management added that it wanted to borrow $100 million more. (A source who attended the meeting reports that Integrated's management was asked the same basic question—"What happened?"—in about eight different ways. Management provided a variety of answers to the effect that it didn't know.)

In its 1988 annual report, Integrated laid no claim to financial strength and admitted a need for equity capital. At year-end 1988, as you may remember, I.C.H. Corp., the junk-bond-minded insurance holding company, was mulling just such an investment. It fell through, and Integrated's March 31 report turned up the disclosure volume a bit: "While the company currently has adequate sources of financing available to finance its operations, the company believes that over the foreseeable future it will require additional equity, capital, or internal sources of liquidity in order to have access to adequate sources of financing." On the evidence, not even tomorrow is foreseeable.

Many are the lessons of Integrated Resources. To start with, even the most successful and celebrated investors can fall asleep at the switch. The list of major Integrated investors at March 31 includes (besides Columbia Savings & Loan and Executive Life Insurance Corp., each a Drexel stablemate) Templeton World Fund and Batterymarch Financial Management. Equitable Life was a major investor as recently as last December 31. What were these worthies thinking of? The poleaxing of the Integrated capitalization is a reminder that when disaster strikes, it strikes fast. That nobody seems to be able to explain why it happened is a reminder that nobody rings a bell. (James S. Chanos, the foremost bear in Integrated, has been short the stock since 1983. His vindication is as sweet as it is lucrative.) The fact that Integrated's senior debt was rated BBB −, or investment-grade, by Standard & Poor's until June 14 is a reminder that every investor must think for himself. That, at this writing, no creditors had plunged the company into bankruptcy and that the common stock continued to trade in positive territory is a reminder that market psychology is hopeful.*

Perhaps the foremost lesson of the Integrated crack-up is that

---

* Three years and eight months later, Integrated (or "Disintegrated," as it was instantly called following its June crisis) has not emerged from bankruptcy proceedings. Under a reorganization plan submitted by the company in January 1993, holders of about $700 million of senior debt would receive between 56 and 59 cents on the dollar. The stockholders and the holders of $676 million of junior debt would receive nothing.

faith runs deep. So-called stub stocks (issued by companies with highly leveraged balance sheets) continued strong on Monday and Tuesday, and no repercussions of the Integrated news had been heard in the junk bond market. There was no visible fallout in the $12 billion to $15 billion market for non-rated and junk-rated commercial paper. When Harcourt Brace Jovanovich (another owner of a "fragile" balance sheet) disclosed Tuesday that it was going to put its theme parks up for sale, its stock zoomed—never mind that it has not yet received a bid. For the time being, institutional investors continue to believe that every day is the first day of spring.

DEFAULTS OF THE FUTURE

October 27, 1989

Now that the high-yield bond market has gone to wrack and ruin, a value-seeking investor may reconsider his prejudices. If junk was barren of value at a premium of 350 basis points to Treasury notes, it must be a little less barren at a premium of 680 basis points. A calculating investor, viewing the world without rancor, would treat distress as an opportunity, not a moral judgment on *certain investment bankers* who made the 1980s a living hell for anyone who could read the plain English in a debt prospectus. His bullishness would be in exact proportion to the market's bearishness.

But there are good reasons to be wary of the high-yield market even now. To start with, the public has met the crisis in junk with an unnerving complacency. It has not yet staged a run, or even a brisk walk, on $35 billion of open-end, junk bond, mutual fund assets. There has been no public uproar yet over the pricing of those funds, which is inexact in the best of times. There has been no investigation into the junk bond holdings of mutual life insurance companies. In short, the public has not yet run for the hills.

Perhaps, as Edwin Levy ventured in these pages two years ago, the public is not yet aware that it has been speculating. Everyone will have an opinion on the great timing issue before the junk market: Will public investors, stampeding out of mutual funds, make the bottom?

In any case, Barrie Wigmore, a full-time investment banker and a part-time scholar, has produced a brilliant new paper that has nothing to do with opinion. Wigmore's thesis is that the credit quality of junk bonds has been falling as the volume of their issuance has been rising. His findings have profound implications for future rates of default and thus for future rates of return in high-yield investments. They suggest that the well-publicized work of college professors in the matter of junk defaults has been overly optimistic. What the gentlemen in tweed have overlooked is the flimsy architecture of a lending boom and the dynamics of the competition among lenders.

It was three long and not uniformly bearish years ago when *Grant's* advanced the theory of the credit cycle (August 11, 1986). The idea was that quality of speculative-grade debt was bound to slip over the course of a major lending expansion. This law of entropy was based on experience and common sense. Knowing Wall Street as we knew it, it seemed a cinch that the idea of financial leverage would be pushed too far. It stood to reason that on Day One of the new era a clever banker would do a deal that violated the canons of mainstream banking. That deal would succeed spectacularly (as Metromedia Broadcasting, the first of the big junk bond deals, did in 1984). Conservative bankers would regret this unsound demonstration, but it would inspire others. Before long, the financial world would be divided into two unequal camps: those who were profitably participating in the new era and those who were disapprovingly standing aloof from it. The progress of the expansion could be traced by the number of defections from the second camp to the first. Borrowing would proceed, on ever more precarious terms, until the old fogies' camp was nearly depleted. What we did not anticipate, lacking vision, was how far the process would carry—beyond Robert Campeau, even, to UAL.

The credit cycle was not an original idea, nor was it immediately a useful one. There was no telling exactly when such a cycle had begun or when it would stop. Writing for the *Harvard Business*

Review in the soul-searching year of 1933, George W. Edwards hit the nail on the head:

> The history of business cycles shows that the stage of prosperity in general is marked by an ever-increasing inefficiency. In the field of security investment, the buying public, swayed by overoptimism, seeks more and more after securities of higher yield, and investment bankers, under the stress of competition, issue securities of higher yield, greater risk, and poorer quality.

"There is a kind of inevitability about the cycle," we wrote in 1986, "with caution giving way to cocksureness and finally to grief." No guess was ventured about which year would usher in grief on a net basis, but the tone of the piece suggested a date prior to 1989. Anyway, the credit experience of the 1920s seemed relevant to the 1980s. In both decades, the public's appetite for high yields was eagerly accommodated: in the 1920s by the 6 percent or 7 percent bonds of foreign governments; in the 1980s by the 14 percent or 15 percent bonds of leveraged corporations. The default experience of the 1980s is still an open book, but the history of the 1920s and 1930s is a matter of record. Markets as diverse as foreign-government bonds, domestic corporate bonds, urban home mortgage loans, and urban business property loans exhibited two important characteristics. First, issuance of debt accelerated as the decade wore on. Second, the rate of default on debt issued early in the decade was significantly lower than the rate of default on debt issued late in the decade. In other words, bonds issued in optimistic times tended to fare worse than bonds issued in skeptical times. Braddock Hickman, surveying the 1900–44 period, neatly synthesized these tendencies. "It will be observed," he wrote of the corporate bond market over four decades, "that the trends in default rates are roughly comparable with trends in net and gross new financing, default rates tending to be high on securities issued during years of high volume and vice versa."

If Hickman's observation is universally valid, the junk bond market entered a danger zone years ago. Bonds issued recently— a credulous period if there ever was one—will blow up at rates unanticipated by the underwriters and their academic apologists. They will fail at significantly higher rates than bonds issued in the early going because fiduciaries by 1986 had almost committed Drexel Burnham Lambert's "The Case for High Yield Bonds" to memory. It was not lost on investors of the late 1980s that Michael Milken was making approximately $1 billion more a year than his most outspoken critic. Applying the Hickman model, you would avoid the debt of boom-time vintage—the debt, that is, that nearly came to constitute the market.

Wigmore, a limited partner of the Goldman Sachs Group, has fleshed out this theory with solid fact. His new, unpublished paper, "The Decline in Credit Quality of Junk Bond Issues, 1980–1988," documents the financial deterioration of the past several years. It shows that the junk crop of 1986–88 is palpably weaker than the issuance of the early to mid-1980s. "Junk bond new issues in 1986–88 experienced a decline in credit quality best illustrated by five traditional credit ratios, which declined 27 percent to 69 percent, depending upon the ratio selected, from 1983–85 averages," he writes. "This decline in credit quality reflected that over 75 percent of junk bond issues in 1986–88 were incurred to finance merger-related transactions at prices and capitalization ratios which entailed EBIT coverage ratios well below 1.0 times."

Reading between Wigmore's carefully documented lines, one may view the junk bond market with new apprehension. Plainly, the numerous academic studies on default rates do not—could not—capture the experience of recently issued debt. "Measurement of default experience requires a long enough period to experience some cyclical adversity and at least to exhaust the liquidity reserves built into the original financing, such as asset sales, payments in kind (paying interest in the form of additional debt securities), zero coupons, deferral of principal repayments or excess borrowing," Wigmore notes. However, as he also notes, one needn't suspend judgment about the probable future credit standing of these untried securities. One can read the documents, compute the ratios, and compare the results with data from prior years, which Wigmore, working at odd hours for the past year, has done.

As you may know, Wigmore is an accomplished financial scholar without tenure. His 1985 book, *The Crash and Its Aftermath*, is the definitive study of the securities markets from the 1929 stock market crash to the 1932–33 recovery. Working at odd hours for twelve years, Wigmore chronicled not only the macroeconomic horizon but also the business and financial landscape, almost tree by tree. (This is the rave of an interested party: *Grant's* has copies for sale at the list price of $49.95.)

The author has lavished the same scholarly care on the contemporary high-yield market. His approach to the problem is direct and understandable. Five measures of credit quality are applied to junk bonds issued from 1980 to 1988. The database comprises 694 publicly underwritten bond issues but excludes financial companies, utilities and private placements, and exchange offers. The five credit tests are coverage of interest expense by "earnings before interest and taxes," or EBIT; coverage of interest expense by "earnings before interest, taxes *and depreciation*," or EBITD; debt as a percentage of net tangible assets; cash flow as a percentage of debt; and common equity as a percentage of capitalization.

As you can see, a great divide was crossed in 1986. Issuance ballooned and credit quality plunged (as Hickman would not have been surprised to learn). Debt as a percentage of tangible assets did not take an alarming bend, but it was the exception, not the rule. Cash flow declined as a percentage of debt, and common equity declined as a percentage of capitalization. No longer did "earnings before interest and taxes" (EBIT) suffice to cover interest expense. Now Wall Street was obliged to fortify the numerator in the customary interest-coverage fraction by the addition of "D," for depreciation. If depreciation, a noncash charge, were treated as an imaginary expense, a marginal debtor would look very nearly solvent. And in truth, according to bull market gospel, the formal interest-coverage arithmetic didn't count anyway. Companies coming out of the LBO shop could always sell assets at a fancy price or refinance their debt at better terms down the road. It was not intended that the LBO capitalization would be the permanent capitalization. Something would turn up to make everyone whole before the principal fell due. There were plenty of chairs for everyone, and besides, the music would never stop.

Concerning the striking decline in credit quality, Wigmore comments: "Pro forma cash flow as a percentage of total debt in 1986–88 averaged only 3.3 percent—down 69 percent from the average for 1983–85. If this ratio held constant indefinitely, it implied thirty years for the average junk bond issuer to pay off its present debts with no dividends and 100 percent external financing of all working capital and capital expenditure needs." But even these figures overstate the comfort and coverages available to junk bond holders, he goes on. The ratios in the accompanying table "apply to all of the issuers' debts, whereas junk bond issues in 1986–88 have been predominantly subordinated issues making up over 25 percent of capitalization. The 1987 and 1988 EBIT, EBITD, and cash-flow ratios probably provided no coverage whatsoever of subordinated-debt interest or principal." Whatever may happen to default rates in the future, it is hard to imagine them falling.

What about the easiest credit test? What about looking up the Moody's and Standard & Poor's bond ratings? Wigmore again:

> The annual proportion of junk bond new issues rated Ba by Moody's or BB by Standard & Poor's declined steadily from over 40 percent in 1982 to single digits in 1987–88. . . . This simple measure of the decline in junk bond credit quality understates the actual decline, however, because the credit ratios within credit-rating categories declined substantially in 1986–88. . . . The average B-rated issuer in 1986–88 had pro forma EBIT coverage of interest 32 percent lower than in 1983–85, pro forma EBITD coverage of interest 18 percent lower, debt as a percentage of net tangible assets 57 percent higher, cash flow as a percentage of total debt 50 percent lower, and a common equity ratio 54 percent lower. The 1987–88 averages were meaningfully worse than these three-year averages.

It's no front-page news that M&A activity drove junk bond issuance. Nor is it surprising that, in the reach to buy companies at bull market valuations, interest coverage received short shrift by bankers and investors alike. How short, however, may not be widely appreciated. "Merger pricing throughout 1986–88," Wigmore writes, "entailed junk bond EBIT coverages of interest systematically below 1.0 times."

Obviously, then, bond buyers expected blue skies, but how deep and unblemished the blue was expected to be is again jolting. "Both junk bond investors and equity investors in the transactions financed by junk bonds had high expectations for growth in issuers'

Perestroika on Wall St.

HB 89

Drexel Burnham defects, en masse, to Morgan Guaranty

EBITD," as Wigmore notes, "for neither party would be satisfied with annual cash flow equal to 3 percent of total debt." He goes on to build a model of those expectations, incorporating some of the standard bull market parameters: 13 percent interest rates, 90 percent leverage, initial EBITD coverage of 1.25 times, EBITD growth of 8 percent a year, capital expenditures of 4 percent of acquisition cost, and resale at eight times EBITD. If you are still with us, this would produce a 30 percent pretax internal rate of return to the equity investors, who claimed to be entitled to it. Wigmore comments from the humble vantage point of the subordinated debtholders:

> Even at 8 percent EBITD growth, the creditworthiness of their investment is dependent upon expectations of consistently improving cash flow for at least ten years. Free cash flow in the first five years is minimal. Assuming junk bonds are one-third of total debt, no free cash flow is available for junk bond principal until the eleventh year. Not until the sixth year does EBITD reach 1.85 times, at which point the remaining debt could be paid off in approximately fifteen years and therefore might be considered refinanceable without growth.

What, then, can be said about future default rates? The model gives no neat answer. It is silent on the prospects for growth and what Wigmore diplomatically styles "lenders' willingness to endure unmet expectations." "It does allow us to conclude, however," the author goes on, "that in the event of an economic environment in which EBITD grew at 3 percent or less, a typical LBO could make no retirements of its junk bond debt within fifteen years and not until the eleventh year would it reach 1.85 times EBITD, at which point the remaining debt could be paid off in approximately fifteen years without further growth."

For the fun of it, we consulted Wigmore's *The Crash and Its Aftermath* to find out how bondholders fared in the Great Depression. The results are simultaneously uplifting and downcasting. "Investors in high-grade bonds in the Depression had no loss in principal value plus 4 percent–5 percent in interest payments," Wigmore writes, "compared with an average loss in value for stocks of 58 percent and a 50 percent reduction in dividend income. . . ." There were no defaults among large corporate bond issues, he adds. As for Treasuries, total returns from 1929 to 1933 amounted to 20 percent to 22 percent. Adjusted for a 22 percent decline in prices, the total four-year returns in Treasuries were on the order of 42 percent to 44 percent. The all-in return on high-grade tax-exempts (also adjusted for the decline in prices) was an even more sterling 50 percent.

So far, so good. However, in what was arguably the grandfather to the contemporary junk market—the market in South American and East European government debt—losses were devastating. "At the lowest point in the market," according to Wigmore, "these bonds were down 77 percent from their highest 1929 prices. Nor was there an opportunity in 1930 or 1931 to get out of these bonds at a profit. The price deterioration was steady beginning relatively early in 1930."

Wigmore ventures no forecasts of junk bond default rates, nor does he dispense any junk bond investment advice. Studying his data, however, one must marvel at the symmetry of the rise in high-yield issuance and the plunge in its credit quality. One must salute the clarity of Wigmore's results. And noticing that even without a recession, much less a Great Depression, junk bond prices have broken, one must wonder about the future.

MORE JUNK FOOD

October 27, 1989

Only a few debt hobbyists, bankers, and professional short sellers have heard about the Church's Fried Chicken leveraged acquisition, let alone read the inch-thick proxy statement. It is the kind of transaction that has fallen between the cracks of the 1980s. Too small to attract much acclaim (pre-Campeau) or notoriety (post-Campeau), it is nevertheless a prime example of the late-cycle credit stretch. To some future financial cleanup committee, it will probably seem unfathomable.

That being said, the motive of the participating commercial bankers, investment bankers, lawyers, accountants, and printers is transparent. Their interest is fees. Some $57 million in fees and expenses will be paid to Wasserstein, Perella & Co., Merrill Lynch, and many others, which is very nearly equal to Church's pretax earnings for the fiscal years 1985, 1986, 1987, and 1988. Church's is now a cog in the wheel of Al Copeland Enterprises, which also owns Popeye Inc. Combined with Popeye, Church's has become the number two fast-chicken company in the United States, behind Kentucky Fried Chicken (a unit of PepsiCo Inc.). Alvin C. Copeland, who founded Popeye's Famous Fried Chicken & Biscuits in 1972, is a native of New Orleans. He was the Louisiana Restaurateur of the Year in 1984 and 1988 and, according to his public relations firm, is a leading sportsman, salesman, and donor to charitable causes. He is forty-five years old.

The Copeland enterprise has everything that some of the bigger leveraged recapitalizations have, including thrilling leverage, a hostile operating environment, negative pro forma interest-coverage ratios, and a strategic design for climbing out of its self-dug hole. Unlike many other leveraged businesses, however, Copeland has a proprietor, president, and chef—namely, Alvin C. Copeland himself—who races power boats. "This activity exposes Copeland to a higher degree of personal risk than were he not engaged in the activity," the proxy admits, although the degree of financial risk to which the buyers of the company's 17½ percent, payment-in-kind, cumulative, exchangeable preferred stock are exposing themselves is something to think about, too.

The narrative of the battle for Church's fills ten relentless pages in the proxy. The first group of would-be acquirers, which included Citicorp Capital Investors Ltd., surfaced in 1987. Over the next two years, competing bidders stepped forward. Inevitably, the questions of who was to own the company, the terms of the change of ownership, and the financial security of incumbent management came to overshadow the prosaic business of selling fried chicken, mashed potatoes, corn on the cob, jalapeño peppers, french fries, and coleslaw to the mid- to downscale Church's customer (who spent, per visit last year, only $3.77).

When the books were closed on 1988, the results showed a net loss of $14 million on sales of $405 million. Discouraging on their face, the numbers were even worse in perspective. Church's had earned $23 million on sales of $540 million as long ago as 1985. The proxy contains an explanation of this decline, which, although unappetizing, is revealing:

Beginning in 1986, the company discounted deeply from Church's menu prices in an attempt to increase customer count at the expense of its margins, despite the fact that its menu prices already established it as a lower-price competitor. The company in 1986 also began purchasing chickens that were larger in size than permitted under the company's specifications, and using lower quality flours in the chicken-frying process. . . . In addition, the higher fat content of the larger chickens, the lower quality flour, and inconsistent supervision of quality control standards produced a Southern-style fried chicken which departed from the company's original product quality and which appealed to fewer customers.

Needless to say, the new Copeland management has improvements in mind. Its financial strategy is to close redundant locations, sell assets, and mortgage real estate. Its operating, or culinary, strategy is to revert to original Church's chicken recipes, to convert selected Church's restaurants into Popeyes, and to roll out a new Church's biscuit, created by Copeland himself. Much hope is invested in this wonder biscuit, which may be topped with honey butter or flavored with jalapeño and cheese and which, to quote an impartial Church's public relations woman, is "out of this world." In the guarded language of the proxy, it "may" produce a "significant improvement" in restaurant chain sales. Not yet, however.

It will have to be a morsel of infinite lightness to countervail the weight of the Copeland debt. The pro forma capitalization is what you might expect. There is a slight deficit in net worth, $34 million in the aforementioned preferred and $449 million in long-term debt. The income statement is also up to the minute. In the six months ended last June, there was revenue of $226 million, interest expense of about $29 million, and a pretax loss of about $29 million.

The proxy was frank about the prospects for the 17½ percent merger preferred. It did not rule out a sinking spell. The stock was quoted last Monday at 7½ to 8¾, down lately from 10, which is a point below 11, which is the stated value for each share converted in the merger. As you might have guessed, the preferred is junior to everything else in the new Copeland capitalization structure. It is behind a Merrill Lynch bridge loan (originally in the sum of $140 million) and a Canadian Imperial Bank of Commerce term loan (up to $258 million). In one of those stunningly frank admissions that nobody seems to take very seriously, the proxy divulged:

> The company believes that cash flow from operations before deductions of interest, depreciation, and amortization expense will be insufficient to make all of the scheduled principal payments on the term loan. . . . Accordingly, the company expects after the merger to sell, over an estimated three-year period, the company's interest in certain Church's company restaurants . . . for an estimated aggregate proceeds of $160 million.

In short, the company means to reduce debt in part by inducing others to borrow. It intends to shift from owning restaurants to franchising them, selling the stores to existing franchisees. These franchisees, or many of them, will need to borrow. Whether such funds will be forthcoming on economic terms will have something to do with the success of the asset-sales program. On October 17, *The Wall Street Journal* reported CHICKEN CHAINS RUFFLED BY LOSS OF CUSTOMERS. On October 23, the *Journal* reported, a little less succinctly, "Price wars between the fast-food giants are starting to clobber the fast-food little guys: the franchisees." Without special knowledge of the situation, one would have to guess that finding a loan will be harder than it used to be.

The Copeland enterprise must sell, but prospective franchisees do not have to buy. They may want to buy, but not at Copeland's price. They may want to buy but may not, in the prevailing credit climate, find a viable loan. It is rarely easy to get out of debt. In the 1990s, probably, it will even be hard to get in.*

---

* Al Copeland Enterprises filed for bankruptcy protection on April 12, 1991.

KLARMAN BAITS A HOOK

February 16, 1990

The bottom-fishing fleet continues to grow, with Carl Icahn, the aeronautical debtor, now reportedly buying junk bonds for the long pull. In Zurich the other day, Salomon Brothers tried to convince the stolid Swiss to do the same. Maybe the Swiss, who have 9½ percent domestic money-market rates, were moved to buy, and then again, maybe they weren't.

Seth A. Klarman, an investor of private capital in Cambridge, Massachusetts, is now, and has been for some weeks, buying junk bonds—a few issues—with conviction. Here is news to ponder. Klarman, thirty-two years old, is president of The Baupost Group. He is an alumnus of Cornell University and of the Harvard Business School (graduating at the top of the class of 1982). Before setting up in Cambridge, he worked for Michael Price and the late Max Heine at Mutual Shares. Price, now president and chief executive officer, remembers the day when Klarman, then very green indeed, was presented with a bonus and a raise. Klarman's reaction was blunt and unexpected. He asked what the extra money was for. Told that it was in recognition of his good work, Klarman replied that he had not made the firm a dime. "You shouldn't pay people unless they earn and produce," he said, leaving his would-be benefactors somewhat slack-jawed.

Also, by way of full disclosure, Klarman is a fast friend of *Grant's*. He has spoken at our conferences and written in our pages and taken our telephone calls, even when he knew full well that the subject under discussion was going to be the end of civilization as we know it. Although himself estranged from the 1980s, Klarman managed to produce exceptional investment results in the long bull market by adhering to conservative investment principles.

In Klarman's case, conservative is not to be confused with Victorian. He and his partners have bought Mexican stocks, big-capitalization stocks, small-capitalization stocks, newly converted S&Ls, and busted junk bonds. They have bought arbitrage stocks and have sold short the bonds of bank holding companies. A favored all-season investment of Klarman's is cash. Cash, he once wrote, is the "preferred steady state, with investments made only when provoked by a compelling opportunity." In the ransacked junk market, he thinks he has found this provocation. "We believe that there are absolutely compelling opportunities in the lower tier," he said recently. "Using conservative valuation techniques—where things would trade in the stock market assuming earnings decreases rather than increases, and assuming no positive asset sales—we think that there are things trading at absurd prices."

Klarman's declaration would be notable for his boom-time credentials alone. During the full-moon era, he was an outspoken bear, not on all junk at any price (for he dabbled in the securities of distressed companies) but on new junk at par. He was bearish not so much on financial leverage as on the financial-leverage fad. "So while we will not attempt to predict exactly when junk bonds will fall from favor," he and Howard H. Stevenson, the other general partner at Baupost, wrote in January 1987, "we confidently predict their demise." And in 1988 he and Louis Lowenstein, another leading bear on junk, wrote: "We believe that because of the tremendous growth in junk bonds outstanding, calculations of the default rate are understated. Bonds do not default immediately; cash must be squandered and business must worsen (or at least fail to improve), both of which take time. Thus, the default numerator lags the rapidly growing total-junk-outstanding denominator in the default-rate calculation." And from the same essay: "Since few of the junk bond mutual funds have significant cash reserves, when investors want their money, *the funds will have to sell, regardless of price.*"

In Klarman's opinion, the climactic selling began a few weeks ago. He notes that the morale of the junk market is exactly the opposite of what it was. As recently as last summer, the downside was unimaginable. Now it's the upside of which no one can conceive. "The people selling these bonds aren't comparing price to value," he contends. "They just want to get out. It's really important to understand that people are selling them because they're down." He recently wrote to his investors:

> We believe there is considerable value in several of the bad junk bonds now being mercilessly dumped by holders. We analyze these situations for three possible scenarios: bankruptcy, survival, or exchange offer. We buy only if there is a margin of safety for us to do well under any scenario. We are psychologically bolstered by the knowledge that most of these junk bonds are being sold for non-economic reasons. As we mentioned in the year-end letter, junk is losing its luster (it still amazes us that it had any).

It would not be quite accurate to call Klarman a "bull on junk." He is bullish on a few specific bonds at specific prices—on the securities that new-era enthusiasts, in their rush to abandon ship, have thrown over the side. The prices in each case are lower than 50, and Baupost has picked up some Bank of New England debentures at 10. (While many so-called bottom fishers will purchase junk bonds in the 80s, Baupost, generally, does not. David Abrams, a colleague of Klarman's, has theorized that the 80s are usually an elevator stop on a journey to lower floors, sometimes—as in the case of the junior Interco bonds—street level.)

Still, Klarman isn't the bear that he was, and his friends have begun to worry about him. They worry that he might be early or wrong. Also—knowing Klarman—they worry that he might be right. If Klarman is right, as he habitually is, they are wrong. If not wrong, they are less farsighted than Klarman, which would annoy them. Anyway, before calling him to gloat over the crack-up of this or that leverage artist, they must now ascertain whether he owns the fallen securities. Alternatively, a rally in the junk market is more likely to cheer him than to irritate him, and that, too, has taken some getting used to. Is this a new Klarman or a new market? If there is now value in junk, won't there be more value by the time the bottom is plumbed? Or (is it possible?) could this be the bottom?

What simplifies these questions is that Klarman is a small-picture investor. If he has views on Gorbachev, the German bond market, the business cycle, or the global yield curve, he does not call his broker because of them. He does not talk about "support" or "resistance," and he might worry as little about the Federal Reserve System as any white-collar worker in the greater Boston area. He invests from the "bottom up," as he says, not the "top down"— "I buy individual values."

The junk bond market did not walk off a cliff in January. It began to tumble down a long flight of stairs last June when Integrated Resources found itself shut out of the commercial-paper market. The summer brought a succession of smaller crises (Simplicity Pattern, Ohio Mattress, and so forth) and then, after Labor Day, the Campeau default. The weekend following the Allied and Federated news, Klarman and his associates, Abrams and Paul O'Leary, got out the files they had accumulated during the boom. Surely, thought Klarman, the time to buy was at hand. But, he relates, "we didn't make a purchase the next day. Nothing happened. It was a big yawn. Most of the fall, it was a big yawn. Gradually, a few sectors of the market settled lower. We were not in the distressed market in any significant way. In fact, for the last couple of years, many of the securities in distress and bankruptcy have been overvalued—relatively few securities, a lot of new players, and they've held the prices too high. Companies like Integrated, Southmark, Maxicare, Coleco—you would have got clobbered in most of them. They all traded too high.

"Toward the end of the year, we nibbled at a few situations. We've had ongoing positions in a couple of situations for the last couple of years. We have bankruptcy investments in some of the Jones & Laughlin mortgage bonds, in some of the Wheeling Pittsburgh claims. A few other distressed securities. That was a small part of our portfolio.

"I would say that by November-December we started to see more things show up. Securities that perhaps had good value but without good covenants, for example, where you had to ask, 'Could you stand the chance of getting screwed based on the very attractive price that you were being allowed to get in at?' You were already down in some securities by 30–40 cents on the dollar, but with the lack of covenants, it wasn't clear what could happen to you."

Paradoxically, says Klarman, the contraction in speculative-grade credit—junk bonds and bank loans alike—has rebounded to the gain of investors. One ever-present worry for the buyers of junk was "event risk"—the possibility that the leveraged company in which they invested would decide to take aboard new senior debt to make an acquisition. "But that risk," says Klarman, "is really a small risk right now. So one of the big reasons that people knocked the bonds down had actually gone away. But the bonds didn't bounce back."

One cause of this selling panic, in Klarman's view, is the new junk bond orthodoxy. In days gone by, all junk was good. Now some junk is bad, intrinsically. There are, in fact, three classes of junk: a top tier of the Krogers, a middle tier of RJRs, and a bottom tier of Tracors or Intercos. The distinction is silly, Klarman contends, because it is an after-the-fact description rather than a before-the-event prediction. If it were clear in advance which junk would not default, people would buy only that. No matter: Unimaginative money has clogged the upper tier, creating opportunities down below. The sum of down-and-out junk bonds, according to Klarman, amounts to $50 billion at par, implying a market capitalization of not much more than $20 billion.

"Normally," says Klarman of the lowest of the low, "this is an opportunity-laden sector. It's under pressure anyway as people try to blow things out to keep defaults off their records, to window-dress, to get mistakes out of their funds before the statements come out. When a bond doesn't pay current yield, it drags down a portfolio's total return, so they sell. And then, on top of that, you've got this tiering effect where anything bad is seen as triply bad, not only for all the normal reasons but also because it's not in the top tier, and the top tier, according to Wall Street, will do well. A diversified portfolio of top tier, and you'll have a great return. A diversified portfolio of bottom tier, and you'll do terribly. What they miss is that, at some price, you will no longer do terribly. In fact, you will do quite well."

The still-unconverted bears, including us, have their doubts. They wonder if the downside in junk bonds must not bear some symmetrical relation (in duration, lunacy, or both) to the upside. They ask, in effect, can a bubble of four or five years' making be deflated in only four or five months? Has the market adequately discounted the crises of Drexel Burnham, First Executive, et al.? Is the bear market in junk bonds a self-contained event or a symptom of the broader distress in banking and credit? If the latter, might not the liquidation have considerably longer to run? In other words, is the junk bond drama a play in one act or the overture to a longer and noisier production?

Michael Harkins, a New York investor who, until recently, had seen eye-to-eye with Klarman on the junk market, remains bearish. "I've talked with Seth about this a lot," says Harkins. "First off, why do we need to stand in front of every freight train? To turn this thing around, you're going to need a whole new class of buyers for junk bonds, just as, in 1980–81, you needed a whole new class of buyers for Treasuries. So it's likely to be a long bottom, not a spike. Second, businesses have been severely damaged by these capital structures. So when you're paying 60 cents on the dollar, it's 60 cents of exactly what? Next, in paying 60 or 70 cents, aren't we just validating the peak prices that Henry Kravis or somebody paid in 1987, 1988, or 1989? For another thing, there are social costs in all of this—the loss of pension funds, for example—and won't that mean changes in the bankruptcy laws? And there's a practical side. In bankruptcy, a bond is a zero coupon with an unknown maturity date. All of the maturity dates are going to be pushed out into the future just because of the overloading of the courts. You can say, 'We'll get more judges and more courts,' but that will take time. Last but not least, the public still hasn't caught on to this junk bond business. Witness the fact that Bloomingdale's was held up Saturday night."

Klarman gives an answer in several parts. He begins by noting that nobody rings a bell at the bottom. "Just about everyone we talk to is saying to us, 'How do you know that they won't go lower? How do you know all of these things won't go down in your face?' " he says. "And my answer to that is, 'We don't know.' We are bottom-up, not top-down, investors. Top-down people would spend a whole lot of time looking at how bad the economy might get or how many sellers there might be. Bottom-up value investors basically look at the values they buy. They leave room to average down, but they buy if they think the values are compelling. We think the values are compelling. Furthermore, we think there's a chance that the likely continuing selling pressure in the market is already being anticipated by the market. If most buyers have stepped back, awaiting better bargains, that suggests that as soon as better bargains emerge, a lot of buyers will step forward. You never know where the bottom is."

As noted, Klarman is bullish in particular, not in general. He is most particularly bullish on Harcourt Brace Jovanovich, the leveraged publishing and insurance company. Bearish on Harcourt at par, Klarman is excited at a quarter of par. "We've bought the subordinated debt around current market prices, which are in the range of 26 to 30 cents on the dollar of claim," he says. "We think that even under a very adverse scenario—where earnings decline, where the stock market declines, where business values decline and they go bankrupt—we think we can still make a profit from our current purchase price. There aren't too many things in the world where, if the business gets worse, the multiple goes down, you can still make money from where you paid. How many do you know? Of course, this is not for the faint of heart.

"I'll walk you through the numbers," Klarman goes on, "but first I want to tell you how ridiculous the markets are. When Harcourt was good junk, which was at the end of August, the market capitalization of all the pieces of HBJ—bonds, bank debt, equity —was $4.6 billion. Harcourt was trying to sell its theme parks last summer. It ended up selling them to Anheuser-Busch for $1.1 billion. The market was expecting, say, $1.5 billion. Let's give the market the benefit of the doubt. Say they got the $1.5 billion. Then the $4.6 billion should have been reduced by the $1.5 billion that they would have used to pay down debt, leaving $3.1 billion of theoretical market cap. The $3.1 billion, since August 31, has dwindled to where you could buy every security of the company, in the market, for approximately $1 billion. So the market cap of HBJ, adjusted for the sale of the theme parks at the hoped-for price, has dropped from $3.1 billion to $1 billion, more than a 67 percent drop. In comparison, the results of the company have been somewhat disappointing but not by any means as disappointing as the change in market cap. I don't know what people were thinking about in August, but they were clearly making the world's most optimistic assumptions. Everything would go well. Every asset was salable. Businesses were annuities."

As Klarman does the numbers, HBJ is worth between $1.2 billion and $1.7 billion, "and possibly more."* The insurance division produced earnings before interest and taxes—EBIT—of $55 million last year. With a book value in the low $200 million range, it would fetch, he contends, $225 million to $275 million. As for publishing, EBIT totaled about $105 million. The company has promised $30 million in cost cutting this year. Thus, Klarman continues, economies coupled with no gain in income would yield EBIT this year of around $135 million. (Depreciation of $100 million and capital spending almost constitute a wash.) Based on recent asset sales, says Klarman, HBJ—publishing alone—could easily fetch $1.5 billion to $1.7 billion as a multiple of cash flow, not including the $250 million or so attributable to the insurance division.

"However," he goes on, "to be much more conservative, you might say, 'Let's turn HBJ into a stock.' Let's assume no leverage at all and EBIT of $135 million. If you assume a corporate tax rate of 35 percent, you'll have approximately $90 million of after-tax income. If you then applied a market multiple to that, you get $1.1 billion. If you applied a better-than-market multiple, which I think you can reasonably do—there are a couple of public comparables that trade at fifteen to seventeen times earnings—this thing, totally unleveraged, would command, I think, a fifteen multiple, then you'd be looking more at $1.3 billion or $1.4 billion. But even if you wanted to use an even more pessimistic value—if you assume that EBIT of $100 million, or $65 million after tax, down from $90 million after tax—and put a twelve multiple on that, you're still looking at $780 million, which, plus insurance, makes $1.03 billion. At that level you wouldn't do particularly well, but you wouldn't lose any money. But I think pretty strongly that a twelve multiple is way below what this thing would fetch in a takeover, based on any one of a number of recent transactions.

"But the point I want to make is that with a value ranging, I think conservatively, from $1.2 billion to more optimistically $1.8 billion and possibly as high as the low $2 billions, the company has only $1.65 billion of total debt, and I think that there's a good chance that the debt is covered. The capital structure is very im-

---

* General Cinema paid $1.5 billion for the company in October 1991. The Harcourt junk bonds moved up sharply, the 13¾s of 1999, for instance, vaulting as Klarman spoke from 59 to 91 under the terms of the acquisition.

portant here. There's $200 million of 13 percent debt, there's $500 million of 13¾ percent senior subordinated debt, and then there's $950 million of subordinated debt, so there are three classes. There is no bank debt; there is no secured debt. There are two interesting implications of that. One is that, if they did go bankrupt, because there's no secured debt, no one would accrue interest in bankruptcy, in all probability. If they filed, cash would go up and would ultimately benefit the subordinated holders. So if they did ever file, it would actually be a big positive for the subordinated debt. Cash would stop going out above them, and there is no cash that goes out below them.

"The company, I think, has a lot of flexibility. It has, at this moment, $190 million or so of EBIT with only $122 million of cash interest expense. That cushion will remain until September 15, 1992, when the payment-in-kind debentures and the 'zero-slash' debentures begin to accrue interest in cash. The first cash interest payment isn't due until March 1993, so they have a three-year window. That's a lot of time for something to happen.

"They have some tight covenants, but they have a lot of flexibility in terms of potentially bringing in some senior debt above everybody, and using that money to retire some of the outstanding debt at a discount. It would be at a discount, but it would have to be considerably above today's trading levels. And I think there's plenty of value, plenty of room, for them to do just that. There are other ways out of it. They could do an exchange offer and convert some of the debt into equity. You could have a raider type come along, scoop up a lot of the debt, and engineer a similar type of restructuring. A bankruptcy may be the best option because it would eliminate the free riders and would provide an effective means of handling the preferred and common without giving them a lot of value."

Klarman spoke before Drexel made the evening news, but he had anticipated some such turbulence and decided to invest anyway. "How did we know in October 1987 that buying Pennzoil at 41, as we did, was a good bargain?" he asks. "How did we know that it wouldn't be 31 or 21 the next day? How did we know that Texaco bankrupt bonds at 90 were going to be a good bargain where we ended up getting 130? How did we know that? The answer is, you never know how low things might go. But it's exactly when all investors are standing around, looking at each other, asking that question, rather than spending their time putting pencil to paper and figuring out the values that you may be getting the best values of your life.

"The activity of the past month, where people have been hitting bids and acting fairly irrationally, getting out of anything that looked like bad junk, in our view is probably one of the best opportunities you will ever have. Ideally, if you knew there was going to be a liquidation of Columbia Savings & Loan or First Executive, you would love to stand there until they were hitting bids and there were no buyers. You'd not only want to know that they were going to liquidate but also that there were going to be no buyers that day. Then you'd get better bargains than we've had so far. On the other hand, I wouldn't wait until the end of that day to start getting in."

Very well, then. This may or may not be the beginning of the end of the junk bear market. Almost certainly, it is the end of the beginning.

PART SEVEN

THE RISE
AND FALL
OF DEBT

"DEQUITY," AND OTHER
POST–J. P. MORGAN CONCEPTS

October 20, 1986

An address by the editor of Grant's *before the Financial Management Association in New York, October 16.*

I wouldn't be anywhere else this morning. In a bull market, we bears do whatever we can to make ends meet and we do it gratefully. Just the other day I journeyed down South to debate a managing director of Drexel Burnham Lambert on the merits of junk bonds before an expectant audience of life insurance executives. Beforehand, it was agreed that my opponent would speak first, then I would try to rebut him, then we would stand together for questions. But before I could say my piece, the fellow from Drexel had rushed off to catch a plane. He said—and wouldn't you know it?—that he had a deal to do. It was a little like trying to stage a boxing match in Las Vegas when one of the fighters is in Atlantic City.

My subject today is junk, of which, according to *The Wall Street Journal,* I am an "inveterate critic." I suppose that I am, even if "inveterate" means "chronic," which suggests "bursitis" or "rheumatism" rather than, say, "open-minded." In finance there's no bore like an inveterate bore, although if you happen to develop a boring turn of mind at the right time on the right subject, there's no telling how far you can go. In the late 1970s, the right idea was inflation. In the early 1980s, it was disinflation. In the late 1980s, I predict, it is going to be credit.

Junk bonds—known, understandably, by the more dignified

term of "high-yield securities" to the people who have gotten rich by selling them—are a symptom of the illness of credit. They are the sneeze for which optimism is the cold. They are no more the disease than the recent preponderance of downgrades to upgrades in industrial bond rating changes is the disease. The disease is a conviction that one can profitably borrow at 15 percent even if one is earning a marginal rate of return on one's capital of no more than 14⅞ percent.

If credit is sick, as I think it is, then the scarce thing should be prized over the thing in surplus. What is scarce, I should think, is liquidity, or even high-grade debt; the thing in surplus is marginal debt, or junk. I have no quarrel with the compound interest tables or with the historical fact that "high-yield" securities have given a good account of themselves over most of the past five years. But I happen to believe that the next five years will be altogether different from the past five. Indeed, in the past two years, the rate of return on high-yield bonds has been eclipsed by—of all things —low-yield governments.

For a bear it is sometimes useful to recall the times in which people have worried for nothing. The truth is that the creditor class is prone to see ghosts, and no financial era is truly serene except in retrospect. Although the world did not come to an end in 1951, for instance, the Committee on Floor Procedure of the New York Stock Exchange, preparing for that contingency, circulated an apocalypse-style memo among the governors entitled "Treatment of Open Orders in the Event of Atomic Attack."

In 1955, as the Dow Jones Industrial Average finally bested its pre-Crash high, the Senate, casting an ill-timed look over its shoulder, held hearings on the putatively ominous parallels between the Eisenhower bull market and the Coolidge-Hoover market. That was a time, by the way, when the balance sheets of the nation's big banks were still heavy-laden with government securities and when memories of the Depression still informed the everyday decisions of bank lending officers.

We've come a long way since 1955—long enough for the nation to have moved from the "debt is poison" idea, which prevailed for a generation following the Crash, to the "debt is panacea" idea, which rules today. Not coincidentally, the length of time required for this odyssey of sentiment was about the time required for one's grandfather, a distinguished banker who briefly drove a taxicab in 1931, to retire from business and move to Florida and to be taken not very seriously about anything.

Like Eberlin's Restaurant, grandfather and his generation have vanished without a trace. You certainly won't find an excess of government securities on the balance sheets of big city banks nowadays, and you won't find the gospel of debt-free capitalization being preached by Harvard-educated investment bankers. Besides, at current rates of growth, the assets of Drexel Burnham Lambert will probably overtake the public debt within our own lifetime, and where will the bears be then? They will be in livery at Drexel, serving canapés.

If there is such a thing as a credit cycle, as I believe there is, then we are well into its mature, or manic, phase. The times, at least as I read them, are pro-debt. People are anti the paying of compound interest but are pro the receiving of it. Periodically, lip service is paid to the dangers of excess leverage, but it has been no easy thing to be short of the shares of leveraged companies in the stock market. Nor is it any accident that Michael Milken of Drexel, the Thomas Edison of junk, was recently canonized on the covers of *Business Week* and *Institutional Investor*. Long before Drexel runs out of money, the press will run out of superlatives to lavish on it.

In 1936 or 1946 or 1956 or even 1966, it strikes me, there would have been no use for Milken's genius, the world in those distant days still being wary of debt. But the liquidity-loving funk of the 1930s has long since been shaken off, and Safeway Stores, a Drexel customer, now will issue bonds with a balance sheet leveraged 45 to 1 without anybody seeming to think much the worse of it. What drives the credit cycle from an excess of caution to an excess of recklessness is that generations forget.

With debt as common as dirt right here at home, it is instructive, I think, that Prudential-Bache Securities was able to market its Global Yield Fund so successfully last summer. What was most revealing about that particular offering were the luminaries enlisted to serve on its board of directors: Nancy Teeters, the former Federal Reserve governor, and Walter F. Mondale, who needs no introduction. One might reflect that when such personages consent to lend their names to a closed-end investment fund, then the market in question is perhaps closer to the top of its move than to the bottom: in this case, the market in debt.

If you accept that there is a surplus of debt in the world, then you may agree that anyone with a contrary bone in his body should think long and hard about the bond market. And you may also agree that, in these circumstances, the burden of proof concerning the most marginal type of debt—junk bonds—should fall to the bulls.

You have been very kind so far not to interrupt to demand to know why this boom in debt has produced the odd result of a massive decline in the cost of borrowing, and why even the United States government, which runs a chronic negative cash flow, which employs the accounting equivalent of disinformation to stitch together the Farm Credit System, and which has bent over backward to cheapen the dollar against the world's important creditor currencies, has enjoyed the fruits of lower rates.

You might have asked, but didn't, why the government should be able to borrow at 100 basis points less than Eastman Kodak, which, although it doesn't have the power to tax, is nonetheless an honest double-A. I'm not sure that I know, but I am sure that the creditworthiness of the Treasury will figure in the international interest rate equation someday. I am bearish on the federal government.

In any case, the most revealing feature of the junk bond phenomenon to me is its timing. The wonderful success of the Drexel corps of leveraged investors has come at a time of credit decline throughout the economy. Bank failures are up, the ratio of consumer debt to consumer income is up, the Treasury deficit is up, and the incidence of corporate-bond downgrades is up. Very low rated junk bonds or nonrated bonds, as a percentage of the assets of junk bond mutual funds, are up, and so, interestingly this year, are junk bond defaults. Since it is so easy to buy junk (and so very lucrative to sell it), the contrary-minded investor might profitably consider nonjunk. He has been well advised to do so, in fact, since 1984 when governments began to excel against corporates of every stripe.

Before I hark back to the 1920s, as I intend to do right now, I am almost moved to apologize for the triteness of the analogy. But I'm nonetheless struck, as you perhaps have been, by the fascinating comparisons between that bull market and this one. The foremost of these, for my money, is the idea of a credit cycle.

In a number of studies that grew out of the financially contrite 1930s and 1940s, it was found that the default rate on debt instruments varied significantly with the year of their issuance. Residential mortgages, corporate bonds, and foreign government bonds of the late 1920s, or New Era, vintage, for instance, were found to have defaulted with much higher frequency than securities issued before the boom got into full swing—when memories of the Depression and debt liquidation of 1920 were still vividly impressed in the minds of fiduciaries.*

The relevance of that finding for our own day, it seems to me, is that one ought first to try to assess the market's attitude toward debt: Is it properly skeptical? If the answer is "no," as I'm sure it is, we ought to be careful. It almost goes without saying that if the road to riches were really paved with promissory notes, then poverty would have been abolished ages ago. Thus, I won't surprise you by predicting that default rates on the current crop of junk will one day prove embarrassingly high.

Reading the new prospectuses, I sometimes wonder if I'm just a scold who is out of step with the modern improvements. Safeway Stores Holdings Corp. ("Holdings," it calls itself), for example, proposes to restructure its balance sheet in such a way as to produce $5.6 billion in long-term debt and $130 million in equity. Now everybody knows—*I* know—that the prospectus is as pessimistic a genre of financial literature as the brokerage house research report is an optimistic one. But if plain English means anything, then a lot of bondholders are going to be in for a lot of anxiety. Here is a passage from the Safeway document:

> Based upon current levels of operations and anticipated growth, Holdings does not expect to be able to generate sufficient cash flow to make all the principal and interest payments when due on the Bank Indebtedness, Debt Securities, and Merger Debentures. Accordingly, Holdings contemplates that . . . the stock or assets of

---

* One little noted nonparallel to the 1920s is the yield curve. Back then, short rates were about even with investment-grade long rates and not so very far below speculative-grade rates. In those circumstances, it didn't pay to carry a lot of bonds in inventory. Nowadays, of course, the yield curve is steeply positive. It pays, and pays well, to hold junk bonds for the rise, which is a fine thing until the day they stop going up.

certain subsidiaries will be sold in order to generate cash to reduce the amount of Bank Indebtedness. No decision has been made as to when such sales would occur, no assets have been identified for sale, and no such decision will be made or assets identified until after completion of a detailed evaluation by Holdings and its subsidiaries of Safeway's assets and operations.

It almost goes without saying, of course—we are all men and women of the world—that the bankers and issuers know the assets far better than we do, and that the hyper-leveraged type of deal has become as routine a financial operation as the appendectomy has become a medical one. We know, too, that this is not the old-fashioned kind of debt, the kind that used to be analyzed on a "depression basis." It is a new kind of debt, a combination of debt and equity that my investment-banker wife, Patricia Kavanagh, has innovatively termed "dequity." *It* is sold not on a depression basis but with a wing and a prayer because, in general, to start out with, the issuers haven't the means to service it; they say they will service it by selling assets, or "restructuring," or doing some other clever thing, but they add, of course, that there can be no assurance.*

I think there can be some assurances. I think it's in the cards that we'll see lots more marginal debt. That is the nature of the manic phase of the credit cycle. It is written somewhere that the marginal underwriter must meet the marginal issuer and that together they must make the acquaintance of the marginal investor. It is necessary that everyone become fully positioned in order to complete the top.

It is the nature of markets to test the extremes of an idea, and it seems to me that the credit markets are currently pushing the extremes of leverage. In the wake of the Crash, a survivor coined a profound aphorism on the subject of mass enthusiasms: "The more intense the craze, the higher the order of intellect that succumbs to it." I submit that our craze is debt and that nearly every genius on Wall Street is climbing on board.

---

* Safeway lived to tell the tale. It sold unprofitable divisions, refinanced its debt at lower interest rates, improved its credit standing, and relentlessly cut its costs. "We're looking in every nook and cranny to get costs out of the company," a spokesman declared in early 1993. "Getting costs out" is a phrase that underscores the fact that, since the buyout, it has been better to lend to Safeway than to work for it.

THE "L" WORD

April 20, 1987

The mugging of the bond market raised the stimulating question of where the liquidity went. All through the rise, bulls kept saying that "the world is awash with liquidity." The phrase became a kind of incantation or brokers' chantey. It seemed a truth so obvious that nobody bothered to ask what it meant.

If the world was awash with liquidity when the long-dated Treasury bond yielded 7.40 percent, where was all the liquidity at 8.40 percent? Had it vanished into the ozone layer, like Right Guard? Had it been rechanneled out of municipal bonds, corporate bonds,

New York Stock Exchange Official Schedule

August 1992

MON	TUES	WED	THU	FRI
3	4	5	6	7
10	11	12 F	13	14
17	18	19	20	21 F
24 / 31	25	26 D	27 H	28

▨ buy growth stocks ☐ buy cyclicals
F - Federal Reserve cuts funds rate
H - Helmet Day - prices may fall
▨ - double header - buy 'em both!

preferred, and common stock into cotton, lumber, gold, and Van Goghs? In truth, "the world is awash with liquidity" is a rubber phrase, wonderfully adaptable to the intended meaning of anyone who uses it.

The late Melchior Palyi defined liquidity as the "capacity to fulfill financial obligations." The world can hardly be said to be awash with that, any more than it can be said to be awash with prudence. The metaphor falls flat. Among living authorities, Henry Kaufman defines liquidity as the ability to dispose of an asset at par, and he contrasts that capacity with mere marketability, which is the ability to dispose of an asset at any price.

On the Street, the everyday meaning of liquidity would seem to be closer to money. Not just money, but big money, as in the Federal Reserve's all-inclusive definition of the monetary aggregate "L," which stands for "liquidity" and embraces M-1, M-2, M-3, savings bonds, short-term governments, commercial paper, and so forth. In that kitchen-sink definitional spirit, *The Wall Street Journal* recently reported that "buying heavily outweighed selling, and several Japanese securities firms also launched new investment trusts, *adding to the increased liquidity* [our italics]." In this case, "liquidity" could stand in, semantically, for "bull market" or "supply of stock" or "gaiety."

Thus, when people assert "the world is awash with liquidity," they apparently mean one of three things: (1) the capacity to turn assets readily into cash is common and becoming more common; (2) the money supply is high and rising; or (3) (the most subjective usage) because markets are tight and money is plentiful, we should all be bullish.

Usage number one is plainly incorrect. One need look no further for proof than Monday's panic in mortgage-backed securities or the recent debacle in perpetual floating-rate notes (you'll recall that that once-thriving $18 billion Euromarket vanished for lack of bids) or the fact that IBM, arguably the most liquid stock in the world, was delayed in opening by almost an hour on March 30. "Order imbalance," they said.

Is the world awash in money (usage number two)? At last report the composite money supply of Japan, Germany, and the United States was up year-over-year by 8½ percent. Briefly, in the early 1970s, it grew by 16 percent; and as recently as 1982, it grew by

10 percent. By past lights, therefore, 8½ percent is perky but not breakneck.

Usage number two cannot so easily be dismissed, however, because the United States is certainly awash with credit. Growth in nonfinancial debt has set postwar records (12 percent to 14 percent) for the past three years, and the electronic velocity of money worldwide is sharply on the rise. As dollars swirl ever faster in financial business, that increased efficiency is tantamount to a bigger dollar supply. The old saying went, approximately: A fast nickel is as good as a slow dime. In any case, the world is spending faster, and the United States is borrowing more than ever before.

What doesn't follow, however, is usage number three, the let's-all-be-bullish interpretation. It is chic to assert that the rise in debt or the rise in the financial efficiency of funds has created the bull market, but maybe the bull market has conjured up the money. And even if money did cause the global upswing, why didn't money prevent the recent U.S. decline? If money was all that bull markets needed, why would we ever have bear markets?

PRINT IT

March 7, 1988

L ate last month a member of the President's Council of Economic Advisers, Thomas Gale Moore, said in a public place that the United States could simply print the dollars it owes to foreign investors if it ever felt it had to. He hastened to add that that was not his idea of sound policy. But, he said, the presses could roll in a bind. The Dow Jones story led with a punch:

> WASHINGTON—The U.S. transition to a net debtor nation is not a significant problem, in part because the country could pay off its creditors simply by running the currency printing press, Thomas

Gale Moore, a member of the President's Council of Economic Advisers, said.

Speaking to a monetary conference sponsored by the Cato Institute, the economist stressed that he was not recommending such an approach, but he indicated that it was clearly an option at some point if worse came to worst.

"We can pay anybody off by running a printing press, frankly," Moore said, "so it's not clear to me how bad that [the transition to net debtor status] is."

What followed was silence. The dollar and the bond market happened to fall on the day Moore spoke—it was Thursday, February 25—but nobody blamed the economist for that. More to the point, nobody seemed to have heard what he said. There was not a word in the New York press Friday. We didn't check the Tokyo papers.

Maybe Moore didn't say it, we thought, and we ordered a tape of the proceedings (they were sponsored by the Cato Institute in Washington). But the audio tape corroborated the broad tape. Yes, Moore had conceded, the United States is a debtor nation, but he noted the mitigating fact that we owe the debt in a currency we can manufacture domestically, at insignificant cost. "Now, Brazil owes their money in terms of dollars," he said. "They, to my knowledge, don't have a dollar printing press. So they've got to get these dollars from somewhere else."

Asked to elaborate, Moore said, "I'm not recommending that we run the printing press. . . . I'm just saying that when we owe money, we owe money in terms of dollars, and it's easier for us to provide dollars than it is for Brazil to provide dollars."

For the information of foreign holders of U.S. assets, Moore works for the president's chief economic adviser, Beryl W. Sprinkel. Moore's job is purely advisory. He does not actually set policy. He is not to be confused with the Treasury Secretary, James Baker, or the Federal Reserve Chairman, Alan Greenspan.

If a foreign investor is nonetheless startled that a senior American adviser would glibly discuss the sovereign equivalent of a Chapter 11 proceeding, he can comfort himself with the fact that this is an election year. The new team perhaps will discuss the efficacy of debt repudiation only behind closed doors.

INTEREST RATES, NTT, AND YOU

March 17, 1989

The Japanese discount rate is 2½ percent, whereas the Japanese prime minister's approval rating is 13.1 percent. Each is at rock bottom, although it is possible that Noboru Takeshita could sink into single-digit public esteem if the Recruit scandal continues to swirl around his salt-and-pepper head. As for the discount rate, it is unlikely to go any lower and may yet, in our lifetime, go higher.

Periodically, in the manner of central banks everywhere, the Bank of Japan clears its throat and challenges inflation to a fight. It has been easy to ignore these pronouncements, for there has been no inflation to speak of at the consumer level, and the inflation of common stock prices has been treated as a public blessing, not

"Here's an idea, Eddie. Let's not call Tokyo on the cellular to catch the opening of the old Nikkei."

a danger. Furthermore, as the Bank of Japan knows as well as anyone, Japanese real estate speculators need low interest rates, and Japanese stock market speculators need high real estate prices. Real estate valuations support equity valuations, and vice versa. The easy flow of bank credit supports the stock market, and the ever-rising stock market emboldens lenders and borrowers. It is a golden circle. Inasmuch as the world needs Japanese liquidity, the risks associated with a rise in Japanese interest rates are considerable.

Thus, a March 8 dispatch by Reuters from Tokyo (it preceded the recent run-up in oil prices) is still required reading for interest-rate-minded investors:

> In its most direct statement yet on inflation, the Bank of Japan warned Wednesday that the risks of higher prices in Japan were mounting and said the central bank stood ready to take "prompt" monetary action to maintain price stability.
>
> The statement, coupled with remarks by the bank's governor, sent yen bond prices plunging on fears of an increase in the Japanese discount rate.
>
> Satoshi Sumita, the central bank governor, said that although price stability is unlikely to be undermined in the short term, he could not be optimistic about future trends.
>
> Pointing in its report to gradually mounting price pressures in Japan, the central bank noted, "The future course of price development needs to be monitored with more vigilance than before."

The report that was mentioned in the story was published by the BOJ, and it concluded (as Salomon Brothers paraphrased it) that "a larger number of manufacturers than at any time since the early 1970s perceive shortages in goods and labor markets, inventories, and productive capacity."

If the fallout from that statement constitutes a full-blown Japanese bear market, as a few observers have optimistically asserted, we should be so lucky. In the past two weeks, Japanese money-market rates have ticked up fractionally, and long-dated Japanese bond yields have been pushed to 5¼ percent from 5 percent. Japanese stocks have stopped going up, stalling in the 31,000 area, which, however, is many thousands of points higher than where they were when *Grant's* first sounded the Nipponomania alarm.

Also, as the BOJ hastened to add, monetary policy *may* be tightened, but it has not been tightened yet.

The view of Japan from lower Manhattan is no clearer today than it was before and is indeed obscured by tax reform. On April 1, Japanese consumers will begin paying a 3 percent value-added tax. Simultaneously, individual and corporate income tax rates will be cut. Also simultaneously, investors must begin to pay a nominal capital gains levy. The net of all this is hard to fathom, but Brian S. Wesbury, a vice president of Stotler & Co., Chicago (he's almost a thousand miles closer to Tokyo than we are), contends that Japanese investors might logically take profits before the April 1 tax date.

We mention this as one possible explanation for the recent weakness in the Nikkei Dow and for the raggedness of the broader list. For some time the market average has risen, but a growing number of issues have fallen. Last summer, when the Japanese market was lower, we described the advance-decline line as "ominous"—as if the slope of the line had clear and scientifically established predictive properties. It turned out to be no more ominous than any other known influence on Japanese securities prices. This time out, we merely note that the broad market has been weaker than the averages. That is not a bullish omen in the Occident.

If you allow the importance to the world of Japanese liquidity, you will also allow the importance of the Japanese stock market. And if you care about the Japanese market, you must also care about the biggest Japanese stock, Nippon Telegraph & Telephone. You may remember the gaudy debut of NTT on the Tokyo Stock Exchange in February 1987. It was not until minutes before the bell rang on the close of the second day of trading that enough sellers could be scraped together to complete the first trade, at about 1.6 million yen. The company's chairman, Hisashi Shinto, called the spectacle "mind-boggling." Just before the initial public offering he had remarked to reporters, only half-jokingly, "One day people engaged in the money game are going to incur the wrath of God."* On April 22, the price of a share hit 3.18 million yen. NTT was the Japanese market writ large: hopelessly overvalued by any Western fundamental yardstick but levitating nevertheless.

---

* One of the best predictions of the era.

The telephone company's capitalization equaled the combined *market* capitalizations of Germany and Hong Kong.

The decline in NTT began on April 23, 1987. The price did not crash, however, and in the days and weeks that followed October 19, the stock found organized support. In November 1987, *The Japan Economic Journal* published a rah-rah piece under the headline MARKET CRASH FAILS TO RATTLE NTT BUYERS. It said, in part:

> "The popularity of NTT is attributed to individual investors' beliefs that since the government made the public offering, it would not inflict losses on the people," said an analyst. Masami Fukuoka, manager of the stock trading department at Yamaichi Securities Co., also said that individual investors consider they are buying Japan itself when they acquire NTT shares. So they buy them without apprehension, Fukuoka added.

Apprehension wormed its way into the picture, however. The company—the second-largest telecommunications business in the world, behind AT&T—became caught up in the Recruit affair. Last December, Chairman Shinto resigned under a cloud. And on March 6, the seventy-eight-year-old industrialist was arrested on bribery charges. In deference to the gentleman's stature and reputation, prosecutors carried him off in a car with opaque windows, the better to screen him from television cameras. "Nippon Telegraph & Telephone Corp. will cut by 10 percent to 20 percent the salaries of thirty-five executives to show their acceptance of individual responsibility in the Recruit stock scandal," Reuters reported from Tokyo last Monday.

On Tuesday, a share of NTT fetched about 1.6 million yen—an epic round trip from the first sale two years ago.* (Some 78 percent of the company, a former public utility, remains in the hands of the government.) Even at that bargain price, however, the valuation amounted to one hundred times projected 1990 earnings and a dividend yield of 0.3 percent. A Japanese observer in New York says that "good support" is available at current levels.

---

* Now less than six hundred thousand. On February 23, 1993, NTT disclosed plans to reduce its work force of more than two hundred thousand by thirty thousand over the next three years and to cut its thirteen hundred retail outlets by a third.

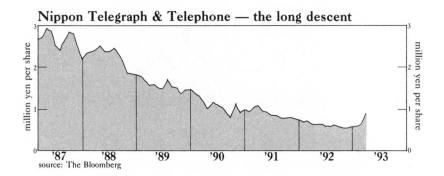

Nippon Telegraph & Telephone — the long descent

source: The Bloomberg

The quiet bear market in NTT is testimony both to the strength and weakness of the Japanese system. What it proves is that a stock can go down after all. As for the Tokyo market as a whole, and for all it signifies to the international credit markets, each day is a new adventure.

TAKE MY KEYS, SIR

October 26, 1990

S had Rowe writes from Dallas:

Just as the top credit professional of the 1980s was the banker, so the top credit professional of the 1990s may be the repo man. If so, "Bulldog" (a.k.a. "Bloodhound"), skip tracer and "credit adjuster" extraordinaire, is a man to know and study. He describes himself, simply, as "a leader in my field."

Repo men and their employers generally do not use their real names for fear of lawsuits or more violent forms of retribution. The

"Credit Card for the 1990s"

AMERICAN E[X]
PESSIMA
3415
1319 37
07/92 THRU 06/9
JAMES D ROBINSON

nicknames "Bulldog" and "Bloodhound" would seem to stem more from qualities of character than from appearance. He does not look like a bulldog or a bloodhound. He looks more like a tank.

Bulldog is in his "mid-forties," stands six feet two inches and weighs 325 pounds. He has a friendly manner of speaking, and his right eye twitches when he concentrates. The effect is unintentionally quite menacing. A sane person would not knowingly upset Bulldog, and if there is anything in this article even mildly offensive to him, it is solely the responsibility of the editor.

I met Bulldog through a car-dealer friend for whom Bulldog has repossessed cars for eighteen years. According to my friend, Bulldog is the best in the business. Only once has he failed to return either with the money due or with the automobile. Never has there been a lawsuit or a problem with the police. Often, the mere sight or sound of Bulldog motivates the borrower to bring his payments up to date.

I had to beg Bulldog for an interview. "Come on," I pleaded, "this is a great story. You are a great talker."

"You're right about that," he admitted. "I'll tell you something. If you are standing in a man's yard at 4 a.m. and that man has a 12-gauge shotgun pointed at your face, you'd better be able to talk pretty good. Why, I've had men point guns at me, and ten minutes later they're giving me the keys to their cars and offering me a cup of coffee."

Bulldog's specialty is repossessing automobiles, although he will work in other areas of the credit arena. He occasionally repossesses bail-bond jumpers. He does not enjoy this sort of work because the laws have become "tedious," and he fears being brought up on kidnapping charges. He told me that he once repossessed a $25,000 set of false teeth against which a Houston finance company had lent $9,000. "Oh, come on," I said, "false teeth do not cost $25,000." "You never saw these teeth!" he explained. "There were four carats in diamonds and rubies and all kinds of gold." According to Bulldog, the Houston finance company had made the same mistake a lot of lenders make. The loan agreement duly noted where the borrower "lived" (at his mother's in Houston). It did not note where he "stayed," which was in Oklahoma City. Bulldog pridefully explained that if a defaulted borrower is alive, he (Bulldog) will find him.

Anyway, Bulldog located his man in Oklahoma City and pulled into the borrower's driveway in his wrecker with the tow sling hanging ominously. The borrower ran out of the house screaming that he was not behind in his car payments. "I'm not here for your car," replied Bulldog. "I'm here for your teeth." "That's fine," said the borrower, dropping the teeth in his driveway. "You take 'em and get away from my house. Them teeth never chewed good anyway." Bulldog Federal Expressed the teeth back to the Houston finance company and rightfully collected his fee ($900, or 10 percent of the outstanding loan balance, plus expenses).

Of the various lenders who engage Bulldog, bankers would seem to be the dumbest. Bulldog tells the story of a Dallas bank that hired him to recover a Bentley against which it had lent a considerable amount of money. Neither the borrower nor the car could be found. Bulldog said that after ninety-two days he traced the deadbeat to Charleston, South Carolina. Bulldog flew to Charleston and confronted his man. "All right, where's the Bentley?" he asked politely. Puzzled at first, the borrower explained that four months earlier he had told the bank that he could not keep up the payments, had parked the Bentley in the bank's own parking garage, and had dropped off the keys. Bulldog flew back to Dallas, located the Bentley exactly where the borrower said it would be, and collected his fee.

Bulldog charges $250 for most automobile repossessions, an amount that is slightly higher than the market. Bulldog believes he is worth it. Any competent repo man can repossess a car in ten or twenty seconds. The hard part is locating borrowers who have "skipped." That is where Bulldog's superior detective skills pay off. Again he repeats with pride that if you are alive, he will find you and that he has never had a problem with the police or with lawsuits.

"With consumer defaults on the rise, business must be fantastic," I speculated. "Not really," Bulldog replied almost sadly. "The problem is the laws are getting more and more tedious, more pro-borrower, and that makes it hard for a man in my profession."* As an example, he explained that Louisiana is a non-repossession state. To repossess property in Louisiana, a lender must work through the sheriff in the parish in which the borrower resides. Most Louisiana sheriffs are not as efficient as Bulldog.

Almost wistfully conscious of his many years in the business, Bulldog speaks of repossessing cars from young folks whose parents he had to confront years before. The young folks have credit cards and move around faster than their parents did, so they are harder to trace. "You know," says Bulldog, "if your daddy and your mama keep up their payments and take care of their business, the chances are that their kids will, too."

I wanted to know about all those credit cards. Did Bulldog ever get hired by credit card companies? He just laughed. "Naw. There's such a thing as credit card fraud, and that's a police matter. There's not much that anybody else can do about those things." Of course. Credit card debt, we know, is unsecured. It is Bulldog-proof, which probably does not bode well for the loan-loss experience of consumer lenders in the next recession.

Having worked for all sorts of lenders, Bulldog is well qualified to offer his prospective employers a bit of advice: "You can either do your credit work on the front end, crossing your t's and dotting your i's and making sure of your customers, or you can face the consequences on the back end, at which point you'll be talking to me."

Unfortunately for the lending profession, there are not enough Bulldogs to go around. After spending a little more time around him, I ventured a little humor. "You know," I said, "I bet that the people who pulled guns on you were probably thinking that if they did shoot you, they might not kill you and then they'd be in

---

* It has gotten worse. "Nobody's financing cars," Bulldog now tells Rowe. In 1993 the repo man was wearing a pair of false teeth around his neck suspended from a massive chain. According to Bulldog, the teeth were a gift from an admirer who had read Rowe's essay.

real trouble. That's why they get nice all of a sudden." Bulldog turned serious, and his eye twitched. "If somebody did shoot me, I expect it would piss me off."

IS IT INFLATION?

March 15, 1991

On Friday bond prices fell, the gold market rallied, and the yield curve steepened. On Sunday, however, *The New York Times* was sure enough of its predictive ground to print an unhedged economic prediction on its front page: AN EXCEPTION TO RULE OF WAR: INFLATION THREAT IS RECEDING.

For years *Grant's*, too, has thought that inflation was receding, but lately we've begun to have our doubts. We note, as the *Times* noted, that the price of oil has fallen, that spot industrial commodity prices are stagnant (the recent rally in the CRB futures index notwithstanding), and that money-supply growth is anemic. We also note that for the past year and a half the Federal Reserve has been expanding the size of its balance sheet as if its chairman were being paid on a piecework rate. Furthermore, the dollar has appreciated against the deutsche mark and gold, but it has lost significant ground against stocks and junk bonds.

As financial semantics is as much debased as any *Latino* currency, a definition of terms is in order. Inflation is a decline in the value of money. It is a broad decline, not a narrow one. Inflation is no more a phenomenon of the oil price alone than deflation is purely a phenomenon of the real estate market. When prices in general decline, that is deflation. Thus, we have no deflation. We may expect deflation in the future, but we have none in the present. What we have is inflation at the consumer level in excess of 5 percent.

We accept as proven the Friedmanite proposition that "inflation is always and everywhere a monetary phenomenon." Ditto, deflation. Significant changes in the value of money are not the result of changes in relative prices, for example, a fall in West Texas crude or a rise in the Dow Jones Industrial Average. They are the result of changes in the monetary order.

Grant's for years has espoused a deflationary view, and we are not quite ready to abandon it. However, we are conducting a free and frank exchange of views, with ourself, on the entire range of monetary issues. What led us to think about deflation in the first place was the truism that credit creation is a process. The Federal Reserve proposes but the marketplace disposes. The Fed may expand its balance sheet, thereby creating the dollars known as "bank reserves" or the dollars known as currency. And the commercial banks, in turn, may lend. Unless the commercial banks have the will and capacity to lend, however, the process will falter. Lately, it has.

Now what? Alan Greenspan has implied that he will stop at almost nothing to forestall deflation. He has reduced reserve requirements and repeatedly lowered the federal funds rate. On February 21, in testimony before the House Banking Committee, he disclosed that he was considering the outright purchase of loans from commercial banks.

Once upon a time, the Federal Reserve did buy commercial loans, and it also lent directly to businesses that could not find other accommodation. It obtained those emergency powers in 1934, a year after the Great Depression officially ended. The program under which it lent (or guaranteed 80 percent of the principal value of the loans of participating commercial banks) was called the 13-b program, and it was not repealed until 1958. It is a sign of the times that the functional equivalent of the 13-b stopgap is proposed now, at a time when there is no depression, great or small, only a "short and shallow recession," and also, strangely enough, a star-burst in equities. It isn't every day that a banking crisis precipitates a bull market. Clearly, credit is sick. Just as clearly, however, the federal government intends to heal it. The question is whether the government can and whether, in the process, it might provoke inflation.

In monetary affairs, as in so many others, intentions and results are separate and distinct. "Adjusted Fed credit" is the basic measure of Federal Reserve intent; it shows what Alan Greenspan would like to do if the banks would only lend and the public borrow. It is defined as the sum of the central bank's assets, mainly its government securities; in banker's talk, its footings. The Fed, as mighty as it is, controls nothing in the world absolutely except its own balance sheet. M-2 is a measure of monetary results. It is defined as the sum of currency, checking accounts, savings accounts, money-market accounts, and so forth. It was formerly imagined that by opening or closing the valves of "repo" or "matched sales," the Fed could manage the nation's money supply. Money was water, and the Fed was the plumber.

Almost nobody believes that today, and the proof is the visible gap between monetary intent (that is, Fed credit) and results obtained (that is, M-2). To shift metaphors from hydraulic to automotive, the monetary transmission is slipping. The Federal Reserve is hitting on every cylinder, but the wheels don't seem to be turning.

So far is economics from being a branch of physics that you can get an argument on almost any monetary assertion that comes into your head. Looking at the graph of adjusted Fed credit, beginning in 1989, you might say, "The Fed's been laying it on with a trowel," but someone else could say, and with equal authority, "No, it hasn't." You and your disputant would differ on the relevant measure of Federal Reserve intent. You would identify the entire balance sheet as the meaningful indicator of what the Fed would like to do. Your debating partner would identify bank reserves as the only meaningful indicator. "Reserves," as mentioned, are dollars. They are what a bank or thrift must lay aside (at the Fed or in vault cash) as a defense against unexpected withdrawals. They are, from the standpoint of the Federal Reserve's balance sheet, liabilities, because they are the deposits of commercial banks. Banks are the Fed's customers.

You wouldn't have to stop arguing there. You could repeat yourself about the Fed overdoing it, and your friend could parry with the fact that the Federal Reserve System's consolidated holdings of government securities (the bills, notes, and bonds it owns outright) peaked as long ago as the week of December 5, at $242 billion. In the latest reporting week, ended March 6, they stood at only $238 billion. To which you could say, "So what?" Because the Fed has cut reserve requirements, fewer dollars of central bank credit are needed to carry the same volume of bank deposits. "Adjusted" Fed credit is adjusted to reflect that fact. The Fed, by that measure, is more than accommodative.

In the old days—before banking deregulation and the Monetary Reform Act of 1980 and last December's reduction in reserve requirements—bank reserves afforded a more direct means of monetary control than they do today. Years ago the Fed would expand reserves and the banks would step up their loans and money supply would ratchet up. The process is more complex nowadays for at least two reasons. First, the ratio of bank reserves to M-1 and M-2 has declined for twenty years. In consequence, the Federal Reserve has relinquished a certain measure of monetary control. In the case of savings deposits, for example, no reserve requirements apply nowadays. The Fed could create bank reserves all day yet not, by that means, cajole an extra dollar of M-2 out of the banking system.

Second, the public itself decides to hold its extra dollar in the form of currency or a bank deposit. If the public prefers currency, it will redeem its deposits. The banks, honoring those requests, will requisition currency from the Federal Reserve Banks. The Federal Reserve Banks will debit the reserve accounts of the banks obtaining the currency. Thus, by withdrawing deposits, the public reduces the reserve base of the banking system. It does not reduce the "monetary base," which you know is the sum of currency and bank reserves. But it does change the mix of the monetary base: It increases the currency component and diminishes the bank-reserve component. Inasmuch as one dollar of bank reserves supports the creation of something like $8 in checking accounts, a currency-seeking public also reduces the banking system's leverage. It inhibits the ability of banks (and thrifts) to make new loans or to buy new securities.

For some time we've believed that the nation's income statement and balance sheet had mysteriously parted company. The CPI kept going up—an inflation of the income statement—but the prices of assets, notably real estate, kept going down—a deflation of the balance sheet. It was our hunch that the balance sheet was the leading indicator of things to come and that the income statement was the lagger.

The stock market rally has cast this theory into the outer darkness where worthless options expire. No less than office buildings, shares of corporations are "assets." The lift-off in the prices of good companies and bad companies this year was not financed by illiquidity but by the opposite, abundant credit.

The most hawkish governor of the Federal Reserve Board, Wayne Angell, regularly stumps for a "price rule" in monetary policy, by which he means that the Fed should steer by the lights of certain commodity prices. Angell watches the gold market but not the stock market. But what none of us knows is whether his favorite prices are tomorrow's leading indicators or yesterday's. Commodities play an increasingly minor role in the American retail price structure. It will be said that that is not the point at all. The point is to identify an index of inflationary tinder, that is, of surplus cash balances. But if that's the case, it seems to us, we ought to consider shifting speculative tastes. In January 1980, everybody wanted gold bullion. In January 1991, everybody wanted the common stock of Ames Department Stores, Wells Fargo, and Household International. Could it be (some readers have asked) that stocks are going up because they constitute a hedge against a future inflation that the equity market seems to anticipate?

Over the years we've broadened our own concept of the "money supply." There are the tangible monetary aggregates, which the Federal Reserve presumes to count and control. Then there is the intangible aggregate, credit. Credit is money of the mind. It is not only a loan but also the expectation of receiving a loan. To be in possession of credit is to view the world expansively. To be denied a loan is to worry.

In recent months the Federal Reserve has indicated that, vis-à-vis the credit contraction, it will pull a Norman Schwarzkopf. By even considering desperate measures in a "mild recession" (successor to the "soft landing"), it has acknowledged the rot of credit and thus the risk of deflation. Understandably, even laudably, the administration means to repair the monetary transmission. If it succeeds, however, who's to say that it will not then drive the car too fast?

Under the so-called price rule, speculators and central bankers spend much of the day watching each other. Speculators wonder if the Fed is going to tighten, and the Federal Reserve wonders if the speculatorrs are going to cause it to tighten. All of which leads us back to the possible significance of the recent bulge in the Federal Reserve's balance sheet.

An old friend of ours, Fred D. Kalkstein, is one who believes that the best leading indicator of inflation is money and that the best leading indicator of money is the Federal Reserve. He's not convinced that 1991 is any different from the last three occasions on which adjusted Fed credit climbed vertically. In 1978, 1983, and 1987, bond yields rose, and he predicts another rise in 1991.

Kalkstein's article of faith is that the authorities are as bearish about the economy as he is. Believing that, he was not surprised when the Fed pushed down the funds rate, swelled its balance sheet, and undertook a number of accounting and regulatory expedients with the aim of reviving credit creation in the banking system. He says he expects more of it. "Obviously," he says, "the Fed must reflate," and it began to reflate, he added—that is, to step up the rate of growth in its assets—before the recession began.

"Recession is a dirty word," he goes on, "and that's understandable. But recessions are necessary. People have to sleep, and businesses and households have to rebuild their liquidity. What the Fed is doing now is what it was doing in the 1970s. It's trying to paper over a recession." Kalkstein went on to assert that the recession is international in scope, not merely domestic, and that the world finds itself increasingly short of capital. He noted that the U.S. inflation rate is currently in excess of 5 percent and that the Swiss inflation rate is in excess of 6 percent. Those are big numbers on which to build a new inflationary cycle, he said.

As for us, we acknowledge that not one single politician is working to bring about the future that we still vaguely expect. On the other hand, both major parties, both houses of Congress, the White House, the Federal Reserve Board, and the Treasury Department are carrying the water of the inflationists. What we have always known is that the government would fight deflation tooth and nail. What we did not expect was that the bond market would be as forgiving of these desperate measures as it has been to date. The rallying cry of the bulls in recent months has been that nothing would prevent the Federal Reserve from pushing short-term interest rates to zero if that were necessary. Thus, a deflation theorist must ask himself: If the bond market doesn't really object to that (its protests have been mild so far) and if the currency market doesn't object (the dollar now is rallying), what *does* stand in the way of Alan Greenspan? If the answer is nothing and nobody, the economy will soon be stuffed with bank credit.*

To restart business activity, the inflationists are depending on the coordinated efforts of bank regulators, central bankers, bond buyers, and currency traders. They need confident borrowers, solvent lenders, and frightened central bankers. They have the central bankers they need, and we will just have to see about the others.

THE SHRINKING CHAIRMAN

July 19, 1991

I n our view," a Wall Street economist fulsomely ventured after the nomination of the chairman of the Federal Reserve Board to a second term, "Greenspan is the best chairman since Marriner Eccles and is more dedicated than any other central banker in the world to fighting inflation."

In our opinion—your editor is speaking—Alan Greenspan is not the best Fed chairman since Eccles. He is another guy with a business suit and a personal computer who thinks he can make an honest woman out of paper money. By the way, Eccles was no prize himself. In the debate leading up to passage of the Banking Act of 1935, Roosevelt's chairman pushed to expand the real estate lending powers of commercial banks. As every American taxpayer may surmise, he got his way.

When Greenspan is praised or blamed for the domestic inflation

---

* Up to this writing, "nothing and nobody" has proved to be the correct answer. The Federal Reserve's balance sheet has continued to expand and the money supply to stagnate. The resulting financial prosperity has, if anything, become more widespread. Nobody so far has entered a strong objection to it except for the short-sellers and the long-suffering bulls on gold.

"By gosh, I guess they have eased."

rate or for the subpar growth in the broad monetary aggregates, we wonder what the words mean. More and more, it seems to us, markets make monetary results. Policy—the volition of people drawing federal salaries—makes fewer results all the time.

It is helpful to recall what it is that the Federal Reserve does. It buys and sells government securities to manipulate the federal funds rate. It influences the term structure of interest rates and thereby the decisions of lenders and borrowers. It does not itself lend (except to banks), and it does not set the terms and conditions of borrowing. It may influence the quoted value of the collateral offered to secure a loan, but it does not determine that value. In theory, any monopolist may control the price or the volume of the commodity it monopolizes. However, it cannot control both at once. The Federal Reserve, a monopoly central bank, tries to control nearly everything: price (the funds rate), volume (the monetary aggregates), politics (the GNP), and price again (the foreign-exchange rate of the dollar). It winds up not controlling much at all.

The conventional language of central banking is heavily freighted with assumptions about cause and effect. People will say, "The Fed is tight," when they mean to say, "You can't get a loan these days." They will say, "Greenspan is doing a great job," when they might have said, "The early stages of a debt contraction feel pretty good, don't they?"

Cause and effect are no abstract matters. If the economy is really a puppet on the strings of monetary policy, Greenspan himself must be treated as a fundamental investment fact, like the price of ethylene. If, on the other hand, the Federal Reserve has lost an important measure of control over money and credit, the chairman must increasingly be treated as a distraction.

That is our theory of Alan Greenspan. The Fed is constrained by other central banks and by the legacy of its own inflationary policies. (Credit contractions do not occur spontaneously but because of preceding bouts of reckless expansion.) The connection between the Fed and the commercial banking system has been made more tenuous by the steady reduction in reserve requirements and the connection between the banking system and the economy has been weakened by the impairment of the lenders' capital and liquidity. In the 1950s the connection between the Federal Reserve System and the banking system was direct and uncomplicated. Today it is neither. In the 1950s the banks still enjoyed a commanding position in the process of credit creation. That they do no more is shown by the boom in commercial paper and by the rise in the process of "securitization," the fashioning of securities out of loans. The Fed is losing market share.

Checking around with various monetary authorities, we found not one who believed just that. "The other side of the argument," observed one, parrying us, "is to note that Greenspan has targeted 4 percent to 5 percent growth in M-2 for the last four years, and that's what we've had." Said another: "If the Fed affects the economy through the fed funds rate, then it's reasonably clear that the Fed can exert important control over short-term interest rates. The size of bank reserves has not been an impediment." And another: "The Fed has fairly close control over M-1 but very little direct control over non-M-1 components of M-2. . . . Does it matter? No. The narrower aggregates are what are important. There are lots of people who [believe] that the Fed has lost a measure of control, but it is based on a misperception of the importance of the broader aggregates."

So much for equal time. More and more, we think, 1991 monetary policy shrinks in significance before the accumulated weight of past monetary policies. During the inflation of the 1970s, for instance, or the easy-money burst of the mid-1980s, banks reached for yield. Finding it, they lent money that they now cannot easily recover. Impaired, they must now lend less. The first-order effect of this change is a pleasing drop in the posted inflation rate and a

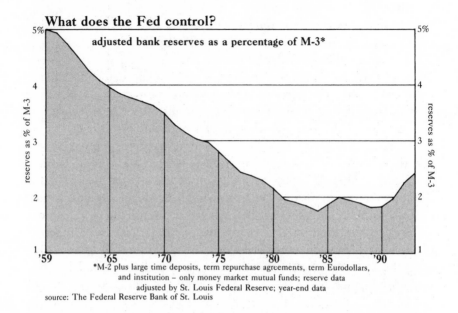

What does the Fed control?

adjusted bank reserves as a percentage of M-3*

*M-2 plus large time deposits, term repurchase agreements, term Eurodollars,
and institution – only money market mutual funds; reserve data
adjusted by St. Louis Federal Reserve; year-end data
source: The Federal Reserve Bank of St. Louis

curious weakness in the growth of the money supply. The second-order effect must be less winning—widespread weakness in business activity and asset values alike. The United States, we think, is entering the second stage of the process. The conditioned response of the market is to believe that the Federal Reserve will save the day by creating more credit. It will try, we agree, but it may not succeed.

Doubting the Fed's capacity to control events, we have little faith in the healing properties of monetary policy. We do not expect the world to end. On the other hand, we expect the bears to eat better, dress better and walk with a jauntier step.*

* Mere wishful thinking.

FLORINS AND PHOTONS

March 27, 1992

W ith your indulgence, we will now compare the coins of Renaissance Florence to the dollars of modern, GOP America. We will appraise the space-age dollar—a mere photon on a computer net —alongside the *fiorino d'oro*, which weighed 3.53 grams and clinked when dropped on a counter. We will size up the Tuscan mint against the Federal Reserve Board and the Clearing House Interbank Payments System and draw a certain number of meaningful conclusions.

If your question is "Why?" we are ready with the answer. The answer is, in our opinion, that something is wrong with the ordinary way of looking at money supply. We are a party to this misconception because we continue to imply in our statistical section that the Federal Reserve is a combination of Archimedes and the Wizard of Oz. Let the Fed expand its balance sheet, the logic of the numbers suggests, and the commercial banks will expand theirs. Let the Fed create more bank reserves, and commercial banks will accordingly make more loans (or buy more securities or otherwise enlarge their footings). Implicit in the neat ordering of the data is a constant rate of turnover of money and a theory that Alan Greenspan is all-powerful. For Wall Street's purposes, we'll be the first to admit, he might as well be.

Repeated reductions in the federal funds rate have failed to restore prosperity, but the Fed can still move markets, galvanize investment psychology, and draw a crowd when its chairman testifies before Congress. The Federal Open Market Committee can create a steep yield curve—it's already done it—and thereby manufacture bank profits, lift the stock market, and demoralize the short sellers. However, we think the Fed's control has been reduced through financial innovation. (It has also been impaired by the shrunken lending capacity of the commercial banking system, but that is another, and more familiar, story.) Money—its nature and movement—is becoming more complex all the time. It may or may not be becoming better.

One of the many things in life over which the central bank has no direct control is the velocity of money: the rate at which dollars move from hand to hand and computer to computer. What interests us now is not so much the rate of turnover of conventional bank deposits but the speed of electronic-dollar impulses on the Clearing House Interbank Payments System, that is, CHIPS, or on the Federal Reserve's own electronic network, Fedwire, or on the new electronic data interchanges, so-called EDIs. One hundred twenty-six banks are connected on CHIPS, and they log more dollar-denominated transactions on some days than there are dollars in M-1. The explosive growth in this monetary traffic suggests that the Fed is not as all-powerful as it used to be. At the least, it's past time to update the familiar schematic of bank deposits anchored by reserve dollars.

Periodically, *Grant's* publishes the staggering, mystifying news that the daily average volume on CHIPS has scaled some new centi-billion-dollar peak. Last month it was $930 billion, on average, every banking day, most of the dollars reportedly dedicated to currency trading. Please note that this has nothing to do with the monetary aggregates. It is the measure of transactions volume. The accounts of the CHIPS member banks are netted up and settled at the end of the day in federal funds (that is, in everyday banking-system money). In view of the vast electronic business conducted, the size of the checks exchanged in settlement is tiny: on the order of $8 billion. It helps to limber up the monetary imagination to consider the ratio of these two numbers, transactions volume to settlement dollars. In February it was 116 to 1. Only the smaller number of dollars is counted in the official monetary aggregates. As for the $930 billion a day, it is uncounted and, by most people, unimagined.

M-1, M-2, and M-3 are the measures of money at rest. CHIPS volume is the measure (one measure) of money in motion. The "M's" constitute a standard basis for judging the effectiveness of

Federal Reserve policy. More and more, though, we've come to doubt that they are enough. In a new book on the subject, Elinor Harris Solomon suggests that they aren't, and she describes the varieties of electronic money with the kind of metaphor you never read in Milton Friedman: "a cloud . . . moving in geosync orbit in the form of virtually weightless photons." That is merely to whet the appetite. The way to think about the new monetary world is actually down to earth. Effective money supply, Solomon says, consists of conventional money plus electronic money multiplied by its continuous rate of use. The key words are "continuous," "weightless," and "cloud." They are not textbook monetary terms, but they are where the nomenclature seems to be heading.

For months we've been asking ourselves why the contraction in international banking has seemed to count for so little in world markets. The Japanese banks, the world's biggest boom-time lenders, are pulling back, growth in world money supply is nil, and interbank lending is down. In short, deflation is the order of the day. Yet the American stock market only goes up, and the world economy, although palpably slowing, has not keeled over. The currency markets are hyperactive. Does the world have an invisible monetary wellspring?

Solomon doesn't address that particular issue, but after reading her essay—it is the lead piece in a book she edited last year, *Electronic Money Flows: The Molding of a New Financial Order*, published by Kluwer Academic Publishers, Norwell, Massachusetts— you may agree with us that it's possible. "In the electronic age," she writes,

> money first consists, as always, of physical cash or deposits. But to this familiar money must be added the more ethereal and information-based money flow. . . . Moneylike value is in motion and continuously available for purchase of goods and services throughout the day. The flow represents all money—whether manifest in physical form or as memory on a computer chip—times the rate of its continuous use. Money flow is a curious mixture of electronic turnover speed plus a not-so-little dash of good old-fashioned "float."

So there is the ether and there are the M's. Helpfully, Solomon tries to unify them. She begins with the monetary base, and she

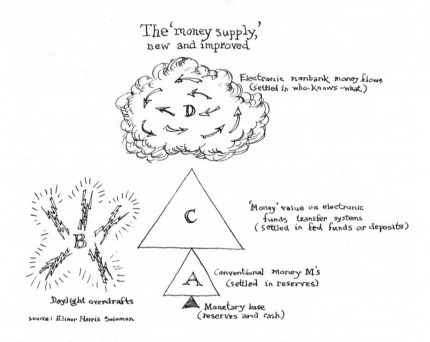

The 'money supply,' new and improved

Electronic nonbank money flows
(settled in who-knows-what)

D

'Money' value on electronic
funds transfer systems
(settled in fed funds or deposits)

C

Conventional money M's
(settled in reserves)

A

B

Daylight overdrafts

source: Elinor Harris Solomon

Monetary base
(reserves and cash)

ends with things you've never heard of (unless you happened to read her interview with the *American Banker* on March 2). The sketch describes the theory, and we will describe the sketch. The base, of course, consists of currency and bank reserves. Reserves are the dollars lying fallow at the Fed and in bankers' vaults. They are there to satisfy the Federal Reserve regulation that 10 cents of every checkable-deposit dollar must be set aside in case the depositors suddenly want their money back. The monetary-base pyramid is the smallest. Next there are the various familiar monetary aggregates, stocks of funds measured (as balance sheets are measured) at the close of business on a particular day. They are snapshots of money in place: See pyramid "A."

By contrast, electronic funds are the monetary movies. They constitute money on the march. (We don't mean to suggest that the conventional M's don't move or that this movement isn't measured; we happen to be interested in money you plug into the wall.) To start with, there's "daylight money," a kind of electronic float: Note the lightning bolts marked "B." Old-fashioned float is created when a planeload of checks is fogged in several hundred miles from the city in which the checks are due to be cashed. Electronic float is a by-product of technology: Funds remitted in the morning are not collected until the afternoon. The lapse between payment and settlement is what creates electronic credit, frequently known as "daylight overdrafts." It is Cinderella credit, as Solomon notes—wiped out at the close of business every day —but the numbers are enormous and therefore suggestive. Average peak overdrafts on Fedwire and CHIPS are running at about $232 billion a day. That is a monetary substance without any evident connection, physical or metaphysical, to the $57 billion in legal bank reserves.

Float would seem an unlikely agent for a monetary revolution. There has always been float. As for debit cards, point-of-sale terminals, and automated clearinghouses, they are new and improved avenues for paying money, but the funds so transferred are settled up in bank deposits: Note pyramid "C." However, a revolution in money is, in fact, under way, and the new monetary material does not always connect with the old. On the CHIPS wire, notes Solomon, end-of-day balances are settled in fed funds. That is, they are settled by the dollars also known as bank reserves. However, as we've seen, stupendous volumes of transactions are settled up with modest amounts of federal funds. The electronic leverage— the ratio of newfangled photons to old-fashioned banking dollars —is enormous. Solomon continues: "There are other instances where settlement appears, at least in part, to be in commodities or barter, or other electronic money or electronic claims to future assets (the Chicago Mercantile Exchange)." These are represented by the cloud "D." Unfortunately, says Solomon, the size of the cloud is unknown.

What are the monetary implications of electronically conducted corporate barter? Of the coming introduction of the "smart," or "integrated circuit," credit card? Smart cards store monetary information in a computer chip, and you spend these atoms as you please. "What happens to the smart card money . . . as it darts around, in pursuit of its function as a medium of exchange, is anyone's guess," ventures Solomon. "We may see money or other assets being downloaded onto smart cards from other electronic money forms owned by nonbanks, such as telecommunications firms with advanced technology. . . . Around the world, the ethereal money nets may 'speak' privately to one another. Through terminals at merchant location or through home personal computer, they may interconnect to transfer 'value' balances without tangible monetary interface. Retail barter flows then may rise dramatically, too, apace with the corporate. All the value-based money contained therein may zoom around outside the banking system entirely, passed on directly from one electronic net to another net, its physical content consisting of magnetized electrons."

The more this new money becomes detached from the old banking system, it seems to us, the greater the likelihood of monetary misunderstanding. What stands to be challenged is the idea of a Fed-centered world. As monetary photons expand, the Fed's influence is bound to recede. If what drives business activity and speculative markets at the margin are clouds of magnetized electrons, the federal funds rate is not as important as it used to be. "As you get farther and farther away from the reserve base and from the money that passes through banks," writes Solomon, "it becomes harder to track down the 'money.' This is especially true if there is bundling of a lot of different kinds of corporate information or settlement in some kind of commodity account (oil or futures, for example)." Plainly, then, the ratio of financial activity to the monetary base is enormous, and it may or may not matter that CHIPS is settled at night in terms of reserve dollars. What matters are the gains and losses and margin calls that the photons produce in the course of a banking day. These, at least, are tangible.

All of which leads us back to the original questions. Is there more to the world's money supply than the sum of the world's M's? If so, is it bullish or bearish? In theory, it seems to us, the revolution in payments technology is potentially expansive. The effective money supply can only rise when the rate of turnover of its electronic component is the speed of light. When the world, wired as it is, is next pushed into a great inflation, the potential for monetary growth may be truly terrifying. "The degree of money pyramiding atop a small real reserve base is unprecedented," notes Solomon. "Sometimes the settlement net is netted down the line, in quasi-money or barter. Indeed, the banking and deposit link may be gone altogether for some electronic money forms." In these circumstances, therefore, the worldwide banking contraction constitutes a smaller threat than a similar contraction would have posed even a decade or two ago (let alone in the 1930s). For ourselves, we don't believe that electronic money has solved the world's credit problem. We don't see how daylight overdrafts, the CHIPS explosion, or even the interesting goings-on in cloud "D" can restore the lending capacity of spavined banks. We do believe, however, that the monetary ether has helped the world's financial markets over the hump of low apparent monetary growth. Such assistance has not been evenly dispensed—the Japanese stock market is on the outside looking in—but it is hard to pretend that $2 trillion of float and frenzy don't exist or have no market effects.

There are many hopeful elements in the rise of electronic money, and one of them is the opening up of distance between credit and politics. The wider the gulf between the creation and distribution of credit, on the one hand, and the Federal Reserve Board, on the other, the better, we would submit. However, it would be a mistake to believe that such a monetary regime is dependent on computer technology. In thirteenth- and fourteenth-century Florence, they had no high-powered printing presses, no open-market operations, and no wall sockets.

The Florentine unit of account, the gold florin, was introduced in 1252 and held its value for about two hundred years. According to another book, *Mountains of Debt: Crisis and Change in Renaissance Florence, Victorian Britain, and Postwar America*, by Michael Veseth, the *fiorino d'oro* was perhaps the most stable unit of currency in monetary history. For that reason alone, it deserves study, and what better time for a short reappraisal than in the midst of our own monetary revolution?

It is interesting and inspiring to consider the calamities that did not result in wholesale devaluation of the Florentine currency. The list includes war, bank failures, government bankruptcy, the Black Death, famine, flood, economic depression, and credit contraction. According to Carlo M. Cipolla in *The Monetary Policy of Fourteenth-Century Florence*, many businesses failed in the mid 1340s for lack of credit—*mancamento della credenza*, as the phrase went. As for wars, they were numerous and costly, but no trace of them is discernible in the city-state's monetary history. "A student of Florentine history who limited himself to the documents of the mint would be under the impression that nothing happened," writes Cipolla. "The currency was debased only twice, and on both occasions the devaluation had purely monetary origins."

Concerning the plague, incidentally, it will not surprise Wall Street to learn that it was ultimately bullish. Per capita wealth and incomes rose (by definition), and the survivors went shopping. Owing to the reduced population, rents fell.

"Unlike modern states," writes Cipolla, "Florence did not finance itself by monetary manipulations. The state received revenues from the mint, but these revenues did not consist of the difference between the face value and the intrinsic value of the currency minted. Rather, they originated in the rights of seigniorage—that is, the tax on the minting activity. If and when a devaluation was decreed, it was not the state that profited from the gap between the face value of the currency and its reduced metallic content; those who profited were citizens in a position to take metal to the mint."

In short, a nearly perfect monetary system and one that functioned without electricity. Electronic money has produced miracles of efficiency. Furthermore, it may hold out the promise of less intrusive federal regulation. Neither advantage should be sneered at. But does anyone expect this post-paper money system to usher in two hundred years of price stability? Query to the technically literate: How much would a gold photon weigh? Would *it* clink on a counter?

PART EIGHT

THE FINE ART
OF CORPORATE
FINANCE

SUMITOMO ON HOLIDAY

February 22, 1988

PARIS—Japan has become such a financial powerhouse that Japanese banks have far surpassed their American counterparts in international assets, while Tokyo has topped New York as a center for international lending. . . .

Japanese banks, which in late 1985 first displaced the Americans as the largest holders of international assets, are continuing to expand their share of the world market and now top the Americans by more than 2 to 1.
—International Herald Tribune, *February 10*

Holiday Inns is no more a triple-A credit than the Holiday Inn at JFK International Airport is the Plaza Hotel. The company's senior credit rating, as a matter of fact, is B1, for "speculative." Holiday did that to itself by recapitalizing last year, borrowing to pay an enormous special dividend and transforming a conventional balance sheet into an ultraleveraged one. In the argot of corporate finance, it became a "stub" company, that is, one whose equity capitalization is sawed off just below the knee.

So when Holiday was able to borrow recently at IBM-type yields, questions were raised. The answers were printed on the cover page of the prospectus. Principal and interest are "payable by drawings under an irrevocable, direct-pay letter of credit issued by the New York branch of The Sumitomo Bank Ltd.," the document said. In other words, besides the money, Holiday had borrowed the credit rating of a Japanese bank. You'll remember Sumitomo. About a year ago it bought a 12½ percent limited partnership interest in Goldman Sachs for $500 million. Standard & Poor's rated the new Holiday securities AA+; the underwriter was Smith Barney, Harris Upham & Co.

"Investment banking. What's your major?"

We'd wager that not many readers have a betting interest in the Holiday notes. "The world's largest hotel and hotel/casino companies, offering business and vacation travelers more than 1,800 hotels with over 350,000 rooms in 52 countries," raised only $400 million, which is a smallish sum of money even in the light of its own outstanding debt. However, the terms of the offering are unusual and thought-provoking. By borrowing on the strength of Sumitomo's credit, instead of its own, Holiday saved some 200 basis points, or $48 million, over the lives of the issues (the 8⅝s of 1993 and the 9s of 1995). The Smith Barney investment banker on the case, William G. McDonald, calls this "a unique form of credit arbitrage." One may wonder what Sumitomo knows that the public market doesn't; how it is able to earn a fee while, in effect, writing Holiday a $48 million check? We do wonder, and we also wonder why Holiday's gain isn't somehow Sumitomo's loss.

Anyway, the deal is revealing of the temper of the times. An American corporation with negative net worth has borrowed on the strength of the pledge of a Japanese bank (which, incidentally, has only a modest stated net worth itself). The American company will use the proceeds to pay down a part of the bank debt it incurred in its leveraged recapitalization. The lead bank in that enterprise was Citibank. Citibank is American. Its credit rating is AA, a notch lower than Sumitomo's AAA. (We lay out the nationalistic facts in case the Gephardt candidacy catches fire.)

What thrusts the transaction into the corporate-finance mainstream is the letter of credit. A letter of credit is a contract. It obligates a guarantor to make good on a commitment when a customer cannot. For years now, letters of credit, bond insurance, and outright government guarantees have augmented the stand-alone credentials of debtors. Possibly that is as it should be. On the other hand, it can do no harm from time to time to poke around, ask some questions, and step back for perspective's sake—to ask, in brief, if this bull market in other people's credit may not mask a bear market in the general run of credit. In particular, one may ask how long the writers of letters of credit can profit by second-guessing the bond market.

To start with, it is important to grasp the numbers; you may have to pause to let them sink in. In terms of its balance sheet, Sumitomo is bigger than the Federal Reserve System ($287 billion in assets as of last September 30, versus the Fed's $261 billion).* In terms of market capitalization, it may be the biggest bank on earth. It is about 10 times bigger than Citicorp ($65.4 billion versus $6.4 billion). As of a few weeks ago, to complete the picture, Sumitomo's dividend yield was 0.21 percent (versus 6.8 percent for Citicorp). Its price-earnings ratio was 90.5 (versus about six for Citicorp, when Citicorp was actually able to show earnings). Its ratio of price to book value was 1,425.5 percent (versus 94 percent for Citicorp). Holiday's leveraged capital structure, while hardly unique today, would have jolted the Street's sensibilities only a few years ago. Indeed, the whole transaction—a leveraged borrower enjoying AA+ standing on the strength of a promise by a Japanese bank rather larger than the Fed—is as much a creation of the late 1980s as are such financial prodigies as the putable, extendable, variable-coupon, renewable note.

Plainly, if stock market stature were the only test of creditworthiness, Sumitomo would need no rating; it would be tops by acclamation. Furthermore, by inference, any borrower bestowed with a Sumitomo letter of credit would similarly be true blue—until, perhaps, the weight of Sumitomo's guarantees subverted its own credit rating. Sumitomo's credit is at the heart of the matter because it is the bank's promise that enabled Holiday to borrow at rates more closely associated with the Treasury than with junk-grade corporations.

---

* It is only an approximate comparison. Included in the Fed's footings, for instance, is $11.1 billion worth of gold certificates valued at the arbitrary official rate of $42.22 an ounce. If the Japanese banks have "hidden reserves," so, too, we suppose, does the Fed.

Where exactly must a Holiday bondholder look for payment? Interest and principal will be provided from drawings under the Sumitomo letter of credit. The bank, in turn, will be reimbursed by Holiday Inns and its parent, Holiday Corp. "These reimbursement obligations of the bank," the prospectus goes on to say, "will be secured by a first deed of trust on three hotel/casino properties in Nevada and by a priority security interest in certain related property." According to the bankers, the value of the collateral—property, casino licenses, and the earning power attached to those assets—is sufficient to cover the liability to service the debt. Overall, as the prospectus notes, payment of principal and interest is guaranteed by Holiday, and the notes will stand on an equal footing with other unsecured debt of Holiday.

Therefore, as the deal is designed, the investor is doubly protected. If the bank failed but the company didn't, the noteholders would be paid. If the company failed but the bank didn't, the noteholders would also be paid. The immediate risk is of a simultaneous blowup at the bank and the company. A less apocalyptic possibility is of a decline in the creditworthiness of the bank. It may tax the imagination to conceive of Sumitomo Bank in liquidation. However, Sumitomo as a double-A, down from triple-A? Why not? Holiday itself, incidentally, has sold more assets and produced more cash flow and repaid more debt than anticipated a year ago. Its own public debt securities change hands at yields of about 11 percent, which in the high-yield market bespeaks confidence.

If the 8⅝ percent and 9 percent coupons of the new notes make a predictive statement, it is that the odds of a fiasco are remote. It is easy to infer from the rating agencies' treatment of Sumitomo—triple-A by Moody's and Mikuni & Co., the Japanese rating agency—that the bank is expected to survive.

What we don't know about Japanese banking could fill an Occidental encyclopedia, but a reading of the numbers never fails to arouse our peasant suspicions. For instance, as of September 30, Sumitomo's equity was $6.1 billion and its assets were $287 billion, for a ratio of equity to assets of 2.1 percent. The stronger U.S. regionals show equity-asset ratios of 7 percent and up; even the weak-sister money center institutions are above 3 percent. Not knowing any better, a layman might assume that the margin for error associated with a 2 percent cushion is thin. Almost certainly, as we should hastily add, the comparisons are rough. To take a ratio of two numbers is to presuppose that the numbers themselves are meaningful; but the quality of equity and assets varies hugely from bank to bank and country to country. Also, there are definitional problems. Under Japanese accounting conventions, for instance, standby letters of credit are treated as earning assets. They are carried on a balance sheet at face value, as if they were loans or securities. Under U.S. rules, letters of credit are tucked away in a footnote and ignored for purposes of asset size. To that extent, therefore, Sumitomo's assets are overstated by U.S. lights (or, alternatively, U.S. banks' assets are understated by Japanese lights). The Japanese must wonder at American accounting conventions, especially the gambit by which one's allowance for bad debts is counted as a form of primary capital. As far as that goes, many Americans can hardly believe it themselves.

As you may have read in the newspapers, the Bank for International Settlements has established new capital requirements for big banks. By 1992 a bank in good standing will show a ratio of equity to assets of 4 percent and a ratio of overall capital to assets of 8 percent. Whether the rules are thought to be stringent depends on one's starting point. As the Japanese tend to show more assets and less equity than the Americans, they begin at a disadvantage. In fact, according to proponents of the Japanese system, so-called hidden assets constitute an important wellspring of Japanese bank capital. This buried treasure is said to include stock holdings and real estate valued at below-market prices. Nevertheless, rules are rules, and Japanese banks are expected to feel the bite. "We can no longer expand our low-profit lending activities as we did in the past because we must limit our asset increases as much as possible," a top man at Mitsubishi Bank told *The Japan Economic Journal* recently.

"Like all Japanese banks," Moody's has commented, "Sumitomo's securities portfolio is undervalued; the difference between market and book value is substantial, and when this difference is given an appropriate weighting and added to equity and reserves, it improves the bank's capital position significantly." When the agency last summer downgraded a quarter of Japanese banks, Sumitomo was not among them.

A Boston friend, apprised of the details of the Holiday-Sumitomo transaction, remarked that, by rights, Holiday's gain should be Sumitomo's loss. Sumitomo's market capitalization should decline by the estimated savings of the guarantee to Holiday Inns. His premise was that the public market's estimate of risk is probably better than a bank's—especially if the bank doing the estimating is out to build its market share or self-esteem. Warming to his subject, our friend contended that there ought to be an item in the Sumitomo balance sheet called "deferred cost of substituting the bank's judgment of credit risk for the market's."

That made sense to us, and we remembered that McDonald, the Smith Barney investment banker, said he expected a lot more Sumitomo-Holiday–type transactions. If our Boston friend was right, the deferred cost of second-guessing the public market's judgments will rise. As of last March, Sumitomo disclosed $20.7 billion worth of contingent liabilities, including $8.1 billion in letters of credit. The Holiday offering will add less than the stated $400 million to that total, by the way, because interests in the letter of credit have been sold, or "participated," to other banks. "As with other Japanese banks," according to Moody's, "off-balance-sheet activity has grown rapidly, particularly in the form of credit support and other guarantees. Sumitomo Bank's ratio of guarantees to true capital, however, is below that of its peers." Of course, that was last year's information.

We asked McDonald about the no-free-lunch interpretation of the Holiday deal, and he said he disagreed with it. He said that the bank was able to exploit a kind of blind spot in the public debt market. This blind spot, he said, is the traditional reluctance to accept a mortgage bond secured by hotels. Whereas the bond market may have refused the security of those assets, the bank did so readily, counting not only the deeds and gambling licenses but also the management and earning power. By lending its good name to the transaction, the bank was able to discover value. Everyone came out ahead, and the lunch was, in effect, on the house.*

---

* In fact, no disaster ensued: As Holiday hasn't defaulted, the Sumitomo credit guarantee hasn't been activated. The balance sheet of the Japanese bank is still larger than the Federal Reserve's, but the former's credit standing is still perceptibly weaker than the latter's. It is weaker than it was four years ago. Sumitomo's senior debt rating was reduced from triple-A (perfect) in 1988 to a weak double-A (merely exemplary) in 1991. In January 1993, Moody's Investors Service placed the bank under sur-

Lawyers lead the 1992 Macy's Thanksgiving Day Parade.

Probably the most encouraging fact we discovered about Sumitomo was that it is rated triple-A by Mikuni, the Japanese equivalent of Moody's and Standard & Poor's rolled into one. Credit ratings of established institutions were thought to be unJapanese when Mr. Akio Mikuni got into the business, but he kept at it, and he has built a following in and out of the home islands (his company is headquartered in Tokyo). He recently delivered a brilliant paper on Japanese banking that he titled, straightforwardly, "Mikuni on Banking." It set the historical scene and explained the dynamics of the Japanese financial rig, without using that term. It described how the big Japanese banks have come virtually to monopolize Japanese financial flows. The banking business was the only business to be in, as Mikuni related the details. Interest rates were regulated, competition was regulated, and corporate bankruptcies were nipped in the bud. As market forces inevitably gain the upper hand, however, he suggested, the good old days will pass into history.

We had always wondered at the paradox of high financial leverage, high savings, and preposterously high stock prices. Our question was why the Tokyo bull market didn't produce a flood of new issues (as a bull market always does in New York) and a corre-

veillance for a new downgrade, proving the point, often made by Michael Milken, that a top-rated borrower has nowhere to go except down. As for the Japanese financial system.

sponding reduction in bank credit as equity was substituted for debt. According to Mikuni, the reason is that, simply, one doesn't issue stock. Custom, usage, and the Ministry of Finance discourage it. "In Japan," he said, "those who issue common equity have to make commitments of dividends in advance. The effect is to make equity finance as costly as bank loans and to make dividends as inflexible as interest payments."

Mikuni told how all this came to be:

> There was no way to escape the omnipresent banks. Years ago, one of Japan's leading export companies told me how it struggled for a decade to raise its equity ratio—to impress foreign investors —and had obtained the desired result by issuing equity and paying off bank loans. All it achieved, however, was to substitute bank common stock ownership for loans. There had been no change in its relationship with its bank!
>
> Other examples of the difficulty of avoiding bank control come to mind. Thus, on paper, Toyota Motor is completely debt free and takes pride in the fact. But over 60 percent of the company's shares are held by banks and affiliates.

Next, Mikuni got around to the mysterious penchant of Japanese bankers for doing unprofitable business—for expanding, apparently, for the sake of expanding. It is the syndrome described by a man from Mitsubishi as "[increasing] our low-profit lending activities." Mikuni proposed the idea that the supply of bank credit creates its own demand. He called it the "great windmill":*

> As long as prices rise—in real estate, in stock values—there is a demand for loans still to be satisfied. Investors need still more money to buy still more land and common stocks. There is pressure for more bank loans to finance further increases in land prices. This is a classic inflationary spiral (if confined to financial values—consumer prices are stable so far). It will go on as long as confidence is maintained. In other words, as long as there are no major bankruptcies.

What drives the banks to lend, in part, is inertia, Mikuni suggested. He described the "window guidance" system for establishing authorized levels of lending. (Mikuni called the Ministry

---

* Now looking more and more like the one that Don Quixote tilted against in the Gustave Doré picture.

of Finance a "franchiser" of banking privilege, not a regulator in the Western sense of the word.) Banks lend because they have lent and because lending got them where they are today, which is rich and powerful:

> The banks acquired their dominant position by relentless pursuit of assets, seemingly regardless of cost. That is their grand strategy to this day, as Western bankers are learning to their cost. Obviously, the practice troubles Western competitors because they see their own margins threatened by our *hari-kiri* loans—there are going to be charges of Japanese "economic imperialism" from non-Marxist bankers in the West! Yet there was an eminently reasonable basis for making such loans in the high-growth era in Japan. Expansion of assets was tantamount to increasing claims over industry. And who would have voluntarily forfeited a greater stake in the world's most dynamic industrial economy?

So much for *zeitgeist*. What one wants to know, of course, is whether a rigged system—*this* rigged system—is viable. Our prejudice is anti-rig because the riggers always seem to come up a dollar short. The Hunts, although billionaires, were not rich enough to buy the marginal silver loving cup offered for sale by the public. When Mikuni speaks of an "endless chain of manipulated business transactions," we naturally put on our doubting hat. Our question is whether the pell-mell expansion of Japanese lending can continue. Or, rather (for we've made up our mind that it can't), when will it stop?

Interestingly, as we say, Mikuni is bullish on Sumitomo. Of the thirteen so-called city banks, the only other institution to win the Mikuni's triple-A is Fuji. A Mikuni research brief, dated January 21, reaffirms that high opinion while noting a drop in profitability caused by a merger with Heiwa Sogo Bank, a spavined savings institution, last year. According to Mikuni, Sumitomo's loans to Third World debtors represent 2 percent of total loans and 54 percent of stockholders' equity. By contemporary American lights, at least, that must be counted a positive. However, spreads between yields on earning assets, on the one hand, and costs of funds raised, on the other, have been under pressure for the past decade, "as loan demand from the corporate sector generally has leveled off with resultant competition among financial institutions," according to Mikuni.

The last word on this subject belongs to an alert American investor who is not a professional bank-stock analyst. He is, however, a seeker of high time-deposit yields, and he reports that the big Japanese institutions, Sumitomo included, are the highest bidders for time deposits in the Euromarkets. What does it mean, he wondered over the phone, when the same Japanese banks are the most aggressive borrowers? Actually, he said, he did know what it meant. What he didn't know was what to do about it.

WILD BLUE YONDER

August 18, 1989

When the Dow Jones Transportation Average soared by 94.06 points in a single session—that was Monday, August 7, Marvin Davis Day—even the bulls might have been taken aback. Senior observers must have rubbed their eyes. As recently as 1957, the Dow Jones Railroad Average (forerunner to the Transports) was quoted at 94.91. That was the *level* of the index. It has now become the increment of one spectacular daily move. When the Transports snapped back to set a new high last month, that, too, was a page out of Guinness. Almost an investment lifetime passed before the Rails could recover the record they had set just before the 1929 Crash. It was not until February 25, 1964, as a matter of fact, that the Railroad average made its way back to 189.13, thereby fractionally exceeding its September 3, 1929, peak. More than thirty-four years had marched on.

The story of the Transports is the story of investment value magnified by debt. It is the story of the power of positive thinking or of mass delusion (bulls and bears will agree to disagree), and of implausible numbers turning up as fact. What was supposed to have been impossible in the post-1987 crash stock market is, after all, what actually happened. Prices recovered to the old highs, then made new ones. Dividend yields shrank. Bankers became bolder and leveraged buyouts more stretched. The substitution of debt for equity on corporate balance sheets proceeded apace. (The last major airline to issue equity to finance an expansion was American, in 1985.) Business activity strengthened—for the airlines, 1988 produced record profits—and many believed that economywide recessions were relics of the past, like the two-year auto loan. By degree, people came around to the view that whatever had happened on October 19, 1987, didn't matter or hadn't happened after all.

Recent goings-on in the airlines are a page right out of the new-era book, and they have prompted some questions around here. For instance, how does a record-low dividend yield in the Dow Transports (1.37 percent at this writing) square with the oft-heard contention that there is no speculation in the financial markets? What about the heated competition among commercial banks to finance aircraft leases and airline M&A activity? What has caused this sudden reappraisal of the prospects for—of all cyclical industries—airlines? Is it the fundamentals of the airline business or the attitudes of lenders? Is it a revolution in flying or banking? And by the way, when did the shadow of coming events begin to fall first across the girth of Marvin Davis instead of across the floor of the New York Stock Exchange? When did the public equities market become the second- or third-best forum for determining the value of an investor-owned business?

Because the bulls have all the money, one should respectfully turn to them for counsel and advice. One should find out what they know, or think they know, and hold it up to the light for examination. By reading the papers and keeping our ears open, we have compiled a Composite Bullish Case. It runs this way:

Standard methods of airline valuation are obsolete. The industry has passed out of the tunnel of regulation (ended in 1978) and ruinous price competition (People Express disappeared in 1986). It has entered the dawn of consolidation. Eight big domestic carriers will compete, and yet, in a way, not compete. Each will have its own hub and turf. Cyclical risk will be leached from the industry

$3,000,000,000

Reverse Obverse Inverse
Support Accrual Tranche
Whole Loan Collateralized
Mortgage Obligations

Scrooge & Marley

December 24, 1991

by new planes, stable pricing, and sophisticated "yield" management. Recessions will no longer be ruinous. The advent of lease finance will permit—is already allowing—more rapid acquisition of modern aircraft. No longer must carriers be constrained by the limits of their own leveraged balance sheets. It is no accident that NWA and UAL, the two recent takeover targets, each owned a high percentage of their own aircraft—what arbitrageurs have learned to identify as "hidden assets."

The bullish case is the kind of story that plays well at investment-banking presentations. And yet, as a reader was recently musing, the boom in new-aircraft orders can hardly be bullish for everyone: for aircraft manufacturers, leasing companies, lenders, *and* airlines. Who bears the financial risk? Who bears the operating risk? It's not front-page news that easy credit has deepened and perpetuated the boom. Homemakers, automakers, and dealmakers have thrived on it. It has increasingly figured in the fortunes of airlines and aircraft-leasing companies. How will the consequences of debt play out when business activity turns down and financial fashions change?

By way of preface, hyperleverage in the transportation field is of fairly recent vintage, even if indebtedness has been rising for years. At year-end 1988, the Dow Jones Transportation Average showed lower working capital and higher long-term debt than it did a decade before, at the start of deregulation. The figures probably understate the growth in long-term debt, as they fail to incorporate off-balance-sheet aircraft leases. More striking is the variability in the financial strength of the component companies. As in 1978, the 1988 Dow Transports encompassed one conservative company (Consolidated Freightways) and a number of middling ones. Unlike the 1978 sample, however, the 1988 Transports included several businesses that did not quite cover fixed charges. Among these emblematic organizations was Pan American World Airways, which is flying on the financial equivalent of one wing. It is a sign of the times that Pan Am is thought to be a credible bidder for UAL, a carrier two and a half times its size and one that does not happen to be bleeding cash. Implicit in the faith in Pan Am is the idea that speculative capital is always forthcoming, at a price, for leveraged transactions. It may not be.

It is easy to forget that the ideal LBO candidate is the antithesis of the typical airline, which is capital-intensive, unionized, and regulated. In the case of NWA, prospective capital spending is billions of dollars in excess of prospective cash flows. Furthermore, every airline is a prisoner of the business cycle and a hostage to the price of fuel. When Forstmann Little & Co. and Kohlberg, Kravis, Roberts & Co. pioneered the leveraged art form in the late 1970s, they conspicuously did not begin with an LBO of United Airlines. It was a decade before they even got around to considering it.

Over the past ten years, three happy trends have smiled on the airlines. First was the fall of People Express and Laker Airways and the resulting consolidation of carriers and fares. Second was the great bull market and all its valuation baggage: The correct analytical attitude has become the superoptimistic one. Third is the junk-credit revolution: What happened on a macroeconomic scale is, in effect, what happened to Dr Pepper in miniature. Lenders and borrowers shed their inhibitions. The success of financial innovators inspired successive waves of imitators. Debt was piled on debt.

The result is a new high on the Dow Jones Transportation Average and brash talk of a new, noncylical era in airline operations. As constant readers might already have guessed, *Grant's* does not happen to believe the Composite Bullish Case. We see in the airline lift-off yet another example of debt in action, making the good times better and casting a shadow over the future. We suspect that easy credit will sooner or later give way to hard, or inaccessible, credit. In consequence, Pan Am will absolutely not be considered a credible bidder for anything. M&A activity will slump and capital will leave the aircraft-leasing business.

The first truth of commercial flight is that results are erratic, have been and will be, barring even bigger change than the dealmakers have thus far proposed. For instance, UAL Corp., United Airline's parent, earned a record $377 million from continuing operations in 1988. However, it lost $4.2 million in 1987. AMR Corp., parent of American Airlines, earned $477 million in 1988, but Texas Air Corp. showed a $719 million loss. The domestic industry last year showed a 5 percent operating margin (after depreciation), the best since 5.7 percent in 1984. However, it fell short of the 6 percent margin earned in 1978, the top of a business cycle and the end of regulation. "In the ten years since deregulation," notes Standard & Poor's, "the industry's operating margin has been an anemic 2.1 percent. This compares to 3.9 percent in the prior ten years, 1969–78. The airline industry's net margin, excluding UAL's large extraordinary gain on the sale of hotels, was 2.3 percent, again below the 1984 level and short of the pre-deregulation peak." As for the second quarter, passenger revenue growth slowed noticeably, and the rise in unit costs at many carriers accelerated. On Monday, TWA announced lower ticket prices for this fall. Other carriers promptly matched them. In short, as Thomas Longman of Bear Stearns has noted, a cyclical industry showed its cyclical stripes.

As we understand the bull argument, what makes things different this time is largely borrowed money: the availability of bank credit for airline consolidations and aircraft acquisition. "These bankers are willing to lend money to fund these transactions," an analyst recently told *Barron's*. "That says something about the revaluation of airline multiples." It says a lot. When commercial bankers get around to seeing the light, the sun is usually over the yardarm. Thus, Bankers Trust's unprecedented role in the pending NWA acquisition—not only arranging $3.35 billion of senior debt but also taking an $80 million piece of equity for its own account—must set a contrarian on edge. Al Checchi, the man who bid with the bank's money (or, rather, the bank's depositors' money), was recently asked about his debts. His response was suitable for framing.

"If the company never did any better than it's doing right now," he told *Business Week*, "I could service my debt."* Never did better? Operating income in 1988 totaled $205 million, the best year on record. The projection for this year is $364 million. (The proxy material contains the usual never-a-look-back projections for the next five years. In 1993, operating income will reach no less than $723 million. You can look it up.) To put that cornucopia in perspective, operating income was $77 million as recently as 1985. Is a return to nonpeak operating income out of the realm of possibility? Or is it not? Bankers Trust and Checchi have their position (the former), and we have ours (the latter).

One of the greatest bull markets aloft is the bull market in new aircraft, and here, too, bank credit has provided the thrust. The total cost of aircraft on option by United States airlines is $100 billion. "Industry aircraft expenditures," comments Philip Baggaley of S&P, "are expected to average $10 billion to $15 billion per annum through the mid-1990s, triple last year's $4.3 billion of operating cash flow. Clearly, most new aircraft will have to be financed with debt and leases, even assuming healthy earnings and growing cash flow."

Bulls welcome the prospect. First, they say, the new aircraft will be more efficient to operate than the old. Second, the old crates will increasingly be retired. Third—our personal favorite—aircraft and airlines have won the imprimatur of the world's bankers. "Aircraft, particularly the newer models, are considered excellent collateral," Baggaley goes on, "and manufacturers, banks, and leasing companies have lined up to provide needed funds."

"Lined up" is, in fact, a bit of an understatement. Japanese banks have piled into the market, and lending spreads have narrowed. Some chapter and verse was provided in a recent *Euromoney* supplement on aircraft finance, appropriately titled "Flying Higher." "Aerospace features alongside property and leveraged or management buyouts as a home for Japanese money," the publication reported. "It is estimated [that] Japanese banks supply over half of the world's aircraft financing requirement, and as much as 75 percent of the non–U.S. aircraft financing."

From that point, the tension in the narrative increased:

---

* A March 8, 1993, *Business Week* story asked, "Can one more airline fit into the U.S. Bankruptcy Court's hangars?" It was referring to Checchi's.

Smaller Japanese banks are fighting for exposure to aerospace, on what some see as dubious risks. The rates now being conceded appear foolhardy to the majors. Mark Lindsay-Bailey, at Sumitomo, says: "Everyone is sitting back and saying you can't be serious that you're going to keep on pruning these margins anymore. Banks are waiting for their chance to price risks at sensible levels."

Another banker, John Sharman of Spectrum Capital, a joint venture of Mitsubishi Trust and a consortium of Western banks, was quoted in the same vein:

"There's very little differentiation in the margin terms in the quality of different carriers. There must be an imperfection in the market, with this degree of oversupply." Sharman says that at the moment "there's a little bit of the 'it's an airplane, let's do it,' approach." Another banker commented: "This is the sort of market where we feel prices no longer reflect the risks."

A company that fairly glows with new-age prosperity is International Lease Finance Corp., Beverly Hills, California. ILFC leases and trades new-model commercial jets. Its portfolio numbered seventy-six aircraft at the end of May (up from forty-nine a year earlier), and its lessees range from American Airlines to Trans World Airlines to Garuda Indonesia Airways. ILFC borrows short and lends long. It borrows in the commercial-paper market or from banks to finance leases maturing in five or seven years. Its balance sheet is highly leveraged. At last report, $1.7 billion of debt was balanced on $433 million in shareholder equity.

If Alfred Checchi, Marvin Davis, and the other financial Wright brothers are aviation novices, ILFC has been around. It claims that it "has never had a significant lease collection problem" and that it "has never disposed of an aircraft at below its purchase price" in its fifteen-year history. A leveraged balance sheet notwithstanding, the senior ILFC debt rating is A−. On May 31 its all-in interest cost was 9.36 percent, an extraordinary feat in view of a then-prevailing prime rate of 11½ percent. And its debt is mainly unsecured.

If you call up ILFC to ask for a copy of its latest annual report, the company will throw in a half-dozen laudatory Wall Street research reports for free. Analysts seem to love ILFC, and the company has requited that affection. The company's assets have exploded, its earnings have risen, and its stock price has climbed. Insiders own almost 60 percent of the stock. The May quarter set new records in sales, net income, and—the other side of the borrowed coin—interest expense. Leslie L. Gonda, chairman and chief executive, was able to describe to his stockholders what seemed to be aircraft-leasing heaven:

> We continue to see a very strong demand for our advanced-technology aircraft as we look into the future with an average of two or more potential lessees identified for each delivery scheduled over the next several years. This positive market environment has enabled us to improve our operating margins. We are also encouraged by declining interest rates which also bodes well for future results.

Interest rates, of course, recently stopped falling. The sudden reversal in money market yields is exactly what ILFC doesn't need. Its leases are fixed-rate (as distinct from GPA, of Shannon, Ireland, which offers variable-rate leases), whereas some 40 percent of its liabilities are variable-rate. The combination of fixed assets and floating liabilities is what got the thrift industry where it is today. Thus, ILFC profits from falling rates and suffers from rising ones. It suffers from flat yield curves, never mind inverted ones.

Operating income, however, is only one string of ILFC's bow. Another and more important source of income is the gain on sales of its aircraft as they come off lease. One of the bullish Wall Street research reports that the company kindly forwarded has a fascinating analysis of the subject. Michael Millman, a Shearson Lehman Hutton leasing analyst, breaks out results over the past two and half years, separating operating income—that is, the business of leasing aircraft—from gains on the sales of those planes. The results give pause. As a percentage of revenues, operating income has fallen to 12 percent or less in recent quarters from 27 percent in the first quarter of 1987. And in alternating quarters beginning in 1987, the company has produced a sizable gain-on-sale to fortify its leasing results. "The company's quarterly, and to some extent annual, results are unpredictable—primarily because of the opportunity-oriented nature of its very profitable remarketing [that

"This is your captain speaking. Any passengers who want to buy some of our new zero-coupon bonds, why, that would be greatly appreciated. We'll be using the proceeds for maintenance."

is, of aircraft] activities," remarked Millman, who, by the way, is bullish.

It is this same unpredictability—the company's ability to turn a profitable aircraft trade at odd moments—that has kept short sellers at bay. The bearish line is that ILFC has become an aircraft-trading company, not a leasing company. It is in the speculation business, like Carl Icahn, and its earnings should be discounted for the observed tendency of all bull markets to come to an end. (True enough, this tendency has not been observed very often in the past several years.) Furthermore, as the bears argue, ILFC is at risk of rising interest rates and a flattening yield curve. It would suffer if the credit protection afforded to aircraft lessors under Section 1110 of the U.S. Bankruptcy Code is diminished in future bankruptcies. It would suffer, most fundamentally, by a decline in traffic. "It all comes down to traffic," a bear said, hastening to add that he was not short yet and wouldn't be, probably, until the great airline/aircraft hurrah had spent itself. He said he was counting on Avmark for a line on the timing.

Avmark, as you may know, is an airline and aviation-economics consulting firm. It is based in Arlington, Virginia, and it says what's on its mind. Recently, Avmark's chairman, Morten S. Beyer, said, "We believe the airlines are a natural resource which should not be pillaged to satiate the larval greed of the Attilas of the stock market."

For better or worse, Beyer wasn't around to pick up the phone when Jay Diamond of this staff called Avmark headquarters to ask some questions of fact. For instance, is the size of the industry-wide order book reasonable or not? And what has been happening in the used-aircraft market? Paul Turk, Avmark's director of publications, got on the phone and echoed some of the chairman's views, regrettably without the metaphors. "Airplanes are ordered in good times and delivered in bad," he said. "Up until now 75 percent to 80 percent of the buying has been for fleet expansion. You begin to see more replacement buying at American, United, and now Northwest. Delta and USAir have relatively young fleets, while Pan Am, TWA, and Eastern will get murdered. Into the next century, about 50 percent to 60 percent of the buying will be for replacement of aging aircraft."

As for the aircraft order backlog—orders and options for U.S. airlines total $100 billion, of which half is firm—it is unreasonable or not depending on one's assumptions. As Turk does the numbers, it is unreasonable. The numbers seem to imply, he said, an 8 percent annual gain in airline traffic into the next century; Avmark projects 4 percent. (Boeing, by the way, making its own assumptions about fleet replacement and traffic growth, finds the size of the order book eminently reasonable.) The consequences of these overoptimistic projections, Turk contended, will be canceled orders and a break in the used-aircraft market. It will mean servicing one's debt "with large aluminum paperweights." Concerning the used-aircraft market, he related what you might expect: Strength in prices for newer, wide-body aircraft but relative weakness in prices for older, noisier, and less fuel-efficient planes. No sense that what the bears are waiting for in ILFC is happening or about to happen.

However, as long as so many investors are positioned for heaven on earth, it can do no harm to cast an occasional glance in the other direction.

What the new-era bulls have rejected or forgotten is that everything in finance has its season. In 1974–75, Boeing common changed hands at four times earnings, or $2 a share. The price is higher today. For most of the past few decades, bankers would as soon have burnt the depositors' money as lend it to a leveraged airline. Now they are lending en masse.

At the start of this essay, note was taken that thirty-four years passed before the Dow Jones Rail Average surpassed its 1929 high. Through most of the century, railroading was an industry in decline, and the Rails' big sleep no doubt reflected that fundamental fact. On the other hand, industries, like companies and neckties, fall in and out of fashion. Periodic bursts of enthusiasm for a type of investment are followed by long spells of revulsion or indifference. A case in point is the sale by Howard Hughes of his controlling interest in TWA at the top of the market in 1966. It was the most serendipitous exit since Calvin Coolidge left the White House in 1929. At the time, of course, it seemed that Hughes was making a gift to the institutional investor. *The Wall Street Journal* of May 4, 1966, captured the spirit of the proceedings:

> NEW YORK—Hughes Tool Co.'s mammoth 6,584,937 ($566,304,582) offering of Trans World Airlines common stock was snapped up by institutional buyers and other investors after reaching the market yesterday morning at $86 a share.
> Merrill Lynch, Pierce, Fenner & Smith Inc., and more than four hundred associated underwriters both here and abroad released the stock for general distribution about 10 a.m. Half an hour later, the manager announced that the offering was oversubscribed and the subscription books were closed.

The story noted the extraordinary size of the transaction and the near-universal enthusiasm it produced:

> The more than $566 million gross value of the sale ranked it as the second-largest underwritten stock offering in American history. It was exceeded only by the $657.9 million secondary sale of Ford Motor Co. shares in 1956. . . .

Even before the public offering price of $86 was agreed on, market specialists were predicting a quick sellout for the shares. They cited the big interest shown by institutional investors. . . .

Managers of mutual funds ranked at the top among institutional buyers of the offering, according to a spokesman for the managing underwriter. He said large buying also came from banks buying for trusteed accounts, from investment counselors, and insurance companies.

Everyone was said to be pleased—"We sold all our shares and we're begging for more," a broker exulted—although Hughes, the man who had more cause for celebration than anyone else involved, kept his own counsel. It was the top of tops. In 1966, TWA changed hands for twenty-three times earnings, a premium over most other carriers (American fetched eleven times earnings and Delta, eighteen times). The capitalization of the Hughes airline (equity at market value plus debt less cash and marketable securities) amounted to no less than $1.08 billion. It was a sum of money considerably larger than the capitalization of the airline acquired by Carl Icahn in 1988, if one inflates the value of the dollar by 5.9 percent a year in each of the twenty-two intervening years.

Now the market has come full circle, but with a difference. Instead of attaching premiums to net earnings, investors are valuing assets and cash flow. Instead of projecting a bull stock market out into the indefinite future, they are projecting a gullible debt market. What nobody would have believed even a few years ago (let alone in 1966) is that Carl Icahn could have raised money in the public markets after issuing a prospectus that might as well have been stamped with a skull and crossbones. "TWA's cash flow is not expected to be sufficient to enable it to repay the principal amount of the senior notes due in 1992 and 1993 or the notes at maturity, in the absence of refinancings," it said in black and white.

The ability of TWA to satisfy its fixed charges and scheduled repayment of indebtedness will be primarily dependent upon the future performance of TWA and its ability to renew or refinance its credit facilities on satisfactory terms. TWA experienced a shortfall of earnings to cover fixed charges during 1985 and 1986, for the two months ended December 31, 1988, and for the three months ended March 31, 1989.

Cyclical? That's airlines. Then again, that's credit, and that's life.*

EUROTUNNEL IN DEBT

June 8, 1990

I n 1802, when Britain and France found themselves momentarily at peace and able to consider a proposition to dig a tunnel under the English Channel, the yield on long-term government bonds in the City of London was 4¼ percent. Bank lending rates at the time were 5 percent. Now that this epic project is closer than ever before to completion, bond yields in the City are 11 percent. Sterling money market rates are 15 percent.

Almost two centuries after Napoleon, engineers have mastered

---

* With each passing day, it becomes harder to believe that any of this actually happened. Where the Pan Am Building used to be, at Forty-fifth Street and Park Avenue in Manhattan, there is now the Metropolitan Life Building; the names were changed in 1992, the year after Pan Am went out of business without, of course, buying UAL. Texas Air, later calling itself Continental Holdings, filed for bankruptcy protection in 1990; TWA followed it in 1992. Carl Icahn, who proved to be no Howard Hughes, resigned his control of TWA, along with his chairmanship of the board, in 1993. NWA has not yet filed for bankruptcy protection, but it has been reduced to petitioning its bankers for mercy.

Probably no other speculative chapter of the 1980s was so wild-haired. Investors came to believe that the airline business had been delivered into a state of permanent prosperity; it was, in fact, as a result of overexpansion, on the verge of ruin. In August 1989, Marvin Davis, the onetime Denver oil man who bought 20th Century-Fox at the bottom and sold crude oil and office buildings at the top, made a bid for UAL, United Air Lines' parent, which was valued at $200 a share. On September 5, 1989, the stock market bid up the price of the stock to 290¾ a share. Nineteen-ninety was a year of modest prosperity for UAL: It showed a net profit of $92 million, or $4.24 a share. The years 1991 and 1992, however, engulfed that little profit with a gigantic loss: in total, $1.3 billion, or the equivalent of $54.06 a share. There is a school of thought in finance which holds that the stock market is efficient. We may all agree that the market is sometimes efficient; however, there are other times—the late summer of 1989, for instance—when it is fanciful.

As for ILFC, it was acquired in 1990 by American International Group, the insurance company, in what must be judged a well-timed sale. On December 15, 1992, the leasing company had the financial wherewithal to place $4.1 billion worth of orders for new jet aircraft. "Our core leasing business has been steadily growing in volume, demand, and profitability . . . ," the chairman, Leslie L. Gonda, said. I picked on the wrong leasing company.

the technology of boring through chalk marl at depths of one hundred meters below sea level. Investment bankers have learned to project uncertain cash flows into the distant future with the invaluable aid of personal computers. However, the Bank of England, the Bank of France, uncounted governments, and debtors worldwide have failed to improve on nineteenth-century interest rates. If Eurotunnel Plc were able to borrow at 2 percent or 3 percent instead of 10 percent or 15 percent, many things would be different today. One would be the price of the company's stock: It would be higher.

Eurotunnel, the Anglo-French construction consortium, is the ultimate bird-in-the-bush investment. It is a start-up that does not expect to open its doors to paying customers until 1993 or to pay its first common dividend until 1998.*

When it raised its first equity capital in 1986 and 1987, the company projected all-in costs of less than £5 billion. It subsequently has raised that estimate to £7.66 billion. At the start, the projected capitalization was £6 billion. Now it is £8.5 billion. In keeping with the spirit of the times, £6.9 billion out of the £8.5 billion is earmarked for debt. In the absence of an operating record, brokers are reduced to quoting macroeconomic forecasts or computer-generated models of internal rates of return. One firm cabled its clients last week, as if it really knew, "We believe that GDP [gross domestic product] in 1993 is likely to be some 6 percent above the level forecast in Eurotunnel's 1987 prospectus." Make no mistake, Eurotunnel is more than an engineering feat. On the revenue-forecasting side, it is also a .45-caliber shot in the dark.

Eurotunnel is a concept investment. The concept seems to be this: Buy now for capital-gains possibilities. Hold until profitability sets in. Then collect the dividends of a steady-eddy public utility. It is hard to apply a valuation to a hypothetical income stream, but brokers have made attempts—precise attempts, thanks to the Lotus spreadsheet. One bullish projection, published in April (before the recent rise in estimated costs) shows net earnings of 8 pence a share in 1996: That will be the company's first profitable year. To put 8 pence in relief, Eurotunnel shares were recently quoted at 550 pence apiece. By 2003, according to the analysis, the com-

* Now 2000.

pany will earn 100 pence a share. The really good news comes rolling in about 2033 when annual earnings will hurdle the 1,300-pence mark. In 2041, the last year of the Eurotunnel concession, the company will earn exactly 2,296 pence a share. The projected total return, 1993–2041, works out to 14.3 percent, which is admittedly more than the current yield on 4 percent perpetual British government bonds. The bonds fetch 10.95 percent. As to the relative merits of Eurotunnel common and British consols, every investor must search his own soul. We can think of nothing exactly comparable to a leveraged, nonrevenue-producing, imagination-capturing, investor-owned undersea railroad, but the Donaldson, Lufkin & Jenrette junk bond index has a duration-weighted yield of 15.66 percent. It is only figuratively under water.

It is easy to ignore an unfinished tunnel if you happen to live several thousand miles west of its construction site—in Brooklyn, for instance. But Eurotunnel is a worthy topic for credit-minded investors anywhere. It is an emblem of the era, for one thing, a showcase of bank debt, technical prowess, the obliteration of national boundaries, and the privatization of ownership. It is the Thatcher government's firm policy to keep hands off the company, and the bank debt carries no public guarantee. In one sense, Eurotunnel is the financial and commercial analogue to the political revolution in Eastern Europe. It is the kind of event that frightens bears and gladdens bulls because it suggests that the universe of the possible is expanding. It limbers up the imagination like the launch of the Hubble Space Telescope or the promised reconciliation of Don King and James "Buster" Douglas.

The Eurotunnel project is a manic-depressive enterprise that leaves its investors alternately high and low. If you are a European reader, you may now be carrying around unwanted Eurotunnel knowledge just as many Americans carry around unwanted Donald Trump knowledge. For late arrivals, the company has suffered a run of trouble fully proportionate to its engineering task. Costs were ratcheted sharply higher last year, management feuded publicly with its contractors, and the enterprise ran afoul of its bank-lending covenants (the "Project Credit Agreement"). Unable to draw bank credit, Eurotunnel ran down its cash and marketable securities. A sense of the melodrama is conveyed by a paragraph from the January 13 *Economist*:

After ninety-nine days on the brink of bankruptcy, the Channel tunnel is once more bankable. Between October 2, when Eurotunnel announced it would overshoot the £6 billion available for construction, and January 9, when its bankers agreed to release more cash, the companies involved in the project wrangled almost without a break to find a way to save it. They managed to persuade the banks that it was worth risking more money, but they did not get to the root of the trouble: the relationship between the tunnel's builder, TML, [Transmanche-Link] and its owner, Eurotunnel.

Eurotunnel is back from that particular brink. It is still in technical default on its loan agreement, but it expects soon not to be. On separate manic notes last week, it reported a step-up in the rate of tunneling and the details of a new proposed financing. On the depressive side of the ledger, it reported an increase in estimated total costs: to £7.66 billion from the range of £7.5 billion to £7.6 billion it had projected as recently as April. As for additional unpleasant surprises on the cost front, Alastair Morton, deputy chairman and group chief executive, said, "I believe completely that this is the last time."* As you may know, the project envisions three tunnels: two to carry the main rail traffic and a third for service and emergency use. Completion of the service tunnel is expected next October. Work on the two main arteries is said to be proceeding fast enough to meet (or even get in under the wire of) the June 15, 1993, scheduled grand opening. Opponents to the tunnel once argued that the French cavalry would invade through it. You hear that argument less and less. Nowadays, opponents contend that the regions to be connected—Kent in southeast England and Sangatte, near Calais, in northern France—are too remote to attract a financially viable share of the cross-Channel market. As might be imagined, feasibility studies have been written to dispel that fear, and 560,000-odd individual shareholders and 208 bank lenders have taken the other side of the bet. Japanese banks, incidentally, account for the largest single share of the bank loans. As might be expected, official Europe is bullish. "The Community of European Railways has launched an ambitious programme to develop a high-speed network throughout Europe, for which the Channel Tunnel

---

* It was not; £8.1 billion is the latest projected cost, not counting the additional expense associated with a postponement of the start of service from the summer of 1993 to December 1993.

"I don't care if we did underwrite them. I ain't bidding on no collateralized fixed-rate multi-tranche tap notes, period."

is a key component," according to the 1989 Eurotunnel annual report.

What makes Eurotunnel's stockholders so susceptible to mood swings is the punitive arithmetic of compound interest. The more the capitalization tilts toward debt, the more precarious the equity owners' grip on the business, and the lower the margin for error in the necessarily inexact revenue forecasts. (New, revised traffic forecasts are soon to be circulated among the creditor banks; according to the *Financial Times*, the data will contain no unpleasant surprises.) The higher the percentage of debt to overall capital, the greater the volatility in the stockholders' returns, if any. Maybe the Eurotunnel planners are better at forecasting interest rates than we are. Then again—a sobering thought—maybe they're not. To date the company has borrowed mainly in French francs, thereby postponing its inevitable entry into the high-yield sterling market. It has borrowed mainly at floating rates. From the new annual:

> The cost of borrowing to the end of the year was just below 9.5 percent before bank fees and margins. This rate reflects the decision to borrow money primarily in French francs initially given that Eurotunnel, up to a certain limit, need not fear currency exposure if it borrows either in French francs or sterling. It is, however, Eurotunnel's long-term objective not to have a significant imbalance between the currency mix of its assets and liabilities. New borrowings in 1990 will be at higher rates as a result of increases in both U.K. and French interest rates.

At year-end, actual capitalization was conservative enough because only a fraction of the promised bank credit had been drawn down. Bank loans and stockholders' equity each (in round numbers) came to £1 billion. Going forward, however, debt will tend to pile up on the balance sheet: The proposed new financing, for example, is highly leveraged. The sum total to be raised is £2.53 billion. A rights issue, on tap for the fall, is expected to contribute £530 million of equity. Commercial banks will lend £1.7 billion, and the European Investment Bank will lend £300 million. Two things may be said about this mix of debt and equity. First, it is longer on debt than the lenders had expected. They were prepared to finance three-quarters, not four-fifths, of the total. Second, it did not seem to shock them. "The banks," commented the *Financial Times*, "do not seem to have extracted a particularly high price [for the higher leverage]. An extra 25 basis points on the entire debt, bringing the average cost to around 160 basis points over LIBOR (assuming no further cost overruns), does not appear excessive, especially as the maturity has been extended by five years." As LIBOR is 15 percent or more, 160 basis points over LIBOR would be 16.6 percent or more. Money lent at 16.6 percent doubles every five years.

On form, the banks wouldn't mind because bigger loans mean greater fees and higher interest income. Even if the banks don't object, however, we can ask some leading questions ourselves. The trouble with creditors, as the 1980s repeatedly taught, is that they always have their hands out. They insist on getting paid whether or not the customers are showing up at the door. "Extra costs will. . . . be compounded by extra interest charges," wrote Tom Rowland in "The Tunnel: The Channel and Beyond." "An overrun early in the tunnel excavation will have to be paid for with extra borrowed cash and the extra debt carried right the way through."

Tunneling is only a little more than half finished. Contracts to design, manufacture, and supply the initial rolling stock for the tunnel shuttle trains were let only this year. The first franc and pound of revenue is (to take the projected opening of June 15, 1993) three years off. In the generic 1980s' leveraged buyout, lenders were led to believe that even if the debtor company failed to cover its fixed charges out of income, it could always sell assets. In the case of Eurotunnel, asset sales—of terminals, boring machines, rails, holes—are possible, but the population of potentially interested buyers is limited.

It is impossible not to wish the bulls well in this thirty-mile undersea trek. Eighteen years work on a previous tunnel project came to naught when the British withdrew in 1975. A Channel Tunnel Company bill failed in the House of Commons by only seven votes in 1929. An earlier tunnel scheme was withdrawn in the House in 1907. There were intermittent schemes to tunnel throughout the nineteenth century. Napoleon III was an enthusiast.

If the past merely repeated itself in continuous cycles, the latest excavation would have failed already. Its success to date may be read as a happy omen for human progress. "This time, things are different," is the bulls' favorite song. Well, *this* time, so far, under the dirty gray waters near Shakespeare Cliff, they are. When the French government recently banned imports of British beef in reaction to an outbreak of "mad cow disease" in the United Kingdom, the British were able to express their ancient feelings toward France in traditional ways. "Given the chance," a London tabloid hypothesized, "the French do not knife a friend or neighbor in the back. Not if they can use a pitchfork." Yet tunneling continues nevertheless.

What, then, has changed? Why after two hundred years is Eurotunnel proceeding now? Is it the inexorable push toward one European market? Is it the Jubilee of Capitalism? Is it a mistake that the fates will presently correct? It was a long and ruminative series of questions to consider over the transatlantic telephone, but a Eurotunnel spokeswoman ventured an answer. She said that the impetus was "partly political, partly economic, and partly that the tunnel is a privately financed project rather than publicly financed, as was the case with the 1970s project."

Which brings us back to credit. If you were a bank, would you lend? We would not, if we were a bank, because it is not obvious to us that we would get our money back on time and in good condition. The margins seem tight in view of the risks. Among these risks are the proposed capital structure (highly leveraged), the projected returns (too dependent on supremely unpredictable events), and the well-known tendency of macroeconomic forecasts to contain the wrong sign. Perhaps the management is right to insist that the latest increase in costs is the last one. However, there is the tendency of costs to rise and of final estimates of costs to come into the shop for adjustment.

The snag in the idea that the tunnel is the epitome of progress is the backward monetary system in which it must finance itself. In the junk bond era, companies borrowed at higher marginal rates than the rates at which they earned or were likely to earn. Banks, reaching for yield (in an inflationary era, banks must reach), lent for the interest and fee income. There is no telling precisely what Eurotunnel will earn or when, despite the official and unofficial projections. What is known about Eurotunnel is that the cost of its capital in French francs is high in historical terms and that the prospective cost in sterling is far higher.

To finance the Panama Canal, the United States government borrowed at less than 2 percent. That anchors the low end of the cost-of-capital spectrum on epic infrastructure projects. Toward the other extreme, the Suez Canal Co. paid 8 percent on a thirty-year bond issue in 1871, and the Northern Pacific Railroad paid 7.30 percent in 1873. The Washington Public Power Supply System paid 15 percent in 1981. In low-interest-rate times, the world was on a gold standard, and the value of money was defined. Now the world is on a so-called information standard, and the value of money is rootless. It is under constant negotiation during trading hours by young people with telephones.

It is all very well that markets make continuous adjustments to bond yields and exchange rates. However, the resulting volatility introduces a special kind of drama into long-term commercial planning. The list of what isn't known about the future is longer than it used to be, even if the brokers' forecasts suggest omniscience all around. Under the tracks of Eurotunnel is the spongy ground of paper money. In years to come, there is no telling how disruptive the settlement might be.*

HOT LIGHT ON GE

September 14, 1990

There being no quadruple-A bond rating, as what's-his-name from Beverly Hills was always saying, the credit of a triple-A company has no place to go but down. By definition, it cannot be improved, but—the times being what they are—it can easily be disimproved. Only twelve American industrial corporations still command the top debt rating of both Moody's and Standard & Poor's.

General Electric, one of that elite number, makes a provocative case in financial evolution. In size and gravitas, it is the ultimate triple-A. Its bonds yield only a little more than the government's, and that interest rate spread is now as thin as a dime. Perhaps investors have come to favor cash-flow-positive debt issuers (for example, GE) as opposed to cash-flow-negative ones (for example, the Treasury), even if the cash-flow-negative issuer can tax and print money. Or perhaps investors are so hungry for extra yield that they have forgotten to ask the most basic fixed-income question in the book: What can go wrong? And the inevitable follow-up question: Am I being paid enough to weather the storm if something does go wrong?

* But interest rates fell, landing on the spongy earth. When, in February 1993, S. G. Warburg Securities reiterated its bullish outlook on Eurotunnel shares, it was able to cite low interest rates and the possibility of even lower ones. At 6 percent, the U.K. base rate hasn't been lower in fifteen years.

General Electric makes aircraft engines, medical equipment, light bulbs, power-generation equipment, refrigerators, satellite heat shields, satellites, television shows, locomotives, electric motors—and loans. It makes all these things by the carload, and its financial parameters never fail to suggest a comparison with the Hong Kong GNP. It is the largest U.S. commercial-paper issuer, with $28 billion outstanding. Its revenues last year totaled $55 billion; earnings, $4 billion, and assets, $128 billion.

General Electric Financial Services (GEFS) is the name of the financial division. General Electric Capital Corp. (GECC), is GEFS's principal, triple-A-rated and fabulously successful company. Employers Reinsurance Corp. is the number two financial holding and Kidder Peabody Group is number three.

In 1980, the forerunner to GEFS competed exclusively with other industrial finance companies. Except indirectly, it did not compete with banks, brokerage houses, thrift institutions, or insurance companies, as GEFS does today. It earned $115 million through secured lending and financial leasing, and its field of operations was domestic. Now, to quote the latest annual, which does not exaggerate, GEFS "is one of the world's leading suppliers of capital, packaging sophisticated financial products uniquely tailored to customer needs." In 1989, the financial division earned $927 million through leveraged buyouts, consumer credit cards, commercial real estate lending, junk bonds, computer leasing, aircraft leasing, auto leasing, auto auctions, railcar leasing, dry van cargo leasing, mortgage insurance, reinsurance, and securities sales and underwriting. It operates worldwide. In the Decade of Debt, the compound annual growth of its operating earnings was 26 percent.

GEFS, as you may or may not remember, played an instrumental role in financing one of the decade's first miracle deals, the Gibson Greeting Cards leveraged buyout of 1982. That year did not mark the beginning of debt (as 1963 marked the beginning of sex, according to the poet Philip Larkin), but it suggested the infinite possibilities of a leveraged balance sheet to a new and historically innocent generation of bankers and investors. With Gibson, the 1980s were off and running, and almost nobody ran faster or farther than GE.

Many of the runners have stumbled (some into the arms of the law), and the rate of expansion of debt is slowing. At the margin, we think, the expansion of private-sector debt may be grinding to a halt. The possibility of stagnation or even contraction has not yet engaged the attention of the corporate bond market, except for the junk bond branch, which thinks about nothing else.

We have a theory: The bear market in junk is of a piece with the bear markets in bank stocks, commercial real estate, and so-called stub stocks (that is, the equities of leveraged corporations). They are of a piece with the bear market in Japan. What each disturbance has in common is the refusal of formerly willing lenders to say yes. The breadth of the downturn raises urgent questions, one of which provoked this essay: If a very good company—indeed, a triple-A company—actively participated in the 1980s, how could it not actively participate in the 1990s? How could a company profit so handsomely by the expansion of debt yet not suffer through the contraction?*

GEFS is the decade of the 1980s under one roof. It financed leveraged cable-television deals, insured mortgages, leased planes and cars, insured municipal bonds, lent against the collateral of commercial real estate, financed leveraged buyouts, and became the largest issuer of private-label credit cards in the country. It became a bank of the future: an unfettered "niche" institution with a triple-A balance sheet. Like the First National Bank of New York in the 1920s or Dai-Ichi Kangyo Bank in the 1980s, it basked in its reputation as the holder of vast "hidden assets." Everyone knew that GE Capital Corp. had taken equity positions in the buyouts it helped to finance. And everyone was familiar with the prevailing, indeed inevitable, direction of equity values in successful leveraged buyouts: up. Thus, as Standard & Poor's put it last fall, "Equity positions, taken by GECC as part of its leveraged buyout financing activity, have grown to a substantial size and are expected to make a large contribution to future earnings as gains are realized." Note the bull market construction, ". . . as gains are realized." A year later, the correct turn of phrase has become, ". . . *if* gains are realized."

We had a list of questions for GE almost as long as its arm. We'd

---

* A logical enough question for the time, but the answer proved not to be the one I imagined. Not only did GE ride out the debt troubles, but it also capitalized on them, growing where others were forced to shrink. It was strong enough to be able to buy depressed real estate and move into the verdant field of bankruptcy financing. I wrote at what would turn out to be the peak of financial apprehension, the stock market's, if not my own.

wanted to ask about the cable-TV loans (reported to total $1.8 billion), the $740 million junk bond portfolio (acquired from Kidder Peabody last March), the buyout portfolio and, more generally, the prospects for consumer lending, now that a business slowdown has been overlaid on a real estate slump. We had hoped to ask if GEFS, to improve its return on equity, has been stepping up the sale of its "hidden assets," i.e., warrants in its corporate-finance clients, such as Tiffany. And we had prepared a follow-up question: In the light of the bear market in stocks, aren't warrant values fast eroding?

GENERAL ELECTRIC CO.—TIME MARCHES ON
SELECTED HISTORICAL DATA AND RATIOS
(IN $ MILLIONS, EXCEPT PER-SHARE DATA)

	1932	1957	1974	1982	1989
Net sales	$147.2	$4,335.7	$13,598.9	$26,500.0	$54,574.0
EBIT[1]	14.7	521.7	1,180.8	3,097.0	12,210.0
Net income	14.4	247.9	608.1	1,817.0	3,939.0
Earnings per share	$0.41	$2.85	$3.34	$8.00	$4.36
Total assets	405.1	2,346.6	9,369.1	21,615.0	128,344.0
Long-term debt	2.0[2]	300.0[3]	1,195.2[4]	3,099.0	16,110.0
Total equity	345.4	1,216.6	3,704.3	10,198.0	20,890.0
EBIT margin	10.0%	12.0%	8.7%	11.7%	22.4%
Net income margin	9.8%	5.7%	4.5%	6.9%	7.2%
Long-term debt/assets	0.5%	12.8%	12.8%	14.3%	12.6%
Long-term debt/equity	0.6%	24.7%	32.3%	30.4%	77.1%
Current ratio	2.3x	1.9x	1.3x	1.3x	0.8x[5]
EBIT/interest	46.8x	46.5x	6.6x	9.0x	1.9x
Return on assets	3.6%	10.6%	6.5%	8.4%	3.1%
Return on equity	4.2%	20.4%	16.4%	17.8%	18.9%
Net income of GECC as % of parent	—	3.2%	7.0%	11.3%	20.7%[6]

[1] Earnings before income and taxes; includes all income sources.
[2] GE gold debenture 3½s, due 1942; Aaa-rated, 40-year-bonds.
[3] GE debenture 3½s, due 1976; Aaa-rated, 20-year bonds.
[4] Five issues, including $300 million of GE 8½s, due 2004; Aaa-rated, 30-year bonds.
[5] Current assets include only those time sales, loans and rental receivables of GEFS that mature in 1990. Including all GEFS receivables, current ratio is 1.2x.
[6] No doubt, GECC has grown in relative importance over the past several years, but the parent company no longer separately discloses its net income.

We'd looked forward to hearing what the brass at GE would say to the proposition that, in a credit contraction, trouble begins at the fringe but eventually visits the center, no matter how strong the center is, or seems to be.

In the time saved by not visiting GE headquarters in Stamford, Connecticut, Jay Diamond, our associate publisher, compiled a fascinating historical table. The information describes the parent company's consolidated finances in a succession of business downturns, starting with 1932, which happens to be the year in which the forerunner to GECC was started. It ends in what may or may not prove to be a recession year, pending statistical revisions, 1989. Evolution has meant more leverage, thinner coverages, lower returns on asssets, and rising contributions to consolidated income by financial activity.

Interestingly, GE's debt rating hasn't changed in the past fifty-eight years, even though its financial profile has. At the bottom of the Great Depression, long-term debt was negligible, interest coverage was massively redundant, and the current ratio was better than 2:1. In 1989, a non-depression year, long-term debt constituted 77 percent of equity, interest coverage was less than 2:1 (surely a remarkably low reading) and the current ratio was less than 1:1.

To the universal question, So what?, we can offer several answers. In the first place, the leveraging of GE is emblematic of the leveraging of America. For another, the stability of GE's debt ratings over the years is proof that "triple-A" is a subjective and relative term, like "thin." By the lights of 1990, GE stands as straight as an arrow. By comparison with its weakest years in the past half century or so, however, the company slouches and has difficulty touching its toes. To us, the second most striking line on the table, after the melting of interest coverage, is the one that shows the rising contribution of financial activity to the consolidated bottom line. Let us agree that the alchemy business has seen its best days and that the warrant value of leveraged companies is going down. In that case, the profit contribution of GE's financial businesses is bound to decline, and perhaps quickly.

On the trip to Stamford we didn't take, we'd meant to ask GE about the significance of GEFS. "Do you see what we see?" we were going to ask the person across the table, apropos of the credit contraction. "And if you do, do you anticipate any circumstances in which the parent's credit might be needed to assist the financial subsidiary's?" The rating agencies seem to agree that, standing by itself, GE Capital Corp. would not command the triple-A debt rating it now does. "Although no guarantee or formal support agreement exists between GECC and General Electric Co.," S&P, for instance, comments, "the parent historically has provided considerable support to its financial services subsidiary, a significant factor in GECC's ratings."

Excusing themselves, the GE spokespeople told us that what they had to say about credit they would say to the rating agencies. So we called the agencies. To our question of whether they worried about the highly leveraged transaction (HLT) portfolio, the real estate and cable-TV loans, and the junk bond and warrant portfolios, their composite answer was, "Yes, a little, but there are offsetting factors." Rodrigo Quintanilla, the Moody's analyst on the GECC case, admitted the potential for problems. He acknowledged that the GECC portfolio is untested by recession. But he cited, among other mitigating circumstances, the subsidiary's presumed call on its rich parent. And he added that, if GECC's debt rating ever did come in for scrutiny, the bonds, not the commercial paper, would be the candidates for downgrade (not that they are now, he added). As for the parent, Martin Knoblowitz, S&P's analyst, said that its diversification and sheer mass were so great that a troubled GECC (if there ever were one) would not immediately threaten GE's triple-A rating. As for the issue of whether the triple-A halo has lost some of its wattage over the years, Knoblowitz said, "We don't go in terms of numbers alone in looking at credit quality."

Next, we turned to a new report on GECC by our friends at Fitch Investors Service. Although bullish, the report is fact-filled, and it can be usefully read by bears and independents. The summary addresses the company's size, intercontinental reach (twenty businesses, each well established in its respective market), and strength-giving affiliation with GE. As for HLTs and commercial real estate, we are advised not to lose any sleep over them: "Fitch does not expect that potential deterioration in related asset quality will hurt the company's financial integrity since profits and the underlying capital/reserve base provide a substantial foundation."

Every financial idea stands on a theory even if the proponent of the idea doesn't consciously know what it is. Our theory is that attitudes toward credit are cyclical. Collectively, lenders and borrowers progress from being brash to being timid, not pausing long at the midfield marker of reasonableness. There are long cycles and short, the long having to do with the passing of generations and the short having to do with the rise and fall of business activity. Once in a blue moon—now, for instance—the long cycle is superimposed on the short one. We are, we think, beyond the manic phase of this consolidated cycle and into the depressive one. In the depressive phase, credit contracts, asset values fall, and business slows down. Among financial institutions, failures proliferate. Failure begins at the margin but eats its way into the middle, like a mouse. Thus, junk bonds show the strain before home-equity loans, and Drexel Burnham Lambert fails before Bank of New England. In a severe contraction, even the strongest lenders are tested, as the process of shrinkage and deflation nullify the financial assumptions that, in the boom, had seemed conservative.

Fitch does not declare a credit theory. It seems to imply, however, that every institution rises or falls on its merits and that good management overcomes problems. The authors salute the capital company's asset quality—"surprisingly good and consistent given the loan portfolio's fairly high-risk profile"—and commend its management. They acknowledge that the GE executives are only human because there were energy-related loan losses in 1986. They do not deny that GE managers are any less human in 1990. But they do not directly address the possibility that real estate and corporate finance produced bigger and more dangerous bubbles than energy, with the corresponding likelihood of large future loan losses at GE.

We do worry, of course—that is our lot in life—and the coolness of Fitch's prose only makes us sweat more. For instance, concerning the most lucrative GECC business line, corporate finance, the authors write:

> Senior and subordinated financing and equity investments in leveraged corporate restructurings total $7.9 billion. This has been a high-profile and high-profitability business for GECC for a number of years. The company's approach can be differentiated from others in the industry by its willingness to take control of and manage businesses, which reduces losses. The portfolio is diversified among over one hundred borrowers and by industry, with a slight concentration in media and cable, which together represent 26 percent of loans. . . .

Strong credit management and a very sizable unrecognized gain from the warrant portfolio are sufficient to cover the variance in credit quality that is anticipated.

So, barring a recession, rabbits of equity will be plucked from the corporate hat. Fitch does have one anxiety. It is that the good old deal days are over:

Of perhaps more concern is the dearth of leveraged buyout activity in the current market environment. However, while this business has represented such a strong profit contributor to the company (a full 25 percent of 1989 results), the slowdown so far has not had a material effect on profitability, as other businesses have provided greater earnings.

The more we thought about GECC's call on the financial strength of its parent, the more circular it became to us. GECC itself has contributed an ever larger share to the parent's net income. To that extent, therefore, GECC is an important source of the very strength that it may one day seek to lean against.

If GE's and GECC's credit ratings cannot get any better, neither can the companies' standing on Wall Street. In a *Barron's* poll this week, GE turned up as one of the stocks most favored by institutional equity investors. As for the bond market, investors increasingly prefer GE to the United States government.

Maybe the credit contraction is a figment of our imagination. Or maybe GECC will glide through whatever contraction there is unscathed. In either case, markets are priced accordingly. If not, there will be some adjustments.

MONEY-GREEN DENIM

January 31, 1992

According to Shad Rowe, our Dallas correspondent, the stock market is now the lender of last resort, having rescued more dying banks than the Federal Reserve.

Junk-bond overcoat

Burlington Industries Inc., the North Carolina textile market, is lined up to become another bull market beneficiary. In 1987, Morgan Stanley & Co. masterminded a leveraged buyout of Burlington, which was then being pursued by the raider Asher Edelman. On the day the transaction closed, the company's net worth fell to $125 million from $1.3 billion, and its long-term debt jumped to $2.8 billion from $300 million. There was nothing unique about this transformation. At the time, investment bankers were fanning out from Jacksonville to Seattle. According to 1980s script, employees were fired, management was decentralized, assets were sold, overhead was reduced, and fees were remitted to the investment bankers by the carload.

Now—and this is according to 1990s script—Burlington proposes to de-lever. It has filed a plan to raise $855 million in common stock, a sale that would put no less than 83 percent of its equity in public hands. Proceeds of the offering (along with $1.25 billion in new bank loans) would be applied to retiring or refinancing its public debt. The announcement of the sale alone was enough to lift the prices of its junk bonds.

In truth, the bonds had come a long way even before the announcement. The company's costs have been falling and its exports have been rising. The textile business, denim in particular, turned up last spring, and Burlington's fourth-quarter operating income before interest and taxes rose by 81 percent from the depressed year-ago figure: to $45 million from $25 million in the three months ended September 28. The Burlington Industries 13⅞s of 1996, which in November 1990 had fetched just 42 cents on the dollar, were quoted last week at 106. The yield has fallen to 12.2 percent from 40.2 percent.

Now the time has come to ask what this round-trip in corporate finance signifies (or will signify if it actually happens). Has it vindicated the promoters? Helped the surviving employees? What does it say about American capitalism in the last decade of the twentieth century? Also—a macroeconomic afterthought—could Wall Street, through its own sheer gluttony, create a fee-based business recovery in this presidential election year?

The first thing to say about Burlington is that it is no Macy's. Its cash shortage is prospective rather than imminent. Late Tuesday, the company reported gains of 5 percent in sales and 81 percent in operating income for the fiscal first quarter ended December 28. In the just-ended fiscal year, cash flow (liberally defined) actually covered interest expense. The 1991 net loss from continuing operations was lower than the 1990 net loss. Also, 1991 EBIT, at $157 million, was higher than 1990 EBIT, at $126 million. EBIT, of course, means earnings before interest and taxes.

A new report on Burlington by Merrill Lynch waxed bullish about the company because "EBITDA" is more than adequate to cover that portion of interest expense payable in cash. EBITDA means earnings before interest, taxes, depreciation, and amortization. It was the promotional concept of the 1980s because it legitimized the convenient fiction that depreciation was an accounting abstraction without any relevance to the valuation of a real-life business. To listen to the investment bankers, paint didn't peel, machinery was ageless, and technology stood still.

The capital investments that the company made before the LBO, according to Burlington's latest 10-K, have allowed it "to operate at substantially lower capital expenditure levels without adversely affecting its facilities or competitive position." It is good that that is so because the 1988 and 1991 financing agreements impose an annual ceiling of $50 million on capital spending through 1995. Either Burlington overinvested during its investment-grade period, or it has underinvested during its LBO period, or both. From 1983 to 1986, for instance, capital expenditures accounted for an average of 5.5 percent of sales and constituted an average of 120 percent of depreciation. From 1988 to 1991, on the other hand, capital spending accounted for an average of 2.45 percent of sales and constituted an average of 78 percent of depreciation. A consultant to the industry who asked for anonymity told our Jay Diamond that the prevailing standards of capital spending are 3 percent and 130 percent, respectively. If so, the company may have some catching up to do, the investments of the early and mid-1980s notwithstanding.

Just as the finance professors promised, Burlington's LBO enhanced efficiency. Margins improved to an average of 8.7 percent in the four years following the 1987 LBO from 4.6 percent in the four years preceding it (we've used EBIT margins, that is EBIT divided by net sales). But they did not improve enough to produce the cash with which the company could meet its maturing debt obligations. Barring just such a refinancing plan as the management last week proposed (and which the stock market, at least up until this writing, seems inclined to allow), the company eventually would have to throw itself on the mercy of its creditors to pay cash interest on its zero-coupon, "step-up" bonds, for instance. "According to our projections, using the current capital structure of the company," Phelps Hoyt, analyst with Duff & Phelps, says, "Burlington will run out of available credit at the end of fiscal year 1994." The problem is not so much a lack of cash flow as the debt-heavy capitalization and the rigor of the amortization schedule. Even the bullish Merrill analyst described the outlook tepidly: "If a business upturn is not sustained and Burlington's results decline, we believe that the company will still meet nearly all of its obligations." Meeting "nearly all" of one's obligations also happens to constitute a working definition of bankruptcy.

In response to the proposed public equity offering, Standard & Poor's put Burlington on "CreditWatch" with "positive implications," but it also issued a warning: "The recapitalization plan would reduce overall financial risk, but the extent will depend on the success of the IPO. If the IPO is not successful, the company will still face financial pressures as substantial debt payments become due and significant noncash-pay interest charges become cash-pay in the 1993–96 period." Hence, the monetary significance of the bull stock market. Its rise has almost come to constitute a new monetary aggregate.

On balance, therefore, we give Burlington's LBO a gentleman's "C." It was neither a stupendous success, à la Cain Chemical, nor a clear-cut disaster, like Federated Department Stores. The company has eliminated 12 percent of its pre-buyout assets and has gotten along with only two-thirds of its pre-buyout sales. Before the LBO, it employed forty-four thousand people with seventy-two plants in ten states (and twelve abroad). Last September it employed twenty-four thousand people with forty-one plants in seven states (and three in Mexico). In effect, it has replaced blue-collar workers with investment bankers.

One telltale sign of the 1980s is complexity of financial structure, and Burlington's is appropriately baffling. There is a Burlington Equity, a Burlington Industries Capital, a Burlington Holdings, a Burlington Fabrics, and a Burlington Industries. There is an employee stock ownership plan, or ESOP, which owns 24 percent of the voting and nonvoting stock (but will own only 3 percent after the offering). With long study it might be possible to understand why Morgan Stanley changed its equity investment in Burlington Holdings into shares of Burlington Capital or, later, why it converted its stock in Capital for shares of Equity preferred or, now, why it proposes to exchange its Equity preferred and nonvoting common for shares in the new Burlington. It appears—Morgan declined to comment—that the firm is about where it stood in 1987 on its investment account. It is almost unimaginably ahead on its fee-and-dividend account.

Morgan, along with the Equitable Life Assurance Society of the United States and Bankers Trust, collectively invested some $122.5 million in equity in the LBO in 1987. They will have collectively extracted $383.5 million in fees and dividends. Morgan Stanley, which invested $43.75 million, will have realized $158.6 million in fees (assuming it takes a customary 5 percent cut on the new equity offering) and another $56.1 million in dividends. Our associate publisher, Jay Diamond, has laid out the details in the accompanying, potentially revolution-fomenting table. It shows that the sum total of actual dividends and actual and prospective fees amounts to 244.5 percent of 1991 EBIT. They amount to 56.6 percent of all the EBIT generated in the years from 1988 to 1991. They represent 325 percent of the company's year-end totals for cash and equivalents for 1990 and 1991. The question we would have asked Morgan is whether its compensation might not be considered excessive in view of the mediocre corporate results obtained. We would have asked, "Are you or are you not the investment-banking equivalent of Lee Iacocca."*

In general, the capitalist class may reflect on the unpaid chits that the Burlington transaction has left in its wake: capital expenditures unmade, workers eliminated (and/or alienated), and frail corporate structures created. Now the same bankers propose that public investors pay $15 a share, or 33.3 times pro forma trailing net income, to buy a majority interest in this worse-for-wear LBO. That would compare to trailing multiples in the low 20s for jeans maker YF Corp., sheet and towel maker Springs Industries, and underwear maker Fruit of the Loom. It is an offer that we would refuse if we were in the market for a nonbiotech IPO.

WALL STREET FEASTS
BURLINGTON INDUSTRIES FEES AND DIVIDENDS SINCE
1987 ACQUISITION (IN $ MILLIONS)

Morgan Stanley:

sub. bridge financing fee 6/24/87	$16.0
underwriting discounts 9/23/87	35.4
dealer-manager fees 1987	1.5
financial advisory fees 1987	29.1
advisory fees through 1989	2.0
fees from asset sales '87–'88	19.8
organization fees 1989	2.5
private-placement fee 1989	4.0
private-placement fee 1989	4.5
private-placement fee 1989	1.0
underwriting discount 2/92[a]	42.8
	$158.6
dividend 8/89	56.1
	$214.7

---

* When, in November 1992, Burlington's management sounded a cautionary note in a telephone conference call with investors, Morgan Stanley's research department rushed in to interpret. SHARP REDUCTIONS IN ESTIMATES said Morgan's headline commentary, referring to the new, diminished profit outlook at Burlington. The investment conclusion, "Maintain Buy," was a classic of Wall Street circumlocution. Nevertheless, the stock price went up.

Bankers Trust:

commitment fee 6/24/87	$ 38.0
annual administrative fee 1987	0.5
facility fee 9/30/88	1.2
annual administrative fee 1988	0.5
facility fee 9/30/88	4.3
restructured credit fee 9/30/88	2.5
annual administrative fee 1988	0.5
commitment fee 12/28/88	1.6
Capital Structure Plan fee 1991	3.8
Capital Structure Plan fee 1991	3.5
	$ 56.4
dividend 8/89	46.1
	$102.5

Equitable:

bridge financing fee 6/24/87	$ 4.5
refinancing fee 9/23/87	3.9
	$ 8.4
dividend 8/89	57.9
	$ 66.3

Total fees	$223.4
Total dividends[b]	$160.1
Total fees and dividends	$383.5

Total fees and dividends as % of:

1991 sales	19.9%
1991 earnings before interest and taxes (EBIT)	244.5%
1990 + 1991 EBIT	135.6%
1989 + '90 + '91 EBIT	81.4%
1988 + '89 + '90 + '91 EBIT	56.5%
shareholders' equity 1991	−141.7%
cash and equivalents '90 + '91	325.0%

[a] assuming 5% underwriting fee for planned IPO
[b] employee stock option plan specifically excluded from dividend payments

KONDRATIEFF FLIES DELTA

May 8, 1992

W hatever the late, famed Russian economist Nikolai Kondratieff would have said, *we* say that no mere business cycle can account for the deepening troubles of the airline industry. It is a long-term decline, we think, distinct from the $99 "fly anywhere" decline of 1983, for example, which bullish Wall Street analysts now seize upon as the relevant analogy to explain away the deflationary business climate of 1992. Last year, for the first time in the jet age, worldwide revenue passenger miles actually declined. Last month a new domestic price war broke out. And last week, following the lead of AMR and UAL but breaking with its own never-look-back tradition in capital spending, Delta Air Lines canceled a sizable new aircraft order. Even before that disclosure, Tony Ryan, chairman of GPA Group, the Shannon (Ireland)–based aircraft-leasing company that's expected to go public any day, quipped to the *Financial Times*, "I often tell people I sleep like a baby. I wake up every ten minutes screaming."

If you have trouble reconciling the valuations of airline securities with the airlines that issue them, so do we. We have been disoriented on this point since 1989, but the public debt of the leading carriers continues to be quoted as if a turnaround were inevitable, not merely probable or desirable. We don't mean to repeat ourselves, but facts are facts. One year ago, Delta's public debt was quoted at 125 basis points over the comparable Treasury rate. Too low, we pronounced, predicting the future losses that duly materialized. The relative scarcity of *Grant's* subscribers, however, is reflected in the current Delta trading level: little more than 100 basis points over Treasuries (the carrier's senior unsecured debt is rated Baa1, or low investment grade), a thin cushion indeed in view of the financial risks.

Meantime, the gap that Delta was opening up last year between its actual and break-even load factors has continued to widen. No wonder that aircraft orders were canceled and plans were disclosed for a reduction in the head count (through attrition, management promises) or that the carrier's financial leverage has increased. One hopeful note is that losses in the twelve months ended last December were narrower than those in the June 1991 fiscal year. On the other hand, earnings before interest and taxes failed to cover fixed charges by a wider margin in December because the ratio of debt to capitalization was higher. The drop in cash was striking, too: to $110 million from $764 million in only six months.

Airlines and aircraft manufacturers constitute a long-running case study in the role of romance in civil aviation. Except for the romance of flight—in Delta's case, the charming story of small beginnings in the crop-dusting business in Macon, Georgia—it is hard to fathom the continued willingness of creditors to lend at a thin spread to loss-making operators. Robert Crandall, chairman of AMR, bluntly told *Business & Commercial Aviation* last month that "new airplanes cannot replace old airplanes on an economic basis." In other words, the increased cost of owning a new plane more than offsets the reduced cost of operating it, which is ordinarily not the kind of sales pitch that generates capital investment. "Simply," said Crandall, "the replacement of the fleet—making the fleet quieter and more environmentally acceptable—increases airline costs. All those things are driving up costs, and fares have to go up to cover them." Instead, of course, fares have gone down.

The open secret about commercial aviation, as Crandall went on, is that it "has not been satisfactorily profitable at any time in its history. The fact is, in the last two or three years it has been dramatically unprofitable. As you look to the future, there is no immediate indication that the profitability problem can be quickly overcome. As a consequence, we have simply to draw down the rate at which we plan to invest our capital."

Asked about recovery from the recession, Crandall gave the answer that would get him fired from a New York Stock Exchange member firm or ostracized from *The Wall Street Journal* editorial page staff: "We are not going to emerge from this recession! The recession is permanent." He predicted that the country will be paying the bill for the 1980s for a long time to come.

Not to put words in the late economist's mouth, but we suspect that Kondratieff would be struck by the confluence of long-term bearish trends in airline and aircraft finance. Last year, for instance, some 20 percent of domestic airline passengers were flown by bankrupt carriers, a fact that goes a long way toward explaining the persistence of low pricing. The chronic lack of profitability, even in good times, has also had predictable results, depleting the carriers' financial strength and deflating the former hope that new-aircraft prices could only go up, not sideways, let alone down. ("A cash-conscious airline industry that's trying to make the most of its existing fleets is generating demand for jet engine noise-reduction kits licensed by a subsidiary of Federal Express Corp.," the *Memphis Business Journal* reported recently, suggesting that there is more than one way to skin the environmental cat.)

As for GPA, Moody's late last month placed its senior debt under surveillance for possible downgrade. It was poor timing for GPA, which was planning to raise $500 million through the private sale of pooled aircraft leases. Moody's cited a number of "structural" issues, including "the traditional relationship between traffic growth and GDP, infrastructure limitations on capacity growth, and airline deregulation." It also mentioned a chill in capital markets, of which none is greater than the recent withdrawal of Japanese bank credit. Up until the time it stopped, there seemed no end to it. Furthermore, Moody's raised questions about the company's growing reliance on aircraft sales, as distinct from leasing income. To us, at least, this is the bedrock issue: "These sales," as Moody's noted, "have increasingly become an important source of earnings and cash flow for GPA to fund new aircraft acquisitions."

Thus, in brief, the issue before airline bondholders is the extent to which dark, secular forces are gnawing away at the safety of their investments. To judge by the hopeful valuations of airline debt in the public markets, the consensus is not to worry, not to listen to Robert Crandall, and not to pay any mind when Standard & Poor's says (as it said last month) that the issuers of $19.5 billion in airline debt are under review for possible downgrade. (Philip Baggaley,

S&P airline analyst, says that he recently attended an analysts' meeting sponsored by Airbus. "They said there will be this many planes, and they will get financed somehow, as they always have been," said Baggaley. "I raised my hand and said, 'Now, wait a minute!' Usually people have an answer ready, but this fellow was utterly dumbfounded. He didn't say anything for about thirty seconds, until someone asked another question, and they went right on. Privately, the Airbus people said that this is a real concern, and they are not sure what will happen.")

Equity investors may say that credit is a lagging indicator, that Kondratieff is dead, and that Delta, at least (when valued according to book value, projected cash flow, or the ratio of price to sales— in short, by anything except net income), is cheap at the current $60-per-share price. We will let the stockholders say those things. To the bondholders, however, who have no claim on the upside if the cycle *does* turn, we ask: What is the profit of reaching for yield when, relatively speaking, there's so little yield?

FLYING BUILDINGS GO PUBLIC

March 27, 1992

John Templeton, the visionary bull, told a visitor recently (and the visitor told *Grant's*) that the news has rarely been more hopeful and the equity market has rarely seemed more picked-over. With GPA Group Plc, the world-league aircraft lessor that plans to go public this spring, there is no such dichotomy. The valuation will almost certainly be too rich while the fundamental news continues to disappoint.

GPA is a credit story as much as a stock story, and it rang a bell with a reader. Suppose, our friend said, Olympia & York had tried to go public two years ago. What would people have said about it?

He answered his own question. They would have said it was unique: mysterious, asset-rich, commanding, profitable. They would have called its president a genius and its business plan a blueprint for the future. Its leverage they would have overlooked or endorsed as prudent and enterprising. If someone had objected that O&Y's earnings were dependent on the appreciation of its assets, they would have replied that buildings—O&Y's buildings, at least—do appreciate because they always used to. If someone had said, what if the credit markets refuse to lend to this brilliant company? the people would not have wasted their breath on an answer.

Now comes GPA with assets that more and more seem to resemble flying office buildings. There are objectively too many aircraft, thousands of new planes are on order (GPA has placed firm orders through the year 2000 for $12.1 billion in new planes and has purchased options for another $9.5 billion worth of new planes), and airlines have begun to cancel orders. Japanese banks, formerly the leading aircraft financing source, are pulling back, and aircraft prices and lease rates are down. Airline operating losses have recently set records, and surplus aircraft spring up in the desert like cacti. A few weeks ago, McDonnell Douglas jolted the stock market by disclosing how it has contributed its part to the surplus: "Some existing MD-11 contracts contain provisions requiring repurchase of aircraft at the option of the commercial customers. In view of the current market conditions for used aircraft, the company's earnings and cash flows could be impacted by the exercise of these options by airlines."

The GPA registration statement makes for good reading, too, and the issues it raises are universal. They include corporate valuation, credit risk, and the state of the world economy. Equity markets are sky-high, but private-market values, in general, are not. Real estate is not. Aircraft values, as noted, have fallen—are falling, reportedly—but the airline business is cyclical. "At February 1, 1992," the document says, describing some of the damage done by the rise in airline bankruptcies, "the Group's portfolio included thirty-six aircraft which were not in revenue service with lessees." Hence, the pressing question: Is the aircraft problem cyclical or secular?

The authorized answer is "cyclical," but you may doubt it, as we do. The nearby numbers describe the trend of GPA Group's finances and plot its ambitious aircraft-acquisition schedule. Note the rise in indebtedness, the decline in aircraft leasing margins, and the rise in aircraft sales margins. Observe the rise in the number of aircraft owned ("aircraft in portfolio"), the drop in number of aircraft sold, and the decline in return on assets. Still, however, in the last twelve months, profit from aircraft sales was almost twice as great as profit from aircraft leasing. In the early going, GPA bought a plane only after it had lined up a customer, and in that respect it resembled a cautious real estate developer. Increasingly, however, it has bought planes on speculation, thereby coming to resemble O&Y.

Boeing is out with an upbeat new forecast for growth in aircraft sales through the rest of the decade. It predicts (according to the *Financial Times*) that aircraft deliveries will average 655 a year between now and 2000—in other words, seven lean years will not necessarily follow the seven fat years of which 1989 was the most obese: 1,791 commercial-aircraft orders were logged. (That was also the year in which the Dow Jones Transportation Average made its all-time high and in which Donald Trump made a pass at AMR: you had to have been there.) "It is not possible to predict how long this period of oversupply will last," says the GPA document, "particularly in light of the possibility that manufacturers may produce a substantial number of aircraft above expected demand in the short term."

Airlines, of course, may cancel their orders; GPA may cancel or reschedule *its* orders, and, indeed, it recently has. To secure its orders and options for 472 new jet aircraft and 76 new turbo-prop aircraft through 2000, the company has remitted a total of $957 million in "predelivery payments." "Manufacturers have on occasion been willing to allow large customers, including the Group, to delay deliveries," the document says, and it discloses that the company exercised twenty-two options, rescheduled twenty options, and dropped thirty-seven others in the last fiscal year and through the first nine months of the current fiscal year (ending this month). "In addition, and by agreement with manufacturers," the document states, "the Group rescheduled the delivery of 22 narrow-body aircraft from 1992 through 1994 to 1993 through 1996." The bullish interpretation of this passage is that aircraft manufac-

GPA GROUP PLC[1]—HOW HIGH IS UP?				
	12 MOS. TO	YEARS ENDING MARCH 31,		
	12/31/91	1991	1990	1989
Indebtedness/total capital	75.7	72.2	64.7	67.3
Aircraft leasing profit margin	12.2%	16.0%	17.0%	14.1%
Aircraft sales profit margin	16.2	14.3	8.4	13.6
Gross profit margin	15.3	15.8	11.1	14.9
EBIT margin	25.1	22.7	19.4	23.6
EBIT/interest	2.44x	2.91x	2.86x	2.80x
Net margin	14.1%	13.9%	12.3%	12.1%
Return on assets	4.4	5.7	7.9	6.2
Return on equity	21.7	25.0	27.1	23.1
Aircraft in portfolio	392	307	240	170
Aircraft sold during period	47	67	73	33

[1] GPA reports are in accordance with Irish GAAP

turers are prepared to be flexible with their large customers. The bearish reading is that there's a persistent glut of the commodity in which GPA is very long. To put the security deposit, $957 million, in perspective, it represents four times the past twelve months' earnings and 83 percent of net worth.

According to an airlines analyst at Standard & Poor's, there is no urgency about the GPA IPO. If the stock market turns unreceptive, there will be no liquidity crisis. On the other hand, he says, if the stock isn't sold, GPA can expect to suffer a downgrade in its senior secured debt rating, now A−. The analyst says that this is not because of mismanagement but rather because of fast growth. Sometimes, of course—witness the real estate business these past few years—the two are almost indistinguishable.*

---

* GPA then proceeded to fly backwards. Its initial public offering was withdrawn in June 1992: The underwriters could not scare up enough investors. It has had to "reschedule" its bank debt, cancel or defer billions of dollars in new-aircraft orders, and warn that the fiscal year ending March 31, 1993, might produce its first net loss in seventeen years. Watching GPA's descent only makes the 1989 airline bubble seem more fantastic.

OPPORTUNITY IN FAT

November 20, 1992

Cholestech is a company tailor-made for the 1992 bull market. Not the least important thing is that its stock symbol has four letters, CTEC. It is therefore a NASDAQ issue, and the NASDAQ market is "the place to be." *The Wall Street Journal* has said so.

Second, the stock price has regularly risen. It has vaulted from its initial offering price of $5 a share last June to $15.625 the other day,* thereby commending itself to brokers and their momentum-pursuing clients. In the third place, no dividend is paid, no net profit is earned, and virtually no products are sold in the American market. Cholestech has essentially one product and essentially one customer. It emerged from the development stage only last December. In these fluid circumstances the speculative imagination is given free play, and the company trades at an imaginative thirty-four times trailing twelve-month revenues of not quite $3 million. (Not earnings but revenues.) Its market capitalization is about $100 million.

Cholestech develops, produces, and sells diagnostic devices that test blood cholesterol on the spot, while you wait, instead of at an outside laboratory. Just hold out your finger. The L-D-X system, Cholestech's one and only revenue-generating product, consists of an electronic analyzer (containing on-board software) and disposable test cassettes.

Maybe the L-D-X is just what this hamburger-eating nation needs to keep itself healthy. One hundred million Americans have high or borderline-high cholesterol counts, according to the National Cholesterol Education Program, and more than 200 million

* On February 25, 1993, it was $8.50.

lipid tests will be performed in the United States in 1992, the company estimates. Lipids, by the way, are water-insoluble fatty substances found in the body (although not in Evander Holyfield's). "Among competitors," management writes, "only Cholestech's L-D-X system can measure total cholesterol, high-density lipoproteins and triglycerides from a single drop of untreated whole blood within five minutes." And it also states that its products "are the result of significant research and development efforts and combine numerous technological advances in fields ranging from materials science and software to optics and dry chemistry. Cholestech believes its technology is also directly applicable to other niche diagnostic test applications where ease of use, precision and accuracy, multitest format, small-volume whole-blood sampling, and immediate feedback are important."

In view of these achievements, it's all the more notable that, in a pending secondary stock offering, half of the 2.5 million shares to be sold will be sold by insiders (the company will offer the balance). An outsider must wonder which part of the prospectus the insiders credit more: the bullish summary language quoted above or five pages of risk factors. The enumerated risks include the fact that Warner Lambert has accounted for some 77 percent of total product sales since test marketing began in the summer of 1991. Warner Lambert, in turn, "has distributed [the products] free of charge to physicians in certain foreign countries." Also, "the company's ability to manufacture consistently sufficient volumes of cassettes remains uncertain." And "the company has experienced difficulties achieving acceptable manufacturing yields on cassettes." And while raising $38 million through private placements and an IPO last June, the company has run up losses of $28 million. Truisms about competition, obsolescence, technological change, and regulation also are given their due.

In life as on Wall Street, nothing is certain, and the selling insiders may have no motive other than taking a profit. With interest rates rising and speculative lipids surging, the public holders may step back to examine their own motives. Have they bid up Cholestech (and so many other companies with four-letter stock symbols) because they deserve to be bid to previously unimagined valuations? Or because 3 percent is a very low rate on a CD?

PART NINE

PUBLIC
FINANCE

THE CANDIDATE'S MONEY

June 5, 1992

H. Ross Perot, the undeclared Ten Commandments candidate for the presidency, has sold short Citicorp, RJR, and the Japanese stock market (or so it appears). He was opposed to the Iraq war, and he has kept his ten-figure fortune despite a demonstrated weakness for undeveloped Texas land in the midst of a worldwide asset deflation. Altogether, he seems a man of parts.

Grant's has endorsed no presidential candidate except for the late Grover Cleveland, and we do not expect to break tradition in 1992. However, every citizen and every speculator must confront the financial consequences of a possible Perot administration. Would they be bullish, bearish, or merely indecisive? (A Washington friend ventures that Perot would be no more successful at dealing with Congress than the intractable Lowell Weicker has been at dealing with the Connecticut legislature. "Nothing would happen for four years," he promises.) The candidate himself has said next to nothing in recent weeks, but his portfolio is eloquent. It has been placed on the public record thanks to the Ethics in Government Act, the title of which might make the Texan smile.

Perot's fortune fills 123 government pages. The disclosure lists 332 categories of assets and 26 of liabilities. No useful magnitudes are stated. Mostly, the billionaire's holdings fall in the "over $1,000,000" category. The candidate has checking accounts in three different banks (Nationsbank, First Interstate, and Northpark National, the latter a Dallas institution) and accounts at five different brokerage firms: First Boston, Goldman Sachs, Jefferies &

Co., Salomon Brothers, and Smith Barney. (According to an operative, an enterprising broker from Shearson Lehman in Dallas called Perot as soon as the filing was made with a message that the document contained an error. When Perot himself returned the call, the broker told him, approximately, "The error is, Mr. Perot, that you have no account with us." Perot promised that he would have someone look into it.)

If one criterion for a successful chief executive is the capacity to keep risk and reward separate and distinct, Ross has the knack. His fixed-income portfolio is blue-chip, while his venture-capital portfolio is venturesome. His commercial-paper portfolio consists of thirty-two issuers, all rated P-1, the best. He owns only a few corporate bonds (most of them convertibles) and not much publicly traded common stock. He owns three investment partnerships that specialize in start-up high-tech firms. "The valuations of the private companies are slightly suspect," advises Jay Diamond, "as the companies generally do not show any sales." We would not be as sure about that as our colleague because many a rising high-tech and med-tech star in this bull market has neither sales nor products.

Professional investors manage a good part of Perot's money, of course, so it is not clear if the candidate himself pulled the trigger on what seems to be a short sale of Citicorp. Mostly, it seems, his short sales are arbitrage positions set up against the relevant convertibles or preferred. A Texas friend relates, however, that there is no doubt about his short position in the Japanese market: For years he's been vocally bearish on the Japanese economy.

As for Perot's real estate holdings, an informed Texas source describes them mainly as mistakes. He says that the man from Texarkana overpaid for the acreage around Alliance Airport, Fort Worth, and that he pulled a boner by signing a master lease on an office building in the Highland Park area of Dallas. When Perot signed the lease four or five years ago, our man says, the building was 85 percent occupied and fetched $14 per-square-foot rents. Now it is 50 percent occupied and receives $10 rents. The characteristic Perot strategy is to buy and wait, our source went on. He did, however, express awe at the way the would-be Outsider Candidate manipulated the federal government to build his airport. "It

Financial assets transition
team – December 1992

was the most unbelievable thing I have ever seen," our informant said.

The candidate has evidently been getting good advice on his municipal-bond portfolio. Nicole Anderes, vice president and the director of municipal research at Roosevelt & Cross, calls it well selected and well diversified, based on the information given. "It is typically in high-grade states and sectors," she says. "Anyone taking a general market stance would want this kind of diversification." (Texas does not tax the municipal-bond income from other states; hence, in Perot's case, diversification pays well.) There are a lot of hospital bonds, but they, too, are high-grade: "For example," says Anderes, "Dallas County Hospitals are backed by a property tax." For whatever prejudices it might feed on Wall Street, Perot holds no New York City bonds except for securities of the better-rated Municipal Assistance Corp.

Locally, according to our Texas friends, Perot is known best for his efficiency, brains, and ruthlessness. His brains, perhaps, present the biggest threat to the republic. As President, would he be smart enough to do nothing when nothing was indicated? Does he understand that the genius of the capitalist system is the diffusion of knowledge among the masses of people? If he does not know that, would he try to govern, CEO-style, from the top down? Not particularly wanting to be governed, even by an accomplished fixed-income investor, we will be watching expectantly.

EAT MY BREAD, SING MY SONG

June 5, 1992

More and more the financial condition of the nation's banks is colored olive drab. It is neither red nor black but government-issue green. Deposits are government-insured, of course, up to the legal ceiling, and have been since 1933. (If the Great Society caused the Los Angeles riots of 1992, maybe the New Deal caused the Wall Street riots of 1986–89. It is an idea for the Bush administration to run up the flagpole.) What is new, even allowing for the recession, is the rising proportion of banking assets that are either government-issued or government-insured: Treasury securities, guaranteed mortgages, guaranteed mortgage-backed securities, implicitly guaranteed mortgage-backed securities, and so forth. As Democrats began the socialization of the liability side of the banking system's balance sheet, so Republicans have pioneered in the socialization of assets. It is a partnership in good government.

Almost universally, Wall Street analysts have applauded recent developments. Banks, they say, have virtually become leveraged bond funds. The art of banking has become the art of buying Ginnie Maes or three-year notes with the proceeds of low-cost deposits. Starting with the five-year note, government yields, at 6.6 percent, top the prime rate, at 6½ percent. In the *American Banker* recently, Sanford Rose contended that the after-tax return on a loan, after taking into account the costs of overhead, administration, and credit loss, is negligible: He guessed that it may amount to less than six-tenths of 1 percent. If so, the preference for Treasury paper seems not merely understandable but also commendable.

Or is it? On reflection, we think it is not. In return for the nationalization of risk and the heavy subsidy of reward, the authorities have demanded a measure of reciprocity. To date, the tangible cost of compliance has been small, but the demands for socially sanctioned credit are rising. The future of banking looks less and less like the kind of business to which a forward-looking investor would assign a high earnings multiple.

Post–Los Angeles, discriminatory lending has moved up on the government's problem list. Enlisting in the campaign to stamp out discrimination with borrowed money are the Justice Department, the Federal Reserve Board, the Office of the Comptroller of the Currency, the Federal Deposit Insurance Corp., the Office of Thrift Supervision, the Federal Trade Commission, and the Department of Housing and Urban Development.

Lenders must reach out to the marginal borrower under the Community Reinvestment Act (CRA).* The amount of required lending is small, but the disclosure burden is great. Bankers also must conform to the provisions of the Equal Credit Opportunity Act, the Fair Housing Act, and the Home Mortgage Disclosure Act. Big banks, to effect a merger, must pay tribute to the government with multibillion-dollar pledges of "community" lending. For the dubious privilege of acquiring Security Pacific, Bank-America, for instance, committed to lend $12 billion over the next ten years to the people to whom bankers do not ordinarily lend, including $7.5 billion in home loans in areas in which bankers do not ordinarily live. Possibly, an investment in the Neighborhood Advantage program is no worse than an investment in Security Pacific common. Still, the precedent is a worry. If, under a Bush administration, the government can extort $1 billion a year per merged institution, why couldn't a Clinton administration (or a Jackson or a Perot administration) get $2 billion or $3 billion?

"In the past year," a team of lawyers with Wachtell, Lipton, Rosen & Katz have recently written, "the Federal Reserve for the first time denied a merger application on CRA grounds. The stringency of on-site CRA examinations has also been increasing. Despite (or perhaps because of) claims by community groups that the

---

* It must be said that most banks have kept their protests to themselves if they had any. The *American Banker*, the industry trade paper, frequently publishes advice on how to comply with the federal laws or turn a good compliance record into a public relations asset. "Imagine paying an advocacy group to monitor your lending," it reported brightly in February 1993. "Well, that's just the arrangement eleven banks in Pittsburgh . . . have had with the Pittsburgh Community Reinvestment Group. And it seems to be working for both sides."

regulators have been too lenient, many banks have received significant (though perhaps selective) criticism of their CRA efforts in their most recent examinations."

It will be said that banks long ago made their pact with the *federales*. The government has chartered national banks since 1864, and the Federal Reserve System has facilitated the leveraged acquisition of Treasury securities almost since its founding in 1914. In return for subsidies, steep yield curves, and monopolistic rulemaking, the government has oppressed the banks with regulations and restricted their freedom of action. It was never much of a bargain, but now, it seems to us, the terms are getting worse.

THE FUTURE IS ITALY

February 12, 1993

Italy is the Roman Colosseum of borrowing and the catacombs of taxation and the Appian Way of compound interest. It has a public debt that is larger and more gross than its gross domestic product. Interest on its public debt amounts to more than 10 percent of its GDP. Italy is not the world's third largest economy—it is number seven, according to the International Monetary Fund—but it does have the world's third largest government bond market. The Italian bond screen, Mercato Telematico dei Titoli di Stato, displays ninety-four issues. Things have come to such a pretty pass that the Italian who recently said, "The state can no longer guarantee everything to everybody," was the Socialist prime minister, Giuliano Amato, himself.

Mathematically, the growth of a country's borrowing may not indefinitely exceed the growth of a country's output. Yet for a decade (or more) in Italy it has.

In the United States, the $4 trillion gross public debt represents about two-thirds of the nearly $6 trillion GDP. Between 1987 and 1992 the U.S. GDP grew by 5.7 percent a year, whereas the U.S. public debt grew by 11.3 percent a year. If those rates persisted, the debt would hit the $8 trillion mark, overtaking GDP in 1999. An American may ask of his own country, as well as of Italy: How much longer?

The lesson of Italy is sobering and hopeful all at once. It is most hopeful that *Italia* is still on the map. Unless he or she is taxed and regulated by New York City, is a veteran of the U.S. armed forces, is employed by the Tennessee Valley Authority, or can remember the Hundred Days of the Roosevelt administration or the more imperial moments of the Great Society, an American may not understand the voracity of the Italian state. In Italy, government spending represents 56 percent of GDP. In America, federal government spending ("investment," in the argot of the Clinton administration) represents 24 percent of GDP. Still, in New York and Rome, life goes on.

We turn to Italy because, barring change, it is America's fiscal destination, and there are questions to answer: What damage has this vast debt done? Is there such a thing as a point of budgetary no return? If so, has Italy reached it? What are the prospects for the Italian stock market and also, not least, for a reader's lira-denominated speculation, the IMI Bank International's thirteen-year zero-coupon bonds? Finally, what does the Italian dilemma suggest about America's financial future?

On to the first question: Is a huge public debt clearly and unambiguously bearish? In the United States, where a rising debt has been accompanied by falling interest rates and a flyaway stock market, many would answer, "No." However, in Italy, we believe, there is no one who would not answer, "Yes." The greater concern in Italy stems not only from the greater mass of its debt, but also from a more virulent case of statism. If in America "entitlements" are the root cause of the growth of the public debt, in Italy what's to blame is the very structure of things.

In any case, Italian real interest rates are among the highest in Europe, the Milan stock exchange is stunted in size and price, and the Italian government's own credit rating is not a reproachless AAA but a diminished Aa3. Italian borrowers were virtually barred from the syndicated European loan market last summer when Efim, the state industrial holding company, went into liquidation. Much to the dismay of the bank creditors, who had assumed that a loan to an arm of the state was a loan to the state itself, the Italian treasury declined to pay. Then, in November, the government reconsidered, and now the Euromarket has begun to accommodate Italian borrowers again. And now Ilva, the Italian state's loss-making steel company, is threatening to become Efim2. It is hard to conceive of such a run of bad luck befalling a purely solvent country.

In public life as well as in business, too much debt can be stifling. The proof of this maxim is that Italy is now running a taut fiscal policy in a time of economic stagnation. We can be sure that if the Amato government had lira to spend, it would spend them. Then, too, as you will remember, Italy abandoned the European Rate Mechanism during last September's currency crisis; to reenter, which is the government's stated top economic ambition, the public debt must be brought in line with the national income.

But how? As this piece was composed in lower Manhattan, we do not pretend to grasp every single nuance. One such imponderable is the resilience of the Italian economy, in which transactions occur aboveground, underground, and underworld. Italians are legendary savers and famous tax evaders. Surely, therefore, the denominator of the Italian debt-to-GDP ratio must be chronically understated.

Also under the heading of "life goes on," Italy has rolled financial rocks uphill before. Great problems have elicited audacious, sometimes larcenous solutions, as in the wake of the tripling of the public debt between 1862 and 1877. Shepard B. Clough, in *The Economic History of Modern Italy*, records that the government seized and sold Church properties "which were not used for religious purposes," sold state property (a little like the RTC), privatized state railroads, and instituted the *Corso Forzoso*, a declaration that the paper money of the banks of issue was no longer convertible into gold. This last gambit, at least, is unavailable to the Amato government, as all the world is now on a full paper monetary standard. (By the way, the lira-denominated gold price must be counted a disappointment to those who are pinning their principal hopes for a gold bull market on the fiscal deterioration of the U.S. Treasury. Until last fall's lira devaluation, gold, in terms of lira, mainly went down.)

Giuseppe Volpi, Benito Mussolini's finance minister in 1926, met still another fiscal crisis by forcing the holders of five- and seven-year Italian bonds, which the Treasury could no longer easily redeem, to exchange them for longer-term consolidated 5s at a price of 87½. This "Littorio" loan lengthened the maturity of the public debt, but not without arousing what Clough describes, perhaps with understatement, as "considerable resentment."

In the Depression, Il Duce created Istituto Mobilare Italiano (IMI) and Istituto per la Ricostruzione Industriale (IRI), a pair of Hoover- and Roosevelt-style public corporations that grew and grew, in debt and political influence if not in efficiency, and survive until this very day. America would look more like Italy if the Reconstruction Finance Corp. were still buying preferred stock in U.S. banks or if the Civilian Conservation Corps were still planting trees. As it is, the Agriculture Department brings a little bit of Tuscany to Washington, D.C.

Statism in Italy is the man who stayed for dinner, and the fiscal crisis is therefore also a political and social crisis. Running up debts, the government has simultaneously run down the nation's capacity to service them.

To turn the tide, the Amato government, just seven months old, has proposed a vigorous privatization campaign, the creation of a private pension system, and an increase in the retirement age (to sixty-five from sixty for men and, chivalrously, to sixty from fifty-five for women). Last summer the government made history by abolishing the *scala mobile*, the allegedly eternal postwar Italian institution for indexing wages to inflation. Besides the lira's undignified exit from the European Rate Mechanism, the autumn also brought labor riots.

An American observer can at least take heart in the relative simplicity of his own country's debt predicament. In the United States it is Bill Clinton versus the laws of compound interest. In Italy it is Amato versus the laws of compound interest compounded again by the state enterprise system. In America there is nothing quite like IRI, not even the former military-industrial complex. In Italy the something-for-nothing political constituency is large, far-flung, and ill-tempered, more so even than in America.

The first impression gained by a week's long-distance study of Italian finance is that reform would be very bullish indeed. Erich Stock, manager of the Italy Fund, tells *Grant's*: "You can imagine what the U.S. market would look like if there were no pension funds. You can imagine what the Italian market will look like once there are pension funds." The second impression is that such a great reform hangs by a thread. Thus, a wire-service dispatch last Friday, only a little more alarming than average:

ROME (February 5) UPI—Prime Minister Giuliano Amato's seven-month-old government defeated a no-confidence motion in the Chamber of Deputies Friday, averting a crisis that his supporters feared could have plunged Italy into chaos.

The four parties of Amato's coalition stuck solidly together to defeat the no-confidence motion presented by the former Communist Party by 321 votes to 255, with eight abstentions in the 630-seat lower house of Parliament.

If Amato, a fifty-four-year-old Socialist, had lost the vote, he would have had to resign his coalition of Christian Democrats, Socialists, Social Democrats, and Liberals. . . . The government is Italy's fifty-first since World War II and was put together after a three-month crisis that followed parliamentary elections in April 1992, in which the traditional coalition parties suffered heavy losses.

Not plunging into chaos is good, but not coming close to plunging into chaos would be better. To the holder of Italian debt it would be infinitely better because the upside of seven-year Italian *Certificati di Credito del Tesoro* is a very finite 11½ percent, after the 12½ percent withholding tax. The downside, in political terms, would be a victory by Achille Occhetto, leader of the former Communist Party, now renamed the Democratic Party of the Left. It is unlikely, from everything one reads, that Occhetto sees the pension-fund issue just the same way that the equity bulls do.

As long as the Warsaw Pact was in place, Italy's non-Communists could make common political cause. Now that the Soviet threat has disappeared, the politicians have lost their cohesion. In some cases they (and their businessmen co-dependents) have lost their freedom: About one hundred people have been arrested on bribery charges. The scandal, which has been unfolding for months, has afforded the public a grim new look under the rock of Italian statism.

The bulls hope that reform is forced on Italy, both by the impossible arithmetic of its own compounding debt and by the terms of a pending 8 billion Ecu loan (the equivalent of about $9.5 billion) from the European Community. To take down the full amount of the loan, observes Daniel Schultz, head of research of IMI in London, Italy must contain the growth of the public debt. If all goes well, the debt will peak as a percentage of GDP in 1994 or 1995.

Italy was able to borrow to the tune of 105 percent of GDP because its population lent to the government. They lent because of their own prodigious savings rate and also because currency controls denied them an overseas alternative. But controls came off two years ago, and the momentum toward financial integration may now be irreversible. Nowadays the government must compete for the people's capital.

The question is: Will the government also allow the people to compete for their own prosperity? Ed Vulliamy, recently writing in the Manchester, England, *Guardian*, observed that Amato's program is the first to attempt an assault on the fiscal beachhead "by cutting spending rather than by raising income."

For a time in the 1980s, Italy was the fastest growing of the four big European economies, but the boom also fed the state, as Vulliamy elaborates: "Italy spent on its massive state apparatus and bloated bureaucracy, with which the ruling cliques bought political power. Civil servants could retire at thirty-five and take a second job on pension. The public utility and health agencies were—and remain—cesspits of corruption. Italy spent lavishly, to little return, on the dinosaur of its industrial public sector, feeding money into the IRI, the state industrial colossus, and other state enterprises, again principally in order to keep the regime in power."

The fiscal crisis has foreclosed a repeat of that idyll, and monetary reforms have reduced the probability of a state-sponsored inflation. As long ago as 1981, the Bank of Italy was relieved of its formal obligation to serve as the buyer of last resort of the treasury's debt, and in 1987 the commercial banking system was similarly unburdened of its bond-buying duties. A year ago the governor of the Bank of Italy was given the right to set key interest rates without the treasury's approval. Most important, until last fall's departure of the lira from the ERM, Italian monetary policy in effect was subordinated to German monetary policy. For all these reasons, the Italian inflation rate has fallen to 4½ percent from 6½ percent over the past two years.

Lately, Italian interest rates have joined in the decline of other European rates. The Bank of Italy's discount rate has fallen to 11½ percent from 12 percent, and the Banca Commerciale Italiana's prime rate is down to 12¾ percent from 13½ percent. Last Friday, following the Bundesbank, the Bank of Italy reduced the proportion of funds that Italian commercial banks must set aside against their deposit liabilities (to a still-astounding 17.5 percent from 22.5 percent; Italy's reserve requirements were, and remain, the highest in Europe). To reduce reserve requirements is traditionally one of the most bullish things a central bank can do for equities.

"Traditionally," an Italian analyst said last week, "investors have preferred short-term bonds because with long-term bonds there was little chance that the government would have the money to pay the yields when they came due. Now BTP bonds are favored; they are five- or ten-year bonds. The government is looking to lengthen the maturity of the bonds because it's finding it more and more difficult to refinance the short-term bonds."

The average length of the United States public debt is five years, eleven months, and falling. The average length of the Italian public debt is about three years, down from about four years as recently as 1987, but up from the bill-length maturities that the treasury was forced to issue in the bad old inflationary days of 1975.

In highly leveraged backward countries, debts are "rescheduled." As Italy is a highly leveraged industrialized country, however, its debts must be "refunded." The question is: Can it refund them?

Barring a change in the rate of growth in borrowing, the government must inevitably fail, although when is a matter of guesswork. The table contains some projections for the next five and ten years, based on the palpably unrealistic assumption that nothing changes. In ten years' time, as you can see, the U.S. debt would be bigger than Italy's is today, as a measure of GDP, although the burden of servicing it would be far lighter. Italy would be still deeper in the hole, but who is to say that 149 percent on the debt-to-GDP scale would spell oblivion? Certainly, though, it would not be bullish.

If there is hope, we think, it is that the Socialist Amato is able to follow the liberalizing example of the Argentine president, Carlos Menem. In the 1930s, Mussolini inspired the Argentine dictator

Juan Domingo Perón, Evita's husband, with his feats of state socialism. Later on, Perón inspired Menem. It is only fair that now, in rolling back the state, Menem should inspire Amato.

Coming into power, notes Carolina Guevara-Lightcap of this staff, who was born and raised in Argentina, Menem made the capitalists despair. On taking office, however, he threw over the unions, embraced the rhetoric of enterprise, and surrounded himself with right-of-center advisers. "The results surprised everybody," she says, "and many cried treason, but Argentina started on its way to recovery. Through November last year the public sector showed a net profit from privatizations of some $3.4 billion, about $403 million more than the IMF minimum. In 1991 the economy grew by 8½ percent; in 1992, by more than 7 percent." Why can't Italy do the same?

We mentioned the lira-denominated, zero-coupon issue of IMI Bank International. A subscriber who bought an odd lot describes his position: "I own a billion lira [that is, at current exchange rates, about $660,500 worth]. I don't get them now. I get them in 2006. To be exact, on June 13, 2006." Compare and contrast with a zero-coupon U.S. Treasury issue of the same maturity, he suggests. The American issue is priced at 40 cents on the dollar to yield 7.2 percent. The lira issue is priced at 20 cents on the dollar to yield 12.9 percent. The lira exchange rate would have to go to 3,000 from last Tuesday's 1,500 or so before the Treasury issue would outperform the IMI issue, other things being the same. Other things may not be the same, of course, because IMI Bank International is under review for a possible downgrade by Moody's (it has been on watch since November). It is rated Aa3. The Treasury is not without risk, as the Clinton administration may be demonstrating right now, but it is backed by the Bureau of Engraving and Printing and the Internal Revenue Service and the Federal Reserve Board.

"Every time I shave," our reader continues, "I make a point of saying, 'We're not going to pay it back.' " He is referring to the U.S. public debt. The lira is just another paper emission of another social democracy, he admits, but capital invested in lira is compounding more briskly than capital invested in dollars.

For our part, we would prefer Italian stocks to Italian bonds if we could only see through the brick wall of Italian politics. If Amato is going to succeed, the Milan market is going to excel because the success of the government must imply the overhaul of the pension system and the privatization of state assets. According to Stock, the Italian market as a whole is valued at 19.7 times estimated 1993 earnings. Excluding the richly priced insurance companies, however, it is valued at 15.5 times estimated 1993 earnings.

Amato may or may not succeed, but he is fighting the good fight, and the Italian bourse is down by more than 40 percent from its 1986 high. President Clinton may or may not succeed, but he seems to be fighting the wrong fight, and the American equities markets stand at new highs. As Amato has demolished the *scala mobile*, Clinton has hinted at raising the minimum wage. Italy may yet show us that there is no such thing as a fiscal point of no return, and America may prove that too much public debt is not in fact a standing bull argument for financial assets. A benevolent observer will purchase a rooting interest in the Italy Fund and remember Amato in his prayers.

ITALY LEADS, AMERICA FOLLOWS
(IN BILLIONS OF DOLLARS)[1]

	U.S.[2]		ITALY[3]	
	1992	5-YR. GROWTH RATE	1991	5-YR. GROWTH RATE
GDP	$5,868.6	5.7	$1,139.5	13.6
Receipts	1,091.6	5.0	517.6	16.0
Outlays	1,381.8	6.6	639.5	15.0
Deficit	(290.2)	14.1	(121.9)	11.6
Gross interest payments	199.4	7.6	118.9	18.0
Gross public debt	4,002.7	11.3	1,196.3	17.6

Government Budgetary Ratios—Historical

Receipts/gross interest	5.47x	4.35x
Gross interest/GDP	3.4%	10.4%
Gross public debt/GDP	68.2%	105.0%
Gross interest/deficit	68.7%	97.5%

Government Budgetary Ratios—Projected[4]
five years forward

Receipts/gross interest	4.86x	3.98x
Gross interest/GDP	3.7%	12.7%
Gross public debt/GDP	88.3%	125.0%
Gross interest/deficit	51.1%	129.3%

10 years forward

Receipts/gross interest	4.32x	3.65x
Gross interest/GDP	4.1%	15.4%
Gross public debt/GDP	114.3%	148.8%
Gross interest/deficit	37.9%	171.4%

[1] conversion reflects average market exchange rate for the period; source: IMF's International Financial Statistics
[2] latest data as of end of fiscal 1992
[3] latest data as of end of fiscal 1991
[4] straight-line projections of government budgetary ratios applying historical five-year compound annual growth rates

Great bull markets almost always end in absurdity, the ruling idea of the rise being reduced to caricature through the forces of imitation and competition. Thus, the bull of the 1960s manifested Meshulam Ricklis ("I am a conglomerate. Me, personally"), the inflationary 1970s brought forth the Hunt brothers, who tried but failed to corner the silver market, and the 1980s gave us Donald Trump, the Beverly Hills office of Drexel Burnham Lambert, and the Tokyo real estate market. A wise man once remarked that financial markets test the validity of ideas by pushing them to their outer limits and beyond—thus the tendency of the junk bond market toward more perilous capitalizations and of the stock market toward more overpriced initial public offerings.

Once in a blue moon, investors will be given the gift of extreme valuations. At these rare moments, stocks or bonds will be higher or lower than they have been in living memory, but they will not seem unduly high or low because people have lost their valuation bearings. So it was in the stock market in 1973–74, when American Airlines fell 90.2 percent, to $4.90 a share from its 1972 high of $49.90 a share. So it was in the Japanese market in 1989, when every stock was going to heaven.

And so it was, I believe, in both the U.S. bond and stock markets in February 1993. For almost two years in a row the stock market had made record highs in valuation. On the evening of February 15, President Clinton, vowing a break from twelve years of Republicanism, promised higher taxes, "bold and persistent experimentation" in government, a smaller federal budget deficit, and economic justice for the malefactors of the 1980s. Next day the Dow Jones Industrial Average dropped by 83 points.

Up until the unveiling of the Clinton plan, stocks and bonds stood at the top of the investment ladder; commodities were near the bottom, one rung above redundant office buildings. The ratio of stock prices to gold prices was the highest in more than a decade. Similarly, bond prices were at a ten-year high in relation to a basket of commodity futures prices.

In the late 1970s, people rushed to exchange their depreciating money for appreciating objects. Shunning stocks and bonds, they bought commercial real estate, oil-drilling partnerships, bags of silver coins, and Chinese porcelain. In the late 1970s, there was passable demand for long-dated Treasury bonds yielding 8 percent and 9 percent. However, by the time the market had finished its absurdum phase, late in 1981, traditional buyers of bonds were almost too demoralized to pick up the telephone. Yields were then in the low- to mid-teens. Never mind that a 14 percent coupon would compensate a buyer for a 14 percent principal loss: At the end of the year, if one's $1,000 security had lost $140 of market value, one would do no worse, having earned $140 in interest, than break even. Imagination overwhelmed objectivity, and the creditor class braced itself for 20 percent interest rates and the ultimate extinction of the bond market itself. There would be no end to it.

Protracted market movements tend to be self-sustaining because they wear out the doubting Thomases and make them poor. By early 1993, bond prices had been going up for as long as many people on Wall Street had been working. Stocks had not suffered a hurricane-force bear market since 1974 (the 1981–82 downturn, by comparison, was almost a zephyr). Inevitably, therefore, journalistic energy was devoted to rationalizing the rise in prices rather than speculating on a more and more implausible-sounding fall. Everything was bullish, the Street believed: Bill Clinton no less than George Bush, a weak economy or a strong one, higher taxes as well as lower ones.

The Wall Street Journal explained the new era to the millions of Americans who did not happen to work in brokerage houses. For example, the paper elucidated on February 8 that the then-current dividend yield of less than 3 percent on common stocks was not, as it might have seemed, a sign of overvaluation. It was rather the proof that a new and younger generation of investors did not urgently need the dividends. They were in the market for the capital appreciation, on which they could bank. Four days later the paper reported that "over the past sixty-six years, stocks have been a more reliable source of dividend income than either bonds or Treasury bills." Professional investors already understood that T-bills were the riskiest class of financial asset because holding too many of them in a bull market was an important cause of job loss; one must buy stocks or bonds, or else. The *Journal*'s story, directed at the nonprofessional, pointed out that interest income from bills is unstable, rising or falling with the level of short-term interest rates. Underneath the headline T-BILL TRAUMA AND THE MEANING OF RISK, a man from a bank answered the objection that 3 percent isn't a very big yield, even from a common stock. "Because the value of a stock portfolio should rise faster than inflation," the paper let him explain, "I wouldn't be averse to consuming principal. . . . That allows you to break the link between the yield on your securities and your spending. I wouldn't be so inclined to consume my principal if I was invested in cash or bonds." As for the risk of principal loss, it went unmentioned, perhaps because nobody quoted in the story had had any personal experience with it.

When investors did lose money, they were frequently indignant, like a professional gambler who is taken in by a tableful of traveling salesmen. A 242-seat Florida restaurant named for the basketball titan Wilt Chamberlain went public at $7 a share (representing a capitalization of $40 million) and fell to less than $6 on the same business day. Was such a thing possible? It was well known that the prices of initial public offerings, like the market itself, only went up. However, the price of a share of Wilt's fell again on the second day, to $4.625. Lawsuits were threatened. Not only had the stock not gone up, but also, incredibly, it continued to go down. On the third business day, the underwriter capitulated: The deal was withdrawn, and the outraged buyers were promised their money back.

It was easy to bridle at the patent excess of Wilt's, but there had been many other such episodes over the past two years. *Grant's* had chronicled them, never failing to cry "Wolf!" Faith, hope, and falling interest rates had become the watchwords of investing. The favorable alignment of interest rates meant a bond dealer could borrow overnight at, say, 3 percent. He could invest the proceeds in a five-year note at, say, 5 percent. The two percentage points of daylight between these two interest rates were manna. They enriched dealers and speculators and healed banks, which purchased Treasury notes as they had once acquired real estate loans. From year-end 1991 to year-end 1992, profits at one hundred large bank holding companies almost doubled, to $20 billion. As long as Treasury bill yields were lower than note and bond yields, an investor was paid to inventory the government's securities.

Businessmen had undergone a process of conditioning almost exactly opposite that of financial investors. Inflation was down, sales were low, and the future was even more uncertain than usual. In those circumstances, the value of inventories—of things, not of securities—tended to stagnate. Inspired by the Japanese success with "just-in-time" inventory management and by the brilliant application of that idea by Wal-Mart, the vast, thrusting, Arkansas-based discount chain, managers kept the bare minimum of stock on hand. Believing that shortages were a thing of the past, they ordered frugally, hand-to-mouth.

By all appearances, then, the sky was bright blue. The money supply, model M-2 (approximately defined as the sum of currency, checking accounts, savings accounts, and money-market mutual funds), was expanding at a rate of less than 3 percent a year. In the white-hot inflation of the late 1970s, it had risen by more than 13 percent a year. In the United States, lenders and borrowers were chastened. In no industrialized country did they appear ready to embark on another great inflation. The composite Wall Street view was that interest rates were not going to rise. As the American saver could not stand 3 percent, a steady stream of funds into the stock market was virtually guaranteed.

But the Clinton administration was different from the Reagan and Bush administrations. As stock prices fell on February 16, James Carville, the administration's campaign strategist, declared, beaming, "I looooooove the stock market falling. In the 1980s the stock market rose 300 percent and real incomes fell. Maybe now the stock market will fall and real incomes will rise."

Even if Carville was having his joke, the political tide was turning. Ronald Reagan had championed enterprise, lower taxes, and less government intervention. George Bush, although he had suffered higher taxes and more intervention, spoke up for enterprise. Now came Bill Clinton, suffering enterprise while championing government and asking for higher taxes.

For a decade or more, caution has availed the investor nothing. As the sun rose, so the stock market went up; as it set, interest rates went down. Anyone who was prepared to worry about the Clinton economic agenda had no doubt been needlessly concerned before. "Bull markets climb a wall of worry" is a trader's maxim, which means that apprehension is a necessary precondition to a rising market. It is a hallowed speculative paradox, but not every concern is baseless and the times do change, sometimes for the worse.

Worse is upon us in the financial markets, I believe (as, to be sure, I have believed before). If something like capitalism was bullish, how could its antithesis, something like statism, also be bullish? It could not be. The world is not going to come to an end, but that is not the point. At a price of twenty-five times the past twelve months' earnings, one of the all-time rich valuations in history, the stock market is armored for every contingency except risk. Whatever else the Clinton years bring, they will fall short of perfection, as a capitalist would use the word perfection.

And interest rates? The administration's domestic monetary policy is one of Federal Reserve credit expansion. Its international monetary policy, as expressed by the new Treasury secretary, Lloyd Bentsen, is, with respect to the yen, one of devaluation. Its banking policy is one of renewed lending. None of these ideas has historically been associated with low interest rates. Worldwide, especially in Japan, deflation has badly rattled the monetary authorities, and competitive currency devaluations have become the order of the day in Europe. If the worst of the debt-related news is out, it follows that the tide of international credit will begin to rise again. In that case, the best of the inflation and interest rate news may already be behind us.

What nobody can know is whether the world, so impaired by excessive debt in the boom years, has regained enough of its financial strength to mount another expansion. In the United States, businesses, banks, and consumers have laboriously been rebuilding their balance sheets. The process has been under way ever since the first wave of savings and loan failures in the mid-1980s. If, as I believe, the economic expansion can continue, an investor must ask, What's cheap? Not stocks or bonds, certainly. Commodities are cheap, some of them (silver, for instance) priced at or near their own cost of production. For a dozen years people have been conditioned to buy financial assets because they appreciate, and to avoid commodities because they don't. They have bid the former up, arguably to the point of absurdity, and the latter down, arguably to the point of value. Accordingly, I have worked up a matched set of thoughts for the Clinton years: Down with paper. Up with things.

New York, March 1, 1993

INDEX